DEEP HISTORY
Country and Sovereignty

ANN MCGRATH AM has led the Kathleen Fitzpatrick Laureate Program on Deep History for the past seven years. She is based at the Australian National University, where she is the WK Hancock Distinguished Chair of History and currently serves on the Council of the National Museum of Australia. Her publications include *Illicit Love: Interracial sex and marriage in the United States and Australia* (2015), which won the NSW Premier's History Prize, and *Born in the Cattle* (1987), awarded the inaugural Hancock Prize. Along with Laura Rademaker and Jakelin Troy, she co-edited *Everywhen: Australia and the language of deep history* (2023). McGrath has also co-directed and produced various films, including *A Frontier Conversation* (2006), *Message from Mungo* (2014) and *Japarta* (2025). Her work has been recognised by the Human Rights Award for non-fiction, the John Barrett Prize and the Archibald Hannah Junior Fellowship at the Beinecke Library, Yale. She has gained memberships of the American Academy of Arts and Sciences, the Institute of Advanced Study, Durham, and the School of Social Sciences and the School of Historical Studies, Institute for Advanced Study, Princeton, and was awarded two Rockefeller Foundation Scholarly Residencies at Bellagio.

PROFESSOR JACKIE HUGGINS AM FAHA is Bidjara and Birri Gubba Juru. She is currently Director of Indigenous Research, Faculty of Health, Medicine and Behavioural Sciences at the University of Queensland. She is also Honorary Professor, Centre for Deep History, Australian National University; POU Atlantic Fellows Social Equity, Melbourne University; Director, National Centre for Reconciliation, Truth and Justice, Federation University Victoria; and Co-Chair, National Apology Foundation. Other roles include Elder in Residence, Australia Progress and Steering Committee Member for Passing the Message Stick and Common Threads, as well as Elder in Residence, Australian Broadcasting Commission. Her publications include *Sister girl: The writings of Aboriginal activist and historian Jackie Huggins* (1998), *Jack of Hearts: QX11594* (with Ngaire Jarro, 2022) and *Auntie Rita: The classic memoir of an Aboriginal woman's love and determination* (with Rita Huggins, 2023). Professor Huggins is in demand as a speaker, mentor, writer and advisor with over four decades experience in Community, academia, government and non-government sectors.

'*Deep History* is a rousing insurrection against the continuing colonial policing of history in Australasia and the Pacific. Indigenous Australian and Pasifika scholars lead in the reframing of our historical narratives, recognising, alongside white scholars, the urgency of truth telling for respectful acknowledgement of First Nations' sovereignty. This postcolonial reframing of the space and tempo of past legacies and contemporary trajectories offers us new and deeper histories for better futures.'

Warwick Anderson, author of *The Cultivation of Whiteness: Science, Health, and Racial Destiny in Australia*

'*Deep History* attempts the timely, difficult, and often discomforting task of blasting open the allied academic disciplines of History and Archaeology to Indigenous ways of representing the past and their sovereign sense of Deep Time. Going beyond the peaceful co-existence models of what was once called "bi-cultural history" in Aotearoa New Zealand and drawing on experiences of settler-colonial rule in the wider world of Oceania, the essays here experiment with a variety of creative strategies to take this challenging conversation forward. The result is an exciting and courageous volume that will speak to all students of decolonisation of knowledge.'

Dipesh Chakrabarty, author of *Provincializing Europe: Postcolonial Thought and Historical Difference*

'This wonderful collection of essays displaying the challenges and achievements of *Deep History*, draws our attention to history's power, for good and ill, and its importance to the sovereignty of a people. From a rich and thought-provoking introduction to the series of exciting, informative, and well-written essays that follow we learn much about the very different forms deep history can take – a long walk, rock art, stories and practices that nourish Country, scientific studies of changes in land and sea, works of historical fiction, and even the conventional historical archive. I came away with a heightened appreciation of the different ways that Indigenous and non-Indigenous histories can and sometimes do communicate with one another, and the vital importance of doing so.'

Ann Curthoys, co-author of *Taking Liberty: Indigenous Rights and Settler Self-Government in Colonial Australia, 1830–1890*

'*Deep History: Country and Sovereignty* has the capacity to open so many new eyes to the profound timelessness of Indigenous history and how it is embedded everywhere – in the land, seas and skies that surround us. It adds new understanding to the connection between the "everywhen" and human and spiritual experience. It is a gift to the children and grandchildren of settler societies.'
Paul Daley, author of *Jesustown* and *Guardian* writer

'A powerful collection of connections to history, Country and culture – offering new insights every Australian should read.'
Terri Janke, author of *True Tracks: Respecting Indigenous knowledge and culture*

'If you have ever wondered what it actually means when we say "sovereignty was never ceded", this expansive volume holds a wealth of answers. Sovereignties of time, place, law, language, knowledge, memory, history, identity, logic, governance and art are explored by some of contemporary scholarship's most critical and creative thinkers. Challenging, compelling, provocative and practical, *Deep History* is a book for head and heart alike. Here is vital and vibrant reading for our truth-telling — and truth-listening — age.'
Clare Wright, Professor of History, La Trobe University and author of *Näku Dhäruk The Yirrkala Bark Petitions*

DEEP HISTORY
Country and Sovereignty

Edited by
**Ann McGrath and
Jackie Huggins**

UNSW PRESS

UNSW Press acknowledges the Bedegal people, the Traditional Owners of the unceded territory on which the Randwick and Kensington campuses of UNSW are situated, and recognises the continuing connection to Country and culture. We pay our respects to Bedegal Elders past and present.

A UNSW Press book

Published by
NewSouth Publishing
University of New South Wales Press Ltd
University of New South Wales
Sydney NSW 2052
AUSTRALIA
https://unsw.press/

Our authorised representative in the EU for product safety is Mare Nostrum Group B.V., Mauritskade 21D, 1091 GC Amsterdam, The Netherlands (gpsr@mare-nostrum.co.uk).

© Ann McGrath and Jackie Huggins 2025
First published 2025

10 9 8 7 6 5 4 3 2 1

This book is copyright. While copyright of the work as a whole is vested in Ann McGrath and Jackie Huggins, copyright of individual chapters is retained by the chapter authors. Apart from any fair dealing for the purpose of private study, research, criticism or review, as permitted under the *Copyright Act*, no part of this book may be reproduced by any process without written permission. Inquiries should be addressed to the publisher.

 A catalogue record for this book is available from the National Library of Australia

ISBN: 9781761170300 (paperback)
        9781761179297 (ebook)
        9781761178474 (ePDF)

Cover design Madeleine Kane
Internal design Josephine Pajor-Markus
Cover artwork Cheryl Davison, *Bringing the Rain*

'From little things, big things grow' by songwriters Kevin Daniel Carmody and Paul Maurice Kelly. Copyright held by WB Music Corp., Sony/Atv Music Publishing (Australia) Pty Ltd Paul Kelly Music, Song Cycles Pty Ltd, 1991.

All reasonable efforts were taken to obtain permission to use copyright material reproduced in this book, but in some cases copyright could not be traced. The editors welcome information in this regard.

CONTENTS

Deep History and deep sovereignty: An introduction   1
Ann McGrath

Part I: Is decolonising history possible? Sovereignty and national education

1   Walking on Sovereign Territory: Carnarvon Gorge   19
Jackie Huggins

2   Good timing? Australian history's changing temporality   26
Anna Clark

3   Deep Time history goes to school: How the new Australian curriculum is learning from the past   42
Beth Marsden

Part II: Archaeology, science and sovereign histories

4   Archaeology and Aboriginal sovereignty   67
Martin Porr

5   Difficult temporalities: Indigenous and Western archaeological ways of knowing the past in Oceania   90
Chris Urwin and Lynette Russell

6   Songs, stories and Deep Histories from Mutthi Mutthi, Ngiyampaa, Barkindji and Tati Tati Water Country   103
Grace Fletcher

Part III: The sovereignty of sustaining landscapes and foodscapes

7   Kai Māori spaces and temporalities in Tāmaki Makaurau   121
Bhaveeka Madagammana

8   For the common good: Local sovereignty and ra'ui in the Cook Islands   136
Bronwen Neil, Antony Vavia and Tom Murray

Part IV: Hard evidence: The languages of rock art and stories

9   History on the rocks   151
    *Laura Rademaker, Sally K May, Joakim Goldhahn
    and Gabriel Maralngurra*

10 Language has Country: Memory, transmission and
    sovereignty in Tara June Winch's *The Yield*   166
    Rosanne Kennedy and Ben Silverstein

11 A place for a stranger: The Wardandi history of
    Thomas Timothée Vasse   187
    Mary Blight

Part V: Walking as a practice of sovereignty

12 *Murrudha: Sovereign Walks*: Tracking cultural actions
    through art, Country, Language and music   207
    *Brenda L Croft, with First Nations Community members:
    Sue and Coral Bulger; Wendy Bunn; Cheryl, Michelle and
    Kobi Davison; Brenda Gifford; Shane Herrington; Leah House;
    Matilda House-Williams; Lois Peeler; Bronwyn Penrith; Maria
    Walker; Iris Walker-White and others*

Acknowlegdments   241
Contributors   242
Notes   249
Index   294

Language note:
In keeping with the larger project of decolonisation, throughout this book words from Indigenous Languages are not italicised.

DEEP HISTORY AND DEEP SOVEREIGNTY
An introduction

Ann Mcgrath

In *Deep History: Country and Sovereignty*, a team of scholars, artists and Indigenous Knowledge Holders gather to interrogate the relationship between First Nations and colonial histories and sovereignties. We pose a range of questions: how do histories make sovereignty? And how do sovereignties make history?[1] Should histories account for multiple sovereignties? And if that is the case, what shifts are required for history's future? This volume considers the competing histories and present-day practices that form and transform the lands, peoples and nations of Oceania, which includes the Pacific Islands, New Guinea, Aotearoa (New Zealand) and the great land mass of Australia. In nations impacted by colonialism, such questions are particularly pertinent.

The enduring cries from Indigenous peoples to have their sovereignty and their history properly acknowledged can be heard across the Pacific and beyond. Indigenous peoples, who have lived on their lands for significantly longer than colonial intruders, have long been making histories. Over millennia, caring for their places and their people, they created stories of the past and the future inscribed in these multitemporal landscapes. As Jackie Huggins has stated: for 'Aboriginal people, our past is still our present'.[2]

This volume considers how sovereignties are enacted through present-day historical practices. The locations discussed in this volume are sites of many-layered time, of dynamic Indigenous ways of being and experiencing their long histories. We observe the strategies by which imperial and colonial powers crafted historical narratives that justified their entitlement to new lands, and how Indigenous people continued to perform deep sovereign histories irrespective of colonialism's attempts to erase them.[3] Through walking, gathering food, gardening, making rock art, storytelling in many media and collaborations with academic historians and archaeologists, Indigenous peoples have performed their history *and* sovereignty through, on and with Country. This all-encompassing term denotes sovereign rights of long, intimate connection – a holistic concept that encompasses self, kin, water, land and sky and all the more-than-human beings that mutually sustain life and play active roles in ongoing stories. Yet, entrenched in school curricula, imperial and colonial histories continue to drive consciousness of what constitutes sovereign histories and what does not. This buttresses denialisms that block even the most moderate proposals towards Truth-Telling and Indigenous justice.

Deep History: Country and Sovereignty complements an earlier book, *Everywhen: Australia and the languages of Deep History* (edited by Ann McGrath, Laura Rademaker and Jakelin Troy), which emphasises Indigenous conceptualisations of temporality and Language.[4] Recognising that the longue durée of Indigenous histories shapes people's sensibilities and everyday lives, this new collection considers how temporality plays out in relation to sovereignty. The contributing authors know the challenges their work presents, and they acknowledge it is not always clear how best to go about it. They grapple with this tension, asking whether it is even possible to decolonise time and history. They consider what scholars can offer, and how they might be able to understand their discipline's ongoing legacies. How might practices of history-making allow for non-linear temporalities and starkly different conceptualisations of history? Is it feasible to realign the practice of history or other academic disciplines to tell the complex historical truths of deep histories?

This book has a broader geographic reach than *Everywhen*, for it spans some of the wider world of Oceania. Applying collaborative practices and learning from Indigenous methodologies, it takes us to villages of Kaivakovu and Larihairu at Orokolo Bay on Papua New Guinea's south coast, to the volcanic island of Mangaia in the Cook Islands, Polynesia, and to Aotearoa. In Australia, we visit lands that include those of the

Noongar and Wiradjuri, the Mirrar at Madjebebe, the Bidjara and other groups at Carnarvon Gorge in Queensland and the peoples of the vast Murray River and Willandra Lakes region.

Origins: Where this collection began

Hawai'i also has a special place in this book's story. On the island of O'ahu, Hawai'i, Jackie Huggins, who is Bidjara and Birri Gubba Juru, and Ann McGrath, a white Australian of Irish–English descent, gathered with a group of Indigenous leaders and scholars from many disciplines. It was the year 2023 – at least according to the European, now near-universal calendar for marking time. After a stay on the American continent, Jackie's plane flew across the Pacific Ocean westward, while Ann's travelled across the Pacific from Australia's eastern city Meanjin/Brisbane, where both women lived and met as young scholars. Our Hawai'ian panel included not only historians like ourselves, but arts practitioners, archaeologists, anthropologists, students, architects, educators and learners. The theme of the conference, organised by the Society for the Study of Social Sciences (4S), had sparked our attention: *Sea, Sky, and Land: Engaging in solidarity in endangered ecologies*. In one of many highlights, a keynote session of Indigenous women leaders, Manulani Aluli Meyer, Mehana Blaich Vaughan and Malia Akutagawa, spoke of their struggles to maintain their sovereign worlds and to pass them on to the next generation. They explained how they were returning to their lands, following Ancestral values, including principles of custodianship, sustainable agriculture and lifeways.[5] In the spirit of connecting with the land and contributing something to the island of O'ahu, four members of our group joined one of the practical events – birdwatching and tending an area near a bird marshland. As the wetlands had dried out due to climate change, we hardly saw a bird, but we certainly pulled up a lot of weeds.

At the conference venue in Honolulu, our panel *Deep History, Temporality and Indigenous Sovereignty* aimed to broaden thinking about Deep History. We shared the digital site that we had developed together with six Australian Indigenous communities over the past five years, part of our laureate program 'Rediscovering the Deep Human Past: Global Networks, Future Opportunities' funded by the Australian Research Council (ARC).[6] One of its key research outcomes, *Marking Country*, is a website co-curated and developed by academic and Community-based Knowledge Holders, with a leading role played by the co-editor of this book, Jackie Huggins. Holding special gatherings on Country, each of the six groups who participated chose how they wanted to convey their deep histories. Their primary goal was to ensure that their intimate histories in relation to land, sea and sky were not lost to their future generations; they also wanted to educate a wider public, including school children. The teams arranged, carried out and filmed important rituals such the wurdu/Wudoo for babies (discussed in chapter 1), undertook historical and cultural mapping, engaged in musical performances, explained the significance of rock art and epic stories across Country and walked on Country of deep Ancestral connection.[7] These practices reinvigorate Country – interconnected and alive with Ancestral, historical and much-storied significance through deep time.

Long histories

The many islands spanning the Pacific Ocean have human histories that go back millennia – from a few thousand years to tens of thousands.[8] In Australia, the scope of Indigenous occupation exceeds the scale of mainstream history; it traverses aeons – across the Holocene and Pleistocene eras. Oceans and coastlines rose and fell; once-joined land masses including present-day New Guinea, Tasmania and many smaller islands were divided off by seas. To its south, the islands of Aotearoa host stories of Ancestors arriving from far across the Pacific, and Ancestral maritime arrivals feature in many other Pacific histories. Ancient accounts of Indigenous connection across the seas are alive – enacted in local and pan-Pacific cultural gatherings and festivals. For example, an Indigenous Hawai'ian elder told the uncle of Gumbaynggirr/Gamilaroi man of New South Wales, Victor Briggs, of how Indigenous Australians journeyed to O'ahu.[9] In the broad sweep of history, this is a reminder that it is only in the past few centuries that the islands of Oceania have been dominated by newly minted histories of European empire and colonialism. This collection explores the role of historical writing and thinking as a means of inscribing and reinscribing the precepts of coloniser sovereignty.

To discuss the complex origins and meanings of our key terms *history* and *sovereignty* would take up many thousands of words. Fortunately, there are many detailed texts devoted to exploring their cultural and legal origin stories and evolution. Like all key concepts, they have changed over time.[10] For our purposes, we will apply more colloquial and flexible contemporary meanings. We take 'history' to concern the past itself, the lived experience of the past, and its diverse retellings in the present. We take 'sovereignty' as a term relating to power, authority and responsibility over lands and people; it can be a dispersed and collective power, not necessarily embodied in one symbolic entity such as a single sovereign or 'Crown'.[11] To this kind of authority, and vital to this collection, we add the *sovereignty of history* – the sway of its powerful narratives and impacts in framing and reinforcing the order and the power relations of the present and the future. In international law, sovereignty had to be performed to be valid. We argue that performing history has been, and remains, a vital tool for doing so.

In considering Indigenous peoples' pasts, the term 'Deep History' can be helpful, for it takes the spotlight off European-generated imperial and colonising histories. The term expands the usual shallow timescales of history. It also signals the long Indigenous histories that took place prior to the arrival of the colonisers, who introduced their Eurocentric chronologies of when history began and how it should be told. Deep History can be used in a fluid way that overrides linear timelines. Instead it can encompass profoundly different takes on history-telling, gesturing towards multitemporal histories enacted in place. It calls for Indigenous history-telling practices to be respected as forms of historical practice and education.[12] We cannot underestimate the challenges, however, that these embodied practices pose to academic history's notions of temporality and chronological framings. They unsettle what constitutes historical evidence, thereby creating new demands on historical methodologies, forms of critique and delivery.

Firstly, periodisation.[13] These chronologies of imperial sovereignty in turn constructed the timelines of national histories – practices that naturalised the authority of these states. By emphasising the key dates associated with European arrival and agency, coloniser nations have asserted an *historically based sovereignty* – one reliant upon their own tellings of their people's landings in places new to them. Whether remaining under imperial powers or becoming republics, in settler-coloniser states like the United States, Aotearoa and Australia, historians have routinely started their studies with the various dates of first European arrivals, which include visits by the first European navigators (whether they actually landed or not), the terrestrial explorers, the 'discoverers', the 'pioneers' – or first European settlers. Or they gave primacy to the kinds of performances of imperial coloniser sovereignty conventionally required in international law: verbal and otherwise recorded declarations of possession by a distant Crown and the official imperially sanctioned and signed inaugurations of coloniser states or nations. Additionally, one of the vital sources of evidence upon which historians have been taught to rely – the state archives – was developed as an 'archive of empire', a key apparatus for constructing state policy and implementation.[14] Archival, historical and archaeological conceptions of time artificially divide and compartmentalise Australian history, sanctioning the primacy of the colonial presence. New histories were superimposed over old landscapes; First Nations histories were disregarded as unknowable. Over the past decades, however, this has changed, with deep histories considered increasingly knowable. Of course Indigenous peoples already held such knowledge; it is archaeologists, other western scientists and historians who have begun catching up.

On lands where Indigenous people's histories stretched back many millennia, we should not lose sight of the way colonisers asserted their new sovereignty claims: in official records, journals and popular publications, they celebrated possession and take-over via the raising of flags and toasting the Kings and Queens of England, France or other sovereigns by inheritance. They sang patriotic songs and commissioned artworks, and established constitutions, laws and judicial systems under the authority of the sovereign. So crucial were the historical enterprises that underpinned imperial sovereignty that some historical accounts were published even before the first colonisers had arrived. Performances of arrival and declarations of sovereignty were re-enacted and reproduced *ad infinitum*. Colonial states established archival repositories and constructed histories that explicitly annulled all that had gone beforehand. First Nations people became history's outsiders.[15]

Later, to justify the inevitability of the introduced sovereignty, colonial nations devised historical plotlines that emphasised their supposed economic, moral and racial superiority and modernity. In several nations, they even expunged the violence associated with dispossession and the oppressions that followed; hence today the call for truth-telling. The timelines of Deep History unsettle the short time scale of colonial histories. From the discipline's beginnings in monastic times, historians have calculated dates by accumulating textual evidence; in more recent times, scientists use techniques such as radiocarbon dating and photoluminescence to ascertain the expanse of Indigenous histories. Australia, for example, now boasts some startling facts about early human occupation. That humans lived at Lake Mungo/Willandra Lakes, at least 40 000 years ago; and in Arnhem Land and Yirrkala 65 000 years ago. As Martin Porr explains, however, such dates and the science behind them can be far more problematic than the wider public appreciates.

Additionally, a fetish for the earliest, 'the first and the last', does not necessarily resonate with Indigenous people, who have their own creation and arrival stories and conceptualisations of time.[16] New Guinea villagers in Orokolo Bay tell of the lou haera, the story people who made the coastline and mountains as they travelled.[17] Perhaps a more significant factor, but not headline-grabbing in the sense of a new scientific 'discovery', is that Indigenous people of regions of early occupation dates in Australia, Papua New Guinea and the Pacific, continue to travel to, conduct gatherings, care for and perform their histories at these very same places today. Concern regarding 'firsts' discounts the longue durée of cultural, present-day association and continuity. Moreover, many Indigenous Australians are not interested in scientific proofs of their arrival on the continent, attesting that 'we have always been here'. While Western-style histories are often reliant upon political change narratives such as the reigns of sovereigns (for example, the Victorian era) or large-scale wars, in Indigenous cosmologies and places of ongoing, embodied connection to place, other knowledges are more important. It is continuity rather than scientifically verifiable dating that they see as the basis of their deep time sovereignty claims. And after all, whether 50 000 or 65 000 years, in terms of their custodianship, and in the context of global human history, this may as well be understood as beyond the scale – as 'forever'.

Everyday sovereignties

For people on either side of the coloniser divide or straddling it, demonstrations of sovereignty and of long histories can be witnessed in everyday life. In Hawai'i, Indigenous elders honoured the 4S conference organisers with beautifully crafted floral tributes from their local gardens. In Aotearoa, the Māori language, and the powerful cultural concepts and protocols it articulates, remain strong. High-profile performances of the Haka at international events, including rugby matches, provide unforgettable declarations of cultural and warrior pride. In Australia's capital, Canberra, the Aboriginal Tent Embassy situated in front of Old Parliament House[18] has demanded recognition of Indigenous sovereignty since 26 January 1972.[19] Its timing directly challenged the current national holiday, Australia Day, which marked the arrival of the first convict fleet at Port Jackson, Sydney.

Non-Indigenous acknowledgment practices that openly recognise Indigenous sovereignty are gathering pace in several settler-colonial settings. For example, when a passenger boards a Qantas flight today, they see a map of Australia that shows the estates of hundreds of Indigenous language groups. When the planes land, the flight attendants honour the Traditional Custodians of the location, paying respects to Elders past and present.[20] At football matches and other sports games, at government, university and community events, Indigenous elders are invited to provide an official Welcome. Radio and television announcers frequently announce the Indigenous nations upon which they are meeting, and many participants do so in virtual meetings too. Weather maps on television screens show the names of cities and towns both in Indigenous Languages and their post-colonisation names. Private corporations, state bodies, universities, schools and colleges acknowledge that they are on the *unceded* lands of their respective Indigenous peoples. Such trends follow the emergence of more inclusive historical narratives and, in Australia, of long-overdue legal recognition of native title in a land where no official treaties had been negotiated. In 1992, the Mabo judgment of Australia's High Court momentously declared that *terra nullius*, the notion that Australia was uninhabited prior to the arrival of Anglo-Europeans, was a 'legal fiction'. Native title had not been extinguished. In North American and Australian universities, prestigious professional academies and funding bodies across Australia are beginning to recognise the intrinsic value of Indigenous Knowledges, allocating research funding to studies that foreground such knowledge, making identified senior appointments, and even acknowledging their institution's roles in acquisitive colonialism.[21]

Sadly, it is not all smooth sailing. In Aotearoa today, governments threaten to dismantle the rights awarded by the Treaty of Waitangi and bilingual language programs. The Hawai'ians are still fighting against huge telescopes being erected on their sacred mountain, Mauna Kea. In 2017, following extensive consultations held by Indigenous nations across Australia, the Uluru Statement from the Heart called for a national reckoning. Among other things, the Uluru Statement asked Australians to acknowledge the long Indigenous history on the continent; 65 000 years in scientific terms, 'always' in many Indigenous reckonings. It demanded Truth-Telling about the nation's history.[22]

The conservative government of the day rejected the Uluru Statement, and in 2023 an incoming Labor government put its recommendations to a national referendum. It proposed two things: to officially recognise Aboriginal people in the Constitution and to provide a secure entity called the Voice which would serve as an official Indigenous body to advise government. The catchcry of the Yes Campaign was 'History Is Calling'. Despite the tireless work of so many people around the nation, the referendum was defeated. Distinguished Indigenous leaders had advocated for constitutional recognition and determined that the Voice was vital for a strong healthy future – towards finally 'closing the gap' – the serious shortfall in Indigenous wellbeing, living standards, health and education. Unfortunately, the campaign became a political football between the opposition parties and the Labor government and grew increasingly divisive. In the lead-up to the referendum, certain conservative Indigenous politicians objected to their people having a distinct status in the wider nation – a stance which arguably rejected their recognition as sovereign on unceded lands. At the same time, a radical Indigenous alliance, the Blak Sovereign Movement, contended that recognition under the colonial constitution would annul Indigenous sovereignty. Among the non-Indigenous population, racism, historical denialism, confusion and ignorance were at play. At centre stage were vital questions of contested sovereignty and contested histories of nation.

Given the shocking and depressing outcome of that referendum, when we attended the conference in Hawai'i, emotions were raw. Long-term Indigenous rights campaigner Jackie Huggins made an emotional address to the Hawai'ian women elders, her on-Country hosts. After such long struggles, amid a history of tragedy and heartbreak, this was yet another blow.[23] Devastated at this lost opportunity, she was particularly concerned about the hurt felt by the younger generation. Empowered, however, by the resilience, courage and drive of her Ancestors, Jackie spoke up, underlining the global solidarity and uphill struggles of Indigenous people in their quest for full sovereign recognition. As the Hawaiian elders pointed out: 'These systems are not our own, therefore we are fighting against them all the time'. Jackie thanked those Indigenous elders in Hawai'i for listening and for hosting us. Despite the optimism Jackie expresses in her chapter in this volume, in October 2024 a conservative government dismantled Queensland's Truth Telling Commission and the Path to Treaty process in Jackie's home state. Such regressive steps cannot, however, stop Queenslanders, your co-editors included, from engaging in historical Truth-Telling at any opportunity. We hang onto those other words of wisdom we heard from the strong women in Hawai'i. The pendulum will swing back over time in favour of Indigenous rights, and the younger generations will be the beneficiaries.

Walking the chapters

To walk you through the rich contributions before you, this book is divided into sections. The first is entitled 'Is decolonising history possible? Sovereignty and national education'. In Jackie Huggins's chapter, she introduces her family story, then explains how her Bidjara sovereignty is enlivened by the immersive practice of walking on Country of deep Ancestral connection (chapter 1). She adopts the ways of her mother and respects her uncle's knowledge. As Jackie explains: 'When I visit, I do as my mother Rita did when she visited there. She would walk around, she would feel the earth, and she would kiss the ground upon which she knew our people had been for tens and tens of thousands of years'.[24] Huggins reflects on the Marking Country website and specifically the making of the Carnarvon Gorge page, which tracks Huggins and Uncle Fred Conway, who shares his ecological, bushcraft and cultural knowledge of this place, culminating in a major art and education site.[25] Tragically, we learn that destructive land practices and climatic pressures led to an inferno that recently destroyed a precious, massive wall of ancient rock art – an archive from which so much could have been learnt.

Anna Clark's and Beth Marsden's chapters (chapters 2 and 3) show how Australian school textbook authors occluded Indigenous people from the possibility of having a history, with the longue durée of Indigenous pasts presented as outside history, as beyond its geographical ambit and temporal scale.[26] They explore the past ways of writing and teaching history that have left long legacies now difficult to overcome. When speaking with Clark, one Indigenous advisor referred to historians as the 'time police'. No wonder, as under a colonising regime, external intrusions, including scholarly ones, constituted forms of policing, if not outlawing, Indigenous ways of life. This impeded their ways of doing history, or their historicities. At last the discipline of history and the education system is attempting to take First Nations' ways of knowing into account. In discussing the new national curriculum on Deep Time, Marsden notes that schoolteachers play a vital role in reshaping perspectives, but they face significant challenges. She urges curriculum developers to respect Indigenous protocols and ontologies and to devise improved ways of presenting the cross-cultural complexity of Indigenous histories.[27]

In the next section, 'Archaeology, science and sovereign histories', archaeologist Martin Porr notes that while his discipline deals in time, it does not theorise what it actually does in relation to time (chapter 4). As noted above, he points out the range of variables that make identifying specific dates of occupation much more contested than the general public knows. Urwin and Russell's chapter (chapter 5) brings together an archaeologist and an Indigenous historian to tackle difficult temporalities in Papua New Guinea and Australia. The living Indigenous pasts and the western disciplines of archaeology and history are strands of knowledge that seem impossible to bring together. But are they? In Urwin's collaborative work, Orokolo Bay's Ancestral places and local Indigenous knowledge of the black sands, pottery, beach ridges and subsurface monuments vitally inform the academic research. The archaeological investigation and radiocarbon dates complement local memory, with oral histories amplifying Indigenous knowledge of generational sequences and geographies. This collaborative research approach and mutual knowledge exchange proves invaluable for negotiating and knowing the past.

In chapter 6, with insights from Brendan Kennedy, a Millu Widungi custodian of the waterways of the Murray River, Grace Fletcher takes us on a journey from a pelican-filled lagoon to a now-dry lake system of ancient human presence: Willandra Lakes. This is the location of a remarkable series of human footprints from the Pleistocene era, a site which enables people to feel the humanity of the deep past in a visceral sense. It also helps us to consider the impacts of climate change. Through the teachings of local custodians such as the Tati Tati, the Barkindji, Mutthi Mutthi and other nations, readers learn that rivers and waterways are part of themselves and their common wellbeing. In turn, everyone should value the health of rivers as living entities that need to be deeply respected and cared for.

In the third section, 'The sovereignty of sustaining landscapes and foodscapes', we learn about foodscapes as enduring practices of Indigenous sovereignty. Examples are drawn from Oceania, the Cook Islands, and in Aotearoa, Tāmaki Makaurau (Auckland), where people practise eco-cosmologies that dictate sustainable food practices – themes also powerfully articulated in the keynotes at the Hawai'i conference. Bhaveeka Madagammana's chapter (chapter 7) provides a forensic look at the Kai/food spaces – a means of appreciating Indigenous seasonal mobilities and complex connections with territory. In Tāmaki Makaurau, Kai Māori Spaces sustain future generations without depleting resources. Through rich linguistic concepts and an architecture of foodscapes, sovereignty is articulated in land management and ways of being in the world. The chapter by Bronwen Neil, Antony Vavia and Tom Murray (chapter 8) also considers the continuity of deep time food practices in relation to sovereignty. On the Cook Islands, named by Russians in honour of the famous British navigator, its people have continued their practice of Ra'ui or culturally based food restrictions, refusing to bend to the way of intruders. Sustainable fishing and other food, travel and living practices become fundamental ongoing activations of continuing sovereignty.

In the next section, 'Hard evidence: The languages of rock art and stories', we learn how Indigenous Knowledge Holders conceptualise rock paintings not simply as art, but as a library, a valuable archive, a classroom blackboard and more. In chapter 9, the collaboration between a historian (Laura Rademaker), two rock art specialists (Sally Kate May and Joakim Goldhahn) and archaeologists, and Indigenous knowledge man and artist Gabriel Maralngurra, depicts how rock paintings and engravings function as history. But, as the authors point out, such knowledge is a gift, and part of a reciprocal kin relationship that must be honoured by family and researchers alike.

Rather than choosing to write standard historical narratives, many Indigenous authors choose to explore and express the truth of their sovereignty via poetry and fictional writing. Rosanne Kennedy and Ben Silverstein (chapter 10) focus on Tara June Winch's *The Yield*, which powerfully reflects on Indigenous memory and sovereignty and the relationship between the Indigenous present and the continuities of historical time. Refusing a historicity of rupture, we learn how Winch brings together multiple times and temporalities: the deep past, the settler colonial past, the settler colonial and capitalist colonial present, and possible Indigenous futures. A key plotline follows the protagonist's work in archiving the Wiradjuri dictionary, with its empowering impact of Language revival on Country.

Moving across the Australian continent to the lands of the Wardanji Noongar people in south-western Australia, Mary Blight narrates the maritime mystery of the French sailor Vasse, who was abandoned by the Baudin expedition in 1801 (chapter 11). Her chapter highlights the factual power of Indigenous memory and oral history, which realigns popular, semi-fictionalised accounts of Vasse's fate at Geographe Bay. The Wardanji cared for Vasse and included him in their Community, yet those who wrote about this story missed this, because they failed to consult Indigenous memory holders. Arguing for the importance of Indigenous oral histories, Blight contends that, unless local researchers listen to Indigenous accounts of history on their Country, they are ignoring their sovereignty.

The penultimate section, 'Walking as a practice of sovereignty', presents a journey from the Snowy Mountains in regional New South Wales to Australia's national capital, Kambri/Canberra.[28] Brenda Croft and her team of collaborators explain how *Murrudha: Sovereign walks* is a culturally appropriate way of doing history and of cultural maintenance (chapter 12). Murrudha is a Wiradyuri term for being 'on track', which evokes following the law and the pathways of song. Through walking and being in places of significance, the team reconnect with their lands and histories, revisiting journeys undertaken in colonial times and the early years of Australian nationhood: in 1834, 1873 and 1927. Asserting their ongoing sovereignty, these groups travelled as a means of diplomacy and political negotiation. In one walk that started at Brungle Aboriginal Mission on Walgalu/Wiradyuri Country, two walamira or clever men trekked 150 kilometres (93 miles) across the Brindabella Ranges to attend the official opening of the new federal Parliament House on 9 and 10 May 1927. Meanwhile the Duke of York and Duchess of York, representatives of the British sovereign, travelled to Canberra in a stately Crossley landaulette imported from England.[29] For the official opening, bedecked in a regal hat, epaulettes and medals, they sat in an elegant horse-drawn carriage. Although the barefoot walamiri men, Jimmy Wiradyuri walamira Nangar[30] (also known as Jimmy Clements) and Ooloogan (also known as George John Noble), were asked to leave, their message got through. Newspapers of the day recognised that they were defending their sovereign rights. With photographers capturing their images in front of the new Parliament House, dual and duelling sovereignties were being played out with theatrical aplomb. The wider crowd supported the Indigenous men's participation, with a well-known clergyman who attended declaring that they 'had a better right than any man present to a place on the steps of Parliament House and in the Senate during the ceremony'.[31] Croft explores her research team's efforts to retrace the steps of these men and others, thereby reasserting Indigenous sovereignty by walking their historical routes.

The contributors to this volume showcase how Indigenous sovereignty can be seen and heard across the oceans. Indigenous peoples often speak humbly of the power they draw from Ancestors, and they also speak of Ancestral futures. Ancestral teachings live on in the present time, in the Everywhen. The whole world needs to listen to these messages of innovation and continuity, for the local and global future, whatever it brings, will be mutual. Indigenous-led and collaborative models for doing history, archaeology and anthropology are essential. Researchers would benefit by venturing out of the classrooms and the academies, as well as beyond the state archives, into the field, in order to take account of different kinds of archives.[32]

Several contributors question whether western-style approaches of history and archaeology can truly incorporate the histories of peoples who live outside their disciplinary logic. This volume demonstrates, however, that First Nations peoples are working hard to take up these challenges across disciplines and across the Pacific. Our collection argues that scholars must look backwards at the trajectory and legacies of their own disciplines before they start to look to the future. School and university teachers alike need to interrogate their past roles in the making of histories that were designed to superimpose imperial sovereignties upon long-held Indigenous sovereignties. Together, we must find ways to ensure that good intentions do not diminish Indigenous knowledge systems and cultural practices.

The keepers of sovereign knowledge of history are generous. This collection explains how walking on Country charges the body and spirit with Ancestral power. Walking together too. We are privileged that Jackie's uncle, Bidjara elder Fred Conway, as well as Kunwinjku elder Gabriel Maralngurra invite you, our readers, to come and sit down on their Country, to learn the stories. Of the rocks themselves, Maralngurra explains, 'He will teach you'. If the people who read this book 'want to ask more questions, they can come. If you want to learn more, we'll tell you … Come and sit down, in a big rock, big cave, I'll explain every little painting on the rock'.[33] In the welcoming environments of such story spaces, whether arriving on the island of Mangaia via a sea canoe, in sustaining inland waterways and bushlands or in Kai Māori gardens, by conversing with people, travelling together and listening on Country, such places and all that they hold have deep histories to teach us all.

PART I

Is decolonising history possible? Sovereignty and national education

1

WALKING ON SOVEREIGN TERRITORY
Carnarvon Gorge

Jackie Huggins

Ngya Bidjara/Birri Gubba Juru marra. My name is Jackie Huggins. I am the mother of John. I am also the daughter of Rita, and Albert and Rose are my grandparents on my mother's side. My father is Jack Huggins. My grandparents are John Henry Huggins the third, and Fanny: all people from Queensland in Australia.

My father was a free man. He wasn't under the Aboriginal protection legislation of the state of Queensland, or of the country, in fact. The Aboriginals Protection Act – or *Aboriginals Protection and Restriction of the Sale of Opium Act 1897* – restricted many Aboriginal people in Queensland to remaining wards of the state, controlling their employment and other aspects of their lives.[1] To be outside this Act meant less restrictions on where you could go, who you could marry, and so on. Your life was not controlled. However, my mother, under the auspices of this Act, was rounded up in the 1920s and put on the back of a cattle truck, removed from the beautiful Country of ours, from Carnarvon Gorge in Central Queensland, and taken over 600 kilometres east to Cherbourg Aboriginal Mission along with five of her siblings. She had 13 siblings in total.

My mum led the life of most Queensland Aboriginal women under the Act in the 1920s. They went into domestic service at the age of 11 or 12, sent to slave out on cattle station properties all throughout the state. My father did not have to do that. Instead, he served in the Second

World War and was a prisoner of war on the Burma–Thailand Railway. While he did come home and fathered three healthy children, he died at the age of 38.

I don't know much about my father's Country, Ayr, North Queensland – Birri Gubba Juru – where he and his children were born, but I certainly know a lot about my mother's. It is also the Country of my uncle, Fred Conway, who has been my cultural and spiritual advisor over many decades. He was a Ranger out at Carnarvon Gorge for thirty years and still takes school excursions there to show, share and teach the Deep History of our Country. He knows every inch of that Country – the Gorge – including the wildlife, plants, birds, where the women's sites are, and the men's sites. He has a talent for impressing upon every visitor how unique that Country is to us, how special and sacred the Country is for most Bidjara people.

We share that place with a number of other groups. Carnarvon Gorge is on part of the Country of the Gayiri, Nguri, Garaynbal (Karingbal), Gungabula, Yiman and Wadja peoples. In 2020, we had a meeting of the Gathering of the Clans, and we hope that, through Treaty rights that are ensuing in our Country, Treaty might become a way for us to get much more out of that than Native Title, as Native Title has not served us so well, so Treaty could assist more in terms of access to legislation. The Mabo Judgement (1992) of the High Court of Australia recognised that native title existed and that the notion of *terra nullius* was a fiction.[2] The Australian Government introduced the *Native Title Act 1993* to allow a process for recognising Indigenous title to land. However, this is a flawed process in many ways, and it generally relies upon non-Indigenous documentation to prove title. Anyway, we lost that because the claimant area was far too great. But Carnarvon Gorge area is clearly Bidjara Country. The people who have claim to that – the Karingbal people – will also acknowledge our connection to that Country. The government determined that they were the last people standing under the Native Title rules of the Commonwealth, declaring the Karingbal own this Country. But the Karingbal people say, 'We know that you own Carnarvon Gorge, and you are the spiritual owners of that place'.

Every year I go back there, to Carnarvon Gorge. I try to make it twice a year sometimes. And in fact, as I write this, I have just returned. When I visit, I do as my mother Rita did when she visited there. She would walk around, she would feel the earth, and she would kiss the ground upon which she knew our people had been for tens and tens of thousands of years.

My mum was a single mum. She was very influential in my life. She grew up four kids without my father, who had passed so young, and she too had a yearning for her Country. As you get older, particularly for our mob, you want to go back to those places. You just yearn for that Country that you came from, even though she was rounded up on the back of a cattle truck and sent to Cherbourg – some 3 hours north-west of Brisbane – at a very young age. Where she ended up was my mother's adopted home. Cherbourg was a mission reserve where our people were put, forcibly removed from their Countries. We had a big inquiry about children being forcibly removed from their families. This was known as the Stolen Generations Inquiry and it was hoped that stolen children could be reunited with their families and communities. Native Title was supposed to fix that too. But unfortunately, it has created all kinds of deep divisions within our communities as well. It is very restrictive as people have to prove they were always on their land and Country to gain native title rights. Of course, this is often impossible for those who were removed from land.

We are relying now on our Treaty that I've been working on, on and off, for the past four years in Queensland. Treaty is an agreement between two parties, and if Native Title is lost then it is lost forever, despite appeal processes. Treaty therefore offers an opportunity for traditional owner groups to negotiate agreements with governments and other stakeholders outside of Native Title. Treaty would acknowledge that sovereignty was always and will always be intact. But unfortunately, due to the Voice Referendum held in 2023, the opposition party in my state of Queensland has said they will not entertain a Treaty if they come into power at the next election. In October 2024, they were elected into power. Hopefully that won't stop us because two Budgets ago the Queensland Government committed funding to pursue Treaty and Truth-Telling, quarantined against COVID and quarantined against natural disasters. Actually, we think this failure of the majority of the Australian people to support the Voice is one of those natural disasters.

Regardless, our Treaty will continue in some shape or form, aided by Truth-Telling. Truth-Telling has to be an honest conversation about what has happened through colonisation and its continued effects on the Indigenous population. It will enable all people to share their truth, officially document their stories, and uncover the untold and unrecognised history of this country. In the state of Victoria, they have a Treaty process and a Truth-Telling Commission that is happening now. Victoria is about five years ahead of Queensland in this regard. Queensland only began their process in September 2024.

Back to my Country, Carnarvon Gorge. This very special and beautiful place called Carnarvon Gorge is in the centre of Queensland. It is an oasis in the desert. It is very remote, but for many decades now, my uncle has been doing the talking up of that Country and educating people – educating whoever wants to listen – about the beauty and the magnificence of that Country.

So when Ann McGrath came to me and said, 'We're concentrating on six sites through Marking Country [the new website], we would love to do one for Carnarvon Gorge', I put my hand up, and so did Uncle Fred. As explained elsewhere, this digital project aimed to present Deep History on Country in the ways that Indigenous custodians wanted to present it to a wider audience. Uncle Fred and I came to a conference at the Australian National University in Canberra and spoke about the work that we're doing.

Ann visited Carnarvon Gorge with another researcher, Amy Way, and we sat there and took photos and videos of the beautiful Country that is Carnarvon Gorge, including the rock art of my Country. It has many sites that are available to the wider public to have a look at, but there are many sites that Uncle Fred has taken me and my family into that he won't show to white people or any other visitors. I feel very special about that.

For me to have come back to thinking about academic history and reflecting on what 'history' means for me as an Aboriginal woman is a bit of a different turn. To explain, as well as publishing histories of my family and many articles, I have done over 45 years in Aboriginal politics in our country, across all kinds of areas: reconciliation, domestic family violence, prison reform, Stolen Generations, you name it.[3] I've been on every board – except a skateboard, and you wouldn't want to see me on that! But that's the extent of my career. And of course, I am an Aboriginal woman historian as well.

I have a deep affection for history. I saw the way that my mother was treated as an Aboriginal single mum, and I saw the way that history wasn't even taught in our schools. And one day I said, 'I want to be a historian, I want to write, I want to teach, and I want to talk about history', and that I did. It was a nice dream come true. The other dream that came true was to see our history taught in curriculums in our Country, which it never was in the sixties. That made growing up pretty hard. We had – of course – the influence from the Civil Rights Movement in the United States and the global Women's Movement to really push us forward in terms of knowing that we could really do something about a dismal situation. So, that is how I came to history.

I was taught by some of Australia's best historians, as Ann was, at the University of Queensland: Raymond Evans and Kay Saunders. Back when I was at university, they were very radical historians. They still are. Along with Kathryn Cronin, they wrote a book – *Exclusion, Exploitation and Extermination* – which is a book before its time that talked about the history and treatment of Aboriginal peoples in Queensland.[4] This has always informed me of where I am now, and that is, as an older Aboriginal woman wanting to make peace with my Country, to go back every year and sit on the ground and to feel the power of the earth come through my feet every time I walk on it barefoot. To feel that indescribable power where you know that you are connected to the Country in every single way. Every sinew, every bone is connected to that place.

So even though my mother was removed from there during the days of the government assimilation policies of removing people from their Country and forcing them to live on government or church-run reserves, we will always stay very connected to Carnarvon Gorge. As a result, my family and I try to go back there quite regularly. But it's a fair way. It's a fair way from where we live now in the city of Meanjin (Brisbane).

It's a bit of a trip, but nevertheless, when you get there it calls you home in every sense of the word. And it is a feeling that others feel too. I have had discussions with my non-Indigenous friends, and their opinions vary. Some people say, 'Yeah, I get that, too', or they might respond that 'I don't feel it as deeply as you', and 'I'm not quite sure'. You know where the truth lies. And I know that our people have always said we're willing to share this Country. I haven't heard much of the reciprocal side, but the response is sometimes that: 'You're taking too much, or you're going to take our backyards'. Never mind, we'll continue to fight the good fight.

Reflecting again on the Marking Country website, it is a project that explores six sites all over the continent, telling the stories of various tracts of Country, and the ceremony, Language and peoples that make them up. There's a beautiful story about performing smoking ceremonies for babies up in the Kimberley. It tells the story of how, when the baby comes into the world, he or she gets smoked by members of their Community to give them protection and guidance throughout their life. It is a beautiful ceremony.[5]

Unfortunately, as detailed in *Auntie Rita* – the book I co-wrote with my mother – when my mum was put onto Cherbourg Mission, she was not allowed to practise her customs and her ceremony, her dance and her songs.[6] Nevertheless, she retained some Language. I can only speak about twenty words of my Language, but these are words that can be a conversation with my family. And the really great thing is, the Bidjara people have just got a grant to foster, learn and share the Bidjara Language. So my whole family is going to be involved in that in 2025. We're going to return to speaking in the tongue of our Ancestors. You're never too old to learn these things, and I would just adore to learn my language. It was taken off us, like so much.

Yet still, the Country is all connected to us. You know we are still here today. Even as a contemporary Aboriginal woman who has done so many things, I still feel very, very connected to where I come from. And this is the kind of message that we want to get out through this book, and through initiatives such as the Marking Country website. That is, we want to share how rich and unique and beautiful our stories are. We want to show how they can be passed on and to share them with other others.

I feel I have come full circle in terms of all the work I've done in my life so far, but coming back to place and Country, and being schooled by one of the finest teachers in the world, my uncle Fred – who just knows so much – has been a great experience for me. The Country, place and space, land and sea are still within us, within us all, no matter where we come from, but particularly for First Nations peoples in Australia.

Waddamooli (in my father's Language).

2
GOOD TIMING? AUSTRALIAN HISTORY'S CHANGING TEMPORALITY

Anna Clark

History has a curious relationship with time. A foundation of empirical research method sits at its core, shaped by ideas and practices of objectivity, evidence, source criticism and chronology. Yet history has also been increasingly understood to be subjective: from the 1960s and 1970s, labour and feminist histories challenged whether history could tell the whole story.[1] These critiques, substantial in their own right, were further animated by postcolonial and settler colonial studies and histories of slavery, as well as movements of postmodernism and poststructuralism – what we might call the 'cultural turn' – along with Indigenous Knowledges.[2] Such approaches fundamentally shifted our contemplation of history as an impartial account of the past to an acknowledgment that the discipline is shaped by, and in turn shapes, its cultural context.

Take 'objectivity', for example. It's a seemingly concrete idea which, as historian Peter Novick's study of American history, *That Noble Dream*, explores, is now understood to be contingent. The field's boundaries, values and methodologies have continuously evolved, rendering even the notion of objectivity subject to change.[3] Similarly, interpretations of historical 'truth' and evidence are now recognised as shifting across eras and place according to who is forming the historical interpretation in question.[4] The concept of time, similarly foundational to historical inquiry, has also been increasingly interrogated.[5] This is important research, showing how time not only organises and sequences historical events, but also influences our perceptions and interpretations of the past at a point *in time*.⁶ As Berber Bevernage and Chris Lorenz have argued, theorising 'the "historical relativity" of time' is critical, and more work is needed to understand how time functions in historical practice and theory.⁷

In response, this chapter explores the concept of time within the context of Australian historiography. I identify three main periods of historical time in what we might call Australian History – that disciplinary historical practice taught in schools and universities which conforms to recognised, authorised conventions of empirical research. These are 'colonising time', 'national time' and, most recently, a critical interrogation of time influenced by First Nations histories and critical theorists, which I tentatively term 'decolonising time'. I've elaborated on the definition and scope of these three periods elsewhere, and I acknowledge the irony of delineating temporal periods in a study that critiques the discipline's changing temporality.⁸ I use them again here, however, more as an organisational tool than any prescriptive marker, and I am open to other principles and approaches that might usefully prod our understanding of Australian history's shifting relationship with time.

Each specified period occupies a relatively identifiable timespan and includes a recognisable body of scholarship. Although I also realise that the definition of 'historiography' itself has been challenged in this latter period of revision and critique – indeed, that decolonising recognition forms an important part of my analysis and in turn prompts a series of provocations for the discipline. I focused on these three periods because they correspond with identifiable shifts in scholarly discourse and societal attitudes, highlighting the dynamic relationship between historical practice and broader socio-political contexts. Towards the latter decades of the 19th century, colonial histories that initially marked out the origins of Australian history gradually gave way to more national narratives.⁹ In this transition, a burgeoning professionalisation of the history discipline prompted historians to chronicle the emergence and ascendency of nation-state. More recently, as in other settler colonial states around the world, Australian historians have increasingly confronted the complicity of their discipline in processes of colonisation.

Such discussion has raised all sorts of ethical and creative questions about historical practice and the discipline's capacity to decolonise.[10] This hasn't been a moment of disciplinary abandonment, but rather a recognition that historians have curated the past, whereby certain narratives were authorised and expounded while others were excluded from the Australian story. The concept of time has played a pivotal role in this settler colonial framework, since it has been used to marginalise First Nations voices by implying that they existed outside historical, linear time. This has effectively positioned them as outside the realm of historical 'progress'. Consequently, until the latter half of the 20th century, First Nations histories and historians were largely sidelined from Australian historiography.

There's been a significant shift in disciplinary paradigms since that period, spurred by calls to recognise and include First Nations perspectives and forms of history-making, as well as insisting on the sovereignty of Indigenous ways of knowing. These interventions have not only extended the temporal scope of Australian history, which now reaches back tens of thousands of years into what has come to be known as deep time, but have also challenged historians to engage with Indigenous conceptualisations of time itself.[11] It's a transformative process not unique to Australia, of course: a growing disciplinary imperative to engage with and incorporate Indigenous Knowledges has propelled new agendas for research, as well as methodological debates, internationally.[12] However, its effect on historical research and practice in Australia has been profound.

Time as colonising

In *Time's Monster*, Priya Satia's potent examination of history's role in European imperialism, she describes the unfolding sense of imperial pre-eminence in the discipline as a sort of self-manifesting destiny. 'The cultural hold of a certain understanding of history and historical agency was not innocent but designedly complicit in the making of empire', Satia explains.[13] Dipesh Chakrabarty has similarly discerned in European imperialism a clash of temporality, 'a moment of encounter between history-rich and history-poor people', which was in turn used to justify the colonial project.[14] Through history itself, the agency of Western empires was seen in historical terms that justified colonisation, adds Satia: 'Where the West was dynamic, the place of progress and history, the East was passive, timeless and unchanging, immune to history'.[15]

Their assessments find resonance in the early colonial histories of Australia, which presumed First Nations peoples lacked a comprehension of 'history' (in that chronological, empirical sense), and therefore existed outside the limits of 'historical time'. Colonial narratives explicitly partitioned Australian history into a simplistic dichotomy of 'before' and 'after' European 'discovery'. Prior to colonisation, the continent of Australia was depicted as an unknown realm, existing as a hypothesis in European consciousness.[16]

Historical maps rendered this imaginary place cartographically, as Terra Australis Incognita – the 'Unknown South Land'. Books, too, described this period when the idea of Australia was mere speculation. *The History of New Holland*, for example, published as the First Fleet set sail to Australia in 1787, described Australia in those terms exactly: 'New Holland was, for upwards of a century, supposed to be part of a vast Southern continent, the existence of which had been long a favourite idea, maintained, on various reasoning, by many experienced navigators, as well as speculative arguers'.[17] On the opening page of his 1837 history of New South Wales, John Dunmore Lang similarly wrote that the 'vast continental island of New Holland … was long supposed by European philosophers to constitute a part of an imaginary southern continent'.[18]

Early colonial history texts continued to underscore the stark division between Australia's apparently unrecorded past and the industriousness and agency of colonists, who were depicted as 'filling in' the continent's supposed historical emptiness with settlements and accompanying infrastructure, people, as well as *histories* of their endeavours. Take the First Fleet journal of Judge Advocate David Collins, for example, which articulated that transformation from the 'silence' of precolonial Australia to the noisy busyness of the early days of settlement, when selecting a site for the colony in a secluded cove on Gadigal Country:

The spot chosen for this purpose was at the head of the Cove near a run of fresh water, which stole silently through a very thick wood, the stillness of which had then, for the first time since the creation, been interrupted by the rude sound of the labourer's axe, and the downfall of its ancient inhabitants:– a stillness and tranquility which, from that day, were to give place to the noise of labour, the confusion of camps and towns, and the busy hum of its new possessors.[19]

It's a vivid, wonderfully written account of the first few years on the penal colony, and Collins is a remarkable interlocuter – he's a curious and diligent writer, and we can be thankful for the accounts he wrote and published. Nevertheless, as a text it does considerable colonising work for the way it lays out that division between (First Nations) emptiness and (colonial) entitlement and industry. George Hamilton's 19th-century reminiscences offer a similar temporal logic of historical absence and presence that Australia represented pre- and post-colonisation: 'Here was a country without a geography, and a race of men without a history', he confidently asserts in reference to this continent's history pre-colonisation.[20]

By constantly drawing comparisons between Indigenous Australia's perceived 'blankness' and the agency of the colonists, colonial histories produced narratives that portrayed the discovery and colonisation of Australia as inevitable. This framing suggested that Australia's supposed lack of pre-colonial history created a void that was awaiting some sort of attempted answer or resolution. Such narratives not only justified but also glorified the colonial enterprise, presenting it as a natural progression towards the occupation and development of an apparently empty land, as this passage from *The History of New Holland* reveals:

Time will shew how far it may be entitled to the approbation of the judicious and disinterested, by either adding to the acquirements of philosophy, or pointing out new sources of national wealth: time will shew how far the knowledge of those lately discovered parts of the globe may be directed to enhance the comforts and add to the lights of polished society, as well as of their own still uncivilized possessors; and how far it may tend to the general happiness of mankind, and the glory of that Being, whose providence has reserved the discovery of them, imperfect as it is, to the present generation.[21]

That a history book was being produced as the First Fleet was *embarking* for Australia highlights the significance of storying the Empire as part of the process of colonisation. The first two editions, both published in 1787, coincided with the planning and departure of the journey to Botany Bay. They responded to the significant public interest in Britain about the creation of the new penal colony and a deep curiosity about the place where it was to be established.

As time progressed, that historical reading of Australia's colonisation evolved from being providential to 'evidenced' by history itself. The relentless expansion of the colony, coupled with its seemingly unstoppable political, economic and cultural development, became focal points for later histories from the colonial period, which described them as a testament to the inherent superiority and destiny of the colonial enterprise. The colony of New South Wales had begun with just a thousand people, 'chiefly male and female convicts' and a small herd of 'seven horse and six horned cattle', politician and historian William Westgarth wrote in 1848. Yet 'These settlements now contain a population of nearly 300,000 colonists, with two millions of horned cattle. There are also twelve million sheep, including those of all ages, and 150,000 horses'.[22]

Emigrants' guides aimed at British imperial migrants and entrepreneurs, along with subsequent colonial memoirs, also crucially narrated the colony's 'origin story' during this period. These accounts often depicted the colony as a blank canvas awaiting the imprint of colonial endeavour, reinforcing narratives of progress and advancement while downplaying or disregarding First Nations' ancient and ongoing histories and cultures. In his 1870 *Handbook to New South Wales*, Frederic Algar was effusive: 'The history of New South Wales, if brief, is eventful, and there are three distinct eras, which mark its progress from a miserable convict station, to one of the most prosperous provinces of the British Empire'.[23] Such ideas not only reveal colonial understandings of historical time, but also confirm just how this temporality – which saw precolonial Australia as 'empty' and therefore without history – worked alongside colonial histories to re-story Australia with imperial narratives that confirmed colonial presence, authority and sovereignty.

Colonial historiography framed historical progression as synonymous with the advancement of colonial interests. It was a mode of history-making that served the colonial purpose of legitimisation, Denis Byrne has argued, in which 'unilinear models of human progress already being advanced in the mid-eighteenth century allowed the non-Western world to serve as evidence of the West's prehistory'.[24] This narrative not only justified the colonial project but also facilitated the marginalisation and exclusion of First Nations histories and cultures. By defining what constituted Australia's rightful historical narrative and its temporal boundaries, even from as early as 1787, the year before the convict colony had established itself, colonial historians implicitly determined which aspects could be omitted or silenced. That Australia's colonisation served as a founding moment for colonial historians was understandable at one level, as Mark McKenna has acknowledged. After all, this was how they actually *practised history* at the time. At the same time we also need to see how that temporal marker between Australian history's 'beginning' and 'everything else' effectively sanctioned the colonial presence by suggesting that preceding First Nations histories were unknowable and insignificant.[25]

For much of the 19th century, colonial histories and chronicles, along with published journals, travelogues, memoirs, and emigrants' guides meticulously documented the daily life of the colony. They recorded the immense challenges of remoteness, desperation and uncertainty, while also revealing colonial inquisitiveness about the land they had arrived in and the First Nations peoples they encountered. These texts emerged prior to the professionalisation of history in the late 19th century, before the advent of more systematic and reified methods of 'scientific' evidence, objectivity, and expertise. Despite that, colonial histories shaped Australian history by marking its boundaries and scope. Colonial historiography also delineated historical time in ways that marginalised First Nations histories on the continent, which spanned tens of thousands of years. Indigenous Australia represented a sort of *historylessness*, as postcolonial scholars such as Lorenzo Veracini and Patrick Wolfe have argued, and the Wiradjuri poet Jeanine Leane has poignantly contended, where 'the dispossession of Aboriginal peoples' was facilitated 'by removing us from western historical time'.[26]

Time as nation-making

From the late 19th century until the middle decades of the 20th, Australian historiography increasingly reflected a more national and scientific historical approach. This was an important shift, moving away from earlier readings of colonial 'providence' to narratives that were now able to substantiate Australia's historical progress with 'objective' evidence. Meanwhile, developments in the discipline itself also contributed significantly to this historiographic turn.

The burgeoning sense of Australian national identity, which was eventually realised with Australia's Federation in 1901, was more than simply local or parochial exceptionalism. The rise of nationalist ideologies in the 19th century was a global movement that positioned 'the nation' as the innate organising principle of culture, identity and governance, and history played a crucial role in shaping expressions of national identity. 'Nations without a past are contradictions in terms', as Eric Hobsbawm and David Kertzer have insisted. 'What makes a nation is the past, what justifies one nation against others is the past, and historians are the people who produce it.'[27] This late 19th-century international geopolitical context was an influential marker of Australian history-writing at that time.

The disciplinary dimension of an emergent national or 'federation' historiography is also vital to consider: the increasing professionalisation and classification of Western historical practice included explicit research methods and qualifications.[28] The discipline underwent a global shift towards what Ian Tyrrell has termed 'scientific history' during this period, characterised by a focus on empirical archival research, rigorous criticism, source analysis and professionalisation within historical studies. This wasn't unique to Australia but mirrored developments worldwide: history programs were developed and professors appointed to universities internationally and in Australia. Textbooks were also commissioned by education departments in newly organised school systems that included the teaching and learning of history. Moreover, the *rules* of scientific historical research, of empiricism using verifiable evidence, archival reading, and source criticism, became more systematic with the establishment of formal history qualifications and professional associations.[29]

That interweaving of disciplinary professionalisation and narrative nationalism created a distinctive temporality in Australian historiography. On the one hand, burgeoning Australian national sentiment frequently evoked its fledgling history, fostering a popular, celebratory historical consciousness. As the Australian colonies moved towards Federation, there were increasing public reminiscences of their 'early days', in the form of museum displays, public commemorations (such as the 1888 centenary of the First Fleet's arrival) and the establishment of historical societies across the continent.[30] This spurt of nostalgic Australian historical affection and official memory making showed how the settler colonies were beginning 'to institutionalize their remembering and forgetting of the past', as Bain Attwood has contended.[31]

At the same time, the sense of historical progress as forward-looking and nation-building became even more pronounced in colonial histories during this nationalising period. Australian history texts from the late 19th and early 20th centuries meticulously catalogued ever-expanding wool exports, acres under cultivation, stock numbers and population growth. Titles of these works, such as Edward Combes's *Material Progress of New South Wales* (published 1885–6) and Timothy Coghlan and Thomas Ewing's *Progress of Australasia in the Nineteenth Century*, published to coincide with Federation, embodied this historical logic. A quick glance at the tables of contents of these history texts, along with their sequence of incrementally filled-in maps of the continent (with rail lines, exploration and pastoralism), confirm that these histories used the discipline's temporality to lay out a sequence of the nation's (future) development.

The historical temporality of inexorable growth and expansion had profound implications. First, historians now possessed the 'evidence' to explain the exclusion of First Nations people from Australian history. Furthermore, some used the concept of linear time to argue that the devastation colonisation caused for Australia's First Nations was outweighed by the overall 'advance' of colonial governance, economy and society. For example, Alexander Sutherland's 1888 history of Victoria, which was published to coincide with the centenary of Australia's colonisation, explicitly quantified the effects of historical 'progress': 'to the sentimental it is undoubtedly an iniquity; to the practical it represents a distinct step in human progress, involving the sacrifice of a few thousands of an inferior race; he subtracts that as a small drawback to a vast good, and finds the balance enormously on the side of the good'.[32] This viewpoint rationalised the subjugation of First Nations people as a necessary sacrifice for societal development.

It was the discipline's own scientific method, which assembled facts and evidence that were housed in the colony's growing museum, library and archival collections. Meanwhile, those same museum exhibits, history textbooks and commemorations used that evidence to demonstrate that First Nations peoples existed outside historical time. GV Portus's *Australia Since 1606* described pre-contact Australian history as a 'dark night', for instance, implying that history had not yet begun in the continent.[33] Similarly, Russel Ward's popular history text *Man Makes History* and AL Meston's *Junior History of Australia* explicitly suggested that First Nations people didn't, and couldn't, inhabit Australian history as they defined it. Despite being the oldest continuous civilisation in the world, Ward insisted, Aboriginal people 'know almost no History'.[34] These examples underscore how the discourse of historical progress was used to justify the erasure of Indigenous peoples from Australia's national history.

Some histories acknowledged the significant duration of First Nations occupation prior to colonisation, yet any sense of deep time fell outside the boundaries of empirical history. 'How long the Aborigines of Australia had roamed over its soil when Europeans first explored the coast, it is for ethnologists to discuss – perhaps with no result', determined GW Rusden, in his 1883 *History of Australia*. In 1916, in his annual lecture to the Australian Historical Society, the New South Wales Director General of Education Peter Board excluded First Nations' history from the emerging national narrative. The national story began with the 'origin of settlement here in 1788', he surmised. For 'what took place before that is geographical rather than human history'.[35] During this period, the term 'pre-history' was typically assigned to the realms of geology, ethnology, archaeology and palaeontology.[36]

While expanding scientific knowledge shed light on Australia's ancient human history, confirming that the continent was anything but empty, it also reinforced the notion that 'Australian history' commenced at the point of European colonisation. Certainly, historical narratives and accounts were authored by or about Indigenous people during this period. Aboriginal activists such as William Cooper, Jack Patten, Bill Ferguson and Pearl Gibbs led notable protests, including the significant 1938 Day of Mourning, and serve as powerful demonstrations of First Nations forms of history-making in Australia during the decades following federation.[37] Moreover, creative writers such as Xavier Herbert, Eleanor Dark and Judith Wright contributed to efforts aimed at exposing and incorporating Indigenous people and perspectives into Australian historical consciousness through their literary works.[38] It's only now, reading back after years of powerful critique, that historians sense the need for a broader historiographical lens to include these counter-narratives mostly made from outside the discipline into the story of Australian historiography.

Overwhelmingly, First Nations people were depicted as the temporal evidence of modern Australia's national progress. 'Australian Aborigines were not simply perceived as an unchanging people in a faraway land', Ian McNiven and Lynette Russell explain, but 'rather they were represented as a relic of Europe's own past and thus were imbued with both great antiquity and timeless stasis'.[39] It's a peculiar and inconsistent temporality, what McNiven and Russell term 'antiquation', in which history is utilised to illuminate the settler colonial past while simultaneously establishing a clear hierarchy between the modern nation and ancient Australia.[40]

Time as decolonising?

Australian historiography began to shift in the decades following the Second World War. Nearly two centuries after Australia's colonisation had begun, what has come to be known as 'New History' disputed the temporality of the history discipline in Australia, especially its assumed timeline and linear tropes of 'progress'.[41] As outlined earlier, this shift occurred within broader, transnational, historical theories and approaches such as labour history and women's history, which sought to document 'histories from below' the discipline had failed to capture. Critically, other movements such as postcolonial studies also emerged during the post-war period, prompting historical recognition of subaltern and First Nations perspectives while also scrutinising the history discipline, including its conceptualisations of time. Australia didn't actually *de*colonise – indeed, I'd argue that settler colonialism is an enduring feature of its historiography. Nevertheless, the aftermath of the war prompted a reassessment of its position within the British empire and its own quest for a national story and identity. While that transnational movement of postcolonial and decolonial critique didn't translate to a decolonised Australian state, it profoundly influenced the history discipline to consider its relationship to power, empire and colonisation.

During this period, rather than exemplifying the social and cultural hierarchies which justified imperialism as a realisation of innate racial 'hierarchies' or inevitable 'progress', Australia's First Nations heritage and culture came to be viewed as proof of the nation's ancient human past. Over time, Deep History became a feature of national storytelling and celebration. This marked a profound shift in the discipline's relationship with historical time. New scientific methods in archaeological research contributed to this shift. When the archaeologist John Mulvaney led an excavation at Fromm's Landing, a cave overlooking the Murray River in South Australia, in 1956, it was the first time radiocarbon dating had been used in Australia. This excavation revealed evidence of human occupation dating back 5000 years, confirming that First Nations people had been here for millennia, and thereby challenging conventional notions of Australian history's established timeline. Mulvaney's subsequent publication of his *Prehistory of Australia* in 1968 reiterated that re-reading of Australia's origin story. His opening sentence rewrote generations of histories which had claimed Europeans had 'discovered' New Holland: 'The discoverers, explorers and colonists of the three million square miles which are Australia, were its Aborigines'.[42]

Subsequent excavations, notably Jim Bowler's work at Lake Mungo in south-western New South Wales, pushed back the date of Aboriginal occupation even further, to 40 000 years. By the early 21st century, as Billy Griffiths eloquently explains, Australian First Nations' claims of having 'always been there' were supported by newly emerging scientific evidence, with colossal timescales dating their presence back to 65 000 BCE. 'The New World has become Old', he insists.[43]

As the 'starting date' for Australian history was stretching ever further into the deep past, the 1960s and 1970s also saw demands for rights and recognition from First Nations activists, writers and historians, such as Oodgeroo Noonuccal, Kevin Gilbert, and Gary Foley, along with the impact of published life stories such as Marnie Kennedy's *Born a Half Caste* and Margaret Tucker's *If Everyone Cared*. Each significant in their own right, these influential figures also collectively challenged the exclusion of First Nations people from Australian history and demanded land rights, social justice and political representation.[44] Furthermore, they insisted that the writing over of Australia's Indigenous history had been an attempt to erase First Nations sovereignty by effectively keeping them at the fringes of the continent's 'history'.[45] Such activists exposed the complicity of so much Australian history, which had defined the boundaries of the discipline to exclude First Nations people from the national story.

Meanwhile, criticism of the history discipline during this period also emerged among non-Indigenous academics and public intellectuals. In his notable 1968 Boyer Lectures, for example, the anthropologist WEH Stanner argued that First Nations people had been actively 'silenced' in Australian history. By the 1970s, this academic critique was comprehensively revising historical research and writing, advocating not only for the urgent inclusion of First Nations histories and perspectives but also for new historical methods to accomplish this. 'The framework of our historical comprehension has been widened in recent years', contended historian Bob Reece in 1979. 'But a great deal more needs to be done if we are to eradicate the tenacious tradition that Australian history began with Captain Cook and the First Fleet'.[46]

The movement for decolonisation was hardly totalising yet the historiography it produced was far-reaching: ideas moved and were shared around the world, unfolding across multiple continents and oceans over several decades. Historians working in postcolonial and settler colonial contexts scrutinised and uncovered the role of the history discipline in perpetuating structures of imperialism and colonialism. They also confirmed that colonised and enslaved peoples had been producing vital histories all along, despite their exclusion from the formal history discipline.[47] And they demonstrated the critical concept of 'time' in that colonising structure, where narratives of 'progress' relegated marginalised peoples to the margins of history.

That epistemological clash has been profound in Australia, where, as Leane insists: 'The construct of "history" defines time as a space that can be measured'.[48] Despite the colonising architecture of the discipline, however, there *was* a rich Indigenous history on this continent, one which also continued after colonisation. What's more, there were fully developed temporalities that encompassed a rich cosmology, sense of time and 'code of truth', as Worimi historian John Maynard carefully explains.[49] For Indigenous historians working at the intersection of disciplinary history and Indigenous Knowledges in Australia, the tension between history's ethical obligation to decolonise and the challenge of that task is a constant, pressing theme. The work of Australian First Nations historians, writers and creative practitioners such as John Maynard, Larissa Behrendt, Tony Birch, Jeanine Leane and Alison Whittaker offer important insights into how history might address these challenges of disciplinary decolonisation.[50] Their interventions – vibrant, creative and critical – occupy an increasingly powerful yet ill-defined place in Australian historiography. Yet as 'hyphenated histories', as Aoteoroa–New Zealand historian Miranda Johnson terms them, these creative Indigenous forms of history-making represent a radical disciplinary break from history – and even a repudiation of it.[51] This is more than just 'history', as Krim Bentarrak, Stephen Muecke and Goolarabooloo elder Paddy Roe insist. 'Within the issue of Aboriginal sovereignty, there is more at stake than the use of lands; there is the right to control the production of Australia's mythologies.'[52]

Such critiques pose significant challenges for the history discipline if it's to revise longstanding historical conceptions of time to incorporate diverse epistemologies and temporalities. Indeed, a significant question arises regarding the translation of Australian First Nations history texts. Can a work of history – that might be gently outlined in sand, sung, painted, and held on Country – be rendered in the framework of chronological historical discourse, given the fundamental divergence in their underlying logics? Can 'our historical imagination ever depart – becoming truly *decolonial* – from the terrain that colonialism has tilled so thoroughly?' as Warwick Anderson recently asked.[53] They're questions that remain to be answered.

At the same time, while extending the discipline into deep time opens up a 'temporal unpredictability' for historians that might be uncomfortable, as Ann McGrath has argued, it also offers the opportunity to consciously engage with Indigenous historical ways of knowing and telling.[54] As the collaborative, edited collection *Everywhen* reveals, sometimes that discomfort helps negotiate the complex conversation between Indigenous temporalities and ways of doing history along with disciplinary practice.[55]

Critically, the consequences of this decolonising period are political and ethical as well as epistemological. If universal assumptions of historical time are just that, how does a discipline of inquiry, with its origins in the Enlightenment principles of empiricism, evidence and rationality, as well as national teleologies, include forms of history-making organised according to vastly different logics without colonising them? And, just as critically, can First Nations interventions in Australia's historical time shift settler colonial institutions and assumptions, as well as its narratives? In contemplating these questions, I'm reminded of an animated conversation I had with Ngemba man, Brad Steadman, sitting in the sunshine by the banks of the Barwon River in Brewarrina.

He said, warmly, but with a hint of exasperation in his voice, that historians were like the 'time police' when it came to authorising and curating Indigenous histories.[56] Yet the invitation, and the challenge, is there for us to at least try and contemplate an approach to historical temporality that's encompassing and inclusive.

3

DEEP TIME HISTORY GOES TO SCHOOL
How the new Australian curriculum is learning from the past

Beth Marsden

In 1928, the Victorian Education Department published a new series of eight compulsory school readers, one for each year of primary school. Of these *Victorian Readers*, the eighth book included an excerpt from 'The old inhabitants', written by the famed correspondent and official war historian, CEW Bean.[1] Written from the first-person perspective, the text describes the so-called discovery of grinding stones in the west of the state of Victoria:

> Those stones spoke of an age before the dawn of history. On the spot where we stood, we knew that someone – some one in the blank, utter darkness before Australian history began, some human being belonging to a time of which no history will ever be written, nor yet even the bare outline of it will ever be known – some woman in a long-forgotten camp must have knelt there and polished those flat stones ... There, just as they had been left in the dim past.[2]

Bean was wrong, of course, about many of the claims he made in this passage. His view that First Nations people existed 'before the dawn of history' in a 'blank, utter darkness' illustrates his perspective: that understandings of the past might only be achieved by non-Indigenous people through the practice of academic or popular 'history'. Bean's choice to characterise the period before European invasion as a 'dim past' reveals the limitations of his understanding and knowledge. His view is also reflective of common settler narratives about First Nations people in 1920s Victoria.

Bean was also wrong when he claimed that 'no history will ever be written' about the time prior to British invasion in 1788. Yet this has only recently been corrected. As Anna Clark shows in her chapter in this collection, historians have constructed a body of scholarship that has positioned First Nations people outside historical narratives of progress. This changed in the second half of the 20th century, as historians engaged with Indigenous knowledge and perspectives of time. More recently, in the past decade, the academic concept of 'deep time' and the field of 'Deep History' continue to expand the scope of history far beyond Bean's 'dim past', aiming to address the challenges of writing histories that extend back 65 000 years.[3] This shift is also evident in histories produced for audiences beyond the academy. In 2023, the decision of the Australian Curriculum and Reporting Authority (ACARA) to include a new course in the Year 7 History Australian Curriculum – 'Deep Time History of Australia' – marked the reach of deep time history into the public consciousness. It signalled its official recognition as knowledge that is of national significance and that every Australian student should learn.[4]

The introduction of 'Deep Time History' marks a foundational change from the usual curricular timeline of 'Australian history' that has generally started in 1788 with the arrival of the first European colonisers in Sydney Cove. Instead, the new course positions students to understand the depth of First Nations cultures and societies extending beyond the limits of this traditional periodisation. It also shifts the typical focus away from invasion and colonisation. Crucially, by establishing a foundation for understanding the continuity of First Nations cultures and sovereignty, it creates possibilities for restructuring the dominant narrative throughout the broader history curriculum.

This recent reform has taken place in the context of a longer history of Australian curricula since the early 1900s. In this chapter, I explore how the new course conceptualises deep time and compare this with past understandings to illustrate changes and continuities in curricular representations of the deep time past, linking these with educational and historiographic debates. However, the contemporary history curriculum continues to reproduce some of the ideas that were dominant in past curricular material, often through claims of disciplinary knowledge and authority about the past. By considering possibilities for a rich engagement with Indigenous Knowledges manifest in the new 'Deep Time History' course, along with its accompanying challenges and potential limitations, this chapter aims to spur ongoing conversation about best practice approaches to teaching the deep time past in school settings. As a former history teacher, now a historian, I'm attuned to the ways academic history and history curricula influence and reference each other.

But what is deep time history and why should students learn about it? Its educative potential is significant, opening the scale and scope of Australian history. It does this by expanding and complicating ideas of time often used to define the history curriculum. Historians Ann McGrath and Laura Rademaker define Deep History as 'the histories that long precede modernity, the medieval era and the few thousand years generally known as ancient history'.[5] Beyond that, deep time history also positions Indigenous knowledge and ways of knowing the past as pivotal to a full appreciation of Australian history. The inclusion of deep time history in the curriculum, then, creates opportunities for students to develop expansive understandings of more than 65 000 years of deep Indigenous history.

Like the academic field of Deep History that deconstructs stereotypical views of pre-colonial Indigenous societies, the new curriculum changes the ways that pre-invasion history has been taught and exposes 1788 as a 'bogus starting date for history'.[6] This both allows for students to learn about the longer history of the continent, and to develop deeper understandings about colonisation. Including more information about the history of First Nations people, unconnected from Europeans, works to foreground First Nations people and history previously 'invisible' to students. This addresses challenges shared in other colonial contexts, such as Finland, where researcher Tanja Kohvakka has argued that the absence of 'prehistory' in Finnish textbooks means students have more difficulty understanding the colonisation of Sápmi, and the impacts on Sámi people.[7] The aim of expanding knowledge of Deep History has been included in recent public education and political campaigns led by First Nations people. As I will explore later in this chapter, the first iteration of the 'Deep Time History' curriculum marks an ambitious and groundbreaking – if somewhat tentative – step in this direction.

(Deep time) history in Victorian curricular materials

School curricular materials offer us a glimpse into classrooms of the past. They provide insights into educational values and standards, as well as the cultural, social and political context in which they were created. They show which stories were privileged and how they were positioned. The texts I explore in this chapter were readily accessible printed materials produced by the state of Victoria's Education Department, between 1900 and 1968. I have selected these as there was no national curriculum during this period. In my research and writing on the history of education systems in Victoria, I have drawn upon these examples as a kind of canon representing wider national trends.[8] All the curricular material I examine here (syllabus documents, mandatory and supplementary readers and curriculum documentation) were selected and endorsed by the Victorian Education Department. This includes the *School Paper* (1896–1968) and the *Victorian Readers* (1928–1965). The *School Paper* was a powerful tool for promoting nationalistic narratives of colonisation, first introduced to Victorian classrooms in 1896. It was designed so that the department could provide locally written material concerning Australian topics. The *School Paper* comprised excerpts from already written texts, often edited for size; it was compulsory reading for all children until 1928. *Victorian Readers* were released in 1928 as accessible texts, to be used in government school classrooms to support children's literacy. They were read over and over and shared across generations, creating a collective engagement with the same narratives across decades.[9] This means, for example, that almost every student in Victorian schools between 1928 and 1965 was likely to have encountered Bean's 'The old inhabitants' by the time they finished primary school.

Historical materials that describe Aboriginal life before the British invasion formed part of the curriculum during this period. I consider these chronologically, to contextualise them within broader social and political conditions, and connect them to historiographical developments and debates. For example, texts that claimed to provide information about First Nations people prior to invasion reflected the nationalistic and scientific focus of the historiography produced during this period. The narratives in these materials reveal several dominant themes, including: the positioning of white 'experts' as the primary Knowledge Holders about the past; the role of scientific knowledge as the method for understanding the past; and persistent tropes and narratives that sought to discursively disconnect and remove First Nations people from the land.

The early 1900s: The settler as expert

Let's start with a piece published in the *School Paper* in November 1900, 'The Australian Aborigines'. This text was an excerpt from a paper written by the British evolutionary biologist, Professor Baldwin Spencer.[10] Spencer had been appointed the foundation chair of biology at the University of Melbourne in 1887 and was involved in the Field Naturalists Club of Victoria and the Royal Society of Victoria. Spencer's position at the University of Melbourne legitimised the Education Department's selection of this text. Yet Baldwin's 'scientific' claims were based upon understandings of evolution now proven to be dubious: 'They still remain in the stone-age, using just the same chipped flints and ground axe-heads as did the earliest men of whom we have any records' and '… the stone-age men were able to persist because they did not come in contact with men who had passed from the stone into the iron age'.[11] His suggestion that Aboriginal people were 'still' in the 'stone-age' firmly positioned Aboriginal people in prehistory, outside progress and modernity – a time before European 'history' supposedly began, and therefore at the base of an imagined social and racial hierarchy.

Although she had fewer formal qualifications, Mary EB Howitt, the author of another text, published in 1910, 'How the Australian blacks lived', had gained some knowledge and experience of Indigenous people. Her father was the 'explorer', natural scientist and anthropologist Alfred William Howitt, and Mary had served as his assistant and secretary. Her family name lent authority to her description of Aboriginal life. Howitt acknowledged that '... I think they were, perhaps, happier before the white people came and took their country from them'.[12] But her description of First Nations life before invasion is derisive: 'They roamed about, and only stayed where there was plenty of food to be found... The blacks did not have houses to live in. They merely made a lean-to...' By highlighting how differently First Nations people lived, representing their lifestyles as antithetical to European notions of ownership and cultivation, white 'experts' such as Howitt and Spencer constructed narratives that sought to legitimise European settlement and connection to the land. Spencer's use of 'stone-age' as a label categorised Aboriginal people as locked in the past, away from contemporary settler colonial society.[13] These narratives, authored by apparent experts on pre-invasion Aboriginal culture, were reinforced by the dominant idea that Aboriginal people were a 'dying race', an idea especially powerful in Victoria at this time. Here, the rate of European settlement, bringing violence and disease, had severely affected First Nations populations. Those who survived often had little choice but to live on remote reserves or missions, away from cities and from the settler gaze.[14]

These texts show some of the types of curricular materials that students engaged with during the early 20th century. These texts privileged white scientific perspectives of Indigenous life before European invasion, affirming settler possession and legitimacy by positioning Aboriginality as primitive. This curricular material also provides a glimpse of how what constituted knowledge about First Nations people, and their history (or lack of it), has been constructed in school materials in past decades. Significantly, these texts reveal some of the ways that settler experts and Western scientific knowledge have been leveraged to construct a standardised narrative that dispossession was natural and therefore inevitable. The authors of these texts constructed Aboriginal people as incapable of living alongside Europeans post-invasion. Representation of pre-invasion First Nations life, culture and society published in curricular material during the early 1900s used European 'expertise' to legitimise claims that sought to diminish Aboriginal connection to the land. These texts reflect developments in the history discipline that Anna Clark has charted further in her chapter, including the way that pre-history was positioned alongside the sciences of geology, ethnology, geography and archaeology.

The 1920s: Knowing the past through science

The influence of this scientific framing is also evident in 1920s curricular material. The previous scientific explanations sought to establish why Aboriginal people could not survive post-invasion. 'The waters of the River Murray', published in 1920 in the *School Paper*, demonstrates a turn towards archaeological knowledge. This was used as a way to situate Aboriginal people and culture in the past. The text explains that the natural erosion of the Murray River's banks exposed the 'remains of aborigines' [sic] camps … the mussel shells from their meals and … the bones of long-buried tribesmen indicate ages of occupation by a race which, in one brief century, has almost ceased to exist'.[15] This encourages students to view Aboriginal culture as something that had already ceased to exist, and that therefore could only be known by using scientific methods of understanding the past – through artefacts, for example. Bean's 'The old inhabitants' does this too. Both texts construct the idea that knowledge of the past can only be accessed through artefacts located and analysed by non-Indigenous people. This framing seeks to negate the potential for Aboriginal knowledge of the past by emphasising the absence of Aboriginal people. Recall Bean's phrasing: 'There were no children here to play'; 'some woman in a long-forgotten camp', and 'some human being belonging to a time of which no history will ever be written'.[16]

By the end of the 1920s, many of the narratives in the *School Paper* were authored by staff employed by the Education Department. Published in 1929, the author of 'Our blackfellows' acknowledged the continued presence of Aboriginal people, albeit in a particularly Victorian way. It begins:

1. Once upon a time no one lived in our State but blackfellows. The white man had not come, and the blackfellow was king of the land ... 3. Then the blackfellow was the master of the soil. But now, very few of them are left in Victoria; they are found, however, in other States of Australia ...[17]

The premise of this text incorporates that of the earlier narratives: that Aboriginal people did not cultivate the land, it was 'empty and silent', and therefore ready to be colonised. The additional claim, typical of Victoria, that there were 'very few' Aboriginal people 'left' in that state, is characteristic of the majority of settler-constructed narratives about Aboriginal people during this period, including in formal academic publications.[18]

These 1920s school texts construct the state of Victoria as a landscape absent of Aboriginal people. Yet they don't go so far as to claim that Victoria did not have any Aboriginal history – or past. By suggesting that it is only through artefacts, and the examination of archaeological sites, that Aboriginal culture and history might be known, these narratives construct the idea that knowing Aboriginal history belongs to white settlers.[19] These ideas are in keeping with the collecting and antiquities craze that swept across Victoria during the 1920s and preceded the formalisation of archaeology as a discipline. That movement, together with the curricular material, emphasised discontinuity of Aboriginal culture, disconnection to land and overall lack of possession of land. It positioned Aboriginal culture, especially that prior to invasion, as something that might only be approached and learned about from a distance. The texts decentre and devalue Indigenous knowledge about the past. Rather, they position settlers as the only actors capable of knowing Aboriginal culture and history from their expert vantage in the present.

The 1930s–1960s: Unsettling the narratives

There are many more examples from the *School Paper* from the 1930s through to the end of the 1960s. From the late 1940s, texts selected for the *School Paper* reveal a growing recognition that ideas about the extinction of Aboriginal people were wrong. These texts reflect developing understandings in broader settler society and politics. These were prompted by changes to Aboriginal people's participation in labour markets and unions, increased mobility – including into inner-city Melbourne – and organised political activity which were made more possible by social shifts accompanying the Second World War. This also contributed to renewed attention to Aboriginal people from the Victorian government, which manifested in the aggressive new assimilationist *Aborigines Act 1957*. Around the same period, new archaeological understandings emerged about how long Aboriginal people had been living on the land that was now called Victoria. Set against these complex social changes, curricular materials claiming to represent historical fact were on unsteady ground.

This is evident in the Victorian Education Department's *Social Studies Course* of 1955. This document is a different type of text to those discussed above, revealing the clash of older established narratives with more contemporary realities. Written for teachers specifically, it provides direct instructions for how to approach the teaching of certain topics. There is only one reference to Aboriginal people in the entire course outline, made in reference to the Grade V theme of 'Our own land'. The topic 'The Australia our ancestors found', included 'the aborigines [sic] of Australia', and instructed teachers that: 'The aborigines [sic] should be treated as in their natural habitat; comparison with the life of the aborigines [sic] to-day will be left to the discretion of the teachers'.[20] 'Natural habitat' is shorthand for pre-1788, and a euphemism for 'stone age'. It suggests Aboriginal people were part of the environment rather than human historical agents and it suggests that they may not be able to survive outside this 'habitat'. The direction to teachers that they should use their 'discretion' to determine whether to compare that 'natural habitat' with 'to-day' reveals a deep unease. It shows an anxiety about how to include historical representations of Aboriginal people and society, and an awareness of the incongruity of a curriculum that continued to locate Aboriginal culture only in the past, when contemporary Aboriginal society was becoming increasingly visible. This course remained in use until the end of the 1960s.

Perhaps to avoid these contemporary issues, in the 1960s the *School Paper* featured more material that claimed to represent First Nations 'mythologies', or stories from the 'Dreamtime'.[21] These were often attributed to settler authors. While these might be described as more positive representations of Aboriginal culture in that they did not trade on well-worn tropes of extinction and racial stereotypes, they were nonetheless highly abstracted. They did not include named actors, time or place, or authors, and were almost always universalised. In these ways, these texts did not claim to represent history, *per se*. Instead, they worked to locate Aboriginal people and knowledge as ahistorical. The narratives were also unconnected from specific tracts of Country or lands, often constructing Aboriginal knowledge, people and culture as homogenous.[22] By directing attention to mythical, homogenous stories of a 'Dreaming', the curriculum could avoid both contemporary political activism and old racial narratives. This period saw a schism emerge between academic history and the history curriculum. The Victorian Education Department seemed unable or unwilling to fall into step with the changes taking place in academic discussions of Australia's past – instead opting for a 'safe', apparently depoliticised approach to representing Aboriginal people and culture.[23]

The 1970s and beyond: Decentralisation to standardisation

In the 1970s and 1980s, the Victorian Education Department became less involved in decisions about the curriculum, as curriculum design was decentralised and schools were afforded greater authority over what to teach and how to teach it. Because of this, curricular materials like those I have analysed so far are difficult to locate, so understanding how deep time history was represented in the classroom cannot be found in government archival materials. Led by organisations such as the National Aboriginal Education Committee, grassroots community organisations and individuals working in schools, bigger changes to Aboriginal education and the inclusion of Aboriginal perspectives in the curriculum were increasingly on the table. By the early 1990s, the history curriculum in Victoria included a 'Koori history' course for senior years, and critical approaches to Australian history more generally.[24] However, the influence of conservative governments at state and federal levels saw these courses diminished. The so-called 'history wars' that followed in the late 1990s cemented the role of history curricula as a site of national political controversy.

The introduction of the Australian Curriculum and Reporting Authority in 2009, followed by the first draft of the Australian National Curriculum in 2010, was a return to centralisation on a new, national level, underscored by standardised testing and teacher professional standards that ushered in a new era of education and curricula in Australia. Much has been written about the Australian Curriculum, and the ways that Aboriginal and Torres Strait Islander histories and perspectives are incorporated across most learning areas.[25] This includes history, with most change taking place at Years 9 and 10 to include what might be described as historical episodes that deal with First Nations experiences since colonisation such as civil rights movements in the 1960s. The first semester-long course devoted to First Nations history, 'Deep Time History' at Year 7, is a significant development.

The rise of deep time history in the Australian Curriculum

As I describe the 2023 'Deep Time History' course, I'll focus on the ways that deep time history is conceptualised, considering the broader social, political, and historiographic factors that underpinned this major reform. I also discuss resistance and setbacks in the consultation process that signal the ongoing contestation and challenges for incorporating deep time history into the national curriculum.

The format of the Australian Curriculum for History is the same from Year 7 to Year 10. Each course is organised into two categories: 'Knowledge and Understandings', and 'Skills'. The 'Skills' are a list of general, transferable historical skills that students should acquire through the course. The 'Knowledge and Understandings' comprise descriptions of content that students should learn through the course.

While the curriculum outlines the content – 'Skills' and 'Knowledge and Understanding' – to be taught, and the standards students are expected to reach, it does not specify *how* the content is to be taught.

There are seven 'Knowledge and Understanding' descriptions in the 'Deep Time History' course. One of these makes a direct reference to deep time: 'students learn about how First Nations Australians are the world's oldest continuing cultures, displaying evidence of both continuity and change over deep time'. There's an annotation to this description that defines deep time as a 'Framework to describe immense scales of geological time used by geologists, archaeologists and anthropologists to investigate the past (e.g. lives of early people)'.

The remaining content descriptions focus on what could be termed 'deep histories of the continent': theories of Indigenous people's arrival to Australia; the movement of Indigenous people across the Australian continent; the response of First Nations people to environmental changes; place-based technological achievements; and the social organisation and cultural practices of First Nations people. The seventh content descriptor emphasises continuity from the deep past to the present by linking heritage sites and material culture from the deep past to the cultural obligations of First Nations people and others to preserve sites and materials. The corresponding descriptions of the skills that Year 7 students should learn in history span both deep time history, and the ancient world. These are the same skills listed for Year 8, and the basis for skill development in Years 9 and 10. In other words, the skills for secondary school history are essentially discipline-specific and remain unchanged regardless of the topics set out by the history curriculum.

The most significant intervention that 'Deep Time History' makes to the ways Australian history is arranged in the curriculum is through its extension of the subject's temporal scope. There's no reference to dates in the content descriptions themselves. The overview of the Year 7 History curriculum, however, describes it as 'a study of history from the time of the earliest human communities to the end of the ancient period, approximately 60,000 years ago–c. 650 (CE), and a study of early First Nations Peoples of Australia'. In this way alone, 'Deep Time History' breaks the mould of previous reforms by aiming to cover more than

65 000 years of First Nations sovereignty rather than a key moment or event. This reframing of Australian history, to acknowledge and include the history of the continent and First Nations people, extends far beyond the point of invasion. It's this aspect of the curriculum that most closely aligns with academic articulations of deep time history.

So, what was the catalyst for including deep time history in the new 2023 curriculum? Several factors seem likely. One is a shifting social consciousness in the Australian settler public, encouraged by First Nations leaders and researchers sharing their stories and knowledge. Research emerging from fields such as archaeology and history have also contributed to a shift in the historical methods by engaging with Indigenous ways of doing history, and through the loosening of the history discipline's reliance on documentary evidence and linear time. Changes like these have been further buoyed by the popularity of First Nations texts for public audiences such as Bruce Pascoe's *Dark Emu*, and the production of documentaries like SBS's *The First Inventors*.[26] The climate crisis is also contributing to re-valuing and re-centring First Nations peoples' intimate knowledge of Country as fundamental to land management practices. For example, recognition of Indigenous cultural fire management strategies is challenging the traditional settler narratives and views of Indigenous knowledge.

Another factor is the ongoing call for Truth-Telling in Australia. The First People's Assembly of Victoria have made clear their view that history education must be scrutinised as 'part of both statewide and localised conversations around the true history of the colonisation of Victoria'.[27] Truth-Telling more generally has so far focused on what we might refer to as 'contested and shared histories', and on representing in more accurate and nuanced ways how First Nations people have experienced settler colonialism since British invasion in 1788. Truth-Telling is also about expanding knowledge of Indigenous cultures and deep histories, not only their histories of grappling with colonialism. In 2017, the Referendum Council released their report regarding the Uluru Statement from the Heart, which included the need to ensure greater recognition of First Nations living on the continent for more than 60 000 years.[28] The most significant driver of change has been the efforts of First Nations educators, who have long been calling for curricula that acknowledge the depth of First Nations sovereignty and connection to Country. More recently, First Nations scholars and educators including Tracey Bunda, Melitta Hogarth and Joe Sambono have been at the forefront of Indigenising curriculum reforms.[29]

These movements towards a more thorough depiction of First Nations histories in the curriculum have not been without setbacks and oppositions. Resistance and reluctance from teachers remain a stubborn barrier, as scholars like Hogarth and Bunda have noted.[30] The consultation process for the drafting of the 'Deep Time History' curriculum demonstrates some of the typical arguments against First Nations histories and perspectives, such as the point some educators made that there was too much emphasis on Indigenous history. One respondent argued for more emphasis on 'cultural roots in Britain/Ireland' claiming that 'Most Australian history is European'. The relentless politicisation of history curricula has also been a factor. In 2021, for example, when the current curriculum was in the proposal stage, then education minister Alan Tudge argued that the curriculum had to 'get the balance right', expressing his disappointment that the secondary school history curriculum 'doesn't even mention Captain James Cook'.[31] Beyond politics and education, the opposition of the majority of Australians to the 2023 referendum that proposed including Indigenous Australians in the Constitution and a permanent Voice to Parliament shows an ongoing resistance to acknowledging First Nations sovereignty. The deliberate damage to culturally significant sites, such as Rio Tinto's corporate destruction of caves at Juukan Gorge in Western Australia in 2020, and the individual vandalism of sites including engravings at Bulgandry, in New South Wales, in 2023 and 2024, show the disregard some Australians continue to have for First Nations culture and history.[32] The current iteration of the Australian Curriculum, and its inclusion of deep time history, will remain in place until 2026. Examining the strengths and limitations of the new course considering the historical precedents helps to locate what might be discarded, retained or expanded in future versions of the history curriculum.

Disciplinary knowledge and skills, and Indigenous knowledge

My discussion of the contemporary curriculum centres on the 2023 'Deep Time History of Australia' course for Year 7 History, part of the Version 9.0 Australian Curriculum, and the *Teacher's Guide*, published by ACARA on 17 June 2024.[33] Rather than comparing it with the current Victorian curriculum, I have selected the National Curriculum for analysis, as it is the main document from which other states are likely to develop their approaches.[34] My analysis is informed by Nikki Moodie's suggestion that reparative scholarship should move beyond only 'critique' to always 'include a theory of change'.[35] This framework is also based on my critique of the historical curriculum, described previously, to show what has changed and what has remained in the new course. As Hogarth and Sambono point out, the current curriculum bears the fruit of long-fought campaigns to include Indigenous perspectives and histories. Acknowledging this and finding ways to strengthen and expand on these aims – by locating and overcoming barriers, for example – is my aim in this section.

To begin, let's return to the way that the curriculum defines 'deep time' and the problems that consequently arise. The definition provided is given as a 'Framework to describe immense scales of geological time used by geologists, archaeologists and anthropologists to investigate the past (e.g. lives of early people)'. In other words, deep time is approached through methods developed in the natural and social sciences. There's no mention of the historical discipline here, nor of Indigenous Knowledges or conceptions of temporality. It does not indicate an understanding of the ways historians are attempting to theorise deep time. I suspect that the scientific orientation of the course could be frustrating to history teachers, who might see little reflection of historical content knowledge in this course. ACARA acknowledged that this issue was raised as part of the curriculum consultation process in 2021, noting that teachers would need 'professional development and access to resources to teach this content', and again in 2024, when they recognised that 'teachers have expressed concern that they are not knowledgeable about the content'.[36]

Opportunities for teachers to develop their knowledge are, however, difficult to locate.

The skills students should attain throughout the 'Deep Time History' course are firmly anchored in the historical thinking framework of the Australian Curriculum: History.[37] These skills are based on historical thinking concepts, developed by British and Canadian scholars and adapted locally, such as 'change and continuity' and 'cause and consequence'. These are intended to help students learn to 'think historically' (to construct disciplinary knowledge) by developing their skills in, for example, assessing primary and secondary sources, to 'identify perspectives, attitudes and values of the past'. This creates a mismatch between the skills and the content of the 'Knowledge and Understanding' descriptions, which are oriented towards natural and social sciences. Consequently, some parts of the curriculum remain locked into a disciplinary tradition, while others are more expansive and suggest a scientific or interdisciplinary approach.

What is required is a more expansive interdisciplinary framework that combines scientific, disciplinary and Indigenous knowledge and skills. This could more adequately allow for Indigenous ways of knowing the past, and of the developments in academic history in this area. ACARA might look to recent scholarship on deep time in the history discipline and work engaged with the politics of Indigenous history-making such as in this collection, which draws together Indigenous ways of knowing the past together with more critical approaches to disciplinary knowledge.[38] The consultation version of the 'Deep Time History' curriculum (that is, the draft that was released for consultation and feedback) demonstrates how this could be achieved. Although this version is scientific in focus, it also created a platform for learning both about First Nations culture and society before invasion, as well as acknowledging how discipline history has contributed to the misinterpretation and misrepresentation of that past. The opportunity for students to develop a critical, nuanced understanding of history is missing from the final version of the 'Deep Time History' curriculum published by ACARA. Significantly, the framing of the course suggests something like reluctance – or hesitancy – on ACARA's behalf to commit to including and centring Indigenous knowledge and perspectives of deep time in a serious way.

This hesitancy is even more clear when we consider ACARA's 2024 publication of a *Teacher's Guide for Deep Time History*. This resource, released in mid-2024, seems to be an attempt to retrofit Indigenous Knowledges to the course by introducing two further ways to consider knowledge in the 'Deep Time History' curriculum: cultural knowledge and archaeological knowledge. The guide states that this knowledge 'is the responsibility of the local Indigenous community knowledge custodians'. As the curriculum documentation does not refer to either of these concepts, this will likely cause confusion for teachers. While the mandatory elements of the Australian Curriculum for 'Deep Time History' on the ACARA website describe scientific knowledge and understanding and historical thinking skills, the Teacher's Guide claims that the course is more concerned with the cultural and archaeological knowledge held by First Nations communities.

ACARA's suggestions that it is the responsibility of teachers and communities to do much of this work, however, could also be viewed as an attempt at outsourcing curriculum development to First Nations communities. The guide also includes the oddly passive statement that: 'It is recognised that the best approach to developing your teaching and learning plan is to work with your local First Nations Peoples'. This comment, along with the direction to teachers that they should develop 'a relationship to learn and implement permissible local knowledges and stories' suggests that all First Nations local communities have the willingness and capacity to work with teachers and schools to develop curriculum materials. These suggestions place a significant load on both teachers and First Nations communities to develop curricula and resources. Even though this might be the best approach, suggesting this in isolation from structural change is negligent. A structured support program is required, which might include time-release for teachers and remuneration to First Nations communities who contribute their time, knowledge and skills to curriculum development in their local high schools. Until this happens, these suggestions remain problematic, if not irresponsible.

Systemic hesitancy

In many ways, the Australian history curriculum reveals a struggle between the incongruity of the national narrative that it helped create and the strength of First Nations people, culture and history that serve to challenge that narrative.[39] The structure of the course is reminiscent of the uncertainty evident in the 1955 Victorian Education Department course outline, which directed teachers to use their 'discretion' when discussing First Nations peoples. ACARA's rollout of 'Deep Time History' also demonstrates an uncertainty, a leaderless hesitancy, a desire to hedge bets. What might the impact of this uncertainty be on educators who may already feel hesitant, or who find themselves contending with a culture of hesitancy? ACARA's advice hardly instils confidence. The *Teachers' Guide* states:

> Teachers may experience some nervousness about teaching this content. Students have been taught about other ancient cultures in History for a long time, and teachers have been comfortable to cover this content. When teaching about deep time history of Australia, you are on the land that you are talking about and the First Nations Peoples of Australia are the longest living continuous culture in the world, so they are here.

It's difficult to develop a generative critique of this advice. These comments validate teacher hesitancy about teaching 'this content', and include the use of the othering 'they' to describe First Nations people. These comments imply that teaching Indigenous history is risky and anxiety-inducing, but teaching about ancient Rome, for example, is safe and comfortable.

There's little in the *Teacher's Guide* that makes it possible to take seriously ACARA's commitment to ensuring teachers are well-prepared to teach 'Deep Time History' curricula. Yet, like the earlier *School Paper* and the *Victorian Readers*, these texts have been created under the authority of government education departments and endorsed for publication. Does ACARA consider the impact that this framing might have on First Nations educators, and on First Nations students in the classrooms of teachers who buy into this idea of being scared or nervous about teaching Deep History, of incorporating Indigenous Knowledges? It's a frustrating suggestion, and disturbingly, it is one that might be used to pare back the course in the next review. This approach to the inclusion of such crucial historical understandings of the history of this continent in the Australian curriculum may invite mistrust in ACARA's processes. It implies a lack of care for First Nations communities and teachers alike, and a lack of clarity that might easily be used as an excuse for teachers to avoid teaching this content, and other content that privileges Indigenous knowledge.

Temporality and continuity

Turning from the curriculum's limitations to its strengths, here I point out some of the opportunities and generative potential of 'Deep Time History' that might be expanded upon in future iterations. As I have demonstrated, many of the historical narratives traditionally used in Australian schools have sought to construct temporal distance between the deep past of this continent and the continuing sovereignty of First Nations people. This new 'Deep Time History' curriculum collapses that distance. It emphasises continuity. There are two ways the course achieves this. The first is through the 'Knowledge and Understanding' description, 'First Nations Australians are the world's oldest continuing cultures, displaying evidence of both continuity and change over deep time'. This description speaks back to the cumulative effect of metanarratives that have claimed that Aboriginal culture has ended, and have sought to represent it as unchanged and unchangeable. The placement of 'Deep Time History' at the start of Year 7 creates a foundation for linking the continuity of First Nations culture, through connections to land, for example, to the Year 9 and 10 history curricula. This might be achieved, for example, by positioning mid-century campaigns for land rights within stories of continuous connection to Country. It is important that student learning about continuity is not undermined by other elements of the high school curriculum reinforcing the dominant settler narrative of history.

There's more potential for students to better understand the continuity of First Nations sovereignty too. A good example is the 'Knowledge and Understanding' description of 'cultural obligations of First Nations Australians about significant heritage sites, including ancestral remains, material culture and artefacts'. This gives teachers a concrete way to construct learning opportunities for students that would bridge the imagined gap between pre- and post-invasion First Nations cultures. This description further creates the potential for learning strengths-based evidence of ongoing connection to Country, and rewrites Aboriginal presence on the land.[40] Locating First Nations connections to Country through cultural obligations towards significant heritage sites now and into the future acknowledges continuing connection to place. Another example is suggested in one of the 'Knowledge and Understanding' descriptions: 'technological achievement of early First Nations Australians, and how these developed in different places and contributed to daily life, and land and water source management'. By showcasing Indigenous knowledge and management of land and water – such as at Budj Bim, or the Brewarrina Fish Traps – teachers will necessarily centre Indigenous knowledge and expertise. Material culture collections in keeping places, museums and galleries present further opportunities for students to learn about First Nations innovations and technologies.

New skills for the new curriculum

More extensive structural reform to the design of history curriculum is also needed. As I have suggested, perhaps the biggest barriers to the success of 'Deep Time History' are the corresponding 'Skills' descriptions. Including oral histories and oral traditions explicitly is essential. This will create more opportunities for students to hear directly from First Nations people, for teachers to utilise online oral histories, for example, and to recognise other forms of knowledge exchange, including through cultural heritage materials. This would mean acknowledging Indigenous ways of knowing and making sense of the past in the same way that discipline-specific ways are positioned. The *Teacher's Guide* gestures towards this, noting the need for teachers to consider 'how this information [Indigenous knowledge of deep time history] has been shared and passed down from one generation to the next'. This advice is well founded, but the curriculum guidelines must support this imperative.

Until that happens, teachers might design learning around a critique of the ways in which disciplinary knowledge has been constructed in the curriculum. The consultation curriculum includes some useful examples. This could mean using the mismatching of knowledge of deep time and the historical thinking skills in a generative way, creating some space for teachers to move away from the rigidity of disciplinary knowledge. Oral traditions, oral history, stories and songlines are one way to do this. These forms of sources are not included in the 'Skills' descriptions. Although they are referenced in the supplementary elaborations, teachers are not provided with a way to reconcile knowledge about deep time passed down via oral traditions, and the primary and secondary source binary embedded in the history curriculum. This means teachers themselves will need to be creative in ensuring the structure of the curriculum does not diminish the authority of stories and oral histories, and to be mindful of the ways they discuss different knowledges. This would allow teachers to develop learning activities that resist traditional approaches – through lists of pros and cons, or debates, for example – that might lead students to think that there are limits or flaws inherent in certain types of knowledge and evidence, which could lead them to diminish Indigenous oral history knowledge as less authoritative. Exploring the ways that historical knowledge about deep time history (including stereotypes and tropes, as ACARA's own 'Deep Time History' draft curriculum suggested) has been constructed through sources would be a powerful learning opportunity.[41]

As a national administrative body, ACARA could do more to ensure that teachers and First Nations communities are supported to work together on curriculum development locally, or risk undermining their own role in developing and administering a national curriculum. In developing more holistic support for teachers, ACARA might consider more deeply the ethics of historical and archaeological research. This could, in turn, be developed to include advice on how best to draw students into that relationship. This includes reconsidering the ways that skills are defined to include more creative ways to engage with non-written cultural materials to understand the past.

Websites that platform Indigenous knowledge, such as Marking Country and Global Encounters, give students the opportunity to learn directly from Elders and communities.[42] These sites showcase Indigenous knowledge about the past, expressed by Indigenous Knowledge Holders. This allows students to learn in ways that replicate how Indigenous knowledge has been passed on in non-textual ways. It allows for an approach that understands that knowledge has been and continues to be recorded in stories and songs, and to develop an awareness that this way of learning is as valid as analysing primary documents.

Looking forward, looking back

Several key aspects of the current 'Deep Time History' of Australia curriculum indicate how much thinking has advanced since the 1900 publication of Baldwin Spencer's 'The Australian Aborigines' and the 1928 publication of 'The old inhabitants' in the eighth *Victorian Reader*. Marking these changes is also useful for reminding teachers how to avoid the limitations of the past curriculum, and for locating what needs more attention in the future as educators and planners move towards the next review and redesign of the Australian Curriculum. Hopefully by the 2026 curriculum review, ACARA will be ready to stop toeing an imaginary line that includes holding tightly to the traditions of history education that have failed generations of settler and First Nations students. To ensure that the much longer and deeper Aboriginal and Torres Strait Islander histories of the continent are positioned as both foundational and ongoing to the story of Australian history, it will be necessary to create a profound structural reform of history curricula through to the senior years. Importantly, these challenges are shared globally. In Canada, the United States, South Africa and Finland, scholarship is growing about representations of deep time and precolonial histories in history and social studies curricula. The New Zealand Aotearoa history curriculum, which positions pre-invasion Māori history as foundational and continuous, provides a strong example to follow. Together with global considerations of environmental and multispecies perspectives, the 'Deep Time History' curriculum is poised to play a significant role in reshaping understandings of the deep time past for the sake of our shared future.

PART II

Archaeology, science and sovereign histories

4

ARCHAEOLOGY AND ABORIGINAL SOVEREIGNTY

Martin Porr

Under the influence of Indigenous rights and self-determination movements, in recent decades archaeology has transformed into a much more diverse discipline than it once was. Many Indigenous communities have embraced the field and have often used its results to assert their sovereignty. While these developments allow archaeology a more positive position in the relationships with Indigenous communities, they generally underestimate the complexities of radiometric dating techniques in archaeological reasoning and the generally undertheorised treatment of time within the field. The relationship of modern archaeological notions of time and their integration into debates about Indigenous sovereignty is a vexed one. Insights gained from considering this relationship have important consequences for future debates about humanity's deep past and Indigenous self-determination. Indigenous communities need to be cautious about embracing archaeological notions of time and archaeological practitioners must be mindful of the complex assumptions on which their treatment of time rests. However, archaeology's multidisciplinary strengths and its positioning across the humanities/science divide mean that the discipline has great potential to support Aboriginal sovereignty and Aboriginal people's aspirations in an informed and responsible fashion.

Some significant intersections exist between archaeological practice, notions of time, and Indigenous and Aboriginal sovereignty. I will primarily engage with Australian cases and experiences here, but similarities and convergences with other settler colonial contexts will be apparent; these relate to each other through shared historical trajectories, intellectual frameworks, and socio-economic and political conditions. I want to emphasise at the beginning that I am a non-Indigenous researcher, originally from Germany and now based in Australia. My reflections are from the perspective of an anthropological archaeologist and rock art and heritage researcher, who continues to work in Europe and Australia. In Australia, I mainly work with Aboriginal people in the Kimberley, especially Wanjina Wunggurr Traditional Owners. Like many other Aboriginal groups in Australia, they continue to struggle to have their cultural heritage recognised. Native Title determinations in 2004 and 2011 constituted landmark decisions in achieving such recognition, however conflicts over the interpretation of Aboriginal heritage continue. Most recently, the decision to phase out the passing of tourism boats through Horizontal Falls within the Dambimangari determination area produced a significant backlash that encapsulates ongoing conflicts between protecting Aboriginal sacred areas and the pressures of economic development.[1] Wanjina Wunggurr Traditional Owners must also navigate different interpretations of the famous Kimberley rock art, which has been a severely conflicted space in the past. It is often a challenge for Traditional Owners to communicate their viewpoints and understandings to the public and other stakeholders.[2] Scientific and archaeological interpretations play an important role in this debate, however they do not always align with Aboriginal knowledge of heritage and history. Integrating – and reconciling – both types of knowledge is an ongoing challenge in balancing public interests and pressures on the one hand, and Aboriginal aspirations for cultural continuity and survival on the other.[3]

These few examples show that archaeology plays an important role in contemporary negotiations surrounding the meanings and significance of heritage. Despite common misconceptions surrounding the discipline, archaeology, as a scientific practice, does not study the past. Archaeology takes place in the present and deals with evidence that also exists in the present. It engages with material aspects of the present to construct and reconstruct past events and processes. Archaeology's engagement with the dimension of time is a complex one and not very well understood. It is therefore important to ask what material evidence means in temporal terms, and how it can inform our understanding of past processes or human actions. Archaeology needs to make inferences about processes of change and continuity at different scales; it also makes assumptions about the character of time itself.

Traditionally, archaeology has employed a linear and universal understanding of time, placing objects and events along a single progression that moves inevitably from the past to the future. However, doing so simplifies the intertwined nature of past and present processes and events. It does not fully capture the personal experience of time and diverges from many Indigenous conceptualisations. The history of archaeology in Australia and elsewhere has shown how archaeological practices and findings can both empower and disempower Indigenous people.[4] Notions of time and how they are used play an equally crucial and underestimated role in these contexts. Notions of time affect the ways in which people define themselves and how they view their place in the world, defining their identities with reference to real or imagined past events and persons.[5] Archaeological practice and its results participate in significant current processes of Indigenous and national identity formation, and it can equally support and undermine them. From these insights, important challenges and responsibilities for the discipline emerge that can have far-reaching political implications.

On 14 October 2023, a majority of the Australian people rejected the proposal to alter the Australian Constitution to recognise the First Peoples of Australia by establishing an Aboriginal and Torres Strait Islander Voice. The associated referendum asked for an advisory body to the Federal Parliament on issues and decisions that affect Aboriginal people. The referendum was related to the Uluru Statement from the Heart, which invited the nation to listen to Aboriginal people and to learn from the original inhabitants of the continent.[6] In public debates surrounding the referendum and numerous online contributions, memes and statements, advocates for the Voice regularly stressed that Aboriginal culture has continued in Australia for 65 000 years. More precisely, the Uluru Statement stated that 'Aboriginal and Torres Strait Islander people were the first sovereign Nations of the Australian continent and its adjacent islands (…) according to science more than 60,000 years ago'. It also outlined sovereignty as a spiritual notion, reflective of the Ancestral tie between the land, or 'mother nature', and Aboriginal peoples. In the Uluru Statement, the scientific determination of 'more than 60,000 years ago' is placed next to the Aboriginal determination of 'from the Creation' and the common-law determination of 'since time immemorial'.

Few people who have used the date of 65 000 years to support the case for recognising Aboriginal people in the constitution know its origin. The date is related to the widely publicised radiometric (OSL) dating of the rock shelter Madjedbebe in Arnhem Land. In 2017, archaeologist Chris Clarkson and his team published a paper in the journal *Nature* in which they argued that 65 000 years ago is now confirmed as the earliest minimum date for the first human presence in Australia.[7] This date quickly entered the public imagination, and it has been widely used ever since, but most people do not know the scientific and physical basis of this age determination, nor are they aware of the issues some experts have raised. So far, this date has not been replicated in any other site east of the Wallace Line and it is about 10 000 years older than all other radiometric age determinations in Australia and New Guinea. Archaeologists continue to debate the issue, although all academic experts agree that the earliest human presence in Australia and New Guinea is at least 55 000 years old.[8] These discussions point to the rarely recognised (or publicised) uncertainties and insecurities of these determinations, which result from the complex methods involved and the fact that dating results always come with uncertainties, which I will go on to discuss in more detail later.[9]

Beyond these debates, which are a normal part of the scientific process, a complex public discourse has discussed, questioned and amplified the significance of the age determination. People have reacted both positively and negatively. As historians Billy Griffiths and Lynette Russell have demonstrated, making the case for an exceptionally ancient presence of Aboriginal people on the Australian continent produced fierce reactions from some sections of the public, which 'dredged up an ugly racist undercurrent in Australian society'.[10] While I do not engage with these deeply problematic responses here, I want to argue that, despite their obvious differences, most reactions to this age determination and others tend to be reflections of a similarly teleological understanding of time and history as traditionally represented in archaeology. This is the dominant Western linear and progressive view, which archaeology and other academic disciplines helped to create. It assumes that the whole history of humanity can be ordered into a single sequence of events running from the deep past to the present. This understanding also incorporates the view that time is progressive and that a 'normal' historical development leads to increasingly higher levels of biological, social or technological complexity.[11] To assess these issues better and relate them to questions of Aboriginal sovereignty, we need to analyse the prevailing understanding of time in archaeology and its historical emergence and entanglements.

The logic of archaeological temporality

In 1797, a letter by John Frere was read to the Royal Society of Antiquarians in London in which he reported the discovery of several stone tools, which should – in his words – 'be considered in that light from the situation in which they were found'.[12] With this comment, the wealthy landowner and antiquarian, who had been an active member of the society since 1771, referred to the fact that he had found the clearly human-made implements under 4 metres of undisturbed soil and gravel. He noted that the sediments included layers of sand that contained shells and layers with fossilised bones of extinct animals. Based on his observations, he made the famous conclusion that the stone tools did not fit into the contemporary understanding of the antiquity of the earth and humanity:

> The situation in which these weapons were found may tempt us to refer them to a very remote period indeed; even beyond that of the present world.[13]

The development of archaeology as an academic endeavour was part of significant intellectual changes during the 18th and 19th centuries. Europe was at the centre of these shifts, but their impacts were felt in all parts of the world, and European thinking did not develop in isolation either. Archaeology was a product of a time of globalisation during which different parts of the world, became increasingly interconnected through political relationships and dependencies, the flow of goods and materials, as well as the exchange of ideas, projections and imaginations.[14] The development of archaeology was equally local and global, and it was connected to other academic fields in complex ways, which were undergoing equally substantial changes of their own.[15] Geology, palaeontology and archaeology contributed to a new understanding of the earth's deep past and, eventually, humanity.[16] These changes had a crucial impact on the view of humanity's past and future.

Archaeology became the source of numerous metaphors about the character of time and history and how these intersect with the material world. The practice of removing layers of sediment to uncover the actions of past people provided the metaphor for understanding the past in the present day. The act of excavation was often imagined as one of movement through time. Fascination with archaeology is always a fascination with the past and the idea of being able to move back through time. The depth of the soil becomes a metaphor for temporal depth. Archaeology consequently becomes a science of discovery, of revealing layers and artefacts that have for a time been hidden from view. While these observations seem straightforward and hardly controversial, they also show that archaeology reflected the dominant view of science during the 19th century, one which, very briefly, assumes that the world exists independently from human observations and perspectives and that facts can be described objectively. It also means that there is ultimately only one true description of the world, which is usually related to the methods of the natural sciences and quantitative analytical approaches.[17]

Many key principles of archaeological fieldwork and observation were already established during archaeology's formative phase in the 19th century. Early practitioners soon realised that stratigraphic sequences could be used to systematically estimate the relative age of different types of evidence. The association of artefacts with the remains of extinct animals or animals long gone from specific regions showed that human life and past environments sometimes differed dramatically from present conditions.[18] However, the possibility of measuring absolute ages in the archaeological record remained extremely limited for a very long time. This situation changed dramatically after the Second World War with the introduction of radiometric dating techniques. These allow researchers to estimate the age of archaeological evidence, calculated in years before the present. In some cases, these techniques are applied to artefacts directly, and in others, they are used to date sediments or other aspects of the contextual matrix.[19]

The most well-known and widely used technique is radiocarbon dating, which makes use of the fact that, through metabolic processes, living organisms incorporate the rare and unstable isotope carbon-14 into their bodies during their lifetime. This uptake ceases with the death of the organism. Carbon-14 decays into carbon-12 at a stable rate: the amount of carbon-14 will halve every 5730 years. Hence, measuring the ratio between these two isotopes in organic remains provides an age estimate in absolute terms. Another widely used method is optically stimulated luminescence (OSL).[20] This process measures the light emitted by a sample of crystalline material when it is heated beyond a specific temperature threshold. At this point, the sample will emit photons captured in the crystal grid of the object during its time in the ground. Because of these physical processes, OSL can measure the time during which crystalline material was not exposed to light. OSL has enabled archaeologists to break through the so-called radiocarbon barrier, which ceases to provide dates beyond approximately 50 000 years ago. Significantly, OSL enables us to date human artefacts and relevant sediments of up to 500 000 years in age.

Measuring the age of archaeological evidence, however, is far from straightforward; different methodological challenges occur at each step related to possible sampling, contamination or processing errors. All radiometric techniques, furthermore, need to be calibrated. In the case of carbon-14 dating, this means controlling for the changing concentration of carbon-14 in the atmosphere and oceans. It should also be noted that all radiometric methods need to be understood in relation to the physical processes they utilise. Any estimation is provided as a probability distribution. Thus, there is no absolute certainty in 'absolute' dating. Greater reliability is only achieved through employing multiple age determinations of a single method, using different dating methods, and applying sophisticated statistical procedures to bring it all together. Age determinations in archaeology will always come with standard errors and deviations. This reflects the dynamic nature of physical reality itself, which needs to be expressed in statistical probabilities, which, for example, reflect the decay rates of isotopes.[21]

Despite the inevitable fuzziness of archaeological dating, archaeology is often perceived as a precise science. Determining the age of an artefact or any other piece of the archaeological record remains a key question for archaeological inquiry. It is also a prominent aspect of the public imagination of archaeology. The fact that archaeology can demonstrate the great antiquity of human presence in Australia is regularly treated as a crucial step in developing the discipline, signalling its greater sophistication or maturity.[22]

Questions surrounding the treatment of time have received increasing academic attention in international contexts recently.[23] Within Australian archaeology, however, critical engagement with the dimension of time itself has been minimal, particularly when it comes to interrogating the reconstruction of historical processes or narratives, and the relationship between archaeological and Aboriginal understandings of time and, hence, implications for Aboriginal sovereignty or self-determination. While I cannot provide a comprehensive survey in this respect, I want to briefly examine the treatment of time in a few influential contributions to Australian Indigenous archaeology from the past three decades.

In archaeologist Harry Lourandos's book, *Continent of Hunter-Gatherers*, 'time' does not feature in the index as a term. However, as in most archaeology studies, time is a central category in assessing and interpreting evidence. Lourandos argues that 'the uniqueness of the hunter-gatherer past, as compared to other human societies, is the extraordinary length of time involved. Time is often scaled in thousands of years. In order, therefore, to understand and analyse these vast periods varying temporal scales need to be employed, and on both long- and short-term time axes'.[24] The discussion continues with reference to methodological issues in describing and comparing different historical processes at varying temporal (and spatial) scales and finding the appropriate explanatory frameworks. Lourandos draws attention to the fact that most theories available from other disciplines (ecology and social theory, just to give a couple of examples) are not applicable to the long-term processes and trends accessible through archaeological methods. He consequently stresses that processes that operated at different temporal scales should be kept apart and discussed separately. Integrating these remains a challenge. The book does not refer to Aboriginal notions of time, nor does it explicitly discuss how archaeological narratives are formed and how they interact with other social or historical processes, or the validity of the distinction between history and pre-history.

In Peter Hiscock's book *Archaeology of Ancient Australia*, 'time' does not feature in the index as a separate entry.[25] Overall, the book involves relatively few general theoretical or reflective considerations. However, it positions itself clearly against the use of ethnographic analogies – or references to contemporary Indigenous interpretations – in explaining Australia's deep human past. The author criticises the use of ethnographic analogy with reference to social evolutionist thinking, which viewed Aboriginal societies as unchanging and unchanged, and, consequently, as representatives of earlier stages of human history. Such thinking was correctly discarded decades ago. Archaeological research has demonstrated in myriad cases that social, cultural and economic expressions in Australia's deep past varied enormously. Equally, the ethnographic present is also not representative of ancient conditions, for example, because of the devastating effects of European-introduced diseases and other disruptive effects of colonial exploitation.

After briefly acknowledging that 'it is inevitable that we will use knowledge of the present in our archaeological interpretations', Hiscock suggests that archaeology can get around this thorny problem by applying 'methodological uniformitarianism'.[26] This orientation assumes that in the past 'the "laws" established for physics, chemistry, geology, biology and other sciences were the same as they are now'. The regularity of these laws equally structure 'the processes of human behaviour and provides a basis for identifying the ancient physical environments in which humans operated'.[27] Seemingly arguing for an extreme form of environmental determinism, Hiscock concludes that this orientation provides an unproblematic basis for archaeological reasoning and developing conclusions 'about the extent and nature of economic, technological and social change over time, without creating the problematic circular arguments that result from telling stories of the ancient past using details simply borrowed from ethnographic records'.[28] Hiscock asserts that his own position is objective, implying that it has an elevated status, and that due to culturally variable perspectives, other interpretations must be erroneous. However, at the same time, such an interpretation cannot explain the multitude of different social and cultural forms and lifeways that thrive in similar environments in Australia and on other continents, including the differences in artistic expressions, economic strategies and material culture across the tropical north or the temperate south of Australia. Such manifestations are difficult to reconcile with the assumption that human behaviours simply reflect the materiality of nature itself, without room for creativity, agency and contingent historical developments.

Finally, in the above-mentioned paper in *Nature* that reports on the results from excavations at Madjedbebe, Clarkson and other authors assert that precisely dating the initial colonisation of Australia has important implications for a whole range of questions. These include the 'timing and rate of dispersal of modern humans out of Africa and across South Asia, and when and where genetic material was transferred between archaic hominins and modern humans'.[29] Such aspects do not form a part of the paper itself, which is instead a report on the excavation materials and the techniques of radiometric dating. The article is mostly about locating the position of objects in time (and space) and less about historical processes, causalities and contexts. Throughout the text, it becomes clear that absolute dating methods can provide data points in time and space of human presence and human activities. They are presented as the key methods that allow archaeologists to reconstruct past processes within a geometric system of spatial and temporal parameters.

Even though the theme of time drives this study, it is somehow invisible. It is certainly not given an independent existence, but rather it is implicitly dealt with as smooth and neutral, without cultural or other dimensions. This basic understanding is also reflected in recent textbooks, demonstrated in how they treat the importance of absolute dating and stratigraphic observations during excavation.[30] In each case, the research aims to determine the sequence and duration of events.

Much archaeological literature recognises issues of scale, particularly in reconstructing past events and processes. However, the relationship between long-term processes and the dynamics and temporalities of human behaviour are rarely discussed.[31] Similarly, discussions about the relationship between archaeological practice and inference on the one hand and historical reasoning on the other are rare. Are the interpretations created through archaeological inference fundamentally different from historical interpretations? Are dimensions and dynamics of individual agency and motivations always inaccessible to archaeological analysis?[32] Archaeology has recently developed more and more sophisticated technologies to detect and reconstruct spatial and temporal patterns of material culture at different scales. But interpreting these patterns and their causes often remains an underdeveloped aspect and requires engaging more extensively with different social theories to explain processes of change and persistence in the past. The recognition of patterns and correlations between data do not themselves constitute causal relationships and, hence, explanations. Furthermore, how should we navigate these questions when it comes to Indigenous knowledge systems and understandings of temporality?[33] As I've mentioned, Australian archaeology still does not engage much with time and temporality as a theoretical problem itself, let alone with the political and cultural negotiations that affect how data points are transformed into meaningful narratives.

Archaeology and chronopolitics

Time in archaeology is created by decisions that are being made in the present. It is important to remember that the archaeological record does not belong to the past. It exists in the present. Its interpretation depends on contemporary definitions, orientations and distinctions. The treatment of time in archaeology is part of the more extensive politics of the imagination of the past. As such, it is subjected to the social power dynamics of the present, or a 'chronopolitics', as archaeologist Christopher Witmore describes them.[34] These processes continue to affect virtually all aspects of archaeology, and they exist in complex relationships with wider political developments. The interpretation of archaeological evidence is never neutral. It is, therefore, important to examine how archaeological evidence is given significance in the present, how it is transformed into different forms of heritage, and how it is embedded into meaningful narratives.

One of the key elements of archaeology's origins is its inherent connection to one of the central dimensions of modernity: a linear and universal understanding of time.[35] This aspect allowed us to recognise the deep antiquity of the earth as well as humanity. There can be little doubt that the origins and structure of archaeology are broadly entangled in establishing the modern world and the worldview of modernity. During the 19th and 20th centuries, the discipline shaped, reflected and amplified people's understanding of the temporality of humanity's past and present in Australia and elsewhere.[36] Archaeology's present theoretical frameworks and methodologies can only be understood in relation to the fundamental modern structures of perception and interpretation, particularly a homogeneous understanding of space and time.[37]

However, as part of modernity's origin narrative, archaeology is similarly affected by the complex temporal structure of modernity and its resulting paradoxes and contradictions.[38] The historian Pratik Chakrabarti has argued that the emergence of a naturalised understanding of time that is independent of local contingencies and conditions was far from straightforward.[39] Using India as a case study, Chakrabarti shows how this understanding of time was worked out during the 19th century in complex negotiations between local mythological narratives, geological surveys, archaeological discoveries, and racial and ethnographic research into contemporary populations. The focus became ordering objects, people and events within a single temporal framework. Engineers often pushed these developments forward, making observations while they oversaw building roads, tunnels or canals. These processes can be understood as imposing an abstract and geometric understanding of space onto the landscape and its many contingencies and temporalities. They are the consequence of a Western worldview and, as such, a part of the European colonial system.[40]

From the 18th century onwards, important changes affected the interpretation of global human diversity by European intellectuals, who needed to integrate an increasing amount of information that became available because of the European-dominated colonial system of exploitation and communication. Human difference became temporalised. The non-European 'Other' was no longer located in space but also in time.[41] The history of the world became a progressive temporality in which humanity moves from simple beginnings towards a more complex and sophisticated future. This process was also conceptualised as a movement out of and away from nature, which was enabled through increasingly sophisticated material technologies.[42] The increased mastery and exploitation of nature through technology became an underlying distinctive theme. 'Primitive' people were seen to be traditional and closer to nature, while 'civilised' people were modern in their advanced understanding and mastery of nature.[43] These views either implicitly or explicitly guided the chronological schemes that have dominated archaeology and anthropology in a dialectical fashion during most of the 19th and 20th centuries. If they follow this logic, archaeological interpretations and narratives reproduce totalising forms of history that suppress the specifics of individual cases and contexts.[44] It can then be argued that they also reflect the universalising approaches to history that are part of the politics of global European hegemony and colonialism.[45]

Archaeology's linear evaluation of the past and its cultural expressions, and the discipline's work sorting these into eras, periods or epochs, do not reflect the past itself. It is rather a negotiation between political and economic understandings in the present.[46] These negotiations then integrate references to material expressions and objects, which participate in these exchanges about what can and cannot be said.[47] Past societies are placed into typological sequences and categories, which contribute to the process of homogenising past variability. In this way, archaeology is mostly concerned with *Chronos*, an understanding of time that is separate from events and objects.[48] It suppresses the multi-temporal character of human life that is always entangled in a multitude of temporalities of persistence and destruction.[49] However, as the past is generally also perceived as a time of historical progression, historical time is not empty or neutral. Following the terminology of historian François Hartog, history also is perceived as a reflection of *Kairos*, the time of metaphysical directedness and purpose, which is usually reserved for religious temporalities of destiny.[50] In the Western modern understanding, this aspect is transformed into the view that history is the successive realisation of humanity's potential and capabilities. It is invariably the economically, materially and intellectually powerful who define and construct these capabilities. In such Eurocentric understandings, those peoples who apparently do not achieve these potentials are judged against the merciless temporality of human evolution or history.

Archaeology is not so much the study of the (deep) past. It is, as archaeologist Laurent Olivier argued, the study of the materiality and temporality of the present: 'A site or an artefact is never wholly contained within the past. It is a product of a dynamic past-present continuum and, as every historical process, its study is affected by considerations of the future'.[51] The decisions and motivations related to different representations of the past are a product of implicit or explicit political decisions, which can be understood as expressing the chronopolitics of archaeological reasoning.[52]

Over the past few decades, archaeology's role in nation-building projects has been analysed extensively in the context of recent European history.[53] The respective interrelationships between political actors and interests on the one hand, and academic or intellectual projects on the other, show how history and notions of time can be manipulated for a range of purposes.[54] For example, the practice of dividing the past into periods and phases is a common mechanism in the fields of both history and archaeology. But it is not an innocent or neutral endeavour. Periods ascribe meaning to evidence beyond their local contexts or relationships, and this is ultimately a political act that is entangled in power relations — and which can be difficult to challenge.[55] These aspects become particularly significant in colonial or imperial contexts in which the power difference between coloniser and colonised groups, for example, is pronounced on many levels.[56]

Archaeology, Aboriginal sovereignty, and the politics of time

In Australia, an important discussion continues about the relationship between archaeology, history and Indigenous knowledge in understanding the past.[57] These recent debates clearly reflect the complexity of conceptualising the past in the Australian context and the different perspectives and orientations that participate in them. These discussions show complex relationships with questions surrounding Aboriginal sovereignty and how archaeologists have or have not engaged with them. After the Second World War, archaeology has played an important role in demonstrating the complexity and antiquity of Aboriginal lifeways in Australia.[58] Simplistic assumptions about the continent's deep human past and its Traditional Owners provided significant justifications for dispossessing Aboriginal people and denying them land and other rights. Throughout the 19th century and beyond, Aboriginal people were seen as not only at the bottom of the ladder of universal historical development but also perceived to be stuck — in unchanged form — in a past period of history.[59]

Archaeological research has contradicted these understandings over the past few decades in various ways. While traditionally perceived as an agent of government-sanctioned development and the destruction of Indigenous heritage, archaeology is increasingly emerging as an advocate for preserving Indigenous and Aboriginal culture and heritage in Australia and elsewhere.[60] These processes are reflected in a recent collection of essays in the journal *Australian Archaeology* (volume 90, number 1) celebrating its fiftieth anniversary and archaeology's development during this time. The fifty papers by professional and academic members of the Australian

Archaeological Association cover many topics, including the discipline's changing relationships with Aboriginal communities and the need to include Indigenous concerns and perspectives. Another key element is the expansion of the available data to allow a more complete picture of the continent's deep past. The dimension of time, however, is not directly addressed. Apart from one contribution on '50 years of radiocarbon dating in Australian archaeology', there is not even a separate chapter on the changing and current impact of radiometric dating methods.[61] There is also no dedicated paper discussing the relationship between archaeology, the discipline of history and the increasingly influential notions of deep time and Deep History.[62] Some might argue that these questions are not central to archaeology's concerns right now and that it is more important to focus on the relationships with Aboriginal communities.[63] However, I would argue that these issues are, in fact, difficult to separate, and that the current situation rather shows a lack of reflective and informed engagement with archaeology's contributions towards questions of Aboriginal sovereignty and publicly and nationally relevant narratives.

These issues were and are particularly on display in the context of the debate surrounding the book *Dark Emu* by Bruce Pascoe.[64] Originally published in 2014 (with a new and revised edition in 2018) for a general Australian readership, the book has deeply affected the perception of Aboriginal societies and their past social and economic formations. Almost like no other book before, it initiated an extensive debate about the misrepresentation of Aboriginal societies and their histories in the public sphere. Pascoe's key argument is that Australian Aboriginal societies before European invasion need to be conceptualised not as hunter-gatherers but as agriculturalists. His critique related to the widely held perception that hunting and gathering was a simple and primitive way of life with little economic and social complexity. This related to an old western understanding according to which hunting and gathering people represented an early stage of human history, with underdeveloped planning and technical abilities.[65] In his book, Pascoe collected evidence to make the case that pre-invasion Aboriginal societies had sophisticated economic, technological and social systems through which they carefully and sustainably managed the landscape and its resources. As such, he argued that these societies needed to be understood as agriculturalists who produced their subsistence – and not as hunter-gatherers who simply exploited resources that occurred in the environment. Pascoe made the explicit link between these understandings about the deep past and contemporary ideas about Aboriginal people, creating a clear and powerful connection about the interdependence between understandings of the past and the present. He assisted in exposing how biases and misconceptions about the Aboriginal past very much determine biases and misconceptions about Aboriginal people today. *Dark Emu* was largely written to rectify these misconceptions. As such, it is motivated by the recognition that histories are written from a political standpoint and are structured equally by the inclusion and exclusion of voices and silences.[66]

While many of *Dark Emu*'s arguments have been widely recognised and praised, it has also been heavily criticised.[67] Significant criticism was directed at the lack of academic rigour in Pascoe's use of historical sources and the book's restriction to material and economic aspects of past Aboriginal societies.[68] A further critique was that the book perpetuated the established Western understanding of human history. *Dark Emu* evaluated past societies along a progression of economic and social forms, from simple hunter-gatherers to more complex societies, without fundamentally critiquing the logic of this conception. Rather, the book's starting point was where settler society had placed past Aboriginal societies and how the contemporary Australian public should instead assess and recognise their achievements more positively.[69] These aspects were consequently an important part of the book's popularity. After all, its vision of the Aboriginal past could be integrated into the current modern value system and worldview, and the related aspirations of many Aboriginal people today. As it argues that past Aboriginal societies had sophisticated structures of economic organisation and political governance rather like those of other so-called advanced societies across the globe, Pascoe's book effectively supports many modern aspirations of Aboriginal equality and sovereignty.

The discipline of archaeology has not substantially participated in these discussions for a long time.⁷⁰ As Pascoe presented himself as an anti-establishment and anti-academic outsider, he also suggested that Australian archaeologists were complicit in perpetuating a simplistic view of past Aboriginal societies. This seriously misrepresents discussions that have been taking place within archaeological circles for a very long time. Key aspects of Pascoe's critique have been debated within Australian archaeology for decades, including the presence or absence of food-producing practices among Aboriginal societies, as well as the prevailing simplistic views of Aboriginal lifeways.⁷¹ However, it is curious that, despite a lot of empirical and conceptual ammunition, archaeologists had very little to say in the context of the *Dark Emu* debate. I would argue that this situation is a consequence of archaeology's reluctance to systematically develop and critically reflect on meaningful narratives about Aboriginal Australia's deep past and relate them to culturally and politically contemporary issues.

Such an assessment of Australian archaeology significantly simplifies a very complex situation, and one can certainly find numerous examples to the contrary. We should also consider that the public perception and evaluation of archaeology and developments within the discipline (including its professional and academic sectors) do not necessarily correspond to each other. However, there is still a general tendency to be foremost empirically oriented and avoid developing theoretically informed interpretations.⁷² At the same time, the public has a great interest in the sensational side of archaeology and its discoveries as well as securely dated evidence. It is especially interested in origin stories. Archaeology's role in discussions about the understanding of Australia's deep past is often reduced to its ability to provide absolute dates for different types of evidence and phenomena. Archaeology is increasingly reduced to the role it can play in an economy of firsts.

Indeed, nothing appears to be more important than archaeology's ability to radiometrically and precisely date past artefacts or other evidence. From this emerges its power to contribute to a global attention economy that follows the same rules of firsts and superlatives, in which antiquity is equated with authority. The latter, however, mirrors and reproduces the above-mentioned global system of historical significance and the evaluation of the so-called achievements of different societies that are ultimately the products of European intellectual dominance and colonialism.[73] These mechanisms have been critiqued in relation to approaches to human evolution or Palaeolithic archaeology elsewhere.[74] The examination of the deep past can easily become a mirror image of the present, leading to a reduction of past variabilities. In this case, only those aspects are examined that are important for specific current questions or aims. The Palaeolithic period is often only of interest because it allegedly contains the origins of aspects of human history that are seen as particularly important in the present. Throughout the research history of archaeology, these have been features such as the origins of art, human hunting, the sexual division of labour and so on. Archaeologists Clive Gamble and Erica Gittins have consequently argued that the most distant periods of human history are rarely represented in all their variability. They are selectively turned into an *Originsland* populated with origins of developments relevant to contemporary agendas.[75] In the context of Australian archaeology, very similar relationships have been observed and analysed for a long time. These intersected with a colonial imagination that systematically underestimated and erased past and present complexities and variabilities of Aboriginal societies and ways of living.[76]

In light of these considerations, we need to ask: do highly publicised archaeological discoveries support or undermine Aboriginal sovereignty? For example, the earliest securely dated in-situ rock art in the Kimberley[77] or the oldest securely dated ceramics found in Australia on an offshore island of the northern Great Barrier Reef?[78] Most archaeologists would certainly argue that these discoveries help Aboriginal sovereignty and aspirations because they allow Aboriginal people to claim an appropriate place in the great narrative of humanity's ascent and progression, especially because they have been denied such a recognition over more than 200 years. As such, Aboriginal people can counter the perception that their past was less complex, and argue that it included significant technological advancements and achievements. However, these advancements and achievements are also defined and assessed against a Eurocentric version of history that is materialistic and technocentric, which is reflected in the examples that are put forward (oldest bread-making, oldest stone houses, oldest agriculture, oldest engineering and so on). In this context, I am concerned about the little-examined intersections between power and time.

If we establish significance using the parameters of archaeological science, radiometric dating and a universal framework of historical assessment, we can just as easily remove or deny it. A site or an artefact that was once established as being the oldest at a global or national level can easily lose this status, simply because another date is produced somewhere else, potentially thousands of kilometres away. For example, how would such a shift affect the significance of the Juukan Gorge rock shelters, which were destroyed in 2020 by Rio Tinto? Would the public care less if these had been dated to just 500 years ago? In the foreword to the report of the Commonwealth Commission that examined the incident, much attention was indeed drawn to the absolute age of the sites that were destroyed.[79] The text, however, also draws on a well-established trope of comparing the age of Aboriginal heritage sites with some of the most famous archaeological sites in Europe or elsewhere. While this rhetoric allows the wider public to easily assess the importance of Aboriginal heritage, it also situates the evidence firmly in the past. As such, this logic might ultimately exclude Aboriginal people from their heritage and the continuity of their ongoing practices.

Furthermore, Traditional Owners are not in control of these processes and narratives and the respective rules are written somewhere else. Archaeologists and the wider public create these rules and they rest on complex and often unacknowledged foundations and historical legacies. In this discourse, is it even possible to change the perception of Indigenous pasts? Can they gain recognition when the rules of the game are still inherently made to reflect the history of Europe? I have said elsewhere that I am suspicious of the equally world-building and world-destroying potentials of archaeology.[80] In a similar spirit, I want to draw attention to the fact that archaeology is equally able to support *and* undermine Aboriginal and Indigenous sovereignty and these negotiations often take place within a framework of unequal power relationships.

Archaeological research can play an important role as long as people realise that engaging with the dimension of time continues to be undertheorised and that we are, in fact, dealing with a multiplicity of temporalities when we engage with archaeological evidence and Aboriginal heritage. Archaeology can embrace these temporalities, which are, in fact, already implicit in many Indigenous archaeology projects that focus on local priorities and social justice.[81] This will require a change in perspective and a more thorough engagement with Indigenous forms of knowledge production and reproduction, which are place-based, local, relational and mediated by Indigenous stories.[82] Following the considerations put forward throughout this book, such a change will also necessitate questioning the temporal or historical logic of the current dominant discourse. Support for Aboriginal sovereignty based on *temporal sovereignty* could potentially transcend the chronogeopolitics of settler colonial policies and its popular narratives. Such a movement can only be achieved if time is not understood as an 'an abstract, homogeneous measure of universal movement along a singular axis'.[83] We need to think of the past as a multiplicity of temporalities and varied temporal formations with their own rhythms. These can be particular to single contexts or can intersect at different scales. In this way, temporalities can continue to reflect locally significant relationships and patterns of contingency without being erased by universally imposed processes and developments.

For archaeology, methodological and conceptual tools are already available that define the discipline in a less rigid way – one that does not exclusively operate within a framework that prioritises linear chronologies.[84] Archaeology has many approaches that allow recognising how the past continuously intersects with the present and how both are continuously created and recreated. We can draw on the fields of contemporary archaeology to interrogate how we approach Indigenous heritage and to recognise that it is not situated in the (deep) past but is contemporary and living heritage.[85] Archaeological techniques of recording and mapping material evidence can be guided by Traditional Owners to allow connections and reconnections with places and landscapes. This work can revive stories and memories as well as family and personal relationships and, hence, contribute to cultural continuation and survival. Such work would engage with and negotiate deep time evidence and contexts through locally significant understandings of place. In this way and if we allow this to happen, the boundary between scientific and Indigenous knowledge and engagements with the past and the world becomes permeable, and this movement can only strengthen the relational understanding of all human practice and the power of Country.

Aboriginal sovereignty, social justice and the future of archaeology

In this chapter I have sought to disentangle some aspects of the intertwined themes of deep human history, archaeological method and theory, and Aboriginal sovereignty. This is a complex topic, and I acknowledge that some of the views presented here are only developed in preliminary forms and require further analysis and interrogation. Since its conception in the 19th century, archaeology has emerged as a powerful agent in structuring the perception of humanity's deep past. Archaeological methods such as stratigraphic analysis have become sources of metaphors to describe how the past is contained in the present. Recently, the enhanced abilities of radiometric dating techniques have further inspired the public imagination. However, the effects of these technologies on creating meaningful narratives are rarely critically discussed and questioned. Nevertheless, archaeology has been historically embedded in wider conversations and negotiations about the shape and character of historical imagination. As such, these processes are linked to wider contemporary social and cultural structures and political power relationships. Within archaeology, these aspects tend to be underestimated and undertheorised. This situation is problematic as the unreflected use of archaeological results and knowledge can undermine Aboriginal rights and sovereignty. However, archaeological methods and interpretations can equally become powerful tools to support Aboriginal people's social justice aspirations.

Because of its continuing shift away from humanities approaches and towards the natural sciences, archaeology often presents its results only in the form of data and as seemingly objective. However, archaeologists need to be aware of the ways in which their practices produce and reproduce persistent (and often colonial) historical narratives. Archaeology needs to engage with the epistemological challenges of how meaningful stories can be inferred from material and other evidence. It also must be mindful of the influences and legacies that affect these processes and how archaeological narratives interact with the public imagination.[86] With its many multidisciplinary strengths and its positioning across the humanities *and* science, archaeology must be involved in contemporary discussions about the relationship between scientific, historical and Indigenous approaches towards the deep past of the continent, with an awareness of its own role in shaping ideas about time and temporality. Only then can archaeology support Aboriginal sovereignty and the aspirations of Aboriginal peoples in an informed and responsible fashion.

Acknowledgment

The author would like to acknowledge that parts of this research were conducted during an Australian Research Council Future Fellowship (FT230100340) and thank the School of Social Sciences, University of Western Australia (Professor Amanda Davies) for institutional support.

5

DIFFICULT TEMPORALITIES
Indigenous and Western archaeological
ways of knowing the past in Oceania

Chris Urwin and Lynette Russell

Our chapter is very deliberately called *difficult temporalities* because we are exploring strands of knowledge that seem impossible to bring together: living Indigenous pasts and the Western discipline of archaeology. A few of the authors in this collection have explored the differences between these strands of knowledges. Although this work is difficult, we argue that these temporalities can be interwoven and brought into conversation with one another to generate new and culturally meaningful histories. Our personal insights into this rewarding process come from our work building archaeological and historical research partnerships with Indigenous communities. We present two case studies from our research in Papua New Guinea and Australia to explore the potential tensions, challenges and opportunities of integrating Indigenous and Western temporalities in two quite different contexts.[1] Before we arrive at our case studies, it's worth reminding ourselves of the potential tensions among these temporalities – or ways of knowing time – and the ways in which these are worked out and understood in the world.

Deep time disciplines like archaeology, geology and palaeontology are preoccupied with relative time, identifying when and in what order sediments, artefacts or fossils were deposited in the past.[2] In theory, as an archaeologist excavates deeper through sedimentary layers, they encounter older and older things and sediments. In the Australian context, the term 'deep time' is increasingly being used to describe the full span of Indigenous history,[3] which according to Western archaeology dates to at least 65 000 years ago.[4] 'Deep time' was first used by geologist John McPhee in 1981 to evoke the earth's unfathomably distant origins.[5] This term is used, in part, because the archive which preserved aspects of Australia's 65 000-year-old First Nations history is a remarkably deep rock shelter deposit on Mirarr Country in northern Australia. Depth can convey richness – like a deep way of knowing – but in archaeology it often invokes distance and foreignness. If even the recent past is foreign, how much more so are the lives and activities that made grindstones and ochred artefacts now buried under more than 2 metres of sandy soil?[6]

Yet the binary of deep and shallow pasts is very much a Western construct. Indigenous communities in Oceania have their own temporalities and historicities (ways of understanding and performing history).[7] These ways of knowing help sustain the relationship between past, present and future. As archaeologist Denis Byrne explains, these pasts are 'always-already imminent in the present';[8] places and material culture are imbued with spiritual and Ancestral presences.[9] In other words, Ancestral places are still populated. How can time be deep, or the past be foreign, if the ancestors still speak, move and act?[10] This is not to say that Indigenous temporalities are without sequence – they may include successions of genealogies, migration places, landscape transformations and Ancestral epochs – but there is no gulf between ancient and recent. Things of the past are close and present kin.

One proposed solution to these temporal tensions has been to develop 'Deep Histories' in which Indigenous social histories, economies, ecologies, and past cross-cultural interactions (as known in oral traditions and archaeology) are brought into conversation with written archives and contemporary Indigenous history.[11] As historians Alison Bashford and Pratik Chakrabarti have recently pointed out, there is a long tradition of mostly white, male authors producing global Deep Histories to account for ancient migrations, Ice Age adaptations and the emergence of language and art.[12] These are ultimately Western cosmologies: ways to narrate and understand humanity's origins. The challenge in Oceania is to ensure Deep Histories are not hegemonic or homogenising but incorporate many Indigenous voices.

As historian Stephanie Mawson has pointed out, 'Telling a meaningful history [of Oceania] that stretches across many tens of thousands of years has presented considerable methodological challenges'.[13] Besides the difficult temporalities involved, for any one person to narrate such a continental history requires substantial skill as a social historian, as well as the capacity to engage cross-culturally and sensitively with First Nations oral traditions while reading the subtle traces of archaeological, genetic and palaeoecological records. Communities and researchers have been investigating these records together for decades at local and regional levels but making sense of such evidence across Oceania and conveying it to a non-academic audience is a major challenge. This is not least because the traditional Western mode of single-author history-writing simply cannot encapsulate the region's diverse Indigenous temporalities.[14]

To understand how cross-cultural Deep Histories of Oceania might be produced and to appreciate the diversity at play among Indigenous temporalities, we first need to understand how Indigenous communities are negotiating archaeological chronologies and the vital Indigenous past today. To this end, we explore two very different case studies: firstly, of a collaborative archaeological project undertaken on Papua New Guinea's south coast; and secondly, of Aboriginal responses to recent archaeological findings and chronologies. These case studies come from dramatically different cultural worlds with their own colonial histories.

In the first discussion, we hear voices from Orokolo Bay on Papua New Guinea's south coast, one of the economically poorest parts of the world yet one where most language groups are in possession of their own land. This study involved interactions between local Indigenous people and university- and museum-based archaeologists from Australia and other parts of Papua New Guinea, as they worked in partnership to understand the past based on archaeology (surveys and excavations) and local oral traditions. Here, conversations about place and history were held in English, local language (Orokolo) and Tok Pisin (Papua New Guinea's lingua franca) at contemporary villages and Ancestral villages where the excavations took place.

In the second example, a different kind of conversation takes place between Lynette Russell and her Aboriginal friends and colleagues in an

Australian context. While Papua New Guinea gained independence in 1975, Australia's First Nations have been fighting for their land rights (with some hard-won successes) since the start of European colonial invasion in 1788. Here, Aboriginal people responded to Russell's survey questions about archaeological dates published in journal articles and publicised through the media. Unlike the Papua New Guinean example, which is based in one place and language group, the temporalities and worldviews of these First Nations people from around Australia are diverse. Along with traditional knowledges, their insights often integrate the results from decades of archaeological research in Australia.

How do Indigenous people in these two very different contexts make sense of Western archaeological approaches, interpretations and dates? How does the social activity of conducting excavations and discussing the results together in place shape how Indigenous and Western chronologies interact? What do the case studies tell us about how to negotiate difficult temporalities cross-culturally? There is much to learn from these case studies about the tensions, challenges and opportunities for narrating the Indigenous past. Our examples blur the boundaries between Indigenous and Western temporalities, showing that these ways of knowing are – to some extent – already inseparably intertwined and mutually inform one another.[15]

Excavating the Ancestral past of Papua New Guinea's south coast

Our first case study shows how Indigenous and Western temporalities can overlap, inform one another and build meaningful multivocal histories. The case study comes from Orokolo Bay on Papua New Guinea's south coast, a place famous for its large villages and elaborate ceremonies.[16] In 2015, Chris Urwin conducted archaeological and oral tradition research in partnership with two village communities: Kaivakovu and Larihairu. He worked with members of the village youth associations to excavate sites in order to work out the history of their ancestors' villages. The collaborative excavations provided a theatre of memory which sparked

Australia and Papua New Guinea.
SOURCES Map tiles by Stamen Design, under CC BY 4.0.
Data by OpenStreetMap, under ODbL.

unexpected conversations about how the oral traditions interrelated with artefacts such as earthenware pottery and animal bone, and buried soil layers. Importantly, the collaborative research showed that the Community understood their history according to multilayered and overlapping temporalities, and that aspects of their cultural chronologies were worked out through their own habitual form of archaeology.[17]

The people of Orokolo Bay have experienced and understood their world according to many coexisting layers of temporality, of which we want to introduce three. Firstly, the world is understood as a product of Ancestral beings in the cosmological past. These beings are the Iou haera, 'story people', who made the coastline and mountains as they travelled.[18] They are still alive in the present and they can be called on to help people catch fish or keep safe on the sea while travelling by dinghy to see family. Secondly, there are genealogies and migration traditions which are about 'human beings', meaning they are ancestors of recent historical memory. These go back twenty-three generations and span eleven migration places. They are known in oral traditions which formerly were memorised and recounted as cycles of song. Increasingly, these oral traditions are being written down because the generation of people who could remember the songs is passing away. Thirdly, there are the ways people experience time day to day. For much of Orokolo Bay's history, time was marked by ceremony. Until the late 1940s, much of local social and ceremonial life was structured by the performance of a ceremony called *hevehe*, which mediated spirits of the forest and sea. In the 1920s–1930s the full ceremonial cycle took nineteen years to complete on average, and longhouse buildings full of ritual regalia were built at various stages of the ceremony.[19] The houses and the process of building them also anchored Ancestral memory, as the central posts (*ive*) of these buildings were inscribed with stories about the ancestors, depicted in raised relief. These three temporalities all converse and overlap, and the lives and actions of the Ancestral beings are woven through the genealogies.

The collaborative archaeological research provided a forum to engage with some of these temporalities. Excavations took place at Ancestral village sites located on old beach ridges 3 kilometres from today's coastline. The location for one of the excavations at a place called Marea Ita was decided by members of the Kaivakovu Village Youth Association. Their uncles had told them that the place was once part of a ceremonial longhouse, but they did not know its specific history. The excavations progressed for six days, eventually uncovering the shadowy traces of longhouse posts – as the young men expected – as well as pig bone and pottery sherds.[20] Each day, one young man called Lare Lako, who owned a garden plot at the site, would photograph the day's finds and then go and find his uncle, Houhii Iaupa, who was living in Kaivakovu village on the coast. Lare would tell his uncle stories about what the excavation team had uncovered. As a result, Houhii shared more and more of the oral traditions with his nephew, and eventually he invited the research team to his house to discuss this site's history which was once an '*eravo* [longhouse], split down the middle' shared between the ancestors of the Kaivakovu and Larihairu villages.[21] The archaeology provided a forum for oral traditions to be transmitted across generations and between cultures (among locals, museum professionals from Port Moresby and archaeologists from Australia).

The collaborative excavations also uncovered thin layers of black sand that remind people of their ancestors' cosmological actions. We tend to think of stratigraphy (sedimentary layers) as the domain of archaeology or geomorphology, and certainly there are ways of understanding these things using artefact analyses and radiocarbon dating, but there are also pre-existing Indigenous Knowledges of these layers, including their temporality. The black sand is known to have been laid by apical ancestors called Miae and Lairua as they travelled across the sky in a canoe. This story and the distinctive sand layers buried in specific places at Popo mutually enforce one another and help sustain knowledge of the past.[22] These sands are regularly unearthed by gardeners today in a habitual and entirely Indigenous form of archaeology. In 2015, Kaivakovu village Elder Paul Mahiro explained that when he could not recall a particular story, he would return to his garden to unearth sub-surface reminders of the ancestors. It is through this agricultural work that Orokolo Bay's people have been re-engaging with their Ancestral sites, artefacts and stratigraphy for generations. As they dig to plant crops, clear vegetation and burn fallow gardens, people uncover material traces of the past.

These material traces include pottery sherds, which are fragments of earthenware vessels acquired through exchange. They were brought to Orokolo Bay annually by the Motu people, who would sail from their homelands in the Port Moresby region, located more than 300 kilometres to the east. They remember this not as barter, but as a relationship with trading partners and close kin.[23] Like the layers of black sand, the pottery

Kaivakovu village families visit the excavation on 19 October 2015.
Photo: Chris Urwin

deposits help anchor local historicities or, as discussed above, ways of understanding and performing history. As gardeners uncover pottery sherds while working at their plots, they gain a sense of their sub-surface concentration and distribution. This knowledge acts to construct, maintain and sustain knowledge of the structure of their ancestors' villages in much the same way as archaeologists interpret the spatial distribution of artefact scatters.[24] Orokolo Bay locals also understand the relative age of their ancestors' villages in the context of beach ridge landforms. There are five main beach ridges between the sea and Miocene mountains approximately 5 kilometres inland. Each of these is an old coastline, and locals can name the ancestors and number of generations that inhabited these places.

In combination, the black sands, pottery and ancient beach ridges are surface and subsurface monuments central to local temporalities, interpreted through lived experiences of gardening and contemporary coastline formation. During collaborative work in 2015, we found that all these temporalities overlapped without contradiction. Pottery from five generations ago is found beneath black sand of the cosmological era. Radiocarbon dates from our research showed that these Ancestral sites are around 650 to 140 years old, and local people have readily absorbed this new scientific information into multilayered temporalities.[25] In fact, Chris Urwin's collaborators had already correctly estimated the age of the scientific chronologies based on their genealogies and observations with how quickly beach ridges had merged through time.[26] The research team was able to use each of these temporal knowledges to build chronologies which combined radiocarbon dates and the oral traditions of village generational sequences, thus ensuring that Orokolo Bay's ancestral places were narrated in culturally meaningful ways.[27] Excavation provided a forum to negotiate ways of knowing the past, and the oral traditions and archaeology mutually informed one another.

Making sense of Aboriginal Australia's Deep History

In our second case study, we examine how First Nations people negotiate their cultural temporalities and Western conceptions of deep time. To do this, we travel south to Australia. Lynette Russell has informally surveyed forty Aboriginal acquaintances and colleagues of diverse backgrounds, ages and genders over the past few decades regarding their perspectives on Deep History and the widespread, commonly repeated claim that 'Aboriginal Australia is the oldest continuously existing culture in the world'. Frequently, these discussions were initiated in reaction to the publication of new dates that advance the antiquity of occupation. In 2017, a new study was published in the influential journal *Nature* showing that Aboriginal people had been present at Madjedbebe in northern Australia at least 65 000 years ago.[28] Russell, along with Billy Griffiths, conducted an analysis of comments left on their co-authored article 'When did Australia's human history begin?' published in the *Conversation* in 2017. This essay garnered a substantial readership of approximately 50 000 and elicited approximately 1000 comments.[29]

In terms of First Nations people's responses, the most common was that archaeologists were merely catching up with what Aboriginal people had always known: that they had always been 'here' (Australia). Griffith and Russell interpreted this as a cultural affirmation statement. Compromising between Indigenous temporalities and Western conceptions of deep time, however, can lead to misunderstandings. For the past thirty years, Russell has argued that expressions such as 'the oldest living culture' imply that Aboriginal culture was static and primitive.[30] This is still a potent personal declaration that affirms one's kinship with ancestors and specific First Nation, and such longevity has implications for assertions of sovereignty. It can also take on a life of its own when endorsed by the media, echoing the language of 19th-century social evolutionists who held the view that Aboriginal people were primitive and unchanging. Numerous Indigenous commentators on the *Conversation* article argued against the concept of attributing a timeframe to the arrival of their ancestors in Australia; rather, they contended that they had always been here. Such an ontology is accepted; it provides perspective, and provides a method of engaging with the past that is not subject to debate around determining exact dates or chronologies. A small number of respondents to Russell's survey put forth an alternative perspective, namely that 65 000 years represents what is in essence 'forever'. Conversely, some individuals perceived the dates as inconsequential compared to the extensive history of Indigenous engagements with Country. As one Aboriginal commentator noted:

> Will we eventually see a figure of 100 000 years? Perhaps ... And that is a good thing, for whatever the precise findings of science, the fact remains that Indigenous people of Australia are Aborigines i.e. native to this land, and their life and culture is a deeply embedded part of the land, having evolved over an incredibly long period of time.

There is a tension here between ontologies and their value systems. Increasingly, dates emerging from archaeological sites are privileged in the media as sources of historical evidence. The press, alongside prominent journals such as *Nature* and *Science*, has cemented the idea that older is better regarding dates. Linked to this is the need for greater understanding of Indigenous ways of knowing globally, which sits alongside the dismissal of the historicity of oral traditions and oral history. Is there any satisfactory way of rectifying these seemingly incommensurable temporalities – or at least, differing measures of significance of such dating techniques?

Certainly, First Nations oral traditions and temporalities and Western science need not be forced into agreeing or placed into the same narratives. Yet Kombumerri and Wakka Wakka philosopher Mary Graham has recently suggested a way forward: to think of Australia as the place where Indigenous people 'became human'.[31] There are echoes here of Professor Eric Wilmot's definition of Aboriginality, which he built on Neville Bonner's idea that an Indigenous nation comprises people who do not have another narrative; rather, they are from the place where they live.[32] In other words, they are a people who originate from Ancestral places.

Regardless of how we make sense of these temporalities, both case studies tell us that Indigenous pasts are already multivocal. Since colonisation, and well before this, Indigenous people in Oceania had been assessing, rejecting, incorporating and negotiating new ways of knowing, some brought by European colonisers, and others by traders from foreign shores or other Indigenous groups. Western commentators, by contrast, seem to privilege what they believe to be 'science' and ignore oral traditions until these are scientifically validated.

In other words, Deep History has a great deal to learn from these holistic ways by which Indigenous peoples incorporate and make sense of alternative temporalities and, often, how these temporalities are allowed to sit side by side: 65 000 years and forever. Native American archaeologist Sonya Atalay has made a similar point about Objibwe epistemologies and philosophies at the time they encountered new worldviews imported by colonists.[33] Their knowledge systems were already multivocal, having tested and incorporated ways of knowing before encountering European people or ideas.

The Orokolo Bay example neatly illustrates how temporalities can work side by side without the contradictions that Cartesian, Western thinkers might assume are present. Excavations created a forum to negotiate cross-cultural ways of knowing the past, with the local oral traditions and archaeological research mutually informing one another. In fact, the multivocal Indigenous temporalities of Orokolo Bay carry more detailed and diverse historical information and are probably more temporally precise. Whereas radiocarbon dates have error ranges spanning up to hundreds of years, the people of Orokolo Bay know each beach ridge and can estimate how long it took to form. They can call the names of ancestors who lived in those places in the 1920s, 1850s and 1700s. How can one properly understand the formation of a landscape without cosmology, lived experience and oral tradition? Without calling the names of the ancestors who still inhabit it?

Both case studies also blur the distinctions that we might have assumed at the start, for it is the Western academy that delineates archaeological and oral traditional knowledge production. The materiality of Ancestral landscapes informs Indigenous historicity, along with archaeological chronologies already factored into Aboriginal thinking about their history in Australia. Building on these two rather different kinds of studies, we feel that the literature that has been emerging in Indigenous archaeology since the 1990s offers a way forward for collaborative and Deep Histories. These emphasise the need for multivocal approaches to the past which interweave – or facilitate conversation between – archaeological information and temporal knowledge held by Elders and Community members.[34] Multivocal approaches to the Ancestral past can produce richer histories for Indigenous and Western readerships and audiences alike.[35] But there's no shortcut to producing these histories. Each history of place, each carbon date, oral tradition and artefact must be negotiated in local contexts by doing the slow, difficult but highly rewarding work of discussing the meaning of the past so we can build cultural knowledge for the future.

Acknowledgments

Chris Urwin thanks the Kaivakovu and Larihairu village communities – especially the village Elders group and youth associations – for contributing so much to our research partnership from 2015 onwards. He pays his respects to the late Henry Arifeae of the PNG National Museum and Art Gallery for his ever-present support and friendship during field work. Lynette Russell thanks the respondents to her surveys.

6

SONGS, STORIES AND DEEP HISTORIES FROM MUTTHI MUTTHI, NGIYAMPAA, BARKINDJI AND TATI TATI WATER COUNTRY

Grace Fletcher

On a cool autumn day in north-west Victoria, Mutthi Mutthi, Tati Tati, Yitha Yitha, Wadi Wadi, and Latji Latji man Brendan Kennedy Millu Widungi (Murray River man) and I walked together on his Country along Tol Tol or Margooya Lagoon.[1] Tol Tol is a deeply historic site of immense cultural and ecological significance for Traditional Owners within the Murray-Darling Basin, Australia's largest river system.[2] Brendan led me through dried creek beds, passing big red gum Grandmother trees and their daughters, pointing out Scar Trees as we walk – some newly scarred, while the thick bark growing around older scar markings signalled an ancient and enduring practice.

Brendan took me to a spot that he calls 'Pelican Point'. Hundreds of pathangal (pelicans), disturbed by our presence, took flight, their wingspans covering the blue sky overhead. Pathangal are Tati Tati's totem and their presence here shows that this is a special place. Trev, Brendan's cousin, introduced me to 'old man weed', which is 'bush medicine'. Ancestral sites are strewn throughout the landscape we walked upon, including middens, ceremonial places, earth ovens, birthing trees and ring trees.[3] These layers of history – both human and ecological – illustrate that this place is rich not only in wildlife, plants and striking landscapes but also histories that intimately and fundamentally involve humans, their environment and water.

One hundred and thirty kilometres north of Margooya Lagoon lies the expansive Pleistocene lake system within Mungo National Park known as the Willandra Lakes Region. The Willandra Lakes are in the south-western pocket of New South Wales, close to where the South Australian, Victorian and New South Wales borders meet. The lakes are in a semi-arid region of vast desert landscapes. Between 50 000 to 19 000 years ago, the lakes were full of relatively fresh water.[4] The Willandra landscape has been shaped by water; this is evident in the undulating lunettes and sand ripples. Yet these lakebeds have held no water for a long time – despite seasonal rains – after having completely dried out some 18 000 years ago.[5] The region seized Western scientific interest when in 1969 and 1974, the wind revealed the Ancestral remains of Mungo Lady and Mungo Man to a young geologist, Jim Bowler. Mungo Lady and Mungo Man lived in the region approximately 45 000 years ago during the last ice age and were buried by Lake Mungo. The Mutthi Mutthi, Ngiyampaa and Barkindji people are the custodians of this historic site, and continue to maintain deeply historical relationships to their Country and ancestors.

Their history is one of confronting dramatic changes in climate due to both the ice age and, more recently, from human-induced climatic changes. Yet the Traditional Owners of the Willandra Lakes continue to care for and live by waterscapes as their ancestors did tens of thousands of years ago. The Mutthi Mutthi people belong to the Murray, Murrimbidgee, Lachlan and Warkool rivers, and the Box, Paiker and Willandra creeks. Barkindji means people of the barka (river), stretching across the Darling River and north towards Willandra Creek.[6] Ngiyampaa are dryland people, whose Country covers the plains and rocky hills of the Darling and Lachlan rivers.[7] Collectively, the Mutthi Mutthi, Ngiyampaa and Barkindji are the Three Traditional Tribal Groups of the Willandra Lakes Region. Barka contains a Deep History and connects Traditional Owners to not only their present Country but the past shapes Country has taken and to the ancestors who have walked upon it for millennia.

My research explores the stories behind both the Deep Historical and enduring sovereignty of water Country for Murray-Darling First Nations people. By periodising this piece in place rather than in time, I engage with the unique temporalities, historical knowledges and practices of First Nations people within the Murray and Murrumbidgee Rivers and Mungo National Park. Indigenous historical practices play an important role in asserting sovereign rights in now-colonised spaces, and I aim to describe the ways in which water connects Mungo's Traditional Owners to Country, Country's history and the history of their Ancestors. Water is the enduring link between the deep past and the present, exemplified through the stories of a set of trackways.[8] The trackways were left behind by ancestors some 20000 years ago and are a rich archive of Mutthi Mutthi, Ngiyampaa and Barkindji Deep Histories.

Mutthi Mutthi women and sisters, Aunty Bernadette Pappin and Aunty Mary Pappin Junior, express the historic and enduring relationship of Traditional Owners to waterscapes and ancestors by sharing their knowledge of the trackways their ancestors created. The Pappin sisters, alongside other Traditional Owners, collaborated with Pintubi trackers and archaeologists in a cross-cultural knowledge exchange to acquire the stories in the footprints their ancestors left. This incredible history provides a tangible connection to a landscape that existed in a different epoch, a time when Australia's landmass was connected to New Guinea and Tasmania, when megafauna walked across the Australian continent, and sea levels were extremely low because of the uptake of water held in glaciers during the Earth's last ice age approximately 20000 years ago.[9]

Brendan Kennedy's deep connection to Country is partly expressed through speaking the Language of his ancestors and living on and caring for Country. He has a deep knowledge of the waterways that have historically and continue to run through his Country, and the songs and stories that his ancestors sang long ago. Deep Historical knowledges held by Traditional Owners of water Country are critical to revitalising threatened ecologies and knowing the Deep History of the Australian continent. Coupled with this is the profound realisation that all of Australia's landscapes and waterscapes have been storied, cared for and walked upon by Aboriginal and Torres Strait Islander people since the Creation.

Deep History and recognition of Traditional Owners' unbroken relationships to Country holds transformative power to see the ways in which every corner of the Australian continent is imbued with Aboriginal and Torres Strait Islander histories. In doing so, Deep History aspires to expand the discipline of history's temporal scales and the narrow chronologies that currently dominate Australian historiography, and to embrace diverse Aboriginal and Torres Strait Islander encultured ways of knowing the past.[10] Colonial visions saw Australian landscapes as sparse, barely populated and untouched, and in doing so, declared Australia as devoid of human history prior to European arrivals.

The term 'deep time' was born out of geology but has been adopted by historians to address the fullness of Australia's human histories that extend well beyond 1788.[11] This realisation dismantles settler visions of Australian landscapes – as *terra nullius*[12] or a wilderness[13] – revealing the many ways in which every corner of Australia's land, sea, skies and waterways are (hi)storied and imbued with the knowledge of Traditional Owners. Echoing Ann McGrath's call to not allow any 'move to the macro scale' to result in a departure from 'the moment, the minute, and *the minute*',[14] this chapter locates moments from the deep past which humanise and make intimate Deep Histories by centring the Knowledges and cross-cultural knowledge exchanges of First Nations people.[15]

Enduring sovereignties over waterscapes

Aboriginal and Torres Strait Islander sovereignty endures over now-colonised spaces. It should be noted that sovereignty is not a word used in Mutthi Mutthi or Tati Tati and it is impossible to capture in English the deep relationship and custodial obligations Traditional Owners have to Country. Brendan explained 'sovereignty is a construct we are using' but that it is a 'coloniser's weapon'.[16] The Deep Histories of Country and the enduring relationships of Traditional Owners to water Country illustrates that wetlands are not merely natural but are socioecological landscapes.[17] Through highlighting the diverse interactions people can have with these places, Aboriginal histories undermine the simple narrative of waterscapes as degraded by human activity. As environmental historian Emily O'Gorman notes, 'new ways of understanding, managing, and relating to wetlands in the Murray-Darling Basin – and elsewhere – are urgently needed'.[18] Deep Historical renderings of the Murray-Darling's waterscapes reveal the longevity of Traditional Owners' enduring custodianship and their essential Knowledges in understanding both the history of place and how to care for it.

The day before my arrival on Tati Tati Country, a public hearing session for Victoria's Yoorrook Justice Commission took place at Margooya Lagoon, 130 kilometres south of the Mungo footprints. The sessions on 24 April 2024 detailed Tati Tati experiences of historical and ongoing water dispossession. Brendan informed Victoria's Minister for Water that the current water dispossession faced by First Nations peoples is a new wave of colonisation. Colonial legal orders across the globe have confiscated and dispossessed Indigenous peoples of their territories and ignored their rights to decision-making powers. The resilience and activism of Australia's First Nations peoples to customary lands have led to authorities in settler colonial states establishing land claim and settlement processes to return lands to Indigenous peoples.[19] Although if those rights are achieved, they are often restricted to the legal constraints of Australian state and territory laws governing land and water management systems.[20] Virginia Marshall equates the Australian states' disregard for Indigenous peoples' rights to water to the same legal fiction that dispossessed First Nations peoples of their land, highlighting a continuity of neglect.[21] Marshall labels the historical disregard and ongoing denial of Indigenous water rights by colonial and legal frameworks as 'aqua nullius'.[22]

In this piece I aim to underscore the struggle for recognition of Indigenous sovereignty and emphasise the importance of recognising Indigenous knowledge and governance systems in the Murray-Darling and Mungo. Deep Historical renderings of Country reveal the long history of Mutthi Mutthi, Barkindji, Ngiyampaa and Tati Tati interactions and custodianship of waterscapes, stretching into different epochs and Pleistocene landscapes. Despite a growing consciousness of Aboriginal and Torres Strait Islander Deep Histories of managing diverse Australian lands and waterscapes, Western water management practices continue to override rights for water. Cultural geographer Sue Jackson highlighted a stark disparity in that while Aboriginal people along the Murray-Darling constitute nearly 10 per cent of the population, Aboriginal organisations hold only 0.2 per cent of available surface water.[23] Tati Tati people have no formal water holdings under Australian law, yet Tati Tati sovereignty and relationship to waterscapes persist.

Socioecological waterscapes – Mungo Lady and Mungo Man

Australian historiography overwhelmingly deals with the past 240 years, leaving the majority of Australia's estimated 65 000 years of history to the fields of 'pre-history'. However, acknowledging the deep past as an integral aspect of the Australian continent's history reveals fascinating stories of interconnected natural and human pasts. The Willandra Lakes Region now lies dry but is a landscape shaped by water. Between 18 000 to 50 000 years ago, the region was an expansive lake system of thirteen lakes, with a shoreline stretching across 200 kilometres.[24] This area was teeming with fish and bird life and home to an enduring civilisation.[25] Contained in the lunettes of the ancient lake system is an astonishing record of the world's changing climate, of a fluctuating lake system, cooling glaciers and First Peoples' interaction with these events.[26]

The high rate of erosion at Mungo makes the wind as much of an archaeologist as the many who have visited the Pleistocene lakes. In 1968, geologist Jim Bowler, while studying the ice-age lake system by mapping the stratigraphic layers of the Willandra Lakes, noticed signs of human activity from the Pleistocene epoch in the form of burnt shells resting beyond the natural shoreline, appearing to have been carried there. Later that year, the wind revealed burnt and smashed bones which had lain undisturbed since the last ice age. Bowler initially hypothesised that these might be the remains of an extinct mega marsupial hunted by people living along the lakes during the Pleistocene. In 1969, a team of archaeologists removed the bones, taking them approximately 800 kilometres east of their resting site to the Australian National University (ANU), where paleoanthropologist Alan Thorne reconstructed the cranium of a 'young adult woman of gracile build and small stature', who had died around the age of eighteen.[27] Named by her descendants as Mungo Lady, she was initially thought to have died 25 000 to 32 000 years ago;[28] this was later revised to 40 000 years.[29] Her burnt remains had been ceremoniously buried in a small round hole near the water's edge, reflecting her community's reverence for the dead. She had remained there for 40 000 years as the lakes dried and her descendants moved to other parts of their Country and as the pastoralists arrived.[30] Mungo Lady's remains proved to non-Indigenous Australia the depth of Aboriginal pasts on the Australian continent.

A year after the 1967 referendum many Australians still underestimated First Nations peoples' deep and enduring connection to their lands and waters. Mungo Lady completely shattered this notion by exemplifying the depth of Aboriginal pasts. Mutthi Mutthi Elder Aunty Mary Pappin Senior wrote, 'I believe that Mungo Lady came to walk with our people to help us with our struggle and to tell the rest of the world about our cultural identity with that land'.[31] To her descendants, Mungo Lady proved to the rest of the world what they already knew: that they and their ancestors have been here since 'the beginning' and their cultures had adapted and proven resilient in the face of extreme climatic changes and socio-political upheaval.[32]

In 1974, when Bowler returned to the lakes, he was met with heavy rains, further exposing the Joulni lunette from which Mungo Lady had been taken without permission six years prior. Bowler noticed part of a human skull and brushed away at it, revealing an intact human jawbone. Two days later, a team from the ANU arrived and excavated the almost complete remains of a man who had died around the age of fifty. The team decided to remove the remains and transport him to Canberra, a distant and foreign place, hundreds of kilometres away from his Country and burial site. For Traditional Owners, this act of removal was inexplicable. Historian Ann McGrath noted the distance both in kilometres and from Mungo Man's descendants' ways of thinking and being.[33] Mungo Man's burial reflected a complex set of cultural practices and belief systems. He had been sprinkled with ochre, with his arms crossed reverently in his lap before he was cremated.[34] Ochre is not a resource available within the region – those who buried Mungo Man would have transported it from at least 100 kilometres away.³⁵ The ceremony reflected deeply spiritual rituals. Mungo Man was missing two of his lower canine teeth, believed to have been removed in an initiation ritual. Over the years his lower molar teeth became worn and scratched, possibly from stripping the long leaves of water reeds with his teeth to make twine. In his old age, Mungo Man developed osteoarthritis, especially in his right elbow. Archaeologist Steve Webb wrote that it is easy to picture him sitting on a cold ice age night, slowly rubbing his elbow in front of his fire in an effort to relieve his discomfort.³⁶

News of Mungo Man and Mungo Lady entered the public sphere, dramatically reframing national consciousness of Australia's past and sparking further scientific interest. Consequentially, a further 104 ancestors were removed from the Willandra Lakes. Despite the growing awareness of Australia's deep past, research in the region was almost exclusively handled by archaeologists, discursively removing this past from Australian history proper and perpetuating the idea of an Indigenous 'pre-history', thus bifurcating history after European arrival from the long Indigenous histories lived out on the same land.³⁷

In 1973, upon learning of the archaeological activities and scientific research out at Mungo, Mutthi Mutthi Elder Aunty Alice Kelly wrote to the New South Wales Parks and Wildlife Services expressing her hurt at the removal of her ancestors. Aunty Alice understood the removal as a violent act of theft: 'The archaeologists are digging up our past … you're taking our past from us'.³⁸ For the traditional custodians, Mungo Man and Mungo Lady, are Ancestors and relatives; 'Please withdraw any further excavation of skeletons from the Walls of China, New South Wales', Aunty Alice wrote; 'they are our tribal people'.³⁹ In 1988 tensions reached boiling point when the Western Regional Land Council placed an embargo on an archaeological excavation at Lake Mungo. The courage and sustained activism of Aunty Alice Kelly, various local Elders and other First Nations peoples helped researchers and government authorities to appreciate the weight of these issues relating to Ancestors, history, kinship and ownership. Mungo is a deeply historic site that transforms colonising visions of landscape as 'sparse' and 'barely populated' into deeply storied and cultured sentient places.[40] Whether it is the footprints of a hunting party in pursuit of game left behind some 20 000 years ago or the songs sung from one generation to the next, the Willandra Lakes Region's Traditional Owners bring to life the stories of Australia's deep past. The Willandra Lakes holds stories of changing landscapes and shifting seasons, and has the power to transform understandings of Australia's past. However, despite the volumes of research and the pilgrimages of archaeologists to one of Australia's oldest sites, Traditional Owners and their Knowledges were long excluded from the research that takes place out at Mungo, their rights ignored. Ancestral remains have been stolen and taken to universities alongside countless cultural artefacts. Through their testimony, teaching and sharing knowledge with outsiders, Traditional Owners such as Brendan Kennedy, Aunty Bernadette and Aunty Mary Pappin Junior have brought the deep past to life and into our present. Their Knowledges and heritage are essential Australian stories.[41]

The Trackways

In August 2003, Traditional Owners and a group of archaeologists walked along the dried Pleistocene lakes of Mungo National Park. Walking several metres in front of Steve Webb was Mutthi Mutthi woman Aunty Mary Pappin Junior, who stopped, turned to Webb and asked, 'Are these footprints?'[42] Aunty Mary – whom Webb refers to as 'hawk eye' – brought the largest series of Pleistocene trackways in the world to the attention of the group and to the astonishment of archaeologists across the globe.[43]

Twenty thousand years before Aunty Mary Junior walked with Steve Webb at Mungo, a family group crossed the drying claypan, leaving behind their footprints. The footprints belong to women, men, adolescents and young children. A woman carried a child, shifting their weight from one hip to the other. Another child wandered off, running up a dune and drawing small crescent shapes into the clay – an image associated with Dreaming – then the child turned and walked back, rejoining the group.[44] A set of prints depicting only the left foot baffled

Webb and his team, who theorised that the Ancestor was playing a hopping game – though this would not explain his impressive 1-metre strides – or that he had one foot in a boat as he propelled himself along a shallow pool of water.

Some days later a hunting party left behind their tracks. A hunter, standing at a height of 6'4", sprinted in pursuit of game, his heels slipping in the mud, accelerating to impressive speeds of 37 kilometres per hour.[45] He spread his toes as mud squished between them, helping him to gain purchase on the slippery lakebed. East of him, four men ran together, the tallest of the men slowing his pace to run side by side with his companions. Kangaroo paws, emu tracks and spear marks missing their target are inscribed upon the landscape. Further down the trackways is evidence that the hunting party speared a kangaroo.

The site holds more than 700 footprints, which are approximately 20 000 years old and of immense cultural, spiritual and scientific significance. Indigenous Ancestors made the footprints as the lakes began to dry. Aunty Mary Junior said that walking alongside the footprints was like 'walking with a family group today, they're the same people'.[46] As the ice age took hold, the world became cooler and glaciers expanded their territory, holding larger volumes of water; sea levels dropped and the air cooled, causing less rain to fall within the Willandra Lakes, creating the perfect conditions for a drying lakebed to preserve footprints for the next 20 000 years.[47] The imprint of an Ancestor's footprints and the mud squelching between their toes have been preserved by Country. The footprints provide an evocative connection to the people who made these footprints and a remarkable glimpse into a moment in time when, during the height of the last ice age, a family group, and some days later a hunting party, walked across the claybed. Their descendants continue to walk in their literal footsteps, caring for Country.

Mutthi Mutthi woman Aunty Mary Pappin Senior said that 'to leave those footprints … was unique. The Aboriginal people were very clever, in making sure that they left a sign for future generations, and we are the generations that's here today'.[48] The three traditional groups of the Willandra Lakes maintain their 'unbroken connection to these footprints as they continue to walk on Country in the footsteps of their ancestors'.⁴⁹ The footprints serve as a powerful invocation of the enduring sovereignty of Traditional Owners. A conference presentation prepared by Chris Little, Dale Patterson, Leanne Mitchell, Daryl Pappin and Dan Rosendhal analysed both the wealth of knowledge facilitated by and the fortuity of having 'the descendants of the very people who made the footprints still living in the region today'.⁵⁰ They continue to maintain and keep culture alive.

The series of trackways held in Country provide a unique glimpse into the deep past, whose stories come alive through a coalition of knowledges. The 20 000-year-old tracks are heading north. Possibly the party was in pursuit of the less dry lakes that still held shellfish, golden perch or other food sources known to have been consumed by Ancestors living in the Pleistocene epoch.⁵¹ A 2005 excavation on the site revealed a further 450 trackways, which were then given temporary protection from the relentless wind by being filled with local sand and protected with hessian sacks.⁵² Ground-penetrating radar technologies revealed a further 2200 square metres of buried footprints. The size and grandeur of the trackways made it apparent to Traditional Owners and the archaeological team that input from other knowledges was necessary to providing further details of the trackway's stories.

Traditional Owners and Webb appreciated that the knowledge of the trackways held by the three traditional groups and by Western scientists would be enriched with the input of Indigenous tracking expertise. Webb felt that his team couldn't interpret the tracks in their fullness, recalling that 'we could take various measurements, but it was as though they were enigmatically hiding information that would make them really come alive'.⁵³ After some enquiries, in 2004 Webb was put in contact with Pintubi woman Cindy Nakamarra, whose mother Mitjili Napanangka, a renowned artist and Pintubi woman, grew up moving through the eastern Gibson and western Tanami Deserts developing essential tracking skills. When she was a young girl, Napanangka's Aunties would share stories from Tjukurrpa⁵⁴ associated with Mina Mina, a sacred site.⁵⁵ Much of Napanangka's artwork incorporated her knowledge of Tjukurrpa and her Country, returning to two essential themes in her work, of her childhood and depictions of landscape soaked with stories from the Creation.⁵⁶

Napanangka's knowledge of tracking, Country and Tjukurrpa were deeply interrelated. Her reputation as a skilled tracker led the Three Traditional Tribal Groups from the Willandra Lakes to invite her to travel to their Country to help learn more from the footprints.

Mitjili Napanangka travelled with two other Pintubi Elders, Paddy Japanangka and Johnny Jupurulla. The Pintubi visitors immediately observed that Mutthi Mutthi, Ngiyampaa and Barkindji were desert people like themselves. Webb recounts that, despite language barriers, the Mungo Traditional Custodians felt a real warmth and gratitude to have the visit to their Country, and that the Pintubi visitors maintained a keen awareness that they were in someone else's Country and brought a digging stick as a gift.[57] Paddy was the first of the trackers to walk onto the site; he hushed his voice and whispered, 'Tjukurrpa', affirming that it was a Creation site. Traditional Owners feel the presence of their Ancestors in the landscape and Paddy agreed that 'the spirits were still there'.[58]

Reading the trackways, Mitjili, Paddy and Johnny shared its story. There are two separate sets of trackways. One is made by a family who crosses the drying clay pan; Mitjili shared the details of a mother shifting the weight of her baby from one hip to the other. The second set of trackways, made only days after the family walked along the lakes, belong to a hunting party. The Pintubi trackers assured the others that the trackway of only a left foot was indeed a one-legged man, pointing to the small round imprint made by a support pole. Mitjili, Johnny and Paddy, upon their return, gave Webb a pole, made out of Mulga, similar to what the one-legged man would have used some 20 000 years ago to walk across a drying landscape. Webb cited the knowledge gained from the Pintubi visit as more than 'we ever could have obtained in any textbook and even a lifetime in archaeology'.[59]

The insights provided by the Pintubi visitors into the footprints connect Traditional Owners to water Country and Ancestors who – similar to today – lived in a changing climate. Today, Aunty Mary Junior and Aunty Bernadette take their grandchildren out on Country to collect ochre and bush tucker, 'teaching kids the old ways'.[60] Aunty Bernadette and Aunty Mary Junior shared with me Mutthi Mutthi

Creation stories of the bunyip, hairybecca, willyag tail and the crow and the canoe dance which Aunty Alice Kelly gave permission to be performed on the international stage. They described to me the deep peace and knowledge of being on your own Country.[61] But there are barriers to practising culture and fulfilling their custodial obligations to Country, which extends to the creeks and rivers along the Murray–Darling Basin. The trackways demonstrate Mutthi Mutthi people's deeply historical relationship and obligation to water Country. Though the Willandra Lakes have long been dry, Mutthi Mutthi Country still covers deeply cultured waterscapes. South of the footprints, along the Murray–Murrumbidgee Rivers, Mutthi Mutthi woman Tanya Charles shares that few animals come to the riverbanks due to the ecological degradation of the Murray-Darling.[62] Endemic species such as mussels, crayfish, golden perch and Murray cod can no longer be collected for food due to the degradation of their habitats. Instead, the invasive introduced species, carp, dominate the waterways. Increasingly polluted waterways threaten the practice of cultural ceremonies that involve being in the water. Yet Mutthi Mutthi cultural practices and custodial obligations to and involving water Country are both deeply historic and enduring. The footprints made 20 000 years ago are a reminder of how deep that connection is, illustrating an enduring and profound connection between land, water and people.

Wangilatha Wangu nga Kiyawatha (singing songs and telling stories)

When Brendan Kennedy and his family walk across Country, they describe it as a living being. The Milloo or the Murray-Darling sustains everything; 'they carry the water, the blood, to the wetlands and lagoons and floodplains that are like the organs'.[63] First Nations peoples have been caring for the surrounding waterways for thousands of generations.[64] Mutthi Mutthi and Tati Tati 'are river people ... [and] are water people',[65] who hold profound ecological knowledge of Country today and the past shapes it has taken. I only experienced a hint of the depth of this knowledge the day I walked on Country with Brendan and his family. Yet it was clear that he knew every creek, scar tree, plant and bird, as well as the fauna that should be frequenting the lagoons but haven't since water regulators have blocked flows. Caring for water Country is a custodial obligation that has been passed down between thousands of generations and Ancestors. 'We've been here for 2000 generations', Brendan told me, 'since the Creation'. Brendan shares Creation stories of the 'Pandyil, the Murray Cod creat[ing] our river, back in Talikara, back in the Creation Times and that's what we live by, Tati Tati people'.[66] Ancestral beings are in the landscape and are a part of the living body that makes up Country.

The footprints in Mungo reveal the layers of history and generations of Mutthi Mutthi Ancestors that have walked upon and cared for this landscape. Brendan testified in the Yoorook Justice Commission that Ancestral beings are all in the landscape; that the rivers are arteries, the creeks are the veins and the wetlands are the organs.[67] It is not merely a question of water rights for First Nations but rights for water itself. The deep past displays the grandeur of ancient landscapes, the Aboriginal past within it and Traditional Owners' enduring relationships to their Country. The deep past is a reminder that every corner of Aboriginal and Torres Strait Islander lands, waterways and skies is storied and has been cared for by Traditional Owners.

Beyond linearity to a history of Everywhen

Goolarabooloo man Paddy Roe asked, 'Why do so many Australians know so little about the deep history of this continent that they call home?'[68] Australian historiography has overwhelmingly dealt with the past 240 years despite the grandeur and depth of Aboriginal and Torres Strait Islander histories and their enduring relationships with Country. Deep Histories reveal an entangled human and natural past which has faced the challenges of changes in climate and transforming ecosystems, and those wrought by waves of colonisation. The deep past and knowledge held by First Nations people of their Country is starkly contrasted by the relatively short history of the Australian state and the extent of the damage wrought by its affiliated systems of water management. Histories of place can be considered as generative sites within a broader national framework, allowing for periodisation to move beyond linearity and into a history of Everywhen. These histories challenge how we think about history and our world, and call for a revision of our national consciousness. Deep History works to expand the temporal scales of Australia's past and centralise the input and Knowledges of First Nations people. In doing so, it holds transformative and unifying potential to see the ways in which every facet of the Australian continent has been storied, sung and walked upon, and has always been cared for by First Peoples and always will be.

Deep Historical and enduring relationships and knowledge of waterscapes offer alternative forms of governance and care for Country to the settler state's in a way that proposes to co-exist with it. The *Uluru Statement from the Heart* invites all Australians to walk together to build a better future, aspiring for an Australia where Aboriginal and Torres Strait Islander children will flourish and their 'culture will be a gift to their country'.[69] This generous invitation comes with the responsibility for all Australians to play their part in preserving and maintaining Aboriginal histories, heritage and threatened ecologies. It comes with the recognition that Deep Histories and modes of Indigenous historical practice are assertions of First Nations sovereignty.

As Australia grapples with some of our most precious ecosystems being under extreme stress and threat of failing, Aboriginal and Torres Strait Islander people offer a salient lesson: 'If you care for Country, it will care for you'. First Nations peoples' Ancestors have maintained deep connections to the Murray-Darling over millennia, a relationship that continues to this day.[70] This relationship constitutes Indigenous claims to water Country or sovereignty. Brendan asserted to the Yoorrook Commission that 'We [Tati Tati] have never authorised and we have never relinquished or bequeathed any of our Country, our water, our culture and our rights and we never will'.[71] Sovereignty has never been ceded by the Tati Tati people, or any Murray River Traditional Owners, and recognition of First Nations land rights must extend to include those deeply cultured and storied waterscapes.[72] Water rights for Murray-Darling First Nations people will ensure not only the revitalisation and health of the Country, but they will also safeguard the cultural and custodial practices that have endured dramatic climatic changes and waves of dispossession.

Acknowledgment

I would like to thank Brendan Kennedy Millu Wudungi, Aunty Bernadette Pappin and Aunty Mary Pappin Junior for their generosity in sharing so much with me. I'd like to extend this deep gratitude to all Mutthi Mutthi, Ngiyampaa, Barkindji and Tati Tati people. Words cannot express how privileged I am to have learnt so much from your people and Country – thank you.

PART III

The sovereignty of sustaining landscapes and foodscapes

7
KAI MĀORI SPACES AND TEMPORALITIES IN TĀMAKI MAKAURAU

Bhaveeka Madagammana

Kai Māori (Māori food) is a fundamental aspect of Māori society. It nutritionally sustains communities and signifies wealth, cultural and social relations and mana (power, balance). Despite growing environmental literature on Aotearoa food, no spatial research has examined the Tāmaki Makaurau (Auckland) historical food practices nor their impact on Tāmaki's landscape. After 1840, Māori food practices in exchange with early colonial settlers dominated the country's markets and supply routes. They were essential to settlers' survival and a significant part of daily cultural and commercial life. Significantly, these food patterns based on seasonal and permanent settlements were developed from food spaces and intergenerational knowledge communally held for centuries before the 1840s.

During the early 19th century, Māori primarily lived in seasonal patterns on the Tāmaki Makaurau (Auckland) isthmus, reciprocally moving between many coastal and inland sites, meaning they could produce various kai (food) across the seasons. These patterns, shaped by numerous factors, were powerful temporalities that indelibly shaped the landscape for centuries. Within their understanding, kai and kai Māori (Māori food) spaces are part of food temporalities that impel deeply cultural, ecological and socially informed practices that feed people and uphold communal health and wellbeing. These integral ancient kai patterns, their spatial changes and the places Māori continually inhabited should be understood as manifestations of kai tino rangatiratanga, which means Māori food sovereignty.

These explorations centre on the period before 1840, when 'Auckland' was founded as a new colonial capital in September of that year. This growing township, purposefully settled as a political and commercial hub, was one of the first actions taken by the infant government after the signing of the Treaty of Waitangi around Aotearoa (New Zealand).[1] After this, intense pressure from settlers and government forces would lead to systematic dispossession of Māori lands. These changes have physically erased centuries of agricultural constructions, which had dominated the isthmus for centuries. Kai temporalities in Tāmaki developed for centuries based on Polynesian practices. By the 19th century, a range of specific material constructions had come to define and nurture kai practices, such as stonefields and hillside terracing. The seasonal patterns of communities encapsulated place-specific kai temporalities. It took them across various regions of the isthmus, such as the Waitemata and Manukau Harbour shorelines and ensured they consumed a range of kai throughout the year, including kūmara, taro, mussels and sharks.

Though there are texts which explore the general kai Māori practices and Māori and Pākeha, or English and European, relations during the early settler Tāmaki township, there currently is no text which explores historical kai Māori practices from a spatial perspective. Historians such as Ben Schrader, Lucy Mackintosh and Russel Stone have expertly studied how Tāmaki Māori engaged with settlers and colonial intrusions during the 19th century and how they continued exercising their autonomy. Other historians, such as Deidre Brown (Ngāpuhi, Ngāti Kahu), have highlighted the critical role that an evolving Māori architecture has played within the development of Māori society and spaces. Māori kai tino rangatiratanga, as an embodiment of Māori food power and narratives, has yet to be foregrounded in written architectural histories. This historical account has been written through a critical engagement with anthropological and ethnographical texts centred on Māori customs and lifeways and inherently understanding the autonomy of Māori communities and the importance of their cultural and spiritual beliefs and practices. It directly follows a Kaupapa Māori framework that approaches colonial narratives embedded within historical accounts from decolonising perspectives, which seeks to critically re-evaluate privileged voices in favour of indigenised perspectives and traditions. While this chapter is centred on highlighting Māori sovereignty, to create more clarity for non-Māori readers, English translations will be made of Māori terms.

Māori changed their food practices in particular ways after the 1840s; understanding the history, patterns and structures which Māori called upon during the period leading up to the 1840s emphasises the immensity of their food temporalities. Māori developed many kinds of food spaces over both vast water and landscapes through purposeful architectures that meant they could reliably feed their communities across the year. These managed food spaces were not confined to cultivated gardens but were located within various seas, rivers, forests and islands.

Kai tino rangatiratanga

Kai tino rangatiratanga can be considered as an embodied spatial force that continually transformed the environment for the sustainable generation of kai. In one way, it is evident in the landscape changes, structures and horticultural gardens that Māori created over the centuries.

Kai tino rangatiratanga is closely tied to three terms, the first being tino rangatiratanga, which can be translated as self-determination, sovereignty and autonomy.[2] It can also be understood as the unqualified exercise of (their) chieftainship, highest chieftainship[3] and absolute sovereignty.[4] The second term, kai tino rangatiratanga, is connected to is food sovereignty, which emerged from global food justice movements. It was championed by La Vía Campesina, a self-described international peasant activist organisation[5] at the 1996 United Nations Food and Agriculture Summit, where they emphasised that food sovereignty is an activist term that is about honouring the rights of people to determine their food practices according to their culture and environment.[6] The final term, kai, can mean food – to eat, consume and drink.[7] Approaching Te Ao Mārama – the world of light, the natural world – through Kaupapa

Māori, the Māori-centric research paradigm, is to conceptualise spaces as shared with immanent ancestral guiding ancestors and gods, embodied within and emanating forth from many natural features alongside a diverse range of animal species.[8] Emerging from the environment through engagement with Te Ao Mārama and primordial parents, kai or food can be understood as nourishing a healthy life.[9]

Māori food sovereignty is a local adaptation of the term in Aotearoa, which Kaupapa Māori researcher Jessica Hutchings (Gujarat, Ngāi Tahu and Ngāti Huirapa) has advocated in her book *Te Mahi Māra Hua Parakore*. Hutchings's text provides a Kaupapa Māori framework, Hua Parakore, tailored to helping communities grow māra kai, Māori food gardens, according to Māori knowledge and shared values. Within this framework, Hutchings states that:

> Māori food sovereignty in Aotearoa puts Māori who produce, distribute and consume food – rather than the demands of global markets, free trade agreements and corporations – at the heart of food systems and policies.[10]

Kai tino rangatiratanga or Māori food sovereignty is an inter-disciplinary term that encapsulates a way of conceptualising, being and enacting Māori-determined kai systems in the environments and significant places that they whakapapa to. Within the context of Tāmaki's history, it is positioned as an underlying drive in the Māori creation of extensive kai spaces.

Early Māori transformations of Tāmaki

Any telling of the kai Māori temporalities in Tāmaki must first understand the broad spectrum of spiritual, practical and place-specific knowledge that Māori communally held whenever they gathered and harvested kai.[11] Taniwha, ancient spiritual creatures, inhabit the Tāmaki region and are associated with specific places imbued with their ancestral presence and narratives. Taniwha can transform into different animals, often acting as cautionary and guarding beings, having the ability to moderate and warn Māori communities of danger or trespassing without regard for the environment.[12] Other ancestral beings that shaped Tāmaki's landscape are Mataaho and Mahuika, associated with geological forces and volcanoes, and the latter with fire.[13] In some traditions, Mataaho rose from the earth, and where he walked is where Tāmaki's volcanic maunga (mountains) and lakes emerged, a process sometimes referred to as Ngā huringa ō Mataaho, 'the writhings of Mataaho'.[14] The importance of these ancestral beings is continually upheld by historical and contemporary whakapapa, the oral histories told by Māori communities.[15] Physical landscapes in a Māori world are imbued with and exist as personifications of immanent beings genealogically tied to contemporary communities.

When Polynesians first arrived on Aotearoa's shore, they brought their food and hundreds of years of their accumulated horticultural and fishing knowledge. Scholars know of six imported Polynesian plants that successfully grew in Aotearoa, of which the kūmara or sweet potato would become the most widely grown. Tāmaki's islands, rather than the mainland, were the first to be inhabited in the area, probably because their climate and geography would have matched their home environments.[16] Subsequently, they dramatically changed the country's flora and fauna. Episodically, Māori burnt large parts of the islands' central ancient forest within a relatively short period, bordering up to the Waitakere and Hunua Ranges, where valleys are still thick with native forest.[17] Pockets of forest were left in valleys and on some islands, where they acted as hunting spaces for wildlife and ecological havens for the practice of rongoā (Māori medicine), which relied on a diverse collection of organic matter.

Like many other places in Aotearoa, early settlements were located along the coasts on the headlands, bays and beaches, where it was easy to fish for kai moana,[18] as early as the 13th century CE.[19] From the 14th and early 15th centuries, Māori also began to occupy the craters of Tāmaki's extinct volcanic maunga due to its inherent geographical defensive abilities, increased soil fertility and visual prominence.[20] From the 15th and 16th centuries, Māori began to purposefully plant on the lower slopes of these volcanic hills,[21] clearing the scattered volcanic rocks and forming them into rows or walls, creating enclosed horticultural plots that were able to demarcate and improve the cultivation process for kai, which was predominantly the growing of kūmara.[22] As māra kai or food gardens were expanding radially outwards from maunga across the volcanic soil during the 16th and 17th centuries, residential features were built into and from the extinct volcanic hills, centring around its upper slopes and crater rims, increasing the space that could support inhabitation while maximising māra kai space on easy-to-cultivate flatter ground.[23] Villages on the hills over the centuries would have incrementally climbed their slopes. This development pattern on the maunga suggests that there was little competition for resources and settlement for centuries. By the beginning of the 19th century, fertile land was plentiful, and most settlements were located on flatter, indefensible sites close to coastlines.[24]

Kai practices and their associated kai temporalities, such as shifting settlement locations, developed for centuries in Tāmaki from Polynesian food practices. Māori purposefully changed Tāmaki's landscape from the beginning of their inhabitation and carefully managed it to maximise kai generation. Kai tino rangatiratanga, Māori food sovereignty enacted through temporal food patterns, was a multifaceted practice that powered the daily and yearly cycles of communities in the region.

Tāmaki makaurau kai practices

A wide range of food spatial typologies were firmly established by Māori by the mid-19th century in Tāmaki. Maunga, or hills, already touched upon, can be considered a prominent architectural feature in Tāmaki before the mid-19th century. The largest hills, such as Maungawhau (Mt Eden), were episodically considered capitals during the 18th century.[25] These hills were centres for large whānau, family and stone-defined food gardens that radiated outwards from their base, occupying most, if not all, of the volcanic fertile soil, including maunga on islands.[26] Maungakiekie and Māngere slopes are extensively terraced and have over 150 terraces across multiple tiers up to their craters' rim.[27] Most terraces were utilised as spaces for houses, storage pits, cooking and stone working, and domestic activities to live and sustain peacetime settlement.[28] Terraces were constructed by excavating back into the earth and then using that earth or even shells or earth from other parts of the settlement to extend the flattened terrace.[29] There was no prescribed pattern to these terraces. Some solely consisted of large storage pits; some were repeatably inhabited as house sites across centuries, while others were used just for cooking. This indicates that terraces and kai structures generally were relationally constructed to communities' needs.

Another Māori typology popular in Tāmaki are pā, fortified villages. Hundreds of these exist in the contemporary Tāmaki region.[30] Māori constructed them from the 14th century to the 19th century in Tāmaki. Pā are essential places of refuge and temporarily occupied in periods of warfare or strife and are consistently closely situated next to māra kai.[31] For pā on the crater's rim on top of the volcanic hills, ditches were typically cut across the rim, allowing fortified villages to be partitioned into higher, more minor defensive positions. Generally, these fortifications were constructed on high ground or near valued resources, trade routes, and across various terrain types. Many in Tāmaki are famed for their ability to overlook a combination of land cultivations, fishing zones and necessary portages and, therefore, are closely related to kai spaces.[32]

The final and most significant spatial kai typology Māori constructed in central Tāmaki is its stonewalled māra kai, its food garden complexes recorded on most of Tāmaki's volcanic soil. Māra means a plot of ground under cultivation, farm or garden.[33] Stone complexes are large areas containing multiple stone structures used as living spaces for growing, storing and cooking food. These complexes covered thousands of hectares of Tāmaki's volcanic soil.[34] One of these structures, stone mounds ranging from 5 centimetres to 2 metres in diameter, were used to grow gourd or kūmara by piling stones that would trap solar heat, creating ideal conditions for plants more used to warmer Polynesian conditions.[35] Ten thousand of these mounds probably existed in Tāmaki and are consistently found in relation to stonewall complexes.[36] Families made stone wall plot delineations to manage their gardens, roughly sized between 25 to 65 metres wide to 80 to 300 metres long and internally divided parallel to its shorter side.[37] Remaining stone complexes become the durable evidence of deliberate and calculated Māori manifestations of māra activities and seasonal food practices.[38]

Modified mountains and gardens once profusely covered the entirety of Tāmaki surface. Colonial dispossession destroyed most of these features, yet they remain today as indelible evidence of kai temporalities. By the 19th century, Māori food temporalities manifested a range of specific physical constructions tailored to ensure peaceful settlements and the protection of food systems.

Most of our information regarding kai Māori practices comes from 20th-century ethnographers such as Eldon Best's and William Phillipp's books. These have been important in re-establishing kai practices, given their closeness in age to the periods they touched upon and their engagement with particular Māori of the time.[39] Later anthropologists and archaeologists such as Helen Leach and Agnes Sullivan are important for contextualising kai Māori practices before 1840. They provided a detailed exploration of the seasonal and ecological practices that were conducted across the isthmus for some centuries.[40] Bringing these writings together, we can illustrate the everyday food practices that have suffused the entire landscape for centuries.

In preparing the māra kai for cultivation, Māori burned off existing vegetation, and any wild fern root had to be meticulously dug out.[41] Māra kai could be used for two to three years before their location had to change, and were positioned to capture northern and eastern sunlight.[42] In some communities, the presence and invocations of tohunga, a Māori priest, played a critical role in the key stages of māra cultivation, especially in harvesting kai.[43] The preparation and storage of kai was another critical part of Māori practice. Large amounts of kai needed to be stored to feed the community over the winter months. The most common way of storing kūmara was in storage pits, sheltered and drained depressions made in the ground. These villages also feature kāuta, typically wooden or stone-enclosed unadorned cooking spaces dispersed amongst Tāmaki stone fields, demonstrating that cooking was done close to the food gardens.[44]

Māramataka, the Māori lunar calendar, is crucial for food garden activities and is used to this day. It determines the start of the cultivation season and fishing patterns, and structures daily lives.[45] Using moon cycles as a calendar, people begin their garden cultivations in Tāmaki around June to July,[46] but more generally, spring or August[47] to autumn the following year.[48] A tohunga priest determined other tohu – signs, marks and symbols – to determine the cultivation of kai.[49] Each phase of the moon within a lunar cycle signals different activities that could be done in relation to kai, corresponding to appropriate times for fishing, gardening and resting. Daily food temporalities were deeply entwined with these lunar signs as a way to guide them in their food activities.

Nearby to the central Tāmaki māra kai stone complexes were large native forests such as to its west and south in the form of the Waitakere and Hunua Ranges.[50] Though these forest areas lacked the central region's flatter terrain and volcanic soil, these were also ancient spaces continuously occupied for centuries. For example, most villages and gardens in Waitakere were concentrated along the coastline, on the ridges, islands and valleys. Waitakere Māori conducted their seasonal movements between these locations, similar to the patterns of other communities utilising the Manukau harbour as a summer fishing location and wintering in valleys between Te Henga and Muriwai, where there are many pā for the storage of kūmara.[51] Many native birds, both sea and land-based, living within the ranges and its many coastal islands, contributed to its rich ecology and were important species to hunt for either their meat or feathers.[52] With its biodiversity, the entire forest was space for rongoā (Māori medicine), where Māori could retreat and find refuge, for it was deeply interconnected to their spiritual, cultural and physical wellbeing.[53] Food practices and, therefore, temporalities were never enclosed and were restricted to what are typically considered 'traditional gardens'. Instead, they were closely related to a multitude of terrains that might be perceived as wild spaces but were, in actuality, managed as food spaces.

Māori fishing was a significant part of this food landscape and was a highlight for communities during the summer when they ventured across the North Island to visit famed fishing spots. Much in the same way as their māra kai practices, by the 19th century, they had accumulated centuries of intergenerational knowledge of the best ways to fish and where they could harvest seafood through a wide variety of techniques: fishing with hook and line and nets, diving with baskets, spearfishing, line cray fishing kapu, carrying dredgerakes, constructing stone traps and weirs. The diversity of fishing techniques and implements reflects the many species of fish Māori encountered in Tāmaki, ranging from mussels and snapper to sharks and stingrays. Fishing gear such as nets were collectively constructed – mainly from dried, smoked or raw flax laboriously woven together. Multiple families worked together.[54] Coastline gathering of shellfish features prominently in Tāmaki, demonstrated by the hundreds of shell middens still dotting the coastline today.[55] Nineteenth-century food practices were largely supported by these gathering and hunting techniques and demonstrate ancient Māori connections to water bodies. They approach them in a similar way to gardening – an engagement with natural and environmental forces mediated by intergenerational knowledge and watchful engagement.

The communities used two main fishing zones in the central Tāmaki region; the first is located southwest of the central region, the Manukau Harbour. This is a huge fishing space where many marine species can be caught.[56] Its low-lying banks, inlets, and estuaries are prized for their availability of sharks, fish and shellfish, spots that would be highly valued and shared between different communities.[57] The second fishing zone was north of the central region, the Waitemata Harbour. A 10-kilometre zone stretching from modern-day Coxs Bay to Ladies Bay is endowed with numerous bays and rocky reefs from which shellfish could be gathered.[58] These spaces have been dramatically altered since colonialism, but many contemporary suburbs had small fresh streams flowing into them from valleys from which people could easily harvest fish.[59] In both harbours, multiple communities prized shark-fishing locations, and fishing for them became the highlight of the summer seasonal pattern.[60]

Both these fishing spaces reinforce the idea that food temporalities, while primarily located on land from settled land-based villages, were in continual contact with water-based environments. Māori had to hold huge knowledge bases about food's material, ecological and geographical aspects to enact place-specific seasonal food-gathering patterns – a distinctive temporality. Tāmaki's food sovereignty is deeply concerned with the health and well-being of salt and freshwater systems – essential centuries-old food systems. Tāmaki's water bodies – both existing and erased – are still powerful reminders of everyday Māori engagement with those environments. Oceanic environments in Tāmaki are for Māori rich, potent food spaces, teeming with fish which can be harvested through considered and detailed spatial and ecological knowledge.

Tāmaki's islands in the Hauraki Gulf, Waitemata and the Manukau Harbour were unique and ancient Māori spaces for centuries in which the cultivation of both land and sea-based food was a major part of life to those communities. Māori consistently inhabited islands similarly to how they inhabited spaces on the mainland, some of which are now regarded as nature reserves. Islands were ideal places for settlements as people could take advantage of its rich biodiversity in both birds and sea life, as well as its warmer climate. Consistently, Māori modified all of the islands to varying degrees through the construction of pā, storage pits, and kāinga in the terracing of the land and kai practices in the form of hangi pits, midden pits and māra kai remains.

Puketutu, in the Manukau Harbour, is a volcanic maunga and a significant place for several Māori iwi or tribes across the centuries.[61] Its food temporalities and garden architectural features continually tie it to Tāmaki's wider volcanic field and the sacredness of food on the island. According to history, its occupation stretches to before the arrival of the Tainui waka, the ancestral oceanic vessels that brought Polynesians to Aotearoa, which occupied it as their initial base.[62] Given its proximity to the other kai landscapes, such as Onehunga, Māngere, Ihumātao and Otuatua, it was uniquely positioned as an ideal place for settlement and seasonal kai practices. As a volcanic maunga, it had extensive stonewall features over its entire land area before much of the island was quarried to construct the Auckland Airport runway.[63] Stone rows and plots of divided māra kai, parallel walls radiating outwards from the maunga, follow the same patterns as the mainland. (Evidence of boundary markers or possibly mauri stones was noticed by an amateur ethnologist well into the 20th century.[64]) These stones evoke ancient beings who guard and protect the māra kai cultivation and reinforce the island's sacredness.

Other islands, such as Waiheke, demonstrate the scale of island inhabitation and Māori engagement with Europeans. Waiheke has pā, likely hundreds of years old, located across the entirety of its coastline situated on ridge lines and hills. Within and surrounding these fortified villages, Māori constructed over a hundred terraces and middens, and nearly two hundred pits.[65] These architectural food features are supported by surrounding karaka trees and māra taro planted in nearby swamps.[66] European timber ships would visit Waiheke as early as the 1790s and begin the deforestation of kauri.[67] Waiheke Māori provided water and provisions to passing European ships, crucial to the early trade networks between Māori and Europeans.[68] The arrival of missionaries in the area in the 1820s meant that Māori on Waiheke had spent decades incorporated into the colonial economy by the 1840s and were well-versed with Christian agents.[69] Like many other Māori communities, those on Waiheke were instrumental in developing the 'Auckland' township by trading with settlers' materials and kai, building on their centuries of kai practices.

Māori inhabited Tāmaki's islands in a temporal seasonal pattern that allowed communities to permanently build and occupy kāinga and adjoining fishing camps spread across several islands, and exchange resources with communities across the Te Ika a Maui. In the same way they inhabited the mainland, food practices on the islands combined defined food gardens with seasonal hunting and foraging practices taking place in the forests, seas and coastlines. The islands can be understood as food islands powered by temporalities situated within an expansive oceanic foodscape. Continual Māori inhabitation of the islands emphasises how Māori food sovereignty extended well beyond the mainland and the central part of the isthmus and was the foundation of island settlements.

Tāmaki makaurau seasonal patterns

All of the Māori villages in Tāmaki, with their associated māra kai regions and fishing camps up until the large-scale arrival of European settlers in the 1840s, were inhabited seasonally. Māori communities had developed permanent settlements from which they projected across the landscape, setting up a series of secondary sites consisting of māra kai and fishing camps. They dynamically rotated between their secondary and primary sites alongside other tribes, which meant that they could produce kai year-round. From this understanding, the isthmus can be seen as an intricate web of overlapping tribal food movements covered by a density of purposefully constructed food sites that stretch over water and land. These food temporalities maximised food generation and also assured peace between various tribes who shared these resources with each other.

Seasonal patterns can be explored through the movements of Te Taoū, a hapū or subtribe of Ngāti Whātua Ōrakei iwi who lived in the central Tāmaki region during the 19th century. They would begin clearing and planting māra kai in late winter, supported by their built-up stores in areas such as Māngere and Onehunga.[70] In early autumn, groups would journey further afield to other coastline sites across the Waitemata and Manukau harbour to plant small māra kai in preparation for their upcoming summer fishing practices.[71] Maramataka would have moderated the start of planting. Food gardens were planted alongside other communities, though they might have had a different connection to those sites; these parties, likely to be family-sized, would negotiate these sites individually.[72] Most of the community would live dispersed within the māra kai or stone food garden complexes. Living in small houses made from either raupō, a wetland plant, or stone, they resided right beside the garden filled with kūmara and, by the 1840s, European food such as corn and potatoes. From here, they carefully tend to the vast quantities of food they would need to get through the winter while harvesting small amounts to feed themselves.

Food practices peaked in summer, marking the beginning of full-time fishing at those sites, which were prepared early in the year and constructed in a staggered fashion that fed people into the autumn, overlapping with the start of a fishing phase.[73] They began their fishing phase in the Manukau Harbour, leaving behind small groups to tend to their primary kāinga while others set up fishing camps along different shorelines covering some 5 kilometres. Seasonal summer sites were also spread along the southern shore of the Waitemata Harbour. In this case, they utilised ancient portage routes to transition between the two harbours and their coastline fishing camps.[74]

In autumn, communities returned to main kāinga areas and began their main harvesting of kumara planted earlier, which required the labour of digging, lifting and storing potatoes, portions of dried fish from Raumati fishing, and pork in storage pits that they also needed to maintain.[75] This autumn harvest was important because it would help sustain communities through winter. Other iwi and hapū had their own seasonal patterns, which overlapped with those of nearby communities.

Central Tāmaki was an Indigenous urban centre by the 19th century, unlike any other place in Aotearoa. Its food spaces and modifications through terraced hills, stone food garden complexes and managed hunting and fishing zones reflected a higher social-political complexity, creating a sprawling urban field of Māori inhabitation.[76] Māori testimony recounts that land during this period was undivided between people and that while Māori tribes had a variety of different stakes and rights to resources, often food practices, whether on land and or water, were done alongside each other. Multi-layered seasonal patterns encapsulate kai temporalities, as they were relational activities that took place in negotiation with other communities, the environment and ancestral beings.

Tāmaki makaurau kai spaces and temporalities

Māori communities constructed vast food landscapes over islands, shorelines and harbours through their intergenerational food knowledge tied together through a seasonal rotational pattern of settlement. Cycles took place over vast distances, which meant that communities could reliably produce food year-round. Wetlands, rivers, seas and mountains were all traversed, transformed, managed and cultivated by Māori in the continual creation of food. Along with food architecture, such as stonefield garden complexes, these areas reflect a sophisticated food system in constant engagement with the natural world.

Building from historical research critically approached from a standpoint that validates Māori sovereignty, food environments can be considered as an indelible physical manifestation of a kai tino rangatiratanga. It compelled a seasonal pattern of living in which a wide variety of locations and environments would be altered to maximise the harvest of kai. These patterns were formed by accumulating generational knowledge on the best locations to grow kai, kai structures and ecological cycles. As I have demonstrated here, Māori temporalities, such as seasonal settlement patterns, the rotation of food gardens, the journeying to fishing sites, and cultivating precious perishable edible biological matter, were intrinsic to the creation of Māori community spaces during the 19th century. By paying more attention to the spatialising of Māori temporalities, we can privilege immanent histories, spaces and practices that underlie the development of Tāmaki Makaurau across the past 650 years. Critically approaching and recontextualising historical accounts from a food perspective, it is possible to see how Māori food spaces transformed and were connected to the entirety of the isthmus and the backbone of its urban settlements.

8

FOR THE COMMON GOOD
Local sovereignty and ra'ui in the Cook Islands

Bronwen Neil, Antony Vavia and Tom Murray

Food insecurity poses a severe threat to traditional ways of life and the stability of urban and rural systems across the globe and here we reflect on how ra'ui, a traditional cultural ban used by the inhabitants of Mangaia to protect and conserve food sources, can inform global resource management strategies during the era of climate change. Mangaia, the southernmost island in the Cook Islands archipelago, is one of the oldest Pacific Islands and the oldest with a platform of exposed volcanic rock; it is 51.8 square kilometres and had a population of 464 in 2022.[1] The practice of ra'ui, part of a Polynesian system of subsistence, traces its origins to the first millennium of the current era, before contact with European settlers, and has continued to be used throughout the past 200 years of the colonial period to ensure supplies of seafood, plant life, animal and bird life at sustainable levels. It is a social tool fundamental to Cook Islands sovereignty, and one which, considered within the framework of eco-cosmology, may offer more broadly applicable solutions.

Our research started with a 24-hour sail from Rarotonga to Mangaia. We sailed on the *Paikea*, a sea canoe owned and operated by our research partner Te Puna Marama Voyaging Foundation. We also received support from the French Government's *Fonds pacifique* and the German-French NGO, Okeanos Foundation for the Sea. The sail was the beginning of a three-week field study on Mangaia and Rarotonga from October to November 2022. This trip, a life-changing one for the

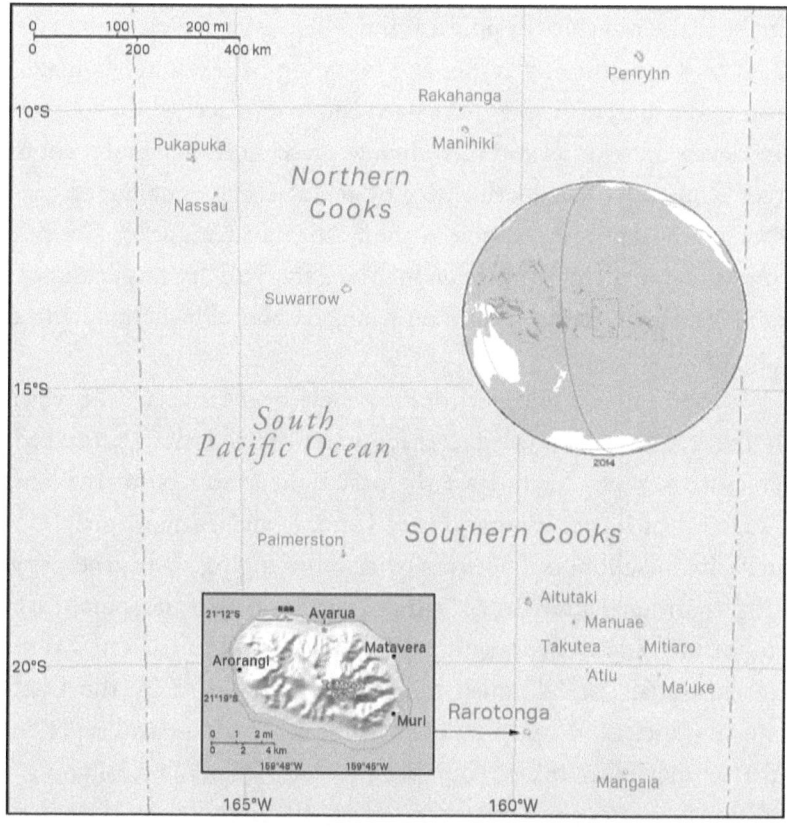

Cook Islands map, 2014.
SOURCE Used with permission of the creator, Ian Macky,
<www.ian.macky.net/pat/map/ck/ck_blu.gif>

researchers, helped us to appreciate the ways in which island societies such as Mangaia, and others across Polynesia, have historically been deployed as a canvas for western projections concerning environmental disaster through mismanagement.[2] For example, in his 2005 international bestseller, *Collapse*, Jared Diamond used Mangaia to defend his social organisation theory that some societies choose failure.[3] We set out to see how the use of a specific environmental management practice, called in Cook Islands Māori ra'ui, could challenge Diamond's thesis.

On Mangaia (see above map),[4] the use of ra'ui to manage resources has been traced back at least to the Ngariki period (500–600 years ago) when the island was ruled by political and religious leaders claiming a direct heritage to Rangi, the Sky Father and founding Ancestor of Mangaia.[5] In more recent times, ra'ui areas have been employed successfully to manage fishing levels for seafood sustainability, to preserve animal and plant food sources, and to protect biodiversity by replenishing endangered species with cultural significance, such as the Mangaian Kingfisher. We reflect on the impacts of reviving ra'ui in Mangaia, and its implications for sustainable future food supplies on Mangaia and elsewhere during this era of climate change.

We have collaborated with local people on Mangaia, who wish to share the traditional knowledge of food security that has guaranteed its inhabitants' survival for at least the past eight centuries for the benefit and survival of future generations of Cook Islander Māori peoples and their Pacific neighbours. We start by acknowledging their generosity in sharing traditional knowledge, which was preserved and passed down as oral history and living practice before the arrival in 1824 of Tahitian, white Australian, and English missionaries sponsored by the London Missionary Society. While our personal cultural heritage and experiences of history inevitably inform our perspectives, we support ongoing de-colonising processes and attempt to reflect on our own subject positions.[6] The 'de-colonising framework' of scholarship acknowledges our culturally informed bias.[7]

According to Jared Diamond's theory, Mangaians precipitated their own demise through exploiting natural resources unsustainably, and were forced to leave their island in search of more habitable land to the west and south, which they eventually discovered in Aotearoa (New Zealand).[8] In this they were allegedly like the inhabitants of Rapa Nui (Easter Island), who were forced to leave their homes in search of new lands after an environmental disaster caused by removing all the trees from their island. More recent archaeology, however, complicates Diamond's thesis and his conclusion that islands such as Rapa Nui offer 'the clearest example of a society that destroyed itself by overexploiting its own resources'.[9] Instead, new scholarship on Rapa Nui has established the critical role of ecological factors that include the impact of rats in vegetation degradation on islands across Polynesia, as well as the social impact of climatic variation and drought during the 'little ice age' (1570–1720 CE).[10]

We offer here a brief re-reading of Mangaian ecological history and present some evidence of current successful environmental management strategies. We will start by introducing the concept of ecocosmology, which has proved useful for undertaking a preliminary study of contemporary ra'ui and other forms of Indigenous knowledge on Mangaia.

Systems of Indigenous knowledge and ecocosmologies

First Nations American anthropologist Lidia Guzy explains ecocosmology this way: 'Eco-cosmologies are indigenous knowledge systems correlating agro-ecology, ethno-forestry, sustainable food production, biodiversity and sustainable living ... Eco-cosmologies can be viewed as indigenous sustainability knowledge systems, however missing in the global SDGs [Sustainable Development Goals]'.[11] As a part of explaining and motivating human behavioural change to accommodate changing environmental circumstances, ecocosmologies take cultural influences and non-tangible heritage seriously.

We use this conceptual framework to explore the deep-time practice of ra'ui. Ecocosmology in this sense denotes a system of mutual exchange and connectedness between the human and other-than-human worlds, within a worldview that values ancestors and the other-than-human (plants, animals, elements such as water, air and fire) as important parts of a fully functioning ecosystem, akin to a home or household. Ecocosmologies are normally defined as ontologies that oppose western anthropocentric cosmologies. The unique ecocosmology of Mangaia includes all the native fish, such as the parrot fish, native animals such as the coconut crab, endemic birds like the Mangaian Kingfisher, and more recent arrivals including humans and their domesticated co-habitants (pigs, chickens, goats, rats etc). It also incorporates the natural elements of earth, sea and sky. The idea is not new and yet its value has to be continually reasserted against the materialist demands of a typical

Western knowledge framework. Scholars in the humanities – including historians, ethnographers, anthropologists, creative arts practitioners and geographers among them – have a role to play in recovering traditional Knowledges in the fields of ecology, land and sea use, environmental studies and biology.

Cultural anthropologists Kristina Tiedje and Lucas Johnston caution, however, that not all 'ecocosmologies' perceive ecological systems as beneficent or positive.[12] Nature may be considered powerful and terrifying, and an unsafe space for interactions with the other-than-human world. While acknowledging those complexities, Tiedje and Johnston point toward ways in which non-mainstream, Indigenous epistemologies are contributing to environmental protection. Sydney environmentalist and scholar Jo Rey has described the reciprocity and respect needed for non-Indigenous scholars to engage productively with Australian Indigenous practices of 'caring for Country'.[13] Such an approach values respect for the other-than-human elements of Country and positive human participation within ecosystems that are characterised by connecting, caring and belonging. The concept of ecocosmology sits well with customary practices of caring for local environments in the Cook Islands and has thematic relationships with other Indigenous research methodologies that have also informed our study of ra'ui.[14]

The practice of re-centring Indigenous knowledge within global decision-making is also urgent. As Aboriginal historian John Maynard has argued in *Everywhen*, 'The knowledge carried across sixty-five thousand years may well be our best defence against a growing global catastrophe. Let us hope that those in power begin to listen before it is too late'.[15] Policy makers on Rarotonga are very aware of the risks that climate change poses to life on the Cook Islands.

Another source of inspiration for our research and fieldwork in Mangaia has been the Cook Islands sociologist Christina Newport, who has written about ocean-going canoes (called in Cook Islands Māori vaka moana) as a unifying cultural symbol and as a metaphor for developing culturally appropriate policy in the Cook Islands.[16] Captain Peia Patai, a Pwo master navigator, conducted an orientation and induction ceremony which enabled us to appreciate the canoes as a research model.

Before boarding the canoe that was to carry us from Rarotonga to our fieldwork site of Mangaia (see photo on page 147), Patai explained the ways in which a canoe is itself an island and a form of floating social organisation with its own systems of administration. While explaining our individual and collective responsibilities aboard the vessel, Patai compared the canoe with the sacred gathering places (marae) that are found throughout Polynesia. The sea vessel was like a sacred island upon which we had duties and responsibilities to each other, and to the greater environment in which we entrusted our lives for the duration of our 24-hour journey from Rarotonga. Aligning western science approaches with traditional eco-cosmological knowledge has been central to Patai's mastery of non-instrument and celestial navigation: a practice that requires constant attention to patterns and changing signs provided by stars, sky, swells, waves, currents, winds, birds and other maritime flora and fauna. For instance, several hours before we could see any trace of the island, the appearance of a white tern flying above the boat's mast showed that we were nearing land. Patai's framing of our journey within a sphere of sacred and secular knowledge practices provided a further guiding context for our understanding.

Questions of sovereignty on Mangaia

Mangaians today pride themselves on their historical resistance to colonialism and the fact that the New Zealand-imposed Native Land Court system has never operated on their island. They note that from the first year of New Zealand administration in 1901, the six kavanas ('governors' or leaders of each of the six districts of Mangaia)[17] refused to participate in the Cook and Other Islands Land Title Court – the division of the Cook Islands Ministry of Justice currently known as the High Court Land Division, that governs land matters in the Cook Islands.[18] While the first step of colonisation was land surveying, this was not allowed on Mangaia.[19] The kavanas were divided at first, and two courts came to operate on Mangaia/Rarotonga: a New Zealand one and another local one belonging to 'the Anarchy'. The British flag was a symbol of 'the Anarchy', based on a myth that Queen Victoria had given the flag to those advocating for self-rule on the Cook Islands.[20] Those opposed to the imposition of the New Zealand court system on Mangaia organised local resistance tactics: for instance, throwing stones on the Resident Agent's roof at night until he was driven out.[21] The right of local residents to apportion their lands as they wished, and pass it down through lines of family inheritance, has been defended and lasts until today. Likewise, the right to impose or lift a ra'ui is a political act that is defended by traditional leaders who resist government impositions in this area of local life and livelihoods.

The Cook Islands were named in honour of navigator James Cook's visit to the archipelago on his third expedition on the HMS *Resolution*, by Russian circumnavigator Adam Johann von Krusenstern. Cook sailed from England in 1776 to Tasmania and New Zealand in 1777, sighting land on Mangaia on 29 March 1777, and meeting his death in Hawai'i in 1779. In an atlas published in the 1820s to 1830s, Johann von Krusenstern noted that James Cook had visited the Cook Islands' southern group, also known at the time as the Hervey Islands.[22] The name 'Hervey' came from Cook's visit to Manuae, another southern island that he visited in April 1777, which he dubbed 'Hervey Island', after Augustus Hervey, an admiral of the British navy. The name of Hervey Islands was later extended to the whole southern group, including Mangaia, but the entire territory, including the northern island group, was renamed the 'Cook Islands' at the time of its annexation by New Zealand in 1901.[23]

Responsibility for implementing a cultural ban on food harvesting or managing natural resources (ra'ui) as well as opening or lifting it is given to the kavanas and the sub-chiefs (rangatira).[24] These officials decide to start or end the ra'ui in a public meeting. The role of the kavana is held for life. If a pāpā kavana is unable to fulfil his duties due to ill health or other reasons, his wife may assume them as 'māmā kavana', with pāpā and māmā being terms of respectful address for older men and women respectively. The head of the island is now the Numangatini Ariki, an honorary title translated as 'king' or 'queen' by Mangaians, the equivalent of 'chief' or 'sovereign'. In the past the Numangatini Ariki was only one of three chief priests who had the power to impose the ra'ui.[25] In 1889, Australian missionary and ethnologist William Wyatt Gill recorded how the office of sovereign traditionally rotated between seaward and mountainside families, a custom that continues today.[26]

Gill noted that both the interior or mountainside royal chief and the shore-side royal chief need to be able to trace their genealogy back to divine ancestors or gods. The chiefdom or kingship/queenship can be passed to the oldest male or female relative in that family and can be declined, in which case it passes to the next in line – a cousin, brother or sister, niece or nephew of the same bloodline. The system of inherited title allows for the distribution of authority to rotate around the main five or six families of the island. The appointment of the king/queen today depends on detailed knowledge of genealogies that stretch back many generations. By the 20th century, some of this intergenerational knowledge was lost, making the selection of the sovereign more difficult. An individual might be a leader in more than one sphere of governance; for example, a pastor and a sub-chief. This increases their authority and gives them the ability to engage with multiple communities when it comes to decision-making about ra'ui.

These locally based and traditionally appointed authorities have key roles in maintaining pre-colonial socio-legal structures. Their decision-making capacity today across numerous areas of government, including traditional management strategies such as ra'ui, provides local pride in their historical and ongoing resistance to colonial structures of governance. They also offer an important witness to Mangaian resource sovereignty and eco-stewardship.

The use of ra'ui for seafood conservation

As part of its growing colonial presence in the Cook Islands, in 1908 the New Zealand parliament instituted the Te Mana Ra'ui ['The Power of Ra'ui'] Act, which declared that 'the ancient right of ra'ui no longer existed in respect of any land which has been investigated by the Native Land Court'. Mangaia was not subject to this court, so the declaration was not influential there. However, it is worth noting that other islands (those that were subject to the Native Land Court) maintained ra'ui zones to manage food sustainability within both terrestrial and marine environments despite the *Te Mana Ra'ui Act*.[27] These marine zones were intended to preserve resources by prohibiting the harvesting of certain species within a specified area of the reef across a given time. Put simply, this prohibition would allow the wild stocks to replenish, aiming to restore an abundance of the resource that could be sustainably harvested at a later date. This was purely for the sustenance of the local people or in the lead-up to a significant event that would require a feast or in more recent times, to host guests.[28] Opening ra'ui for hosting guests is debated within some communities. They would argue that the marine resources should be available for the island's residents only – with survival, satisfaction and perhaps material gain in mind as a reward for their commitment to abstaining from resources.

With increasing pressure on fisheries and food security observed worldwide and locally within the Cook Islands, Mangaia re-introduced their local customary marine tenure system to combat threats of food security. Ra'ui areas on Mangaia, much like the other Cook Islands, are owned and operated by the community and traditional leaders of the affected, often adjacent, district(s), as opposed to employing legal enforcement through government and ministry.[29]

The strategy of ra'ui was also re-introduced in 1998 on the main island, Rarotonga, in response to a failing marine resource management system implemented by the government. It had failed due to lack of community compliance. The ra'ui sites were reinstated with the criterion that the protection had to be community-led.[30] What gives strength to establishing and regulating Mangaian-protected areas is that by not having legislation of government and other authorities overriding ra'ui, power (mana) is maintained under the traditional leaders (aronga mana) while under local leader (ariki) sovereignty.[31] Traditional power is not displaced, hence there is greater social goodwill to abide by the local customary tenure.

At present it is the spiritual and socio-cultural attributes of ra'ui that fortify local commitments to maintain their abstinence from resources. Many spiritual contexts apply within governing processes and tend to act as a guide for community decision-making.³² The success of food security rests upon the community or district refraining from harvesting within a ra'ui for the greater good of present and future generations. Survival in the outer Cook Islands seems to have developed a culture of food distribution that ensures the entire village eats; a 'love your neighbour' attitude where care and concern for a neighbour's wellbeing is traded reciprocally – a form of mutualism where everyone takes care of everyone. In other cases, commitment to ra'ui relies on enforcing sacred taboo, which can vary between sites. For ra'ui to succeed, the objective of the common good must outweigh considerations of personal material gain.

Diverse views still exist when it comes to establishing and committing to ra'ui zones. One socio-economic impact concerns potential financial loss to the fishers who regularly harvest within a ra'ui zone.³³ However, most inshore fisheries are subsistence-based and there are no currently known records of ra'ui breaches over the past two decades, although there is a wealth of anecdotal accounts of such breaches.³⁴ Fisheries management officers recount that men and women are sometimes caught fishing in the exclusion zones and a notable justification is to paraphrase a biblical verse: 'If you see it, take it! Otherwise, it's a sin'. This is a widely held view and has also been used in the context of current debates about deep sea mining in the Cook Islands.

Having ra'ui closures to limit reef access does not mean completely giving up subsistence or artisanal-based livelihoods. Respecting a ra'ui zone could restrict access to food sources within certain parts of a reef, but neighbouring reefs could prove to be equally or more productive, as marine resources spill over from protected areas into unprotected ones. For example, since there are no physical barriers around ra'ui sites, parrotfish that have been allowed to grow to full size in protected areas may then be fished in unprotected areas. Ra'ui areas provide a chance for marine life to recover in adjacent parts of the reef, since ra'ui zones rely on customary, not physical, boundaries.³⁵ The marine fisheries office has seen substantial improvement in the size and stock of marine life. For example, the parrotfish, popular for eating, has recovered from the dwindling numbers and small sizes that resulted during the period of overfishing.

An intermittent ra'ui has allowed coconut crabs, which dwell in ground burrows below coconut trees, to reach advanced ages of 50 to 70 years, with correspondingly large shell sizes of more than 30 centimetres in diameter. These are saved for eating on special occasions, such as a visit from the Numangatini Ariki or the return of athletes from the Cook Islands Games. And although it was never a food source, the population of Mangaian Kingfishers are another important part of the ecosystem that has recovered in sufficient numbers that it is now off the 'Red List' of Endangered Species. This was achieved by a ra'ui on the species across the whole island for several years. The ra'ui zones are intimately connected with the ecocosmology of the whole Cook Islands group.

In his safety briefings to passengers and crew, traditional voyaging teacher Captain Peia Patai underlines the significance of the ocean-going canoe as a marae or sacred site, where unity, a strong sense of community with the sea and its inhabitants, and co-operation with the natural power of the ocean are essential for preserving life on board the canoe. The canoe can also be understood as a metaphor for the success of multi-species island communities such as Mangaia. In this sense, the lens of ecocosmology is useful for observing the role of the sacred within resource management philosophies on islands such as Mangaia, both historically and today.

On Mangaia, the traditional leaders and a range of local stakeholders have implemented a series of ra'ui zones that have gradually increased marine, plant, animal and avian biodiversity on the island. Additionally, population decreases and changes in agriculture may be helping to make these strategies more effective. The continuity of traditional Cook Islander knowledge and its authority is crucial to implement ra'ui effectively and sustainably. This brief study of ra'ui shows that, contrary to Jared Diamond's highly popular and influential thesis in *Collapse*, the global lessons to be derived from islands such as Mangaia and Rapa Nui are not those of ecocide, human 'covetousness' or 'selfishness', as posited by archaeologists Paul Bahn and John Flenley.[36] On the contrary, the deep-history practice of ra'ui on Mangaia offers an excellent example of successful long-term eco-custodianship that demonstrates the capacity of collective action. The island of Mangaia, with its long history of resilience and survival in the face of major climate fluctuations and its capacity to resist colonial powers and economic globalism, may offer important clues for averting looming climate challenges and crises in other societies.

Sunset over the Pacific Ocean, seen from the *Paikea* on her journey to Mangaia, with research collaborator Teriimana Tehei, October 2022.
SOURCE Bronwen Neil and Te Puna Marama Voyaging Foundation

Author and crew member Antony Vavia on the *Paikea*, nearing Mangaia, October 2022.
SOURCE Bronwen Neil and Te Puna Marama Voyaging Foundation

Acknowledgments

Our sincere thanks to the Cook Islands Office of the Prime Minister and the people of Mangaia for welcoming us to their island and sharing their knowledge and hospitality with our team. The sea canoe *Paikea* is owned and operated by our research partner Te Puna Marama Voyaging Foundation and we offer personal thanks to Peia Patai and Cecile Marten for their assistance. We acknowledge financial support for this research from the French Government's *Fonds pacifique* (Embassy of France project NB 2218) and the Okeanos Foundation for the Sea.

PART IV

Hard evidence: The languages of rock art and stories

9

HISTORY ON THE ROCKS

Laura Rademaker, Sally K May,
Joakim Goldhahn and Gabriel Maralngurra

When I was a kid, old man Thompson Yulidjirri introduced me to rock art. He took me up Injalak Hill, showed me the rock art and told me stories as we looked. Old Thompson took us to Injalak Hill when I was a kid, when we were school kids. We used to go up. Old Thompson used to take us there, tell us the stories, and how it was done and how it was painted, and how people used to live up there during the wet and come down in the dry, and what they caught. They would paint up on the rocks. It was like a classroom, a big blackboard, and now it's still going, because we carry on our culture and telling stories. So, the story will never be forgotten. It will be there for more than a thousand years, and a bit more.[1]

The Old People taught Old Thompson the same way: walking Country and painting the rocks. Probably his dad took him up Injalak Hill or maybe Paddy Compass. And they were travelling. In those days, when they were having ceremonies at Gunbalanya, Croker Island, Goulburn Island, there was a base camp at Gunbalanya, and people used to go up the hill to see, visit family and stayed there. And, they wanted to paint something, just to put their mark, or something, just to let people know that he was here, he done this painting. That's what it's about.

Hard evidence

Rock art from Injalak Hill, west Arnhem Land.
Photo: Sally K. May, permission courtesy of Julie Narndal Gumurdul

**Barramundi fish painted using X-ray technique,
Injalak Hill, west Arnhem Land.**
Photo: Sally K May, permission courtesy of Julie Narndal Gumurdul

Our co-author, artist Gabriel Maralngurra, has been going up Injalak Hill all his life. The old man Thompson Yulidjirri showed him the rock art. These were Gabriel's history lessons. Yulidjirri told the stories of individuals, only a generation or two earlier, who had 'left their mark' for their descendants, but he also told the stories from way back. As Gabriel explains, his people have a very Deep History indeed:

> [Australia's history] goes way back. Very long time, from the beginning, I don't even know, but that's how we've been told, from the Ancestors, the creation time, when we were living on the rocks, and painting on the rocks, telling stories to their kids, to everyone.[2]

Western scholarship, rock art and the beginning of 'history'

First Nations peoples have lived in northern Australia for some 65 000 years, at least according to archaeological evidence. It was only relatively recently, only thirty years ago, though, that some academics still considered the pasts of Australian Indigenous people as not really *history*.[3] These pasts were of some other quality; they were not the kind of pasts that determined events and shaped the future as 'history' is supposed to do.[4] First Nations people were presumed to lack an intellectual framework that would enable their pasts to constitute 'history'. Instead of 'history', First Nations people's pasts were merely 'myths' when told by First Nations peoples themselves, or, when told by scholars, they were 'prehistory'.

The idea of 'prehistory' as opposed to 'history' emerged in the 19th century when the academic discipline of archaeology was taking shape in European universities. Writing became the line that divided people's pasts and cultures among the various academic 'experts'. The written record was the domain of historians, and whatever came before writing fell into the new field of archaeology.[5]

But this separation of writing from material sources of evidence wasn't always the case for European scholars. For centuries, scholars had used the Bible as their main source to explain the creation of the world and its content. Then, the rediscovery of other texts about northern Europe in the 16th and 17th centuries, such as Cornelius Tacitus's *Germania* from the first century AD, broadened the source base from which scholars developed their ideas about the deep past. 'Discoveries' and translations of Icelandic sagas followed, witnessing to times that existed before written literacies in Scandinavia.[6] But how could these histories be known without writing?

One way was by rock art. In 1748, for instance, a pair of unsuspecting Swedish farmers uncovered a Bronze-age tomb packed with engraved stone slabs. This was the spectacular Bredarör cairn on Kivik.[7] Some interpreted the engraved procession of human-like beings and the war chariot depicted on the slabs as a reminiscence of a triumphal Roman ceremony, arguing that Roman forces once must have reached far beyond the northern lines of the empire, a bold statement that could not be evidenced from written sources.[8] Scholars saw that studies of rock art could complement scant written sources, revealing histories of times without writing.[9] Before there was a discipline called 'archaeology', European scholars had viewed and interpreted rock art in light of both written and oral sources to write their histories.[10]

By the late 19th century, this older relationship between academic history and rock art studies was obscured and even lost altogether with the rise of the discipline of archaeology. From the perspective of Western scholars, the division between historians with their writing and archaeology with material culture made sense. After all, the study of written documents requires one kind of expertise and method, the study of material culture requires another. Historians called their times 'history', and archaeologists – except for 'historical archaeologists', who applied archaeological methods to contexts and cultures that could also be known through a written archive – studied the newly coined '*pre*history'.[11] Rock art, as material culture, became understood largely as evidence of 'prehistory' – the domain of archaeologists – rather than as a historical source.

On the chronological scale, 'prehistory' dwarfed history in that it covered the entire past of human species until Mesopotamians started writing things down about 5200 years ago. After that, it becomes complicated, as different peoples in different parts of the world adopted written literacies, or not, at various times. Even across Europe, 'history' supposedly began at different times. In southern Europe, the ancient empires were deemed to have a 'history' that stretched deep into antiquity. In northern Europe, however, early historians assumed that 'history' commenced only with the introduction of Christianity.[12] 'History', according to western scholars, had different start dates, depending on the particularities of whether and why people wrote, or when they encountered others who wrote about them.

Of course, this implicitly meant that for many peoples around the world, 'history' began when European colonisers arrived on their lands and shores, bringing their writing with them.[13] In the Americas, 11 October 1492 marked the end of 'prehistory'; Rodrigo de Triana saw land and history supposedly began. In the same way, until recently, much of settler Australia considered Captain Cook's 1770 charting of the country's east coast as the beginning of Australia's 'history'.

Telling histories beyond writing

But there are many more ways of knowing and telling the past than by the writings of Western academics. Historians at universities do not have a monopoly on history. So, what about the peoples of these continents and their ways of recording and remembering the past? These historical methods pre-dated and then co-existed with European writings. Europeans mistakenly deemed cultures that used literacies other than written script to know their pasts – oral traditions, art, song, dance, monuments – as not to have history at all, when, in reality, it was simply that European historians did not know how to interpret them. Without writing, the pasts of Indigenous peoples were classed as being before or beyond history.[14] As Ann McGrath and Lynette Russell have put it, for too long, Indigenous peoples were made out to be 'history's outsiders'.[15]

Claiming that 'history' only started when Europeans turned up sounds ridiculous now. But it was plausible for those shaped by Eurocentric beliefs associated with social Darwinism. In this understanding, just as 'savage' or 'primitive' cultures supposedly develop into 'civilisations', so oral societies would gradually and inevitably embrace written literacies.[16] The view assumes a hierarchy of knowledges that places Indigenous Knowledges (and material culture) at the bottom.[17] According to such a view, orally transmitted knowledge is unreliable, overly emotional, and biased; it is believed to lack an archive that might be consulted to establish the hard facts of the past.[18] This viewpoint assumes the 'primitive' culture has no real memory of the past apart from 'myths', unlike literate 'civilisation' that supposedly self-consciously writes its own history and plans its destiny.[19] That is putting it bluntly, of course, but these kinds of assumptions about writing and history persist, not only in popular discourse, but reverberating through the legal systems of settler societies, with devastating consequences for First Nations peoples seeking to use oral tradition to prove their claims to land and sovereignty in settler courts. In British Columbia, in 1991, the Supreme Court found that, despite abundant oral evidences confirming the Gitksan and Wet'suwet'en people's history of land ownership, an absence of *written* evidence meant that this history was impossible to prove.[20] It is for good reason that many Indigenous Australians today consider offensive the use of the label 'prehistory' to describe their pasts.[21] The 'pre' could suggest First Nations people needed Europeans for their histories to begin.

Historians and archaeologists know about these problems.[22] Archaeologists have been talking about it since at least the 1990s (and sometimes quite heatedly too).[23] Many scholars in both disciplines are working hard to unpick the racist assumptions and the colonial heritage at the core of our disciplinary practices, and First Nations historians and archaeologists themselves are leading the charge.[24] Choctaw archaeologist Joe Watkins writes of the tension between his belief that archaeology is a powerful and effective method for understanding the past, and his feelings of betrayal by other archaeologists who, he felt, did not take Indigenous people's concerns about his discipline more seriously.[25] Another archaeologist could never forget the challenge from a Tanzanian researcher: 'Why do you whites say our history is prehistory?'[26] These are old habits. For archaeologists working in settler colonial contexts, the 'historical' period remains more or less interchangeable with the 'colonial' or 'contact' period. 'History' often still starts with, and is defined by, the presence of Europeans.[27]

Historians have been somewhat oblivious to the debates going on down the corridor in archaeology about so-called 'prehistory'. But over the past fifty years, historians have been rethinking their archives and turning to oral and Indigenous Knowledges as sources of history. In the United States, the New Indian History, also driven by Native American historians, sought to bring First Nations voices into the writing of history and centre their perspectives.[28] In Australia, the field of Aboriginal history exploded from the 1970s, with the *Aboriginal History* journal seeking to draw on knowledges from linguistics and oral history to produce a fuller understanding of Aboriginal pasts. And the plural – 'pasts' – is deliberate. These movements drew attention to the multiple ways of understanding and conceiving the past, challenging colonial histories that aspired to be definitive, comprehensive and universal. Reading the archive 'against the grain' is now commonplace for identifying First Nations experiences and perspectives within the colonial archive.[29]

Some historians are challenging their discipline's limits by turning to 'Deep History', that is, histories that stretch as far back as the human story might be told.[30] Deep History transcends the divide between prehistory and history, drawing together oral, written and material sources. Most, however, remain wedded to a 6000-year timeframe for the discipline at the most, and, therefore, at least implicitly, to the presence of written documents.[31] Nevertheless, historians increasingly accept that there are ways of knowing the past beyond the traditional text-based archive; there are other kinds of archives, other 'houses of memory', beyond the repositories of written documents usually built by colonial authorities.[32]

Archivists, too, are pointing out that there are other repositories of records and documents beyond the archival boxes if we are looking for evidence of the past.[33] As Eric Ketelaar famously proclaimed, 'everything is an archive' if approached in the right way.[34] Historians increasingly understand that all peoples have histories, and that these are known, understood and shared in rich and manifold ways.[35]

Where are First Nations archives?

The bulk of the Aboriginal past, stretching millennia before colonisation began, has been left out of 'history' as taught in universities, partly due to academic historians' blinkered evaluation of writing as the only legitimate form of record. But, some might ask, even if historians wanted to study these Aboriginal pasts, where are the records and archives they might use to investigate them?

Well, First Nations people have been saying repeatedly that they *do* have archives. There are vast First Nations repositories of knowledge of the past, if only others cared to listen and understand them as such. One such record is art, and rock art in particular.[36]

Gabriel Maralngurra explains that rock art 'tells us about the history of the painting, because it's been painted there for a long, long time'.[37] This is not only the case for his people, the Bininj of west Arnhem Land, but also has been insisted upon by knowledge holders from across the continent. As Wakaman Elder Carol Chong said:

> Rock art is our record and our keeping place of our knowledge, lore and culture. Rock art is a powerful link between our country, our past and our people, and we want to protect and preserve it for future generations.[38]

Maung Elder Ronald Lamilami likewise explained that rock art sites are his people's 'libraries': 'it tells stories ... from father to sons, to their sons'.[39] Continuing the metaphors of writing and script (or is it a metaphor at all?), his son Leonard Lamilami described his clan's paintings as 'like a dictionary for us, like a bible'. Again, his brother Patrick Lamilami explained in 2016 that rock art is 'our library, it holds our stories'. He continued:

> Our rock art sites are like history books to us that have stories to pass on to future generations. This is why it is important to protect these places. By playing the didjeridu, telling traditional stories

and visiting rock art sites I help keep my cultural life and heritage strong for my people.⁴⁰

Traditional Owner Ron Marks from the Barengi Gadjin Land Council in Victoria also spoke of rock art as a repository of knowledge:

> Here, this is our library – this is our art gallery. It warms the heart to know that for thousands of years – stories have been written on rock on sites such as this.⁴¹

Similarly, Dharawal elder Shayne Williams explained:

> It's important to protect [rock art] because *that's where our literacy is*. Our literacy mightn't be in the form of books, but it's physically manifested into the land, like the rock engravings, for example, and paintings. This platform ... is *like a big book to us* ... And they're like our libraries: we go there and that's where we learn about our culture and heritage so, to destroy them, is like pulling down the British Library or the State Library of New South Wales or the Australian National Library, for example. Can you imagine how devastated people would feel if that happened?⁴²

As these knowledge holders proclaim, rock art is an archive abundant in sources, documenting a long Aboriginal history that stretches back millennia.⁴³

Many non-Indigenous archaeologists working closely with Aboriginal Traditional Owners in their study of rock art have already embraced rock art as an archive replete with historical records. Archaeologists Paul SC Taçon and Liam M Brady describe it as 'an archive of deep-time human experience'.⁴⁴ Robert Layton calls it 'a record', created 'to be remembered'.⁴⁵ Anthropologist Howard Morphy also describes rock art as a 'tangible record' and laments the failure of other anthropologists to engage with it.⁴⁶ His insights have yet more pertinence for historians. Whereas other kinds of repositories of memory, such as song, dance and music, have been threatened by the devastation of colonisation, much rock art remains through the millennia. Morphy, therefore, calls it 'the most durable ... record of all'.[47] Taçon writes of rock art as a uniquely 'enduring' historical source, with rich insights into past lives.[48]

Given these testimonies, perhaps it would be better to think of rock art not simply as art but also as *document*, that is, a fixed means of conveying knowledge.[49] We suggest that, as documents created by observers of happenings or participants in activities, rock art can also provide evidence about the past. That is, it can become, in the terminology of archivists, a *record*.[50] The stunning galleries of art, curated and preserved in rock shelters or across plateaus, are therefore also *archives*. They are collections of records, selectively created and curated. Like written archives of paper documents, rock art is produced, preserved, curated and valued through various historical processes.[51] It has its own authors, archivists, conservators and interpreters, each of whom plays a role in the keeping of historical memory for the Community. It can be 'read' by those who understand the literacies of such a text. Like a written archive, it reflects the interests, priorities and concerns of that community.[52] Indeed, we suggest that, in many ways, these records might be considered a better archive than the repositories of paper that academic historians are used to, and often esteem above all else.[53]

Of course, rock art is not the only archive that holds records of deep Aboriginal histories. In Australia, rock art is actually only a surface manifestation of the richer archive that is Country itself.[54] As Aboriginal Australians declare, the landscape itself holds the songlines and stories of the continent.[55] Rock art simply makes this deeper record visible: it is a manifestation of the knowledge held in Country. As Koorie scholar Shannon Faulkhead points out, some records cannot be stored in institutions. Sometimes, they are embodied in people themselves. Sometimes, they are kept in the landscape, in Country.[56]

In contrast to these archives, the colonial archive that many academic historians predominantly rely upon has not always been a welcoming space for First Nations people, although many are finding ways to turn its power to suit Indigenous interests.[57] Colonial archives have been an integral technology of surveillance and control of Indigenous lives by settler-state authorities.[58] They served to establish Western systems of knowledge as powerful and effective on Indigenous land, subjugating Indigenous Knowledges and authorities.[59] Though they contain records of Indigenous Knowledges and culture, these Knowledges are often dislocated from Indigenous people themselves, both physically by their removal from Country to faraway institutions and legally as they became (supposedly) owned by governments and holders of collections under Western intellectual and copyright laws.[60] Indigenous people were made to be 'subjects of the record and not the owners'.[61] First Nations voices are often muted and rare in the colonial archives. However, as leading First Nations historian Lynette Russell points out, knowledge about First Nations people held in public archives can become Indigenous knowledge through restorative reclamation processes.[62] Nevertheless, as First Nations lawyer Terri Janke explains, 'we are captives because we do not own the archives, written records and documents about our lives. Our stories are not told by us'.[63]

First Nations people are subverting and transforming all this. The colonial archive, once used as an instrument to separate Indigenous families, has now become the means through which Indigenous people are finding kin, restoring culture and connection and, importantly, seeking redress.[64] Nonetheless, colonial archives remain sites through which colonialism has been and continues to be enacted.[65]

Alternative archives such as rock art have been a way for Indigenous peoples to control the nature and terms of their own representation and to represent others. Anthropologists Severin Fowles and Lindsay Montgomery describe the Indigenous rock art of the American West as a 'counter-archive' for the way its narratives challenge colonial accounts through the firsthand testimonies of Native American peoples.[66] In Arnhem Land in Australia's Northern Territory, Bininj recorded their own interpretations of visiting Macassans and invading Europeans.[67] And so archaeologists studying colonial and contact contexts within Community-led projects are now learning to interpret rock art as an alternative archive that counters those of Europeans.[68]

In Australia, the stories marked on the rocks belong to and arise from the Country itself. They are part of the land, and the land is part of the story. Sometimes, we know who the artist was, perhaps someone in living memory or who might still be alive today. Sometimes, it is the work of the Ancestral beings who live in a kind of time that is not fully grasped by disciplines of history and archaeology. Sometimes it is the work of Spiritual Beings such as the *mimih* in west Arnhem Land.[69] In the Kimberley, even the birds are artists: there, the Kujon, a little grey sandstone shrike thrush bird (*Colluricincla woodwardi*), created rock art.[70] The Country listens and speaks.[71] The art on the rocks not only conveys evidence about the past through images, it communicates. It knows. Treating images carelessly or disrespectfully can provoke spiritual attacks, leading to sickness or death. The land and its people might become sick if art is not visited, maintained and cared for.[72]

This kind of knowledge confounds academic knowledge. It goes beyond what scholars are trained to perceive and understand.[73] As Morphy points out, these modes of 'narrating and preserving history' through art on the rocks 'pose a genuine challenge to the form, content, and character of history as it is understood in the Western tradition'.[74] But rather than excluding these sources as outside of history, we suggest they be used to reframe how we think about history itself.[75]

But who can read First Nations rock art?

It may be all well and good to understand rock art as an archive, but can outsider scholars actually read it? And, perhaps more to the point, should they?

Historians are getting better at 'reading' images. Some historians are already engaging with visual sources, especially when it comes to First Nations histories. In Australia, a leading example is historian Jane Lydon, who uses historical images to rediscover and interpret the stories of First Nations people in the early years of photography in Australia, showing other historians how to understand visual sources.[76] Such work demonstrates that written documents are not necessarily superior for conveying information across times and cultures, nor is writing necessarily more readily understood and interpreted than visual sources.

Archaeologists, for whom this is probably obvious, will remind you that Lydon began her career as an archaeologist.

That said, First Nations visual sources and archives have a different nature and providence to images in the colonial archive. This is not simply a matter of encouraging historians to engage with visual and material culture – although we would support this, and collaboration with archaeologists is a productive way to do so. Rather, recognising First Nations rock art as archives and documents requires an expansion of the discipline's very approach to the past itself, as well as our practices and epistemologies of coming to know the past.

The question of how an academic historian might 'read' Aboriginal rock art reflects the disciplinary impulse to objectify the archive. That impulse is to establish a divide between the agent (i.e. the researcher) and the object (i.e. the source) and, vicariously, the First Nations people who own it. Our extractive academic model is to 'delve' and 'mine' the archives to uncover their 'treasures' and 'secrets' (ignoring the labour of archivists who carefully ordered and prepared them).[77] The divide between academics, whether we define ourselves as historians, anthropologists, archaeologists or something similar, and 'our sources', would normally presume that this is also a temporal divide. The researcher works in 'the present' to unlock the secrets of sources that come from 'the past'. What this model does not consider is that such sources might actually be acting on us. Understood properly, rock art cannot be domesticated, controlled or studied; it reveals itself when and to whom it wishes.[78] It has an agency of its own.

Terri Janke, in her recent work on ethical research and engagement with First Nations communities, wrote about finding better ways to engage with Indigenous Knowledges – that is, ways that uplift First Nations peoples themselves. Janke insists that Indigenous Knowledges should not be objectified and commodified by outsiders. Instead, she extends a First Nations relational, embodied understanding of knowledge into the academy and beyond. In universities, as our liberal assumptions would have it, knowledge is disembodied and 'out there', ideally for anyone to use freely. But perhaps knowledge is not best understood as disembodied and 'free' but as existing always in relationships with others.[79]

Given this, any engagement with First Nations archives can only be attempted with the authorisation of, and in close collaboration with, the First Nations people who own them. Aboriginal rock art is not readily objectified and 'mined' for information as academic historians traditionally would have it. It will only share its insights when approached in proper relationships with its owners. This imperative for collaboration with First Nations people is not simply a matter of research ethics (although it is necessary for ethical practice). It is a question of intellectual integrity.

This is a stance of receiving knowledge as a gift and sharing in reciprocal relationship, rather than of extracting and mining information. Such a stance will not consider the academic historian or archaeologist the source of First Nations empowerment.[80] Nor can it become an opportunity to store up even more knowledge for the universities. Given Australia's history of colonisation, the ongoing settler suppression of Indigenous sovereignties and the denial that First Nations people even have a history, non-Indigenous people are the ones who need to do the listening in any dialogue. By learning to see 'history on the rocks', with the communities for whom this history is cultural identity and law, we hope visions of the 'past' and how we might come to know and understand it might expand.

In the meantime, Gabriel Maralngurra invites you, our readers, to come and sit down on his Country, and learn the stories from the rocks. He will teach you:

> If [the people who read this] want to ask more questions, they can come. If you want to learn more, we'll tell you ... Come and sit down, in a big rock, big cave, I'll explain every little painting on the rock.[81]

Gabriel's Country is in west Arnhem Land, and he invites you to come up to Injalak Hill, but the Australian continent is scattered with the most stunning deep time rock art archives. You will not need to travel far to see them. But go in the right way, with permission, with a guide. Learn from the First Historians and listen to what the oldest of archives are still saying about the deepest of histories.

West Arnhem Landscape.
Photo: Sally K May

Acknowledgments

Gabriel Maralngurra sadly and unexpectedly passed away after this chapter was written but before it went to print. We use his name with permission of his family and wish to express our gratitude and condolences to them.

We are deeply indebted to the many Traditional Owners of west Arnhem Land for their intellectual and practical assistance with our work (especially Jeffrey Lee and Josie Gumbuwa Maralngurra). The staff and artists of Injalak Arts have been central to the development of this work. We are grateful to Laureate Professors Ann McGrath and Paul Taçon for providing leadership, mentoring and encouragement. Dr Jess Urwin gave vital feedback on earlier versions of this chapter. We also acknowledge the Australian Research Council as this research was funded by grant nos. FL170100121, FL160100123, SR200200062 and FT210100118.

10

LANGUAGE HAS COUNTRY
Memory, transmission and sovereignty in Tara June Winch's *The Yield*

Rosanne Kennedy and Ben Silverstein

I am writing because the spirits are urging me to remember, and because the town needs to know that I remember, they need to know now more than ever before.

The Yield

In 2007, political philosopher Aileen Moreton-Robinson, a Goenpul woman, published *Sovereign Subjects*, a significant and influential collection of works by Indigenous scholars on Indigenous sovereignties. Introducing that collection, she situates each contributor's standpoint in the 'everyday actualities of their sovereignty in their relations with other Indigenous people and communities'. Despite this experiential knowledge, or perhaps because of the variety of Indigenous standpoints and sovereignties, Moreton-Robinson refuses to provide a 'quintessential definition of Indigenous sovereignty'. Rather, she argues that the writer's task is not to define sovereignty so much as it is to 'reveal its multiple manifestations' and to identify the many ways its force is refused acknowledgement or recognition by colonising assertions 'in a variety of contexts and texts'.[1]

We are interested in some of the ways in which sovereignties are practised and made apparent today through relationships with deep time. As non-Indigenous scholars, we write from standpoints that differ from those of contributors to *Sovereign Subjects*; our position is external to, but always in relationship with, Indigenous sovereignties. It is from here that we take up Moreton-Robinson's project of considering manifestations of Indigenous sovereignty and the contexts of their emergence. Contemporary Aboriginal articulations of deep time, we argue, refuse a sense of temporal rupture between past and present. Rather, they perform memory work that evokes a sense of the past in the present that we have elsewhere called the 'deep present'.[2] Indigenous temporalities may acknowledge European periodisations of human history, but they resist incorporating Indigenous pasts and presents into this schemata.

These themes and practices are central to Tara June Winch's award-winning novel, *The Yield*, which is fundamentally concerned with the work of memory.[3] The novel transmits and activates memories of both a deep past – the long history of Indigenous presence on the continent – and more recent settler colonial pasts. It also addresses ways of living in a present that is constituted via these pasts, its characters' lives haunted by memory and forgetting. Winch brings together multiple times and temporalities: the deep past, the settler colonial past, the settler colonial and capitalist colonial present, and possible Indigenous futures. In refusing a historicity of rupture and instead weaving these temporalities together, the novel constitutes a deep present that is evoked through the transmission and activation of memories of a deep past and practices of speaking Wiradjuri Language on and in relation to Country. In her author's note, Winch details the archival and oral sources on which she draws and which she imaginatively reframes in the novel to braid the stories and temporalities of the three main characters into a compelling and memorable narrative. Winch works with the impact of intergenerational trauma caused by policies and practices of removing Aboriginal children and forbidding them from speaking their Language or connecting with kin – registered in the central character Albert Gondiwindi's stories of his Stolen Generations childhood living in a boys' home. In this context, she informs readers that Australia had the most rapid rate in the world of extinguishing Indigenous Languages, many of which are endangered today. Trauma permeates other stories of characters burdened by the grief of loss, dysfunction and incarceration.

The need to remember is at the heart of this novel. Indeed, remembering and transmitting memory to present and future generations is represented as imperative, and the novel itself is an act of cultural remembrance. Set in locations based on actual placenames in Australia – such as Massacre Plains – the novel could be regarded as part of the Truth-Telling about the nation's past called for in the Uluru Statement from the Heart.[4] Yet, despite the weight of trauma and grief, *The Yield* is also – and even more forcefully – a novel of repair and hope. That hope, we argue, is communicated in the novel's active remembrance and circulation of Wiradjuri Language, a Language of people and Country in what is also known as central New South Wales. Speaking Language represents and fosters positive forms of attachment to Indigenous lifeways, kin and Country.

We argue that the novel's cultural imaginary of a deep present is achieved through its transmission and layering of different temporalities. *The Yield* is part of a constellation of works in the creative arts, in research and in public heritage projects that are developing imaginative modes to transmit cultural memories of deep Indigenous pasts in the present. As such, it contributes to a resurgence of Indigenous culture in Australia, especially evident since the inaugural National Indigenous Art Triennial, *Cultural Warriors*, which opened on 7 October 2007, and continuing with artists such as Kamilaroi Bigambul artist Archie Moore representing Australia at the 2024 Venice Biennale.[5]

Here we focus on the novel's remembrance and transmission of Wiradjuri Language, through its narration of Albert Gondiwindi's act of writing a Wiradjuri dictionary and recording the spoken Language. Significantly, *The Yield* circulates Wiradjuri Language into the reading public through the form of the novel, which both stories the words it introduces and presents them in a dictionary appendix.[6] In producing a partial Wiradjuri dictionary, the novel acknowledges and participates in current reclamation projects of Indigenous Languages that have been endangered by colonisation.[7] The contents of that appendix – titled

'The Dictionary of Albert Gondiwindi: A work in progress' – are drawn from one such project, led by Stan Grant, Sr and John Rudder, who compiled the new Wiradjuri dictionary.[8] But, vital as such a project might be, reclamation and regeneration of Language goes beyond simply restoring a mode of speech or understanding.

The novel's work of activating and performing Wiradjuri has implications, we argue, for understandings of law, authority and sovereignty in the Indigenous present. First Languages are entangled with and are a part of Country. Throughout *The Yield*, speaking a First Language brings together place and people, past and present, human and more-than-human. For Albert Gondiwindi, the Language of Country 'is the way to all time': remembering Language demonstrates knowledge that grounds Indigenous claims to sovereignty in Country.[9] Specifically, the novel's innovative representation of Albert's use of Language to story Country – drawing on the deep past and Ancestral memory – advances a conception of sovereignty that might be situated alongside but is not synonymous with a state's purported authority to pronounce law. We argue that, through Albert's dictionary, the novel invites us instead to understand sovereignty as fundamentally relational and embedded in Country. This is a sovereignty that emerges and is practised through speaking Language, through Wiradjuri storytelling, and through history-making: the deep present is rendered a time of Indigenous sovereignty.

Archiving Language

Utilising the capacious and elastic form of the novel, *The Yield* draws on and imaginatively incorporates historical records, oral storytelling and the sustaining memory of Aboriginal presence on Country through deep time.[10] Through free indirect discourse we gain some access to the interior, subjective perspectives of the three main characters: Albert Gondiwindi; his granddaughter, August Gondiwindi; and the long-deceased Reverend Greenleaf, each of whom represents a different historical period and a different sense of temporality. Rather than follow a linear chronology or resolve contradictions between European historical periodisations and Indigenous temporalities, the novel engages potentially contradictory conceptions of time, preferring to position these temporalities in sometimes abrasive relation. For example, the 'deep time' of the Ancestors and of the earth, which Albert Gondiwindi, one of the two central characters, calls 'the real story of time' – that 'ropes and loops and is never straight' – is juxtaposed with the 'church time' that arrived with European settlers.[11] Church time is communicated through the serialised letter of Reverend Greenleaf, which spans his establishment of an Aboriginal mission in 1880 and ends with his incarceration as a German immigrant – and therefore an 'enemy alien' – and death in 1915. The novel conveys the bureaucratic, machine time of the settler colonial and capitalist present through the story of a rapacious mining company (suitably named Rinepalm) that plans to raze the old Aboriginal mission, which has subsequently become home to the Gondiwindi and Falstaff families.

The first nine chapters alternate between August's story – which takes place in our own present time – and Albert's story and the story of his people. Albert's story, which unfolds via a dictionary, moves between three times: the recent past of his adult life and his family; the settler colonial past of the Aboriginal mission and his Stolen Generations childhood; and time travel with the Ancestors into the deep past, through which they impart their knowledge in the present. We meet Albert's granddaughter August in chapter 2, as she returns to her family home for Albert's funeral after a decade in London with little to show. She quickly learns that her Nana must move, as the property they called home is to be destroyed by a mining company. The proposed mine is supported by many of the town's residents for its implausible promise to bring jobs to a struggling part of regional Australia. Greenleaf's voice is introduced in chapter 10, and is loosely based on an archival document, 'A Plea for the Aborigines of Australia', written by Reverend John B Gribble, who founded an Aboriginal mission in Wiradjuri Country where the novel is set.[12] In the fictionalised version of this letter, Greenleaf gradually realises that his Christian benevolence has in fact implicated him in exterminating the very culture and people he claimed to 'protect' and love, and wonders whether he himself has 'become the beast'.[13] After Greenleaf is introduced, the novel roughly follows a repeated sequence of three chapters, each foregrounding the voice of one of the main characters. Albert's dictionary chapters, with their multiple temporalities, are followed by August's present-day narrative, which includes her memories of the haunting disappearance of her beloved older sister Jedda, missing since she was taken aged 10. From August's narrative, which readers will recognise as the time of present-day Australia, the novel moves into the settler colonial past through Greenleaf's 'plea' to a member of the British Society of Ethnography.

The Yield provides a container that includes remediated documents from the archives, a partial dictionary, and the stories of various characters. As an affective and malleable literary form, the novel helps to make memorable the dry historical facts or, for that matter, dictionary definitions that, as Albert points out, 'any fool can look up', by wrapping them up in story.[14] This insight helps us to think through the relationships between the varied voices that move this novel along. August's story is one of returning home from London after having run away a decade earlier, trying to escape the grief that had descended on her and her family after Jedda's disappearance. Jedda's body was never recovered and her fate – unknown to all except her murderer and Albert, who keeps it to himself but shares his discovery of her fate in his dictionary – renders her a haunting presence throughout much of the novel.[15] August finds herself a foreigner not only overseas but also, after a decade of absence, a foreigner at home. Learning to repair the emotional and cultural ties that enable her to experience a sense of belonging once more, her story serves as a kind of narrative glue between disparate elements – including both the dictionary and the archival letters. It brings the layered temporalities of the Ancestral past, of the colonial past on Greenleaf's mission, and of the past of August's family and her poppy Albert into the present, revealing their urgent significance today.

In the months before his death, Albert's efforts to remember the recent and the deep past are represented not only as his legacy, but as a cultural necessity. He writes and records a dictionary that will transmit Wiradjuri Language so that it does not become 'extinct', like the black rhino August has read about in a newspaper.[16] In transmitting Language through technologies of writing and recording, he produces a resource for cultural pride and survival. The novel opens with Albert teaching readers how to pronounce the Wiradjuri word for Country – Ngurambang – pronounced Ngu-ram-bang. Directly addressing the reader in the second person, he tells us: 'If you say it right it hits the back of your mouth and you should taste blood in your words'. He then issues an imperative: 'Every person around should learn the word for country in the old language, the first language – because that is the way to all time, to time travel! You can go all the way back'.[17] Country is a capacious term in Aboriginal English that speaks to much more than place, including, as described in Bawaka Country, 'humans, more-than-humans and all that is tangible and non-tangible and which become together in an active, sentient, mutually caring and multidirectional manner in, with and as place/space'.[18]

From the start, Language is linked to Country and to Indigenous conceptions of temporality as going 'all the way back'. In *Everywhen*, Ann McGrath and Laura Rademaker describe 'Country' as a term 'denoting pride in belonging to certain places and long-held sovereignties. Sites of family and knowledge, they are abiding Indigenous domains. A word spoken with affection and emotion, Country denotes discrete tracts of Ancestral, richly storied and nurtured land – an Indigenous or tribal estate connected with thousands of generations of people and their sovereign nations'.[19] Country emerges as such through relationships across time, relationships that place and story people. Belonging to a language group is a means of belonging to Country – to a region designated by kin relations, cultural traditions and Language. They continue: 'Together, language and landscape amplify historical associations, reinforcing the authority of the land's custodians, which is based on a deep-time sense of belonging. Their appreciation of enduring Ancestral connection with special places over a great span of time confers a unique historical vantage point'.[20] Gurindji/Malngin/Mudburra artist and art historian Brenda Croft reminds us that Language and Country emerge and become together: 'Country has Language and Language has Country'.[21] Language emerges from and with Country. Language is more than words and direct translations; Language is story.

A key practice of settler colonialism in Australia, guided by the ideology of white supremacy, has been stamping out – extinguishing – Indigenous Languages. This is an impossible project. As McGrath and Rademaker write, '[s]uch languages are not altogether gone. They cannot disappear, for they belong to the land. They have been "asleep", awaiting their awakening'.[22] Many Indigenous or First Nations people see First Languages as a means of connecting and reconnecting with Country; or with the grounds and waterways of their tribal domains, their Nations. For Noongar novelist Kim Scott, 'language comes back and one makes oneself an instrument for it and for the spirit of place'.[23] In a physical, spoken way, mother tongues connect Indigenous Peoples with deep Ancestral pasts. Viewed from this perspective, *The Yield* both tells a story of the 'awakening' of an Indigenous Language, Wiradjuri, and simultaneously transmits it – through definitions and teaching an audience of Indigenous and non-Indigenous people how to pronounce words.

The novel opens with a shift from communicative memory – memory that is transmitted orally, from one generation to the next – to cultural memory – memory that is recorded and can be activated in the future.[24] In the field of memory studies, it is argued that important aspects of a culture are committed to archives and only become cultural memory when they are activated.[25] *The Yield* narrates a story about producing an archive of Language, which takes on political as well as cultural significance – especially given colonial efforts to extinguish Indigenous Languages. When Europeans arrived in Australia, over 270 Indigenous Languages were spoken and passed down between generations. Colonial governance regimes, like those at the Aboriginal mission where the novel's character Albert was sent when he was taken from his mother, forbade him from speaking his Language, and sought to push Indigenous languages to the brink of extinction. Albert tells us his wife Elsie gave him an English dictionary which prompted him to write his own dictionary recording his Language, Wiradjuri, 'even if that language isn't mine alone', a language which is now listed as endangered.[26] We learn that, dying of cancer, he continues to work on his 'big book' – the dictionary he has been recording, to archive and transmit the Wiradjuri Language to future generations. But as he lies dying, the pages blow away in the wind;

the wind that, as part of Country and all that constitutes it – human and more-than-human beings, landforms, the weather and its unpredictable velocities – was the source of many of these words.[27] Crucially, Language and Country remain intertwined.

Story, as Albert uses it to explain the words in his Wiradjuri dictionary, is a mnemonic device.[28] Albert's chapters – those that centre his point of view – all take the form of defining specific words by telling stories about their significance to him. By communicating the deeply felt significance of a word in his own life, Albert increases the likelihood that the word will be remembered. Whereas dictionary definitions are easily forgotten, stories stick; embedding words in stories enables them to be more readily remembered. In Albert's dictionary, these words are shared in a 'backwards' order, reflecting the 'backwards whitefella world' he grew up in. So it begins with yarrany, a spearwood tree, from which Albert 'once made a spear in order to kill a man', and then begins again with English words that start with Y, first 'Yellow-tailed black cockatoo – Bilirr' and takes us all the way (back) to 'Australia – Ngurambang'.[29] This practice of translating English words into Wiradjuri departs from a tendency the linguist Jane Simpson identifies in Australian missionary dictionaries, which often present Aboriginal-to-English word lists but do not go the other way, representing an Aboriginal Language as a source to be mined, not to be spoken.[30] In structuring a dictionary in that manner, First Languages are rendered as 'static and archaic' and without a future.[31] By contrast, Albert Gondiwindi's dictionary presents multiple forms of reversal.

Illustrating the possibility of a non-linear approach, Albert also tells us that we need not tread a linear path through the dictionary; we can instead find our own way. We can move from policeman or policewoman – gandyan or gandji to gaol, or shut place – ngunba-ngidyala, to incorrect, wrong – wamang.[32] We might assemble a story so we can read, in other words, of the ongoing violence of settler colonialism that continues to burden and disrupt the lives of the Gondiwindis, as for so many other Indigenous people across Australia. We could reflect that '[s]ome days everything seems wamang still'.[33] Or we might move from the husk of seeds – galgan, from which all life comes, to burnt grass – bimbayi, learning from Albert's Ancestors how to clear a field, how it might then yield tubers that could be roasted and ground into flour, before turning to harrow, plough – gungambirra, and on to wheat – yura, which evokes a memory of the Gondiwindi flours that 'were meant especially for the body of the Gondiwindi'.[34] Those flours might come next, as buwu-nung or dargin, which need to be separated into the mature seeds that should be replanted, while other seeds can be dried out in the sun, ground into a fine flour, and made into a porridge or bread. This, Albert tells us, 'is our harvest, since forever'.[35] Organising relations on a conceptual map in this dictionary might tell a story of Country and the work of sustaining and caring for that Country, the labour of regeneration and repair performed in ways that connect practice in the present to the practice of ancestors in deep time, since forever. This alimentary mode of relationship – that is, the relationship to burning, planting, ploughing, harvesting, grinding and preparing food to nourish the Community – continues to endure through and beyond colonisation.

One might narrate a story thus, building a world through connections and relationships that follow a logic other than that of the English alphabet. Or one might approach each word as itself already storied by Albert Gondiwindi. For instance, explaining the word for younger sister – minhi – he tells us that when he was little and in the Boys Home, he was always thinking of his younger sister, his minhi, across the way in the Girls Home: 'I never forgot her. She was just a baby, Mary was, when we were both taken away; that's a sad story with a happy end because we found each other again'.[36]

In reflecting on Albert's practice of producing a dictionary, we want to mention three points. First, situating definitions in story positions words as relational; they are filled with and evoke sensation, feeling and kin, rather than simply gesturing to the objects they reference. For example, the way Albert shares the word for a younger sister, a minhi, carries with it a relationship with place framed through the work of caring for Country, the fraught relationship between a brother and sister, the pain of rupture and separation within a historical experience of colonisation, the work of memory and the attenuated joy of a return to relationship. Dictionaries produced by missionaries in contexts of colonisation, Laura Rademaker writes, tend to 'reduce' Indigenous Languages, containing them 'in a form they could recognize and control'. Rachel Gilmour describes this as a strategy that displaces Indigenous culture and re-creates an Indigenous language as a 'vehicle of Christianity'.[37] Albert's dictionary, by contrast, reiterates and reproduces language within story of and as Country from which meaning emerges.

Second, Albert's narrative about minhi provides a personal memory of the Stolen Generations – of children separated from their families and culture to be denied affective and practical relationships with their kin and traditions. This was a colonising project designed to extinguish Aboriginal cultures in the interest of producing a monolithic white culture grounded in British knowledges and traditions. In defining minhi, Albert recalls a conversation with a fellow 'roving man' who comments: 'The family trees of people like us are just bushes now, aren't they? … Someone has been trimming them good'. Albert comments: 'I wouldn't ever forget these words because they sounded like sad poems'.[38] Here the novel anticipates Moore's exhibition, *kith and kin*, winner of the Golden Lion for Best National Participation at the Venice Biennale 2024, which uses graphic forms to engage audiences in recognising the impact of settler colonial violence in disappearing Indigenous people and diminishing Indigenous populations.

And third, as we consider below, storying Language here is a way of grounding authority in Country, of speaking the language of sovereignty as it emerges in, from and with Country. Morgan Brigg and Kombumerri and Wakka Wakka philosopher Mary Graham quote cultural historian Stephen Muecke's imagined settler/stranger saying: 'I come from a place where the word is sovereign', to which an Indigenous person might respond: 'That is not a place, it is a story; stories without places will pass, like your time passes … My place is sovereign'.[39] Albert, August tells us, 'had a story for everywhere'.[40]

We read the dictionary here as a technology of memory – it is a means for Language to be committed to memory through a written record.[41] The words in Albert's dictionary come from multiple sources: from the mission's archives, which include records of births, deaths, relationships, rations; from Greenleaf's letters and word lists; from the diaries and records of early anthropologists and explorers; and from Albert's time-travelling visits with Ancestors who share stories about beings rather than offering simple meanings. His dictionary is a container of sorts for the words of these Ancestral beings. In translating the experience of being in relationship with Ancestors into the form of the dictionary, Albert Gondiwindi produces another object, in the form of the cassettes and pages that hold his dictionary. These are sharable, rendering the Language transmissible, even in Albert's physical absence (though his return in some form is, we think, assured). The cassette recorder, in particular, is a vital technology; the recording of Albert's voice is an index of his presence and, when replayed, a trace of his being in the present, which the Community cherishes. This future transmission is not smooth. Indeed, one family member – Aunty Nicki – interrupts its circulation; unbeknownst to her family, she hides both the dictionary and the recording in her office in the Local Council, an institution of the settler state for which she works, straddling two communities. There are multiple mediations of Albert's dictionary at play in these scenes: the written text and recording of Language which he remembers with the help of elders and ancestors; the technological difficulty of accessing recordings held on anachronistic media; and the investments and motivations of people who may or may not want the dictionary to become part of the public record in the present.

In the novel's narrative, August re-connects to her Country and kin in part by searching for material evidence to demonstrate that the family has deep roots in the land, which is at imminent risk of being razed by a tin mine. She and her Aunty Missy visit the Historic Museum Australia, seeking artefacts such as carved message sticks, axe heads, anvil stones, shields, shovels and milling grinding stones from their Country, which will provide evidence in a potential native title claim to block the mining company.[42] Albert's dictionary, for which they also search, provides vital evidence of connection to Country for that claim. Outside of the novel's story, the dictionary also functions to transmit Wiradjuri Language in the present, and in this way, facilitates knowledge about the value of recovering nearly extinct languages and the urgency of language reclamation projects.

These projects awaken Language and demand its utterance. To speak that Language is to speak of Country, authority and sovereignty. Speaking Language brings it back from the edge of extinction, saving it from the fate of the black rhino – 'extinct', 'gone forever' – envisioned early in the novel.[43] By transmitting Wiradjuri Language to future generations, Albert fulfils transgenerational custodial duties, carrying the past into the present, and thereby representing a temporality of continuity.

Memory and sovereignty

As we noted above, *The Yield* begins by addressing the reader in Albert Gondiwindi's voice, speaking of Country and guiding us to do the same, teaching us how to say it, how it feels: 'I was born on Ngurambang – can you hear it? – Ngu–ram–bang. If you say it right it hits the back of your mouth and you should taste blood in your words'.[44] And the novel also ends with his demand that we, the readers, say it, hear it, feel it: 'Ngurambang! Can you hear it now? Say it – Ngu–ram–bang!'[45] The novel and the stories that fall between these opening and closing injunctions can be read as moving us from those first, almost tentative moments of saying the word to a sense of right feeling; it 'decolonises the throat and tongue'.[46] Why must we say and hear Ngurambang? In part it is the importance of the word itself: the word coming from and returning us to all time, to deep time. But there is a more performative aspect to moving beyond knowing and reading and writing the word to speaking and hearing it, both rendering it as what Winch describes as a 'language in motion', and giving voice to Country by speaking its Language.[47] This is why Albert devotes his last days of life to writing the dictionary.

One of the dictionary's effects is to canonise past knowledge, holding it and transforming it from a hidden archive (as in Greenleaf's letters) into working memory, into presence, into living performance.[48] Albert Gondiwindi insists that speaking Language is a way of knitting himself and other Wiradjuri people together in relation to Country, Ancestors, history and more. Rather than the 'ersatz' language of a written dictionary, a kind of container for an externalised knowledge or a cultural reference memory, speech might reiterate a working memory: it has what memory studies scholar Aleida Assmann, inspired by Walter Benjamin, terms an 'aura'.[49] Certain kinds of speech, moreover, connote authority, and we want here to consider the kinds of lawful authority that are practised or performed through speaking First Languages.

The legal scholars Shaunnagh Dorsett and Shaun McVeigh remind us that the word 'jurisdiction' derives from the Latin *ius dicere*: to speak the law. Jurisdiction, then, 'is the practice of pronouncing the law', declaring both the 'existence of the law and the authority to speak in the name of the law'. It is a 'practice of authority and the creation of lawful relations'. This manner of understanding jurisdiction – foregrounding the 'diction' in the word – helps them to convey the sense in which jurisdiction is productive, not just descriptive.[50] Though they were drawing here on traditions of imperial sovereignty, their approach might also help us to consider the practice of speech in relation to Indigenous sovereignties that are often its counterpoint. Speaking an Indigenous Language – here Albert Gondiwindi speaking Wiradjuri – can be understood then as performative in the sense described by JL Austin.[51] It constitutes both Country and Law. Not in the sense that these did not exist prior to their utterance in Language, but rather that Country, Law, People, and Language emerge together, the relationship between them (re)iterated and renewed, over and over again. It is this understanding of the emergence of these relations, manifested in speaking Language, that forms what might be called a sovereign claim to land. As Albert says in his dictionary, 'speaking our language' is 'singing the mountains into existence'.[52] The authority of First Law – the 'laws that have governed relations between and within First Nations and between the human and non-human since the beginning of time' – is vitally based in its utterance in Language that emerges from Country.[53]

In wanting to rethink the relationship between law's authority and sovereignty, we find Dorsett and McVeigh's approach compelling in part because of the way it re-situates the starting point for inquiry. As they note, discussions of authority in Western political philosophy tend to centre the question of state legitimacy, sometimes embodied in the sovereign. Rather than taking sovereign legitimacy as our starting point, the legal scholar Sundhya Pahuja suggests that 'treating "who speaks the law" as the first question invites us to pay close attention to the issue of law's authority'.[54] This approach turns our attention to an understanding of how authority is established, understood and practised in this contested settler colonial context.[55] Authority may be closely linked to sovereignty but should not be collapsed into it as though they are the same thing; authority to speak the law may be considered rather to come first, prior to the claim of sovereignty.

We acknowledge that scholars disagree regarding whether the term 'sovereignty' might usefully describe Indigenous forms and practices of (political) authority. Kahnawà:ke Mohawk philosopher, writer and political strategist Taiaiake Alfred, for instance, has argued that sovereignty can only be understood as 'supreme political authority, independent and unlimited by any other power', whereas Indigenous law is based on relational autonomy. Consequently, '"sovereignty" is inappropriate as a political objective for indigenous peoples'.[56] Similarly, Mary Graham, writing with Morgan Brigg, understands sovereignty to be an imposed force. Drawing on a Hobbesian political philosophy, Graham and Brigg characterise a sovereign as the supreme power whose authority is based on the idea that it is necessary to overwhelm, subdue and civilise a state of nature characterised by a war of all against all. By contrast, Aboriginal politics is based on an understanding of people in relation – with each other, with Country, with totems, with other-than-human beings. People are not at war with each other but rather only emerge through a 'complex, refined, and multifaceted system of obligations and dispositions'. This displaces sovereignty's basis, leaving Country as a site of relationism.[57]

Others seek to wrest the concept of sovereignty from the reductive – or perhaps provincial – understanding it has accrued in European political philosophy. Thinking historically or ethnographically, they aim to re-imagine sovereignty in ways that 'release … it from a Western legal concept'.[58] Lenape Indigenous Studies scholar Joanne Barker, for instance, argues that we might consider each articulation of sovereignty in its historical context, insisting that the meaning of sovereignty itself 'is embedded within the specific social relations in which it is invoked and given meaning'.⁵⁹ This may prompt a turn to understand sovereignty through its Indigenous articulations, tracing the ways it is referred to, practised, or made material. Osage anthropologist Jean Dennison pursues this task by turning to Osage nation practice and arguing from this location that entering into the politics of sovereignty may not necessarily mean engaging in a 'zero-sum contest for power' in which the singular sovereign emerges as a sole ruler but rather of being entangled in multiple and 'deeply interconnected' sovereign claims, each of which expresses an authority in 'an ongoing process of engagement with other authorities'.⁶⁰

Closer to Wiradjuri Country, Aileen Moreton-Robinson describes a sense of relationality at the centre of Aboriginal political belonging. But where Graham locates relationality in opposition to sovereignty, Moreton-Robinson thinks them in connection: sovereignty, she writes, 'is grounded within complex relations derived from the intersubstantiation of Ancestral beings, humans and land'.⁶¹ In her relational account, the origins of Indigenous sovereignties are 'in and of the earth', as people and other beings are 'the embodiment of our lands'. Indigenous sovereignties function through what she calls 'the logics of relativity'.⁶² She explains that in Goenpul ontology:

> The structure and form of the land is the fabric of ancestral metamorphosis and activity. Ancestral power and presence permeate the land. In this respect the metamorphosis of ancestral beings into the physiography denotes their and their human descendants' sovereignty.⁶³

We understand Moreton-Robinson to be saying that those creative Ancestors made all life, made Country, and that through the very forms of Country – the rivers, hills, grasses, trees, rocks, human and non-human beings – their presence is passed on today, in the present. In Goenpul ontology, Ancestors 'established the Aboriginal ways of life providing laws for governance, social institutions and human and non-human activity', setting out 'what behavior is and is not allowed'.⁶⁴ They then become Country, become part of the land, where their traces – the signs and stories of their being – remain as a sign of their sovereignty.

For Kombumerri/Munaljahli legal scholar Christine Black, the land might be understood as the source of law; more accurately, she reveals, *'the Land is the Law'*.[65] This is not a sovereignty of supremacy and dominion, but rather a sovereignty in which people and all life, place and law, are created and emerge together in relation. In the words of Wiradjuri playwright and activist Kevin Gilbert, land is 'not merely a source of sustenance but also a living spiritual entity, an inextricable part of the life of the tribe'. The land is the Dreaming, it belongs to people who in turn 'belonged to it – now and forever'.[66] We might think of this understanding of relational sovereignty as a positive transmission of attachment, connecting and transmitting the deep time of Language and Country in the deep present.

These are themes Winch takes up in *The Yield*, in which – for Albert Gondiwindi – it is the richness of language that represents the basis of sovereignty. Language produces law, but it further orders the world through conceptual maps, organising constellations of relationships that are productive of authority, of sovereignty. Stan Grant, Sr and John Rudder note in describing their Wiradjuri dictionary that it is not just words that constitute a language; rather, Language constitutes 'ways of thinking' and modes of classification. Language for them is 'about people, their lives, how they relate to each other and how they live together in the world'. The words are secondary: 'A good speaker of Wiradjuri could actually use some English words and still speak Wiradjuri'.[67] This articulates authority not in a register of purity or authenticity but under the sign of relationship with and as Country.[68] The Language Albert asks us all to speak exemplifies a relational approach to sovereignty; we can read *The Yield* as an extended elaboration of the organisation of authority on Gondiwindi Country

In Albert's dictionary, to take one example, the word for magpie – garru, or wibigang, or dyirigang – is necessary but insufficient for understanding. A simple word (or three) might flatten meaning. The dictionary contains so much more, sharing knowledge in a deeper sense. It tells us that:

Garru is a messenger bird. They can be vicious like the plover but the ancestors said they brought spiritual messages, that the garru love to talk if you can make friends with them. So I tried that, and now they come down here into the garden when they aren't nesting, and I'll say garru nguyaguya milang mudyi – magpie, my beautiful friend – and he'll be calm and gentle. He told me about his ancestor, the first magpie, and about how important it is to protect his babies from the goanna, that's why he is the way he is, and I told him how I understood completely.[69]

Here Albert's story is authorised by the source of knowledge – knowledge of the garru shared with him by his Ancestors. Being in good relation with those Ancestors enables Albert then to be in good relation with the garru – speaking to them in the Language they share through their common belonging in Country – and learn from him a story of the garru's Ancestor, the first magpie, and about the relationship between the magpie, his babies and the goanna. Winch presents this knowledge, representing relationships between the human and more-than-human world, with and in Country, as a basis of authority. Ancestors, magpies and Albert all speak, and they speak of law, of proper disposition and of Country. This organisation of relationships grounds Language in Ancestral knowledge, in turn grounding authority in the deep time of Gondiwindi or Wiradjuri Country.

A Gondiwindi/Wiradjuri sovereignty emerges, then, as a force, experience, or sensation of relational being, with Language at its centre. It is a sovereignty counterposed to Western sovereignty. In the epigraph to *The Yield*, the Christian Saint, Augustine, who shares a part of his name with August Gondiwindi, asks: 'In the absence of justice, what is sovereignty but organised robbery?' These words suggest both a critique of rapacious colonising sovereignty and the possibility of a more just and moral model. In multiple voices speaking in relation, *The Yield* presents an extended elaboration of this possibility. Wiradjuri scholar Wendy Brady describes a 'sovereign Indigenous nation [that] is formed through the ancestral and communal relationship', practising a sovereignty in which 'each individual is part of the fabric of both authority and power that is interdependent on the other'.[70] This interdependence is not restricted to the individual people who live in Country today but extends, as we have seen, both to more-than-human beings and to Ancestors who may not be alive in the strict sense of the word but who are entirely present, constituting each moment as a deep present.

This relational sovereignty of the deep present may at times appear to be submerged by an ongoing invasion and colonisation. We have argued that, as well as telling truths about traumas suffered by Indigenous people in this colonial context, *The Yield* is also a novel of hope and repair. Hope, here, is to be found in the enduring presence of sovereignty and the ongoing capacity of the Gondiwindis and others to live accordingly. Within the novel's narrative, August begins to heal from the burden of grief and loss she has carried since losing Jedda, not only her sister but a 'witness' to her life, someone who 'saw' and validated her.[71] This healing comes in part from recognising that Jedda is not 'gone forever', 'extinct', like the black rhino, but will 'always be, exist' – ngiyawaygunhanha – that 'a person exists beyond the living and the dead'.[72] Like the Ancestors, Jedda lives on forever, in the form of the dancing brolga, the burralgang.[73]

Repair also comes through August's return to her Country, which facilitates a sense of connection and reawakens her capacity to take on her relational responsibilities. What gives her hope is her realisation that 'there was an expanse behind her, their lives meant something, their lives were huge. Thousands of years'.[74] There, or 'here', she found that instead of 'living her life in a box of to-do … she cared about something and her family for the first time in forever'.[75] The importance of narrative comes to the fore; unlike a simple list, plotting events into the form of a story produces moral meaning.[76] Awakening 'from a stony sleep' she 'find[s] herself standing on the edge of something larger than she'd ever been able to see before'.[77] This glimpse of Everywhen is made possible by both August and Jedda's returns, but also by Albert's awareness of the importance of memory and its transmission. Alert to the fragility of Language in a context of colonisation, of its vulnerability to being buried, ploughed over and forgotten, like the bones of the Aboriginal people from the mission, Albert created a durable archive of Wiradjuri.[78] He did so by committing his memory of the Language to transmissible cultural forms – to writing and recording – thereby bequeathing Wiradjuri to future generations.

When August visits the Historic Museum Australia, we learn that she shares Albert's sense that 'pass[ing] on everything that was ever remembered' is 'urgent'.[79] Poppy wrote in his dictionary that 'once you find a piece of something you know about, afterwards you end up getting given more and more pieces of the puzzle everywhere you go'.[80] August wanted to tell the museum people 'that something was stolen from a place inland … that she thought they should understand it was all so urgent now, to tell them that she wasn't extinct … All the hidden pieces were being put back together, she wanted to say'.[81] Her awakening to the 'deep past' of the Gondiwindi comes from learning that Gondiwindi artefacts are in the museum, that they evidence Gondiwindi domestication of animals, construction of fisheries and milling techniques dating back 18 000 years.[82] These are pieces of a puzzle that is given shape by learning that Poppy has recorded the Language with all its stories of the Ancestors, and drafted a native title claim that, in the novel, promises to interrupt the mine and secure a Gondiwindi future on Country.

The 'sole statue' in Massacre is of 'a soldier in metal regalia, draped in ammunition and slouch-hatted, leant against his gun', cared for by a council worker with grace and respect.[83] The statue of the Anzac war hero, a familiar presence across the Australian memorial landscape, is 'a tangible, material [form of] heritage through which … [colonial] settlers assert their presence and claim to belonging and "ownership"'.[84] Gondiwindi memory endures these claims of colonising possession. Albert has learned the importance of translating story to tangible cultural forms that can be transmitted to future generations, although that tangible form of heritage exists to share intangible forms. As August and Joey write in the foreword to Poppy's dictionary, which they printed out for local kids: 'Maybe you are looking for a bench, or a statue by the banks of the Murrumby to honour the people who have lived by the river. Better, there is water returning, nudging what was dead. Better the burral-gang congregate here often. Better these words and better we are still here and that we speak them'.[85] Through the act of printing and distributing the dictionary, August and Joey actively transmit memory of the deep past to present generations, to the burral-gang, to Country. Through her act of writing *The Yield*, Winch shares Language that conveys stories of Ancestors that have been passed on through the generations, through Country. In so doing she is working to ensure that Wiradjuri lives today and can be lived in Country, in relationship with these stories.[86] *The Yield*, then, not only represents processes of recording and transmitting the memory of the deep past; it gives that world imaginative and material form for readers today. In activating memory from the deep past to the colonial past, and rendering the settler colonial present as also a deep Wiradjuri present, Winch communicates Indigenous temporalities and ontologies, grounding Indigenous sovereignties in the present.

11

A PLACE FOR A STRANGER
The Wardandi history of Thomas Timothée Vasse

Mary Blight

Early in 1801, when Western Australia was still thought to be an island separate to the eastern half of the country,[1] a French expedition arrived at Geographe Bay, Wardandi Noongar Country, in the southwest of Western Australia.[2] During ten days of exploration, a seaman called Thomas Timothée Vasse was washed away and presumed drowned. Two hundred years later, in 2001, Vasse's great-nephew Alain Serieyx published a book, *Wonnerup the Sacred Dune*, imagining what his life would have been like if he had survived. A postface in the book by Wardandi Traditional Owner Bill Webb states that his people hold an oral history of when Vasse lived with them.[3] Bill Webb notes that Serieyx, not realising that Wardandi people still live on Country, did not consult them when writing his book.[4] Bill Webb invites anyone interested in this oral history to visit the Wardan Centre at Injidup in the south-west of Western Australia.[5] Hoping to redress this gap in the historiography of the Baudin expedition, I visited Bill on 21 August 2021. The interview with Bill included a drive to where Wardandi people first saw Vasse in 1801, and the location where he later died. Bill gives permission for this information to be incorporated into a discussion of Vasse's fate and I am grateful for his generosity in sharing it.[6]

This story highlights how local Indigenous people continue to carry out their obligations to Country and to those who died there. This is a vital element of their Law and the sovereignty over deep time and into the present. Aboriginal author Tony Birch has pointed out that 'a sovereign right to land and the interpretation of the past in Australia are inextricably linked'.[7] Indigenous oral histories like this demonstrate the sovereignty of traditions, beliefs and knowledge, which existed before settler invasion of Country or boodjar. In Wardandi oral tradition, the coming of Europeans to Wardandi boodjar had been predicted. Bill explained that:

> My dad he said, 'It was said to us for thousands and thousands of years there would come a man to this land one day who would shape and change it out of all recognition. He is not a sharer, he's not a carer and he will never ever put back the things he has damaged. And overnight he will turn the place into desert.' So overnight is like, what, 180 years. There's a third more desert added to Australia.[8]

When I asked him why Wardandi people looked after Vasse he replied:

> I think we were inquisitive. We knew for thousands and thousands of years that they were going to be here some time or other and it's more like that inquisitiveness, 'Oh they have finally arrived. What are they, who are they? Are they the ones where the prophecy said the men would come to the land and wreck it?' So, we were standing about going, 'Are these the ones?' There was the French first. We were going 'Are these the ones?'[9]

Wardandi people are Bibbulmun people and therefore part of the Noongar Language group, whose society is based on kinship systems, rather than acquisition and ownership of land. Noongar academic Len Collard says that according to this world view:

> People simply did not arrive in another person's *kaleep* [hearth or fire] and assert ownership unless they had some form of relationship with that land in a previous existence.[10]

The word 'wardan' in Noongar means ocean, and Wardandi are therefore ocean people. In the early 1800s, Noongar people believed that their loved ones would return after death from the ocean in the west, from a place called Kuranup, and would look white.[11] Noongar scholar Dr Len Collard and Dave Palmer have explained how Wardandi people would have thought that the 'coastal explorers were djanga or returned spirits of their noitj moort or dead relatives coming home again'.[12] Wirloman Noongar academic Clint Bracknell points out that Kuranup is connected to the concept of the Dreaming, or the Everywhen, showing 'the importance of coastal landscapes in perpetuating Noongar understandings of space and time'.[13]

After James Stirling established the Swan River Colony in 1829, many Noongar people initially welcomed British colonial settlers as djanga.[14] Bracknell identifies this as a 'historical practice of finding a place for strangers', and evidence of 'a relationality integral to Noongar time concepts', reaching back over thousands of years.[15] In 1801, the arrival from the west of two French ships conformed with this world view. Bill Webb confirmed that the Wardandi considered the French explorers to be returned relatives:

> We call that the djanga, the dead. Because when we die, we ash them a little bit. We thought all our dead were coming back. So, they came ashore, and they did their research.[16]

Therefore, two longstanding Noongar worldviews, a prophecy that a new, destructive man would appear on Wardandi boodjar, and a belief that the dead would return from kuranup, out on the ocean, with a white appearance, shaped the way that Wardandi people dealt with the Baudin expedition when it arrived on boodjar, thirty years before the Swan River colony was established in Western Australia.

This oral history, as told by Bill Webb, comes from his Ancestral grandmother, Elizabeth Hill, born in 1850, who passed the story down to her many children.[17] She was told this history by her mother Kammingurt, a Wardandi yok (woman) who was born around 1829.[18] Len Collard and Dave Palmer have commented on how important 'story, song and performance' are in Noongar culture and family life.[19] In 2001, at Margaret River in the south-west of Western Australia, Bill's mother Vilma Webb, along with dramaturge Margot Edwards, director Phil Thompson and Noongar actor Kelton Pell, staged a two-act play called the *Deadwater Chant*. The play, developed on Country under Vilma's guidance, dramatised the story of Vasse and Wardandi oral history about his time at Geographe Bay.[20] Linda Barwick has commented on how 'Indigenous embodied practices of knowing' can, when the past is remembered and re-enacted, make 'all history "now"'.[21] Bracknell concurs, saying that this connection to the past via performance creates 'collapsing notions of time', making the past present and creating a 'temporal transcendence'.[22] The history of Vasse is another strand added to Wardandi knowledge, showing an ongoing obligation from Deep History times to care for strangers.

Exclusive use of written archives in Australian history privileges colonial narratives and leads to incomplete histories. The Wardandi history about Thomas Timothée Vasse introduces a cross-cultural and corrective dimension to the historiography of the Baudin expedition, bringing it to life, and adding a vividness and richness to its narrative. Settler George Fletcher Moore discussed the Wardandi oral history about Vasse in 1838.[23] Recent books about the Baudin expedition discuss Moore's 1838 report, with Jean Fornasiero et al. considering it a 'local myth' and Paul Gibbard noting that it 'endures in Wardandi oral history'.[24] Graham Seal says that Moore did not see Vasse's bones in 1838, and deems the story probably not true.[25] On the other hand, Noongar academic Len Collard says that the story of Vasse is 'one of the earliest accounts of Nyungar helping a European'.[26] Whereas Brendan Cullity, a vigneron from the south-west of Western Australia, says the reluctance to accept this oral history is due to several reasons: Moore was informed of it thirty-seven years after the Baudin expedition arrived, disbelief that he could speak enough Noongar to find out this information, and suspicion that Wardandi people were lying.[27] Vasse's disappearance is therefore a mere footnote in many books and writings on the Baudin expedition and yet this Wardandi oral history adds a new dimension to its historiography by challenging the idea that Vasse drowned at Geographe Bay.[28] Parallel with Narungga, Kaurna, Ngarrindjeri academic Lester Rigney's principles of Indigenist research, here I aim to centre a Wardandi voice, allowing presentation of an overlooked history.[29] I delineate this Wardandi history and how Moore came across it, investigating and correlating it with archival research to show its contribution to the history of the Baudin expedition.

How Vasse was left behind by the Baudin Expedition

The Baudin expedition arrived at Geographe Bay in Western Australia on 30 May 1801 at the start of the Noongar season of Makuru, winter, remaining there for ten days.[30] Their ships were the *Géographe*, captained by expedition leader Nicolas Baudin, and the *Naturaliste*, under the command of Jacques Félix Emmanuel Hamelin. The expedition had a large cohort of scientists – including zoologists, astronomers and botanists, among others – under instructions to study the Indigenous peoples of New Holland.[31] In mid-1800, Thomas Timothée Vasse, assistant helmsman on the *Naturaliste*, had left an administrative job in France with the Ministry of Finance, joining the Baudin expedition under Hamelin without his family's knowledge.[32] Baudin had problems managing his crew for the entirety of this troubled voyage. Hamelin thought of leaving Vasse behind at Île de France (Mauritius) 'for some misconduct', but changed his mind when too many other crew members quit during the stopover there.[33] After several days spent measuring the depth of water in Geographe Bay, scientists and sailors went ashore on 4 June 1801. Two groups explored the area, having several cautious and curious encounters with Wardandi people. Yawuru academic Shino Konishi has discussed the Baudin expedition and the emotional reaction of the French explorers to Wardandi boodjar (Country), offering significant insights into cross-cultural encounters.[34] Naturalist François Péron came across a sacred grove by the river, with a garlanded tree at the centre, saying that its 'majesty and reverence' inspired 'sweet emotions' as he stood there.[35] The French made many useful observations of the landscape managed by firestick farming, noting signs that a much larger group of Wardandi people than they had encountered were resident in the area.[36]

At the end of the day on 5 June, due to carelessness and stormy weather, the *Géographe*'s longboat sank near the shore, leaving a group of scientists stranded for two days. The expedition's efforts then turned from exploration to rescue. Baudin suffered great anxiety, watching from the *Géographe* as Hamelin and the crew struggled to both locate those stuck onshore and retrieve the wrecked longboat.[37] While Hamelin was occupied, Pierre Bernard Milius, second in command, took charge of the *Naturaliste*.[38] Alexandre Le Bas de Sainte Croix (known as Le Bas) was the officer responsible for the longboat when it sank, and Baudin sent him with a team of men ashore to work on its retrieval. Eventually, at 3 o'clock on the morning of 8 June, Baudin, realising that the longboat could not be saved, sent rowboats from the *Géographe* and *Naturaliste* to bring everyone back onboard, including the stranded scientists.[39] Le Bas and his crew returned to the *Géographe* through difficult seas.[40] He reported his failure to retrieve the longboat to a displeased Baudin, who remained silent, 'for his condition did not permit' the reprimand on Baudin's lips.

The next day, 9 June 1801, Milius, stuck aboard the *Naturaliste*, became curious to see what was happening. He decided to go ashore with a rowboat crew that included Vasse and Léon Brèvedent. Watching from the *Géographe*, Baudin assumed that Milius went for 'amusement'.[41] As Milius approached the coast, a squall came through, overturning the rowboat and nearly drowning everyone. Luckily, the crew and boat were washed ashore.[42] Brèvedent noted that they then had to drag the rowboat nearly eight miles to relaunch it.[43] Arriving where the longboat had sunk, and drenched to the skin, Milius was astonished to find just one crewman from the *Géographe* present. Weapons, equipment and clothing were scattered onshore. Not realising that Le Bas had already departed, Milius thought the crew had gone into the forest to collect wood. According to Milius's journal, his men, thinking of old adventure stories they had heard, speculated that the Wardandi had eaten their friends.[44] This was despite Wardandi people leaving the scientists strictly alone for the two days they had been stranded ashore, so this idea reflects prejudices the French carried against Indigenous peoples. Milius calmed his crew as they checked the forest. Finding no-one, he realised that Le Bas and crew must have returned to the *Géographe*, hidden in the mist and rain. Night was falling, the weather worsening, and it was now clear that it would be difficult for Milius and his men to return to the *Naturaliste*. Crew on the *Naturaliste* noticed this perilous situation and sent a rowboat to retrieve them.[45] Baudin saw the two rowboats from the *Naturaliste* approaching the shore and gave orders that 'port fires' be lit on the *Geographe*, signalling its location every quarter hour. The *Naturaliste* also 'set off rockets every now and then' to help this new group stranded ashore to locate it.[46]

The weather worsened as they tried to retrieve Milius and his crew. Some could swim, plunging into 8-foot-high waves to bring ropes from the rowboats to those waiting on the shore. One by one the crew were pulled out to the boats, as waves loomed over their heads, pounding the shore.[47] Brèvedent saw everyone else fastening the rope under their arms before being hauled out, but Vasse considered himself a strong swimmer and refused to do so.[48] While being dragged out to the boat, Vasse lost hold of the rope. Milius saw him tumble in the waves and become buried in the sand. Two men onshore, still awaiting their turn, searched for him, to no avail. Eventually the boats departed, with Milius regretting that he could not save this 'excellent mariner' while lamenting the fact that he had lost a hunting dog on this ill-fated trip.[49] Breton, a crewman of the *Géographe*, noted in his journal that Vasse was drunk.[50]

Milius returned to the *Géographe*, reporting Vasse's disappearance to a disapproving Baudin. The arduous trip back to the *Géographe* had given Milius a high fever, and he was so fatigued he could barely speak. Baudin allowed him to rest and then sent him back to the *Naturaliste*, ensuring that lanterns were on the rigging to guide him.[51] It was now late in the day of 9 June 1801, and Baudin was extremely worried about the safety of the ships. They were too close to shore, and he had never seen the barometer so low, indicating that the storm was intensifying. The wind howled, the rain lashed down, and waves pounded through the forecastle of the *Géographe*. Both ships put up as much sail as possible, moving away from the shore, no longer visible due to the rain and mist.⁵² Baudin later noted that the loss of Vasse was caused by the 'rashness of two officers', saying that Vasse 'least deserved' to be a victim of these misfortunes.⁵³ He named the location *L'Anse des Maladroits* (The Inlet of the Clumsy), a name that did not stick, as the area is known as Wonnerup Inlet today.⁵⁴ And so, the Baudin expedition left Geographe Bay, assuming that Vasse had drowned.

Wardandi oral history concerning Vasse

Bill Webb's oral history concerning Vasse comes from his Ancestor, Elizabeth Hill, daughter of Kammingurt, who told her this oral tradition. Deep History research looks at Indigenous histories going back many thousands of years.⁵⁵ According to Patrick Nunn and Nicholas Reid, the wealth of deep time histories held by Indigenous peoples in Australia is considered 'exceptional' when compared to other oral traditions around the world.⁵⁶ There are many examples in Noongar oral traditions, as Wirloman Noongar academic Clint Bracknell has noted, such as Wardandi yok Ngilginan who spoke to ethnographer Daisy Bates of the nyitting or cold time, likely referring to the ice age which finished 15 000 years ago.⁵⁷ There is a Wardandi oral history of the time when the sea levels rose at Cowaramup Bay in Western Australia as the ice age ended, told by Bill Webb's father George Webb.⁵⁸ This aligns with research by Nunn and Reid on inundation stories around Australia dating back to the sea-level rise that occurred 7000 years ago.⁵⁹ David Rose has pointed out that Indigenous society in Australia was based on reciprocity, rather than competition, leading to a conservative society of great stability, maximising the 'precision of replication' of culture.⁶⁰ Nunn and Reid go on to say that this culturally conservative approach means that people are given the authority of learning a story so that they can tell it the 'right way', leading to great accuracy as it is passed down the generations.⁶¹ Oral histories, according to scholar Martha Rose Beard, who is working on an Irish oral history archive, are 'performed', showing subjective aspects of the history recounted.⁶² Bill Webb related the oral history to me in a narrative style, with a solemnity conveying its significance in Wardandi history.

Here is Bill Webb's oral history of what occurred the day after Vasse was left behind:

> Our ancestral grandmother was out walking along the beach, and he was on the beach the next morning. And so, they looked after him. The women were nurturing him more because he wouldn't go off hunting and gathering with the blokes. They would give him separate supplies of food and that. And he only had a few possessions. I don't know what he had. His bag maybe. He'd make sure that was his, his last little memory of being left here. They looked after him, but he always wandered to the beach to see if any boats were coming.[63]

> To our knowledge he was about three years with us.[64]

Bill Webb described a large meeting with other clans, held every four years, that Wardandi would attend. Vasse had been with the Wardandi for around three years when the next meeting was due:

> Every four years the three nations would gather together. The Wongi and the Yamatji and the Bibbulmun. We are the Bibbulmun nation, not Noongar. There is an area at Wave Rock. Like any government we would meet there to determine the laws and customs in those three nations. Acknowledge each other and stuff.[65]

The distance from Wardandi Country or boodjar to Wave Rock is around 415 kilometres, a significant journey to undertake. Due to his anxious vigil for the Baudin expedition, Vasse refused to go with the Wardandi. Later, while returning to their boodjar, Wardandi people discovered his body:

> When they came back, they must have gone up along the coast and went up from Augusta towards Cape Naturaliste. Then when

they came into the bay and started walking along, they found
Timothy Vasse had died on the beach. Near what we call the
Whale Tree. So, they found him there, but they just left him there.
They thought 'we better leave him here because his mob will come
back and get him'. So, when the English came down to the area,
they told them about it and then we don't know what happened to
Timothy Vasse.[66]

Bill is unaware of what happened to Vasse's bones after Wardandi people told colonial settlers about them:

I think they must just have got it out of the way you know. So, we
don't know what happened to him. He was just rotted away, his
bones and that; but his jacket, you know. We said, 'Hey one of
your mob there, we left him for you to come pick up'. 'Course they
didn't come and get him. That's the story of Timothy.[67]

While showing the location where Vasse died, Bill said:

See that last big tree there? That's where his remains were
discovered in the sand dunes. That's where they found him. So, it's
the Whale Tree but it's also Timothy Vasse's final resting place. We
must have gone down across the Barrabup and then back along the
coast here and as we came down through here to go to Wonnerup
they saw him on the beach. I think he must have perished from
the lack of food when they left. Because he relied on the women to
feed him all the time. He would walk from Wonnerup all the way
through to Kerajenninginup, that's Cape Naturaliste.[68]

It should be noted that the area Bill Webb indicated as where Vasse first appeared is near where the longboat sank, correlating with where Milius and his crew were rescued. Bill Webb's knowledge of the locations where his Ancestors first saw Vasse and where he died, and the importance to him of showing them to me, reflects Barwick's idea that, for Indigenous peoples, the past is 'ever-present within the landscape'.[70] While the

A place for a stranger

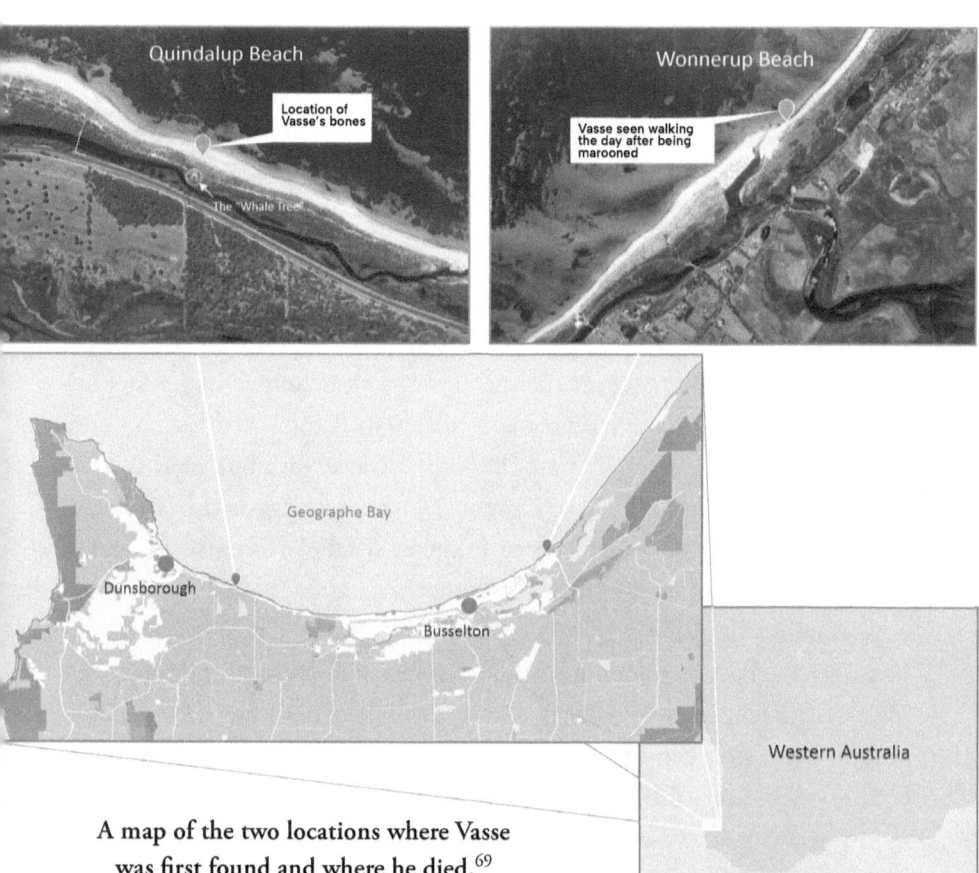

A map of the two locations where Vasse
was first found and where he died.[69]
Illustration: Sam Blight

history being related here is linear, with its dates and sequence of events, it is essentially one of a relationship with this stranger, Vasse, who came ashore on Wardandi boodjar and lived and died there.

Bill Webb knew that the Baudin expedition did return two years after Vasse was marooned:

> It was about two years later that one boat came back and it was a hazy sort of day. I don't know whether they could see that he was on the beach or whether he was doing something else. But he was always there. He would walk all the way to Cape Naturaliste. He might not have been on alert by that time. It being a bit hazy as well, they just went on through.

Indeed, in March 1803, the *Geographe*, and its new consort ship the *Casuarina*, returned to Geographe Bay, heading home to France.[71] On the evening of 10 March 1803, they moored near where the longboat had sunk and, according to scientist Péron, everyone looked at the beach, thinking of Vasse. Two fires, larger than those seen on their first visit in 1801, sent up smoke near the shore. The weather was fine and the sea calm, inviting 'a search – fruitless, perhaps, but at least easy, as well as sacred' according to Péron.[72] He added that everyone felt sad when Baudin ordered their departure the next day, without going ashore.[73] Konishi has commented on how emotional Péron's writing is, and how it has been seen as 'hyperbolic and extravagant', but in this case one wonders what would have happened if his feelings had been acted upon.[74] A journal entry by officer François-Michel Ronsard, however, does not mention Vasse, commenting that the carcases of several whales were floating in the water when they arrived, and a boat was sent to investigate. They anchored overnight, but it was misty, and the coast was obscured. Ronsard reports that at 6 am the next day they set sail, and around 8 am they came to the location of their last anchorage, two years before, on 9 June 1801. The French then realised the previous night's mooring was near where the longboat had sunk. Not wanting to retrace his steps, Baudin pressed on.[75]

After returning to France in 1804, Péron, Louis de Freycinet and others authored a book on the Baudin expedition, with the first part published in 1807.[76] During this time, a newspaper article appeared stating that Vasse had somehow survived the fury of the sea, living with an Indigenous group for two or three years. He had then appeared 300 or 400 miles south and met an American boat. The article claimed that Vasse had been arrested on board by the crew of an English cruiser, taken to England and detained. Péron and his friends asked the Navy Minister to investigate this rumour and he found it to be false.[77] Still certain that Vasse had drowned, Péron and his companions produced maps and reports of the expedition, naming the river near where he had been lost the Vasse River.[78] Vasse's parents were not informed of his presumed death until 1808, and his father refused to believe it, sure, until his death, that his son lived in America.[79] This was despite the first volume of the Baudin expedition discussing Vasse's presumed drowning.

The idea that Vasse survived was compelling. Rumours in France of his survival against all the odds, several years after his disappearance, and his father's conviction that he had gone to America, show a horror of being left behind in a remote part of the world, with no hope of returning home. The information from Bill Webb about Vasse living with Wardandi people for around three years adds to the poignancy of the story, as he may still have been alive when the Baudin expedition came through Geographe Bay in 1803. While discussing this, Bill Webb shivered as he contemplated how close Vasse may have been to rescue by his compatriots.

The colonial settlers find out about Vasse's survival

The next episode concerns how Wardandi people told colonist George Fletcher Moore in 1838 of Vasse's survival and subsequent death. The Vasse district at Geographe Bay, as it was now known, was colonised by the Bussell family and others in 1834, subsequent to the colonisation of the Swan River colony in 1829. After their invasion of Wardandi boodjar in 1834, settlers quickly became antagonistic toward Wardandi people, due to settlers occupying Wardandi Country without negotiation or treaty.[80] In September 1835, settlers fired upon Wardandi people for taking an axe.[81] In June and July of 1837, a massacre of Wardandi people was led by several Bussell brothers (Charles, Vernon, Lenox and Alfred),[82] assisted by district constable Elijah Dawson, soldiers of the 21st regiment and other settlers.[83]

In 1838, Advocate General for the Swan River Colony, George Fletcher Moore, travelled to King George's Sound on 'a most unpleasant duty' as Advocate General.[84] Moore was very interested in Noongar Language, and studied it seriously from 1833, becoming a fluent speaker and producing a Noongar dictionary.[85] During this voyage, Moore visited the Leschenault, Vasse and Augusta districts. At the Vasse settlement

Wardandi people informed him that they remembered Thomas Timothée Vasse being left behind by the Baudin expedition. Moore noted in his diary:

> Some natives of that neighbourhood recollect him. They treated him kindly and fed him, but he lingered on the seacoast, looking out for his vessel. He gradually became very thin from anxiety, exposure, and poor diet. At last, the natives were absent for a time on a hunting expedition, and on their return they found him dead on the beach, his body much swollen (as they described it) – perhaps dropsical.[86]

The Wardandi people who talked to Moore offered to take him to see Vasse's bones, but his ship was about to depart. Moore noted that the location of Vasse's bones was at Wonnerup, a place with 'only two settlers with their establishments, and some soldiers' and that the Bussell settlement was six miles south of the location indicated.[87] Upon his return to Perth, he wrote to the *Perth Gazette* in May 1838, discussing the Wardandi oral history about Vasse. He summarised the history of the Baudin expedition, the circumstances in which Vasse was lost, and how Wardandi people cared for him. Moore said Wardandi people had 'treated him kindly and relieved his wants to the extent of their power by giving him fish and other food' but he daily became 'weril weril (thin thin)'. He noted that Vasse's 'remains had not been disturbed, even for the purpose of burial, and the bones are yet to be seen'.[88]

The violent history of the colonisation of the Vasse explains why Wardandi people would have told Moore, a visitor, about Vasse, rather than the settler families living in the area. Due to his expertise in Noongar Language, George Fletcher Moore was regarded as a dependable informant on Noongar people. In October 1836, he accompanied Colonial Surveyor Septimus Roe on an expedition, searching northwards to Shark Bay for an inland sea, when he heard a report about it by Noongar people.[89] In October 1837, after Lieutenant Bunbury and settlers at York, east of Perth, perpetrated a punitive expedition against Balladong Noongar people during July and August, Moore was sent to York to announce, in Noongar, that hostilities were at an end, and there would be no more killing.⁹⁰ Georgiana Molloy, an avid collector of botanical specimens at Augusta and the Vasse, is known to have used Wardandi people as guides for this work.⁹¹ By 1838, however, the Molloys had not yet moved from Augusta to the Vasse district. Ever since their invasion of his land at Geographe Bay, the situation between settlers, including the Bussell family, and Wardandi birdiya (leader) Gaywal was tense. Settler John Garrett Bussell understood some Noongar, but did not think that Noongar Language was more than a primitive collection of words, which author William Lines has pointed out led to 'a lack of interest' in what Wardandi people had to say.⁹² This, plus the many violent incidents following settlement of the area, including the massacre in 1837, may be the reason that Wardandi people turned to an outsider, George Fletcher Moore, to communicate their knowledge about Vasse.

In April 1841, Georgiana Molloy, wife of Captain Molloy, now Resident Magistrate of the Vasse district, wrote a letter to a friend in England. She said that a Dr Carr,⁹³ recently arrived in Australind, was down at the Vasse district 'to reclaim the Bones of Mons. Vasse, the Gentm. from whom this river takes its name', guided by Wardandi people.⁹⁴ She stated that Wardandi people had seized and killed Vasse, an idea not supported by George Fletcher Moore in 1838 or by Bill Webb's oral history. She said 'some society in Paris' had commissioned Dr Carr to retrieve the bones.⁹⁵ Dr Carr returned to England aboard the *Parkfield* on 21 April 1841, but it is unknown whether he had Vasse's remains with him.⁹⁶

In February 1841, two months before Dr Carr visited the Vasse district, a larger massacre of Wardandi people had occurred at Geographe Bay. Known today as the Wonnerup massacre, it was led by the Bussell brothers: John, Charles, Vernon and Alfred (Lenox was, by then, too unwell mentally to join them).⁹⁷ Resident Magistrate Captain John Molloy, with the participation of soldiers of the 51st regiment and other settlers, were involved.⁹⁸ The massacre was an aggressive response to the spearing death of settler George Layman by Wardandi leader Gaywal at Wonnerup, after many years of settler violence towards Gaywal's family. Following this, the fact that surviving Wardandi people later helped

Dr Carr to search for Vasse's bones in April of 1841 demonstrates strong feelings of obligation towards Vasse, a stranger who died on Wardandi boodjar.[99] The survival of the Wardandi history of Vasse, after these violent events, also shows the strength of this oral history tradition. In 1865, demonstrating the continuation of this history, ethnographer Augustus Oldfield reported that Wardandi people told him, during a visit to the area, that Vasse had 'lived many years among them' and had 'self-died'.[100]

In accordance with a prophecy going back thousands of years, the arrival of the Baudin expedition in late May 1801 on Wardandi boodjar at Geographe Bay in Western Australia was expected by Wardandi people. The arrival of a pale man, from the ocean, where kuranup is located, also conformed with Wardandi beliefs about the return of loved ones after death. Thomas Timothée Vasse was the first stranger to remain on the shores of Wardandi boodjar, left behind by the Baudin expedition in 1801. He was followed within thirty-four years by the English, who stayed this time, beginning the foretold environmental destruction of Wardandi boodjar that continues today. Wardandi Traditional Owner Bill Webb's information that there was a prediction for 'thousands of years' that strangers would come who would try to destroy Wardandi boodjar explains continuing Wardandi interest in the story of Vasse.[101]

Survival of the Wardandi oral history about Vasse is an example of the continuity of Wardandi Noongar culture, heritage and sovereignty, despite the violent colonisation by settlers of Wardandi boodjar. As shown in this chapter, the Wardandi oral history was told to settler George Fletcher Moore in 1838, and again to Augustus Oldfield in 1865. More recently, it has been told to me by Bill Webb. Without this Wardandi oral history, there is no information that Vasse survived and Wardandi people cared for him, revealing the gap it fills in the historiography of the Baudin expedition. The power of this history should be heard, and to ignore it would be to ignore Wardandi sovereignty on boodjar. Indigenous voices should be included in Australian historical research, and this Wardandi history adds interest, poignancy and new information concerning the Baudin expedition. Jackie Huggins says that for 'Aboriginal people, our past is still our present'.[102] Wardandi people still remember Thomas

Timothée Vasse, telling his history as a castaway to those interested, part of a strong, living culture today. This demonstrates the sovereignty Wardandi people have always held over Country, and its accompanying and continuing obligations to those who live among them.

Acknowledgments

The oral history component of this chapter was provided by Bill Webb, a Traditional Wardandi Owner, and his contribution to this research is gratefully acknowledged. The advice and guidance of Dr Paul Gibbard of the French Studies department and Professor Len Collard at the School of Indigenous Studies at University of Western Australia is also gratefully acknowledged.

PART V
Walking as a practice of sovereignty

12

MURRUDHA: SOVEREIGN WALKS: TRACKING CULTURAL ACTIONS THROUGH ART, COUNTRY, LANGUAGE AND MUSIC

Brenda L Croft, with First Nations Community members: Sue and Coral Bulger; Wendy Bunn; Cheryl, Michelle and Kobi Davison; Brenda Gifford; Shane Herrington; Leah House; Matilda House-Williams; Lois Peeler; Bronwyn Penrith; Maria Walker; Iris Walker-White and others

'Murrudha' is a Wiradyuri term meaning 'on track'.[1] Australian First Nations pathways are sites of embodied sovereign actions, and walking enables corporeal and customary engagement with Country; reimagining and reinvigorating journeys and customary acts, ways of being since time immemorial. Walking represents the inter-temporality and spatiality of Indigenous cosmologies, which colonisation disrupted but did not erase.

The ongoing colonial practices of displacement, dismissal and denial of Indigenous rights continues to severely affect Australian First Nations communities. The inspiration for '*Murrudha: Sovereign Walks* – tracking cultural actions through art, Country, language and music' (hereafter *Murrudha: Sovereign Walks*) was an indirect outcome of my creative-led PhD project, which closely engaged with my patrilineal Gurindji Community, and specifically the Wave Hill Walk-Off Route, site of a sustained protest and a significant turning point in Aboriginal land rights struggles – the route formally placed on the National Heritage List in 2007.[2]

I have always been interested in knowing more and engaging with the traditional custodians on whose homelands I live, work and travel through, which is a key element of Critical Indigenous Studies/Theories. As such, I considered that the walk undertaken in May 1927 by traditional custodians from Brungle Aboriginal Community over the Brindabella Ranges so that they could be *present* at the opening of the newly constructed Parliament House in Canberra warranted the same official acknowledgement.

Murrudha: Sovereign Walks aims to track cultural actions through art, Country, Language and music. I led the project together with non-Indigenous Professor James Pittock of the Fenner School of Environment and Society at ANU, the project commenced in 2020 and will run through until at least 2026.[3]

The team works in close consultation, development and engagement with respective First Nations Community members and organisations associated with the project's cultural and geographical remit, including Ngambri/Ngunawal/Walgalu Peoples from the Canberra region, Walgalu/Wiradyuri Peoples in the Brungle/Gundagai/Tumut region and surrounds; Meneroo/Ngarigo/Ngarigu Peoples of the High Country in the Snowy Mountains, and Dharawal/Dhurga/Djirringanj/Walbunja/Yuin Peoples ranging from the coastal areas of La Perouse to the Far South Coast of New South Wales.

Additionally, there are cultural connections across the Victorian border to members of the Yorta Yorta Community. Disciplines encompass Indigenous Knowledge-Holders, performing and visual arts practitioners; those involved in storytelling/storywork, Language reclamation and reinvigoration; Elders and Youth; and academics and Community-based practitioners.

The project's framework is grounded in culturally respectful inclusivity, and our goal is to have continuing discussions and disseminate information with respective First Nations communities for the life of the project, and beyond.

Murrudha: Sovereign Walks historical framework

The Meneroo/Ngarigo/Ngarigu women in 1834, Molonglo/Ngarigo/ Ngunnawal woman Nellie Hamilton and her Countrywomen in 1873, Wiradyuri walamira (clever man) Nangar and Ooloogan in 1927, and other Australian First Nations Peoples' individual and collective acts of walking in, on and through Country are embodied Indigenous sovereign actions of self-determination.

These culturally performative acts of literal and symbolic Indigenous sovereignty justify national recognition by all, particularly given that these feats of cultural maintenance and transmission have been disrupted by the ongoing un/settler colonial project of displacement.[4]

Murrudha: Sovereign Walks considers how the *act* of walking in, on and through Country – traditional sovereign homelands never ceded – can be re/memorialised and reinvigorated by and for respective First Nations communities, with support from non-Indigenous allies.

The ANU Murrudha team, in consultation with relevant First Nations family and Community members, is proposing to nominate these journeys as sites of national cultural significance on Australia's National Heritage List, with the first nomination being the Nangar/Ooloogan walk from Brungle to Canberra in time for its centenary anniversary in 2027.[5] The outcome of the 2024/25 nomination will determine future nominations – the 1873 Queanbeyan to Cooma journey, and the 1834 Lhotsky trek from Canberra up into Ngarigo/Meneroo High Country homelands.

The infinite links – across Ancestral time and space – of these three pathways incorporates Indigenous communal positionalities, spatialities and temporalities. These pathways exemplify what has come to be called the 'Everywhen' – simultaneously embodying these respective communities' Ancestral past, their present and their futures.

Since the earliest days of colonial contact, there are well-documented examples of First Nations peoples undertaking sovereign actions of walking their Country. *Murrudha: Sovereign Walks* draws inspiration from three historical events, as follows:

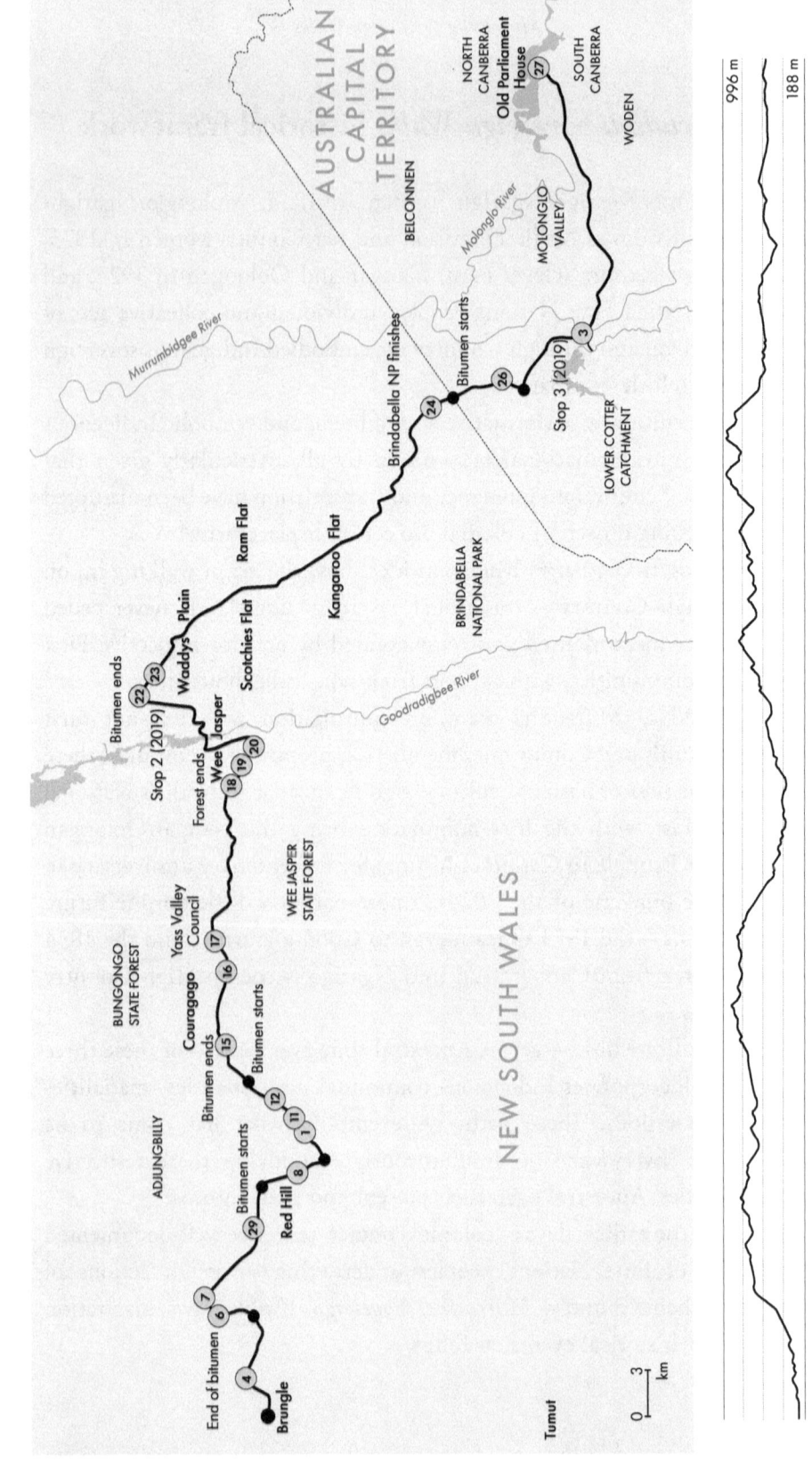

Johann Lhotsky (c. 1795–1866), a naturalist born in Lemberg (Lwów), Galicia (now Ukraine) who arrived in Sydney Australia in 1832.⁶ Two years later Lhotsky journeyed south from Sydney to the Limestone Plains, which would be formally selected as the site for the national capital of Australia in 1911. In 1834 he stayed at Yarralumla Station (now the residence of the Governor-General).

Lhotsky continued into the alpine high country through the traditional homelands of the Meneroo/Monaro/Ngarigo/Ngarigu, following tracks established on ancient First Nations pathways. It was while undertaking this journey in 1834 that Lhotsky 'notated a song he heard at a corroboree',⁷ which was published in 1836 – somewhat floridly – as:

A
Song
of the
Women of the Menero Tribe,
near the
Australian Alps.
Arranged
with the assistance of several Musical Gentlemen,
for the
Voice & Pianoforte,
most humbly inscribed as the first specimen of
Australian Music,
to
Her Most Gracious Majesty
Adelaide.
Queen of Great Britain and Hanover.
By Dr. J. Lhotsky, Colonist, N.S.W.⁸

Left: Murrudha: Sovereign Walks (map subject to change following ongoing consultation with First Nations community members) – tracking cultural actions through art, Country, language and music. Overview of three diverse Murrudha walks for National Heritage List nominations. The first nomination will be the Nangar/Ooloogan Brungle to Canberra 1927 walk.

Lhotsky's translation is poignant, arguably revealing the irrevocable and deadly impact of colonisation on Ngarigo People in less than half a century of settler colonisation:

> Kon-gi, kawel-go, yue-re, con-gi, kawel-go, yue-re Kuma gi ko-ko, kawel-go, Kuma-gi, ka-ba ko-ma, gi ko-ko, koma-gi, ko-ko, kabel-go, Komag i ka-ba, ko-ma-gi yue-re

Lhotsky's translation revealed his empathy for the Meneroo/Ngarigo Peoples' despair at the colonial onslaught:

> Unprotected race of People, Unprotected all are we, And our children shrink so fastly, Unprotected all are we.[9]

Travelling further south to Tasmania, Lhotksy compiled a short vocabulary of Tasmanian Aboriginal words, publishing both this and the song in *The Journal of the Royal Geographical Society of London* in 1839.[10] On returning to Sydney, Lhotsky published a record of his travels, with his sympathetic observations of First Nations peoples evidently at odds with the colonial authorities of the day:[11]

> ... In such and similar reflections, I was engaged, when I perceived a short distance from the way, the first Aborigines I met with since I left Sydney; a very striking contrast with the period when Captain Phillips [sic] saw in Sydney Cove, tribes of 50 and 60 of them – now not one to be found in a space of about 90 miles. I shall have more occasion hereafter to explain, why I consider this extinction of an entire race of men [sic], as one of the greatest blames of all the different governments, which have succeeded each other in these Colonies, whilst the present success of civilizing the Aborigines of Van Dieman's Land, shews clearly, that all other failures were and are owing to the whites and not to the blacks. The tribe I saw, was composed of a few individuals, amongst whom a rather handsome young girl was remarkable.[12]

Lhotsky considered his treatment by the colonial authorities to be extremely poor, as acknowledged in contemporary accounts, and in April 1838 he departed for London, on the barque *Emu*, arriving in London on 17 July 1838. It can be argued that he was considered by his colonial masters to be just as much of an outsider as the First Nations Peoples whose lands he travelled through. Lhotsky died destitute at the Dalston German Hospital in London in late November 1866.

Almost four decades after Lhotsky's journey into the Snowy Mountains, in a bitterly cold May 1873, Molonglo/Ngarigo/Ngunnawal woman (Queen) Nellie Hamilton (c. 1837–1897) trekked from Queanbeyan to Cooma along with a number of her Countrywomen and their children. Due to being Indigenous, they had been refused passage on the mail coach. Their forced journey on foot saw at least one of the group fall ill and die shortly afterwards.

Nellie had travelled to Cooma following the death of her husband Billy Hamilton. She was invited by his Ngarigo/Ngarigu Countrymen and women, most likely to participate in cultural mourning activities. Nellie was a woman noted for her outspoken determination, with the following declaration attributed to her in the early 20th century:

> Yah, yah! Your law! I no tink much of your law. You come here and take my land, kill my 'possum, my kangaroo; leave me starve. Only gib me rotten blanket. Me take calf or sheep, you been shoot me, or put me in jail. You bring your bad sickness 'mong us. And what is that over there (pointing to the Queanbeyan jail)? Yah, blackfellow have no jail, bail he want 'em.[13]

An Anglicised revised version published four decades later still reveals Nellie's fury:

> You come and take our land and kill our game and let us starve, and if we take a sheep or kill a calf you shoot us or put us in gaol. You bring your disease and give it to us – we had nothing like that until you came and stole our land – you give us rotten blanket and bad rum.[14]

A key figure in the local region moving between Ginninderra Station, Queanbeyan and Tharwa, and as discussed above, to Ngarigo Country when cultural obligations required, Nellie died on New Year's Day, 1897, in old Queanbeyan Hospital. She was buried in unconsecrated ground outside the Riverside Cemetery alongside the Queanbeyan River.[15] As the *Argus* newspaper reported:

> The cemetery is located not far from an acknowledged corroboree/ cultural gathering site near the junction of the Queanbeyan and Molongo Rivers. In 1862 a gathering was noted as drawing representatives from three communities: During the last eight or ten days two or three tribes of blackfellows from Braidwood, Yass and Bland Plains [Riverina region], have visited this town ... assembling nightly for 'corroboree'.[16]

In 1927, just over half a century on from Nellie Hamilton's walk from Queanbeyan to Cooma, Wiradyuri walamira (clever man) Nangar (c. 1848–1927)[17] also known as Jimmy Clements, and Ooloogan (c. 1840– 1928)[18] also known as George John Noble and Marvellous, undertook a three-day, 93-mile (150-kilometre) trek across the Brindabella Range.

Departing from Brungle Aboriginal Mission, nestled between Gundagai and Tumut on Walgalu/Wiradyuri Country, the two walamira (clever men) journeyed across the mountain range in order to be *present* for the official opening of the new federal Parliament House on 9 and 10 May. Now they were on Ngambri/Ngunawal homelands in the recently established national capital, Canberra. Contemporary press clippings acknowledge their participation as defending their sovereign rights to their traditional Country.[19]

Nangar was born around 1848 near the foot of Gaanha-bula (Mount Canobolas), an important bornung (initiation) place. Gaanha-bula, meaning Two Shoulders (Gaanha – shoulder, Bula – two) is known as the Eldest of Three Ancestral Brothers – the other brothers being Wahluu (Mt Panorama) and Galbman Ngiiliya (Mt Macquarie).[20]

The son of King Billy Lambert, whose Country stretched between the Belubula and Cudgegong rivers, and the nephew of Queen Nellie

Nangar (also known as Yangar, Jimmy Clements and 'King Billy') Wiradyuri walamira (clever man) on the front steps of Parliament House (c. 10 May 1927).
SOURCE A3560, 3108, Museum of Australian Democracy and National Archives of Australia. Photo: WJ Mildenhall.

Hamilton (d. 1897) of the Canberra/Queanbeyan region, he is associated with Wiradyuri clans from Mudgee in the north to the upper Murrumbidgee in the south. His Country included most of the eastern border of Wiradyuri Country.

Ooloogan (also known as George John Noble and 'Marvellous'), Wiradyuri walamira (clever man) and dog at Bachelors' Quarters.
SOURCE A3560, 419, Museum of Australian Democracy and National Archives of Australia. Photo: WJ Mildenhall.

Ooloogan was born at Muttama, central western New South Wales, in around 1840. He was known for his travelling showman skills. He demonstrated customary tool-making and utilisation at country shows in the high country down to the coast in the region. Although not much is known about his earliest days, he almost certainly completed the burbong (initiation) ceremony between the ages of twelve and sixteen, as this was the final step to manhood and an essential step to becoming a walamira (clever man).[21]

~~~~~~~

Gather 'round people, I'll tell you a story
An eight-year long story of power and pride
British Lord Vestey and Vincent Lingiari
Were opposite men on opposite sides[22]

As noted, it was the formal recognition of another sovereign First Nations action that became the impetus for *Murrudha: Sovereign Walks*.[23] This national heritage-listed 22-kilometre track is on the homelands of the Gurindji, Malngin and Bilinara Peoples at Wave Hill in the Victoria River region of the Northern Territory. Throughout different seasons, over half a decade from 2011–2016, I (Brenda L Croft) walked sections of the track, guided by Gurindji family and senior Community members, retrac(k)ing segments solo, to embody aspects of creative-led multidisciplinary doctoral research framed by Critical Indigenous Performative, Collaborative Autoethnography and StoryWork methodologies.

The combined action of physical and psychic corporeal engagement with my patrilineal Country and re/memory provided the impetus to

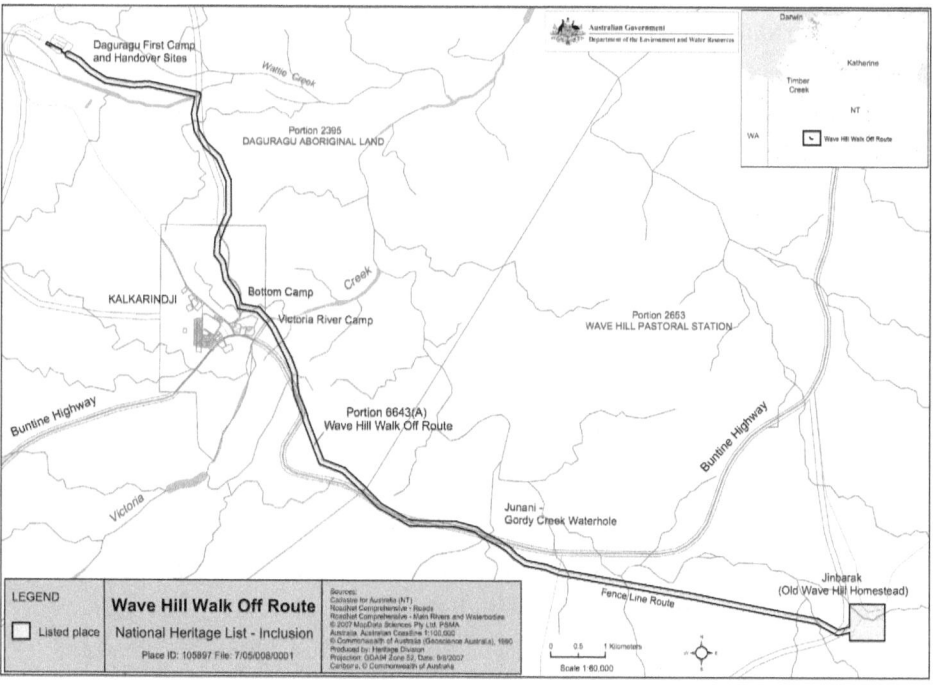

National Heritage Places – Wave Hill Walk-Off Route
SOURCE Australian Government Department of Climate Change, Energy, the Environment and Water website, <www.dcceew.gov.au/parks-heritage/heritage/places/national/wave-hill>

approach the First Nations communities whose customary homelands and Ancestors are associated with the 1927 action by Nangar and Ooloogan – Ngambri, Ngarigo, Ngunawal, Walgalu and Wiradyuri.

The prominent Ngambri Elder, Matilda House-Williams, called for such histories to be documented. In 2008, she conducted the first Welcome to Country protocol held at Australia's parliament house, inaugurating the incoming government of Prime Minister Rudd:

> **Dr Aunty Matilda House-Williams:** [They're] still not in the records of history. And lots of other things that happened, not only here and around this ... general area of Canberra [and] Queanbeyan. Very little knowledge [got passed] down because other [non-Indigenous] people only wanted to write what they thought was the best ... exclud[ing] Aboriginal people from history. Because if nothing's written about [them], then it means no Blacks live[d] here. How can you [I] say you're from here when you're not even in the [history] book? Because if a white man didn't write it down for you ... come on, come on now [sarcasm]. The ... people that [made] this part of the world, an Aboriginal world [and] history was Aboriginal people. It was Aboriginal people. They loved the land and they cared for the land. They cared for the rivers ... But you wouldn't ever know that an Aboriginal person ever camped on [the] river [here] ... In this part of the world, it was rivers and mountains that kept Aboriginal people together.[24]

The ancient pathways taken by Nangar and Ooloogan on their trek to the white celebrations of the national capital embodied a powerful act of sovereignty – of self and communal-determination – that deserves official recognition on the National Heritage List. Similarly, the action by traditional owners and affiliated groups in walking off misappropriated Gurindji homelands during a blistering dry season in 1966 was finally acknowledged as a national act of Indigenous self-determination – albeit over four decades later:

... they picked up their swags and started off walking ...
... this is the story of something much more ... [25]

Brungle Aboriginal Station

Brungle Aboriginal Station[26] was established as an Aboriginal Reserve by the New South Wales Aborigines Protection Board[27] in 1888, a century after the arrival of the First Fleet at Sydney Cove. One of the oldest Aboriginal Reserves in New South Wales, Brungle has been the home Community of many significant Aboriginal leaders throughout the 20th century and remains one to the present day.

Nestled in the foothills of the Snowy Mountains between Tumut and Gundagai, it is a sanctuary for its residents. Brungle matriarchs such as Aunty Bronwyn Penrith, interviewed below, have played a particularly significant role in the cohesiveness of the Community, with many of the First Nations Elders associated with Murrudha, sharing family connections and cultural ties to Brungle Community.

Australian First Nations Community members regularly travelled between Warangesda (Darlington Point) – Brungle – Yass (Hollywood Reserve) – Cowra (Erambie Reserve), through Dhurgha, Gundungara, Ngambri, Ngarigo, Ngunawal, Wallabalooa, Walgalu, Wiradyuri and Yuin/Yuwinja homelands.

Nangar and Ooloogan were renowned for their capacity to cover hundreds of miles across the state in unexpectedly swift time, including their work touring the show circuit.

Aunty Bronwyn Penrith (BP) in conversation with Brenda L Croft (BLC)

BLC: What do you feel when you go home to Brungle?

BP: Ah, brilliant. I usually open the window as I come over the hill from Gundagai and breathe.

BLC: Is it an exhalation like a 'Hah' [exhales]?

BP: More an indrawn breath for that freshness, and feeling alive and part of the Brungle Valley. Sometimes I 'cooee', ask my daughter.

BLC: Do you hear anything there?

BP: Not there. I stop [later] near the old place where I grew up, in the car and moon at night, it's just beautiful. You can almost see us living there, and people fishing on the banks, you know? Smoke from the fires, and that. I can see that in my mind's eye now, even now. So, I was very lucky to have, to live my early life as part of that community, it's a bygone era.[28]

Aunty Bronwyn Penrith recounted her grandmother telling her when she was a child: 'Those old men (Jimmy Clements and John Noble) could travel with the whirlywinds', using storytelling as an explanation for the swift travels by both walamira across mountainous terrain.[29]

The initial focus for *Murrudha: Sovereign Walks* has been on the 1927 trek by Nangar and Ooloogan from Brungle Aboriginal Community to Parliament House, their destination a site of long-standing protest where both Wiradyuri walamira (Bamblett, 2024 pending) stood their sovereign ground. The proposed nomination would be in 2025/6, in time for its centenary anniversary in 2027. The other pathways – Hamilton and cohort (1873) and Lhotsky's travels where he recorded the Song of the Women of the Meneroo (1834) – are planned as future nominations.

Key elements of *Murrudha: Sovereign Walks* encompass reactivating embodied, culturally guided, corporeally immersed actions of sovereignty in, on and through traditional homelands – Country-Kin-Country. Reclaiming and asserting connection to Country and Culture is a collective sovereign action ensuring cultural reclamation, reinvigoration, reimagination and transmission. Significantly, these are acknowledged positive predictors for improved Indigenous Health and Wellbeing, nationally and internationally.[30] Our work not only imagines but also creates equitable Ancestral Futures, recentring First Nations rights over non-Indigenous Australians' privileged expectations.

Murrudha: Sovereign Walks also presents annual Non-Traditional Research Outcomes generated by First Nations and non-Indigenous creative-led, bioethically and environmentally sustainable researchers. Through multi-disciplinary, multi-modal, multi-literacies and culturally appropriate research processes, collaboration with cultural practitioners and Knowledge Holders is a priority.

Working 'at the speed of trust' demands incorporating Language reclamation and reinvigoration, in hand with contemporary culturally appropriate land-management stewardship.[31] This includes Critical Indigenous Performative and Collaborative Autoethnography, StoryWork and StoryMapping methodologies.

Murrudha: Sovereign Walks Timeline

Since 2019, the ANU team has held annual workshops, events, exhibitions, public programs and symposia, with an international event held at the Embassy of Australia in Washington DC, USA during NAIDOC Week, July 2024, which accompanied an exhibition that included images of Murrudha participants on display until February 2025.[32]

2019: The beginning of the project

> It really is a mark of resistance, grace, and resilience to walk so far to protest in such a dignified manner and to speak to the authorities at the time, even though they weren't listening. These walks, these Sovereign Walks, enable us to explore not only the history, but also how the land has been managed in the past and what we need to do to restore it.[33]
>
> *Professor Jamie Pittock*

In the five years since, *Murrudha: Sovereign Walks* has held annual gatherings and workshops, presented on panels at national and international First Nations- and creative-led research symposia, with each year's events consecutively adding to further 'tracks' being rewalked and re-embodied.

September and November 2020

Murrudha: Sovereign Walks In September 2020 a reconnoitre to Brungle (September) took place with Brungle Community member, ACT Parks Indigenous Ranger Dean Freeman; ANU First Nations graduate, archaeologist and cultural advisor, Dave Johnson; and Professor Brenda L Croft. The group met with Dean's parents, Buddy and Phyllis Freeman, to discuss the Murrudha proposal and view Aunty Phyllis's extensive archives on Brungle Aboriginal Reserve and its families.

In November, a Murrudha group undertook a test walk, completing 80 kilometres of the estimated 130 kilometres, commencing from Brungle and travelling over three days to near Uriarra Crossing.[34] Leaving Brungle, the group walked up Honeysuckle Creek Road through the state forest to Tumorrama Hall, then onto Wee Jasper and across the Brindabella Range to Uriarra Crossing.

8 December 2021

Murrudha: Sovereign Walks – Track #1 The Murrudha team submitted two panels to the Art Association of Australia and New Zealand (AAANZ) Annual Conference: Impact, which was held online due to Covid restrictions. The two panels consisted of ANU Murrudha First Nations and non-Indigenous team members, and First Nations Community members from Canberra and Brungle. Panel topics included developing methodologies and theoretical frameworks, creative-led research approaches, and outcomes to date.

30 May–3 June 2022

Murrudha: Sovereign Walks – Track #2 The Murrudha team submitted two panels to the AIATSIS (Australian Institute of Aboriginal and Torres Strait Islander Studies) Annual Research Conference, held on Kabi Kabi Country, 30 May–3 June.[35] The second Murrudha panel focussed on the work of Will Kepa, First Nations ANU MPhil candidate, manager of

Murrudha: Sovereign Walks Panel II, AIATSIS Annual Research Conference on Kabi Kabi Country, 31 May 2022. Left to right: Jilda Andrews, Lisa Slater, Aunty Sue Bulger, Shane Herrington, Rohit Rao, Aidan Hartshorn.
Photo: Brenda L Croft

Yil Lull Studio in the School of Music with Djinama Yilaga (Happy Place), comprising Dhurga/Yuin singers working in Language reclamation as part of Murrudha. I'll now hand over to some of the participants in the project to give their thoughts.

> ... what I've really loved within this project is how we can think about and use culture and artistic practice as tools, and also metrics that we can engage with health and wellbeing. Listening to artists and seeing artwork, people talk about their cultural practice. We're really thinking about Indigenous health and wellbeing through cultural practice and creative practice as well ... I'd just like to share with you my understanding of how Murrudha is operating, in a way. It's really Brenda and her team, and also led by community as well, have placed the walk, the incredible journey from Brungle through to New Parliament House in 1927, and used

that as almost a backbone, really of something that we can focus and think through and return to. Keeping 'on track', honouring the actions and the situations of people that have gone before, and thinking about that as a sovereign act ... How to act with sovereignty, what that feels like and what that looks like and what it means. If you think about that as the spine or the tree trunk, there are several projects that have come off that, then, that give meaning to that spine or that trunk of that tree. And when those branches come off, they flourish in all sorts of different directions. So through these two panels, we hope that we're giving you an idea of not only the action or the project that binds it all together, but the ways that the project is guiding or inspiring or leading outwards, which I think is really, really important. We're all linked, both of the panels, all of us here that have been brought here through Brenda and through this project. I like to think of it as a spine, because it's bodily, and it's really helped me understand how we're related and how our projects speak to one another as well. That there is something there that's centring it all ... it's beautiful.[36]

Dr Jilda Andrews (Yuwaalaraay cultural practitioner and ANU Research Fellow)

I've been with National Parks for the last 16, 17 years and I've been with National Parks as an Aboriginal educator, delivering cultural education to schools, unis, TAFEs, but also to the general public ... local cultural education, so delivering talks about our people, where we come from, where we went to, and being able to sit on this panel as part of the 'Sovereign Walks'. There's lots of different pathways through Country, and this particular walk is one walk that has a very strong platform, but also there's lots of other pathways through Country ... Delivering education to our own community ... gaining knowledge from our Elders, from our own people, and running programmes to educate our people about culture ... it's been very challenging at times, but very rewarding – rewarding because seeing young kids starting off very young, and then later on in life seeing them as actual leaders in the community, and my son [Aidan is] one of them.[37]

                        Shane Herrington (Wolgalu Knowledge Holder and Indigenous Ranger)

My role in this project is working with Aidan [Hartshorn] and Shane [Herrington, Aidan's father], Dean Freeman [from Brungle Community], who couldn't make it here, and Paul House, who's Auntie Matilda's son. Working with them to map out the route that the two men, Jimmy Clements and John Noble, might have taken when they walked their walk of sovereignty from Brungle Mission to Old Parliament House in protest. Mapping out that potential route, if it is to be on the National Heritage List or the Registry, what would it look like now? How would people be able to walk it now? Because as we saw in the previous talk as well, being on Country, walking on Country, is really important, and it's integral for people to revive culture stories and connect. And it's really challenging now, because as we know, Country is really fragmented because of the kind of policies that were put in place before and the kind of maps that are made, and how land is owned now. And working around that, working around who has power right now, so that you lot can reclaim power ... I'm not from Ngunnawal or Ngambri Country. I was born on Dharug Country, Sydney, but I grew up in India. My parents are both Indian. Working with people here and working on this project has helped me understand what my place here could be, what my place there [India] could be, in another country that experienced colonialism but in a different way.[38]

                        Rohit Rao (non-Indigenous ANU Graduate)

We have, Shane and I, been to the spring that starts the Murrumbidgee River, and to see horse tracks. Would you call them that? Horses have trampled the spring that is the source of the

Murrumbidgee River. So we say we don't want them there. There are other places where you can ride horses. We don't want them trampling a river that is very important to us … We are bombarded with people who have friends in high places who say that they should have horse riding in Kosciuszko National Park, northern Kosciuszko National Park, but give them a place where they can ride their horses, because that's their heritage. But not trampling the very start of the Murrumbidgee River.

Brungle Mission, or Brungle Station, Brungle Reserve, 100 years after the First Fleet arrived, it was set up as a camp with fences so that Aboriginal people were told to stay in an area of, say, two kilometres square, and, 'That's where you have to live. That's where you have to find your food. That's where your people will be.' That was government policy. 'That's where you must live.' Straight away those traditional practices are taken away. No longer are you free to go walking on those trails that so many of their ancestors did. They were forbidden to speak their language, and if they did speak their language, they were punished or humiliated in public. You have a whole generation of grandchildren growing up without language, and we are part of that now. But we have reclaimed our Wiradyuri and Walgalu language, and thanks to the people who have done that and kept that language, we can now reclaim our language, and hopefully soon speak it fluently throughout our country.

… part of the current story of this walk, that we've adapted to so many things in our history over thousands of years. We can adapt now to our own story of how we can now recreate this walk and bring it back to country to us, so that it's ours.
> *Aunty Sue Bulger (Walgalu/Wiradyuri Knowledge Holder, former Chairperson of Brungle Tumut Local Aboriginal Land Council)*[39]

… when Shane [Herrington] was talking about the stories, how 'The Man from Snowy River' and these romantic national stories are covering over Walgalu Wiradjuri stories ... is thinking about the importance of telling stories differently and different knowledges and cultural practices, and how important those stories are to interrupting that national myth that is also a bigger part of damaging the country.[40]

Dr Lisa Slater (non-Indigenous academic)

~~~~~~~~~~

I was up late last night trying to finish the track for [Djinama Yilaga] and I played it to them at breakfast this morning and just that moment of just sitting there and sort of observing them listening to the song is very, very special to me that they hear this music that they've created and they're trying to maintain their song and their culture and revive it and their language and things like that. And a very touchy emotional subject as well for these ladies writing about their family and their Mum. So that was just, I really feel honoured to be able to share that moment with you guys after breakfast this morning, if I may say. But just the blessing in general to work with people who are trying to keep their culture alive and it benefits me because I'm a musician and I look for just about anything I can within song and within our own songs.[41]

Will Kepa (Iamalaig, Kulkalgal – Torres Strait Islander Peoples, PhD candidate, Manager of Yil Lull Studio, ANU School of Music)

I'm a Ngarigo Yuin woman. My grandfather is a Yuin man and the Yuin Nation is from Sydney all the way down to the Victoria border and in between the ocean and The Great Dividing Range. It's all my grandfather's Country, all related to just about everyone there ... Djinama Yilaga started in 2019 ... For me, it's a very spiritual thing that happened and it was like the ancestors would just open up these doors for me ... my vision is to actually have a bigger South Coast choir singing in Dhurga language ... It's about my connection and it's about really our loss of culture through our Nan being taken away and that big void that's there now in our life because we don't live on our Nan's Country. We spent all our life on our grandfather's Country. But we've always been told we follow our mother's line ... if we follow our mother's line, Ngarigo is our Country, our mother's, our Nan's Country ...

This is a song about my grandmother and it's a song about me also and intergenerational trauma. I always wondered what it meant for me and my family and the only thing I can think of is when I think about my Nan, I cry. My Nan was a young 10-year-old girl from Ngarigo Country and she had a little sister Mary. Their father was Alex Brindle, and he was a Black tracker for the Cooma police. Well, my Nan was stolen away from her Country at the age of 10 and taken on a train down to Cootamundra, her and her younger sister Mary. And at Cootamundra Girls' Home, they were taught to cook and clean and look after other people's babies. And when they were ready, they were sent out into service, into white people's homes. And I don't know whether they were ever loved or cared for in those homes.

At the age of 16, Nan left the service and she met my grandfather, Reggie Walker. They got married at Kiama and they spent their whole life living on the South Coast, Yuin Country, away from my Nan's country. They had lots of children and they moved up and down the coast living in the bean paddocks, picking beans, out in the forests, cutting sleepers for the railway, fishing on the beaches, living by the creeks and in old humpies. But my Nan, she never got to go back to her Country. My Nan and Aunty Mary, they both married Yuin men and they both ended up at Bodalla and they both died there. And they both were buried at the Moruya Cemetery and they're buried in unmarked graves so we don't even know where we can visit them. So this song's for my Nan ... [singing].[42]

Cheryl Davison (Ngarigo/Walbunja Peoples)

Murrudha: Sovereign Walks – Track #3 symposium panel, Drill Hall Gallery, ANU, 13 December 2022. Left to right: Jamie Pittock, Leah House, Aidan Hartshorn, Dean Freeman, Jilda Andrews, Shane Herrington.
Photo: Brenda L Croft

December 2022

Murrudha: Sovereign Walks/Still in my mind: Gurindji location, experience and visuality – Track #3 This event brought together the outcomes from my creative-led doctoral research project 'Still in my mind: Gurindji location, experience and visuality', at its final exhibition venue, the Drill Hall Gallery at the ANU, and the next gathering of *Murrudha: Sovereign Walks* participants. Panellists participated in public programs associated with the exhibition, referencing the Gurindji Walk-Off from Wave Hill Station. Murrudha panellists gave oral history presentations detailing their timeless connections to place, from Brungle to Canberra and the High Country.

A week of events comprised the exhibition opening and an accompanying symposium, a film screening with Q and A. Music performances celebrated songman and First Nations cultural activist Kev Carmody, who was awarded an honorary doctorate and who provided the Occasional Address to graduating students. It also included Djinama Yilaga choir and a photographic shoot with Kev Carmody and Jim Everett puralia meenamatta.

Participating were Gurindji community members from Kalkaringi, Daguragu and Darwin, and non-Indigenous 1966–75 Walk-Off supporters plus Brungle–Canberra *Murrudha: Sovereign Walks* participants, ANU Murrudha team members and other First Nations community members. All events were documented by Ronin Films for proposed future broadcast and teaching resources. Leading academics and cultural custodians found the symposium extraordinary, powerful and deeply moving.

20–24 November 2023

Murrudha: Sovereign Walks – **Track #4** In mid-December 2023, a four-day gathering/workshop was held for Murrudha participants and community members at the ANU School of Music and School of Art and Design.[43] In comparison with the previous year's public programs, this event prioritised community engagement. Panel presentations were by and for First Nations community members from Brungle, Canberra, Melbourne, Sydney, Tumut, Cummeragunja and Wagga Wagga. Oral history interviews with Brungle, Cummeragunja, Tumut, Sydney, Wagga Wagga community members were recorded by Ronin Films. The photoshoot involved participants in the research project Naabámi (thou shall/will see): Barangaroo (army of me).

A further photoshoot was staged on the steps of Old Parliament House, now the Museum of Australian Democracy, with descendants of Nangar (Jimmy Clements) and Ooloogan (George John Noble) referencing the historical image of Nangar (Jimmy Clements) taken at the same site on 8–9 May 1927. I have shared some of the participants' feedback in the box that follows.

Murrudha: Sovereign Walks

Descendants of Nangar and Ooloogan on the steps of Old Parliament House/
Museum of Australian Democracy, 24 November 2023.
Front row: Dean Freeman. Middle row, left to right: Cheryl Penrith,
Aunty Soni Piper, Aunty Lois Peeler AM, Aunty Coral Bulger.
Top row: Cheryl Spencer, Wendy Bunn, Aunty Bronwyn Penrith.
Photo: Prue Hazelgrove

Post-gathering feedback

Dr Lois Peeler AM (Yorta Yorta/Wiradyuri/Wurundjeri Peoples, Elder/ Knowledge Elder): Dear Brenda and Monika – I just wanted to express my appreciation to you both for the great effort in bringing together Mob and for your assistance during my visit.[44]

Aunty Coral Bulger (Walgalu/Wiradyuri Peoples; Elder): Hi Brenda, Thank you very much for all your hard work on projects and respect to our Mobs, greatly appreciated ... Yindyamarra Mandaang guwu (respectfully thank you – Wiradyuri language). Best wishes and warm regards, Coral Bulger.[45]

Wendy Bunn (and her sister Cheryl): Dear Sis Brenda 🙏 😊 ... I would just like to extend our sincere gratitude and appreciation of your continuous, tireless work and dedication towards this important, significant project regarding our heroes, old Uncle Jimmy (Nangar) Clements and old Great Grandfather, George John Noble (old Marvellous). It is quite the honour and privilege to be invited to represent our ancestors and to be a vessel and voice on their behalf in creating awareness and truth telling of their profound journey almost 100 years ago, and be a part of an incredibly significant moment in Aboriginal Australian history. Jimmy and Johnny's story is a huge piece of the woven fabric that makes up this country's Aboriginal history and their story needs to be told and shared with the wider audiences. I am so excited and immensely proud to be amongst such amazing, inspiring, dedicated and passionate leaders and individuals in making sure our heroes, Old Uncle Jimmy and Old Uncle Johnny, are rightly honored and respected by our efforts in gaining the recognition they so rightfully deserve ... 😊. Thank you! Warm regards, Wendy & Cheryl xx.[46]

July 2024

Murrudha: Sovereign Walks – **Track #5** Most recently, a contingent of twelve people associated with *Murrudha: Sovereign Walks* – First Nations community members, a non-Indigenous research assistant and ANU staff members – travelled to the US to participate in multiple connected events which were held at the Embassy of Australia, Washington DC, during NAIDOC (National Aboriginal and Islander Day Observance Committee) Week celebrations.

My exhibition, *Naabámi (thou shall/will see): Barangaroo (army of me)*, was officially opened by Australian Ambassador Hon. Kevin Rudd AM and Dr Aunty Matilda House in her final role as 2023 NAIDOC National Elder of the Year on 8 July at the Embassy of Australia, with a performance by Djinama Yilaga.

Aunty Matilda House-Williams, 2023 National NAIDOC Elder of the Year, speaking at the opening reception with Ambassador Kevin Rudd, Embassy of Australia, Washington DC, USA, 8 July 2024.
Photo: Timothy Croft

Aunty Matilda – one of the key drivers of *Murrudha: Sovereign Walks* from the outset five years ago – was accompanied on stage by her granddaughter Leah House, a Murrudha First Nations Community member and Naabámi participant, and my niece Maddie Croft, also a Naabámi participant, both of whom assisted Aunty Matilda with her possum-skin cloak.

This stunning customary attire had been worn by Aunty Matilda in February 2008 at the official opening of the 42nd federal parliament during Ambassador Rudd's tenure as prime minister. Ambassador Rudd was clearly affected by Aunty Matilda's acknowledgment of his time as prime minister, particularly his national Formal Apology to Stolen Generations and their descendants that same year.

The ambassador expounded on the strength of Australian First Nations women in his speech, drawing connections from Barangaroo, Cammeraygal sovereign woman (c. 1750–1791) – the inspiration for 'Naabámi' – through to the women and girls present at the opening and represented in the exhibition portraits. Djinama Yilaga performed songs in Dhurga Language to a capacity audience, moving many to tears, particularly the youngest member and only male, Kobi Davison, the nephew of Cheryl and Michelle Davison, and Iris Walker-White, aged 11 years.

Attendees included Native American Community members from cultural institutions including the National Museum of the American Indian, staff from the National Endowment for the Humanities, staff from the National Museum for Folk Life, staff from the National Natural History Museum, staff from the Kluge Ruhe Aboriginal Art Collection, University of Virginia, Australian expatriates, Australian politicians attending Australian–US Trade talks, members from Capitol Hill, local students and interested members of the general public.

On Tuesday 9 July public panels included Elders, singers/performers, emerging leaders and young people who will be our future activists, many involved with both 'Naabámi' and *Murrudha: Sovereign Walks* – Track #5. It is only fitting to close the chapter with their collective voices of generous appreciation: people who relish walking together, being together, the love of family, and their solidarity with the sovereign struggles taking place across North America.

Djinama Yilaga performing at the opening reception for *Naabámi (thou shall/will see): Barangaroo (army of me)*, Embassy of Australia, Washington DC, USA, 8 July 2024 NAIDOC Week celebrations. Left to right: Maria Walker, Michelle Dixon, Kobi Davison, Michelle Davison, Aunty Iris Walker-White, Melanie Horsnell.
Photo: Jeff Snyder

Marntaj (OK, finished, all right, goodbye); Wallilu (all is well, 'til we meet again)

Having now had more time to reflect on our visit to Washington and our participation in the Murrudha Project, I now know what I am called to do with whatever time I might have left in terms of telling our story with integrity and with truth … Nooringe Brenda, it was such a privilege for us to be invited to Washington DC. There were a number of highlights for me personally, firstly to be present for the Opening of your Exhibition and to be greeted by the images of many family members and friends, but most importantly to see my Mother's portrait, I truly had the sense that she was waiting for us. In addition to this, I confess to not understanding the exhibition in

Murrudha: Sovereign Walks – Track #5 and Naabámi participants with Ambassador Kevin Rudd in *Naabámi (thou shall/will see): Barangaroo (army of me)*, Embassy of Australia, Washington DC, USA, 8 July 2024 NAIDOC Week celebrations. Left to right: Prue Hazelgrove, Melanie Horsnell, Brenda Gifford, Brenda L Croft, Michelle Davison, Kobi Davison, Ambassador Kevin Rudd, Aunty Matilda House-Williams, Aunty Iris Walker-White, Leah House, Maria Walker, Michelle Dixon, Sasha Croft, Aunty Bronwyn Penrith, Maddie Croft.
Photo: Jeff Snyder

its entirety, until I read the catalogue on our arrival and the story of Barangaroo and Dilboong has had a profound impact on me and the realisation that we are not just our Mother's army but of something that is so much bigger than us on an individual level and am humbled to have been included. I also appreciated the opportunity to spend time with both Matilda and Bronwen, both of whom have been lifetime friends and to meet and get to know a little about Leah … Having the opportunity to visit the museums and learn a little of other cultures was also very special. Finally, it was a pleasure to meet your family, the love you have for them and they for you was obvious and lifted my heart and spirit. The hospitality extended to us from everyone was something that I will always treasure.[47]

Iris Walker-White (IW-W)

First of all, thank you for the wonderful opportunity to travel to Washington DC to be a part of the opening exhibition, Naabámi, at the Australian Embassy. It was an absolute honour to be there and perform with Djinama Yilaga and be in the presence of our beautiful Elders, Aunty Matilda House and Bronwen Penrith, our kin and also share our time with Brenda Gifford, Terry and Monika Duggan. I appreciated all the love and support that our nephew Kobi received from all. It was so encouraging for him and we were so happy that he and Christopher formed a bond instantly. The portraits are so special and we recognised many relatives and friends but it was even more special to see our mother Deanna Davison looking down on us. It was very emotional. Visiting the African American museum and the Martin Luther King Monument was so powerful and made me reflect on our own struggle back home here when we were growing up in the sixties and seventies but I was even more overcome with emotion at the Native American Indian Museum as it reflected our own lives as Native Australians. All our love, Michelle Davison.[48]

Michelle Davison

My time in Washington was great, it was good to hear the choir, beautiful especially Kobi the future of our music is in good hands, and I look forward to his development, Brenda's support was great, something as little as seeing Art Pepper's saxophone at [the] Native American museum was a highlight, because he is one of my favourite horn players, and learning more about the Native American Indians history and similarities with our mob was interesting, thanks again Brenda Gifford.[49]

Brenda Gifford

Thanks so much Brenda for the opportunity to be a part of your exhibition and to sing for you. The Embassy visit was the highlight of my presence there. I enjoyed every day there being with you all and, it was fun, now can't wait for England lol. You are such an inspiration for us all I reckon. Keep doing what you do. Sending lots and lots of love your way and also to Christopher xxx.[50]

Maria Walker

I've made memories with my grandmother that's the most important part for me, I am not sure I'll have another opportunity like this trip again so I'm just so thankful to have had this experience. I've made some beautiful new friends and made the most of each day outside of the commitments making the most of site seeing and exploring. It was just such a beautiful experience and I can't believe I got to be a part of it. Thank you Brenda and all your team that made it happen 🎅🖤.[51]

Leah House

Being in Washington for the Naabámi opening and panel talks was really special to me. Not only was it inspiring and empowering for my own practice and development, it was incredible to hear and be present in all these important discussions and conversations. These conversations ranged from the big ones on stage to the little interpersonal conversations between participants and complete strangers. Hearing what this project meant to everyone and what impact it has had first hand is something that will always stay with me and continues to grow as the work grows. I love to help people share their story, to listen, and share that with others. I feel humbled and thankful to be a part of the sharing of these stories, this trip demonstrated the importance of the sharing of these stories and the relationship and community that is built in that process.[52]

Prue Hazelgrove

First, may I recognise an appreciation of the extraordinary foresights of Brenda Croft to imagine that the photographs can be exhibited at the Australian Embassy in Washington. For me these photographs represent the Emergence of the forgotten and voiceless, out of the darkness of Colonisation and us Aboriginal Women stood, strong in our Power. I loved the conversation with all of the travelling Party at breakfast each morning. The ladies and Kobi from Djinama Yiliga, and mine have been woven together three generations ago with the marriage of my Grt Grandfather [and] their Grt Grandmother as an older Couple and over those many generations I have remembered the stories of our Family connection and retold them, of who we are in our South Coast connections. I was very proud to hear our Language sung at the Australian Embassy and felt this had a lasting impact on the listeners, in ways that other communication may not. The amazing accomplishment of Brenda Gifford's journey through her craft, I appreciated that real and honest truth-telling took place to the American audience for NAIDOC conversations delivered by the two panels of speakers. The opportunity to visit the African American History Museum and the First Nations American Indian History Places and tast[ing] their food, was and remains such a highlight for me. I heard the Stories and felt their loss from this window into the History of America thru their eyes. It runs parallel with our own First Peoples experience of Colonisations and dispossession. For me it feels like we 'broke Bread with Americas People of Colour'. I wish to thank you all for your company on this experience of travel ... I love that we travelled together the Old and Wise and the young voices were all much appreciated. Thank you, Brenda and all you Mob, it was an experience that will stay with me forever. Sincerely, Bronwyn.

Bronwyn Penrith

Memories were made when we went and I had lots of fun so thank you Brenda and everyone who came. My favourite thing was when I was singing in the embassy and I had the most fun with Christopher, Leah and you. PS thank you Christopher [age 13] for playing with me ... Thank you all for making the so little time so so so special.[53]

Kobi Davison

ACKNOWLEDGMENTS

We wish to honour the custodians of the lands upon which the co-editors work – the Ngunnawal/Nambri people of Kambri, Canberra and the Turrbal, Yuggera and Yugambeh of Meanjin, Brisbane. We thank our families for their support, especially Uncle Fred Conway and Milton Cameron. We are grateful to UNSW Press, particularly Harriet McInerney, Paul O'Beirne and Jocelyn Hungerford for sharing their enthusiasm and professionalism. This volume would not have been possible without the conscientious work of our super-efficient Research Assistant Jess Urwin, who performed important organisational and liaison work, and provided perceptive comments on each of the chapters. Our funding came from the Australian Research Council's Laureate program 'Rediscovering the Deep Human Past: Global Networks, Future Opportunities' (FL170100121). Finally, a big thankyou to the fine contributors to this volume – many of whom have been strong supporters of our seven-year venture, the Research Centre for Deep History, Australian National University – and who are our friends and colleagues.

CONTRIBUTORS

Mary Blight completed a double major in Indigenous Knowledge, History and Heritage, and French at the University of Western Australia (UWA) in 2020. She completed honours in French at UWA in 2021 and was awarded the Leon Tauman Memorial Prize in Honours French for her thesis on the Wardandi oral history of Vasse. She is currently enrolled in an MPhil in Indigenous Research and Development at the Centre for Aboriginal Studies, Curtin University.

Anna Clark is an award-winning historian, author and public commentator. An internationally recognised scholar in Australian history, history education and the role of history in everyday life, Anna's most recent books are *The Catch: Australia's love affair with fishing* (Penguin 2023) and *Making Australian History* (Penguin 2022). She is currently Professor of History at the University of Technology Sydney.

Brenda L Croft is from the Gurindji/Malngin/Mudburra peoples from the Victoria River region of the Northern Territory of Australia, and has Anglo-Australian/Chinese/German/Irish/Scottish heritage. Since the mid-1980s she has been a leading member in Australian and international First Nations and broader contemporary arts/cultural sectors as a multi-disciplinary creative practitioner (artist, curator, educator, scholar). Brenda's creative-led research encompasses Critical Indigenous Performative Collaborative Autoethnography and Storywork methodologies, working particularly closely with her patrilineal family and Community, as well as national and international First Nations/Indigenous communities. Brenda is Professor of Indigenous Art History and Curatorship, living and working at the Australian National University on unceded Ngambri/Ngunawal lands. In 2024, Brenda was the Gough Whitlam and Malcolm Fraser Visiting Chair of Australian Studies, Harvard University, on the Ancestral Homelands of the Massachusett.

GRACE FLETCHER currently works for the Australian Government contributing to a range of policy and engagement projects. Her research at the Australian National University focused on the practice and places of Deep History as sites of convergence which offer to enrich understandings of Australia's recent and deep pasts. Grace has presented the findings of her research after recently being invited as a speaker on the themes of Indigenous temporalities, sovereignties and Deep Histories at the 2023 4S Society for Social Sciences Conference in Honolulu.

JOAKIM GOLDHAHN is an archaeologist and research fellow at the University of Adelaide, South Australia. He earned his PhD from Umeå University's Institution for Archaeology and Saami Studies in Sweden in 2000. His career has focused on exploring the European Bronze Age and the enigmatic world of rock art. Goldhahn has conducted fieldwork in various regions and cultural settings, including Australia, Denmark, Kenya, Norway, Scotland, Spain and Sweden. In Australia, he has been involved in multiple Community-led research projects, working closely with Aboriginal stakeholders and corporations in western Arnhem Land.

PROFESSOR JACKIE HUGGINS AM FAHA is Bidjara and Birri Gubba Juru. She is currently Director of Indigenous Research, Faculty of Health, Medicine and Behavioural Sciences at the University of Queensland. She is also Honorary Professor, Centre for Deep History, Australian National University; POU Atlantic Fellows Social Equity, Melbourne University; Director, National Centre for Reconciliation, Truth and Justice, Federation University Victoria; and Co-Chair, National Apology Foundation. Other roles include Elder in Residence, Australia Progress and Steering Committee Member for Passing the Message Stick and Common Threads, as well as Elder in Residence, Australian Broadcasting Commission. Her publications include *Sister girl: The writings of Aboriginal activist and historian Jackie Huggins* (1998), *Jack of Hearts: QX11594* (with Ngaire Jarro, 2022) and *Auntie Rita: The classic memoir of an Aboriginal woman's love and determination* (with Rita Huggins, 2023). The first collaboration between Jackie Huggins and Ann McGrath was the edited collection with Kay Saunders, *Aboriginal Workers* (1995). Professor Huggins is in demand as a speaker, mentor, writer and advisor with over four decades' experience in Community, academia, government and non-government sectors.

ROSANNE KENNEDY is Associate Professor in Literary Studies and Gender Studies at the Australian National University on Ngunnawal and Ngambri Country. Her research has addressed issues of testimony, truth-telling, human rights and memory in settler colonial and comparative global contexts, particularly in relation to Stolen Generations. She has also published on environmental humanities and eco-memory.

ANN MCGRATH AM has led the Kathleen Fitzpatrick Laureate Program on Deep History for the past seven years. She is based at the Australian National University, where she is the WK Hancock Distinguished Chair of History and currently serves on the Council of the National Museum of Australia. Her publications include *Illicit Love: Interracial sex and marriage in the United States and Australia* (2015), which won the NSW Premier's History Prize, and *Born in the Cattle* (1987), awarded the inaugural Hancock Prize. Along with Laura Rademaker and Jakelin Troy, she co-edited *Everywhen: Australia and the language of deep history* (UNSW Press 2023). Ann has also co-directed and produced various films, including *A Frontier Conversation* (2006), *Message from Mungo* (2014) and *Japarta* (2025). Her work has been recognised by the Human Rights Award for non-fiction, the John Barrett Prize, and the Archibald Hannah Junior Fellowship at the Beinecke Library, Yale. She has gained memberships of the American Academy of Arts and Sciences, the Institute of Advanced Study, Durham; and the School of Social Sciences and the School of Historical Studies, Institute for Advanced Study, Princeton; and was awarded two Rockefeller Foundation Scholarly Residencies at Bellagio.

BHAVEEKA MADAGAMMANA is a PhD candidate at Waipapa Taumata Rau University of Auckland's Te Pare School of Architecture and Planning and is part of the Māpihi Māori and Pacific Housing Research doctoral group. His research explores architectural histories of Aotearoa through employing Indigenous and decolonial approaches to research.

GABRIEL MARALNGURRA was a renowned Australian Indigenous artist. He also worked as a translator, artistic mentor, tour guide and researcher in Aboriginal and colonial history and art from western Arnhem Land. He was one of the founding members of Injalak Arts and served as its co-manager. He sadly and unexpectedly passed away after his chapter was written but before it went to print. We use his name with permission of his family.

BETH MARSDEN is a non-Indigenous historian and post-doctoral research fellow in the Research Centre for Deep History in the School of History at the Australian National University. Her research focuses on Australian colonial and Indigenous history, particularly history of education and schooling, from the late 18th century to the present. She is currently writing a national history of First Nations schooling. A former history teacher, Beth is also currently working to develop resources for the teaching of Deep History in Australian schools.

SALLY K MAY is Associate Professor and ARC Future Fellow in the School of Humanities, University of Adelaide. Her research, which is based on more than twenty years of fieldwork in northern Australia, focuses on relationships between people, landscapes, material culture and imagery.

TOM MURRAY is a writer/director/producer and professor in screen media and creative arts. His award-winning feature documentaries include: *Dhakiyarr vs the King*, *In My Father's Country*, *Love in Our Own Time* and *The Skin of Others*. Tom's work is interdisciplinary and investigates and acknowledges the history of colonialism, Indigenous culture and knowledge systems, screen and audio production, documentary media, environmental history, ethics and reciprocity, embodied and affective knowing, creative scholarship and inter-cultural storytelling. He has been a consultant to numerous state film funding agencies and worked across Australia and the Pacific region to develop documentary media skills and scholarship. In 2014 Tom was awarded the Australian Academy of Humanities Max Crawford Medal, the highest award in Australia for outstanding achievement and promise in humanities research. He is an Australian Research Council Future Fellow and Founding Director of Macquarie University's Creative Documentary Research Centre (CDRC).

BRONWEN NEIL is Professor of Ancient History in the School of Humanities at Macquarie University (Sydney). Her research interests are ancient cultural history, with a focus on visual and material representations of religious leadership and environmental stewardship. She was the founding director of the Centre for Ancient Cultural Heritage and Environment (CACHE) at Macquarie University, a former Von Humboldt fellow (Bonn, 2008–2009), and is an elected fellow of the Australian Academy of Humanities and head of its Religion section. She has published widely, with her most recent monograph being *Dreams and Divination from Byzantium to Baghdad (400–1000 CE)* (2021), funded by an ARC Future Fellowship (2014–2019).

MARTIN PORR is Associate Professor of Archaeology at the University of Western Australia and a member of the Centre for Rock Art Research and Management. He was a Senior Alexander von Humboldt Research Fellow and is currently an Australian Research Council Future Fellow, working on contemporary heritage aspects of rock art in Europe, Australia and South Africa. His research has so far concentrated on decolonising approaches in archaeological research, the integration of Indigenous philosophies into archaeological reasoning, and Australian rock art, among numerous other topics, and he has conducted fieldwork in Germany, France, Spain, South Africa, Thailand, Australia, India and the Philippines. Before his academic career, he was employed at the *Landesmuseum für Vorgeschichte* (Halle/Saale, Germany), and as Museum Director of the *Städtische Museen Quedlinburg* (Germany).

LAURA RADEMAKER is an Australian Research Council DECRA Research Fellow at the Australian National University. A historian of Indigenous Australia, she is a winner of the Australian Historical

Association's Hancock Prize and the Academy of Social Sciences in Australia's Bourke Award for her interdisciplinary and Community-based historical methods.

LYNETTE RUSSELL AM, Sir John Monash Distinguished Professor, is an anthropological historian. She is the author or editor of over twenty books. Her current research endeavours involve the comprehensive examination of Dutch, Spanish, Portuguese and Makassan interactions and connections. She is Deputy Director of the Australian Research Council's Centre of Excellence for Indigenous and Environmental Histories and Futures, as well as ARC Kathleen Fitzpatrick Laureate Fellow (2020–2025). In 2025, she takes up the role of German Research Fund Mercator Professor 2025–2027, at the University of Potsdam. She is an elected fellow of the Royal Geographic Society, the Royal Anthropological Institute, the Royal Historical Society, the Academy of Social Sciences Australia, the Australian Humanities Association and the American Academy of Arts and Sciences.

BEN SILVERSTEIN is a lecturer in Indigenous Studies and honorary member of the Research Centre for Deep History at The Australian National University on Ngunnawal and Ngambri Country. He has researched in colonial and Indigenous histories, engaging questions of race and settler colonialism as well as contests over sovereignties and colonial government. He is the author of *Governing Natives: Indirect rule and settler colonialism in Australia's north* (2019).

CHRIS URWIN is an Australian Research Council DECRA Research Fellow (2025–2027) at Monash Indigenous Studies Centre (Monash University), conducting archaeological and museum-based research with Indigenous communities in Australia and the Pacific. He has also held positions at the Smithsonian Institution (USA) and Museums Victoria. His research focuses on how people build places through time, and how personal and Community histories are constructed when artefacts are collected and exchanged.

ANTONY VAVIA is a senior research fellow at Te Puna Vai Mārama (Cook Islands Centre for Research) and a lecturer at the Auckland University of Technology (AUT). With a PhD from AUT focused on small subsistence-based Pacific Island fisheries, he brings a unique blend of marine science and ethnographic expertise to his work. His research interests delve into the intricate relationships between traditional ecological knowledge, cultural practices and using tools within marine science to supplement the development of sustainable/appropriate resource management strategies. Currently, he is collaborating on several innovative projects that address pressing issues in fisheries management across the Pacific region, and learning more about ocean-related policy making.

NOTES

Deep History and deep sovereignty: An introduction

1. See: Andrew Canessa and Manuela Lavinas Picq, *Savages and Citizens: How Indigeneity shapes the state* (Tucson: University of Arizona Press, 2024); Manuela Lavinas Picq, *Vernacular Sovereignties: Indigenous women challenging world politics* (Tucson: University of Arizona Press, 2019).
2. Judy Skene and Limina Collective, 'Experience and identity: Jackie Huggins and writing history', *Limina: A journal of historical and cultural studies*, vol. 2 (1996): pp. 1–7.
3. For various team publications on Deep Histories, see: Ann McGrath and Mary Anne Jebb (eds), *Long History, Deep Time: Deepening histories of place* (Canberra: ANU Press, 2015); Ann McGrath, Mike Jones, Ben Silverstein, Amy Way with Ruby Ekkel, 'Marking Country: Mapping deep histories', *ANU Historical Journal II*, no. 4 (2024): pp. 161–78; Ann McGrath, 'What is "deep history"?', *Teaching History*, vol. 56, no. 1 (2022): p. 4; Ann McGrath, Laura Rademaker and Ben Silverstein, 'Deep history and deep listening: Indigenous knowledges and the narration of deep pasts', *Rethinking History: The journal of theory and practice*, vol. 25, no. 3 (2021): pp. 307–26. We owe inspiration also to Andrew Shryock and Daniel Lord Smail, who use the term 'Deep History' to apply to hominid history and gesture towards a valuable interdisciplinary practice bringing together science and humanities, albeit at that time without a cross-cultural emphasis. See: Andrew Shryock and Daniel Lord Smail (eds), *Deep History: The architecture of past and present*, new ed. (Berkeley: University of California Press, 2011).
4. Ann McGrath, Laura Rademaker and Jakelin Troy (eds), *Everywhen: Australia and the language of deep history* (Sydney: UNSW Press, 2023). This volume was co-published with the University of Nebraska Press. In my earlier study of intermarriage across colonising borders, I argued for the importance of negotiations across gendered sovereignties and their transgenerational continuity; Ann McGrath, *Illicit Love: Interracial sex and marriage in the United States and Australia* (Lincoln: University of Nebraska Press, 2015).
5. Dr Kamanamaikalani Beamer is Chair at the Hawaiʻinuiākea School of Hawaiian Knowledge and was the special plenary speaker. His address was entitled 'Aloha 'Aina: Hawaiian Knowledge Today'.
6. Rediscovering the deep human past: global networks, future opportunities (FL170100121). For further information, see also: <re.anu.edu.au/overview/>.
7. See the Marking Country website: <marking-country.re.anu.edu.au/woddordda-ngarinyin-intro/>; McGrath et al., 'Marking Country: Mapping deep histories': pp. 161–78.
8. For a popular introduction to Pacific history, see: Nicholas Thomas, *Voyagers: The settlement of the Pacific* (London: Head of Zeus, 2021); Nicholas Thomas, *Islanders: The Pacific in the age of empire* (New Haven: Yale University Press, 2010); Anne Salmond, *Tears of Rangi: Experiments across worlds* (Auckland: Auckland University Press, 2017); Anne Salmond, 'Star canoes, voyaging worlds', *Interdisciplinary Science Reviews*, vol. 46, no. 3 (2021): pp. 267–85.
9. Victor Briggs, *Seafaring: Canoeing ancient songlines* (Broome: Magabala Books, 2023).

10 See: Aileen Moreton-Robinson, 'Introduction' in *Sovereign Subjects: Indigenous sovereignty matters*, Aileen Moreton-Robinson (ed.) (Sydney: Allen & Unwin, 2007). She does not provide a set definition, noting that this is experiential knowledge and has multiple manifestations. Note the discussion in chapter 10 of the current volume. See also: Larissa Behrendt, 'Aboriginal sovereignty: A practical roadmap', in *Sovereignty: Frontiers of possibility*, Julie Evans, Ann Genovese, Alexander Reilly and Patrick Wolfe (eds) (Honolulu: University of Hawai'i Press, 2017), pp. 163–78; Evans, Genovese, Reilly, and Wolfe, *Sovereignty*, pp. vii–vii; Robert J Miller, Jacinta Ruru, Larissa Behrendt and Tracey Lindberg, *Discovering Indigenous Lands: The doctrine of discovery in the English colonies* (Oxford: Oxford University Press, 2010); Andrew Fitzmaurice, *Sovereignty, Property and Empire, 1500–2000* (Cambridge: Cambridge University Press, 2014).
11 See the above citation for references to discussions of sovereignty. The term has been hijacked in some ways by the 'sovereign citizens' who espouse an individualistic, anti-state ideology originating in the US, and who assert that they exist outside the state and its powers.
12 For a more sustained discussion of approaches to history, and an Indigenous critique of historical evidence as the Country's teachings, see: Ann McGrath, 'People of the footprints: Rediscovery, Indigenous historicities and the science of deep time', *Interventions: International journal of postcolonial studies*, vol. 22, no. 2 (2022): pp. 181–207.
13 Kathleen Davis, *Periodization and Sovereignty: How ideas of feudalism and secularization govern the politics of time* (Philadelphia: University of Pennsylvania Press, 2008).
14 Asheesh Kapur Siddique, *The Archive of Empire: Knowledge, conquest, and the making of the Early Modern British world* (New Haven: Yale University Press, 2024).
15 Ann McGrath and Lynette Russell, 'Introduction' in *The Companion to Global Indigenous History*, Ann McGrath and Lynette Russell (eds) (New York: Routledge, 2022).
16 Jean M O'Brien, *Firsting and Lasting: Writing Indians out of existence in New England* (Minneapolis: University of Minnesota Press, 2010).
17 We discuss temporality in more detail in the collection McGrath, Rademaker and Troy (eds), *Everywhen*.
18 In 1972, this was the current Parliament House. It was replaced by a massive new building in 1988. This anniversary year marked the 200th anniversary of the first colonisation/invasion, the first fleet of convicts. Yet another reminder of the links between history, sovereignty and the nation state.
19 Gary Foley, Andrew Schaap and Edwina Howell (eds), *The Aboriginal Tent Embassy: Sovereignty, Black Power, land rights and the state* (New York: Routledge, 2014).
20 See: 'Reconciliation at Qantas', Qantas website, 2024, <www.qantas.com/au/en/qantas-group/sustainability/reconciliation-at-qantas.html>.
21 Ross Jones, James Waghorne and Marcia Langton (eds), *Dhoombak Goobgoowana: A history of Indigenous Australia and the University of Melbourne, Volume 1: Truth* (Melbourne: Melbourne University Press, 2024).
22 'The Uluru Statement from the Heart', Australian Human Rights Commission website, 2024, <humanrights.gov.au/our-work/aboriginal-and-torres-strait-islander-social-justice/publications/uluru-statement-heart>; Mark McKenna, *Return to Uluru* (Melbourne: Black Inc., 2021); Megan Davis and George Williams, *Everything You Need to Know about the Voice* (Sydney: UNSW Press, 2023); Melissa Castan

and Lynette Russell, *Time to Listen: An Indigenous Voice to parliament* (Melbourne: Monash University Publishing, 2023). The bark petitions were another dramatic intervention, asserting the sovereignty of the Yirrkala people. Clare Wright, *Naku Dharuk: The Bark Petitions: How the people of Yirrkala changed the course of Australian democracy* (Melbourne: Text Publishing, 2024).
23 Jackie Huggins and John Sanderson, *The Reconciliation Journey* (Melbourne: Macmillan Education Australia, 2009).
24 For more of Rita's story, see: Jackie Huggins and Rita Huggins, *Auntie Rita* (Canberra: Aboriginal Studies Press, 1994); Jackie Huggins, *Sister Girl: The writings of Aboriginal activist and historian Jackie Huggins* (Brisbane: University of Queensland Press, 1998). For a study of Jackie's father, see: Jackie Huggins and Ngaire Jarro, *Jack of Hearts* (Broome: Magabala Books, 2022).
25 'Walking deep history: Carnarvon Gorge', Marking Country website, 2024, <marking-country.re.anu.edu.au/carnarvon-gorge/>.
26 Ann McGrath and Lynette Russell (eds), *The Companion to Global Indigenous History* (New York: Routledge, 2022).
27 One step in that direction is work undertaken by the Ngarrngga Unit at the University of Melbourne, whose expert Indigenous curriculum developers are working to integrate the Carnarvon page created by Jackie and Fred into teaching resources. See: 'Welcome to Ngarrangga', Ngarrangga website, 2024, <www.ngarrngga.org/>.
28 McGrath, Rademaker and Troy (eds), *Everywhen*.
29 'Royal Visit', *Argus*, 20 July 1926, p. 11; 'Royal tour Crossley landaulette', National Museum of Australia website, 2024, <www.nma.gov.au/explore/collection/highlights/royal-tour-crossley-landaulette>.
30 Laurie Bamblett, 'Nangar (c. 1848–1927)', *Australian Dictionary of Biography*, 2024, <adb.anu.edu.au/biography/nangar-33736>.
31 Mark McKenna and Peter Read, '1927 – Jimmy Clements, John Noble, and the opening of Parliament House', *Australian Dictionary of Biography*, 2024, <adb.anu.edu.au/the-quest-for-indigenous-recognition/jimmy-clements>; *Argus*, 10 May 1927, p. 19.
32 Various scholarships are available for anthropology and archaeology fieldwork as fieldwork is generally a required part of their practice. One fund that is available for historical fieldwork is the Minoru Hokari Scholarship; details here: <study.anu.edu.au/scholarships/find-scholarship/minoru-hokari-memorial-scholarship>.
33 Gabriel Maralngurra, in conversation, 10 August 2022, cited in chapter 9.

1 Walking on Sovereign Territory: Carnarvon Gorge
1 For more on this Aboriginal Protection Act and missions such as Cherbourg, see: Thom Blake, *A Dumping Ground: The history of Cherbourg Settlement, 1900–1940* (Brisbane: Thom Blake Historian Publishing, 2023).
2 AIATSIS, 'Overturning the doctrine of Terra Nullius: The Mabo Case', AIATSIS website, 2024, <aiatsis.gov.au/sites/default/files/research_pub/overturning-the-doctrine-of-terra-nullius_0_3.pdf>.
3 Some of these works include: Jackie Huggins, *Sister Girl: The writings of Aboriginal activist and historian Jackie Huggins* (Brisbane: University of Queensland Press, 1998); Jackie Huggins, *Sister Girl: Reflections on Tiddaism, identity and reconciliation* (Brisbane, University of Queensland Press, 2022); Jackie Huggins, 'Experience and identity: Jackie Huggins and writing history', *Limina: A journal of historical*

and Cultural Studies, no. 2 (1996): pp. 1–7; Jackie Huggins, 'The 1967 Referendum: Thirty years on', *Australian Aboriginal Studies*, no. 1 (1997): p. 3; Jackie Huggins, 'Reflections on the reconciliation journey', *Journal of Australian Indigenous Issues*, vol. 21, no. 4 (2019): pp. 72–77; Jackie Huggins and Maria Dimopoulos, 'In conversation with Dr Jackie Huggins', *Journal of Australian Indigenous Issues*, vol. 26, nos. 1–2 (2023): pp. 53–55.

4   Raymond Evans, Kay Saunders and Kathryn Cronin, *Exclusion, Exploitation, and Extermination: Race relations in colonial Queensland* (Sydney: Australia and New Zealand Book Company, 1975).

5   See the site here: <marking-country.re.anu.edu.au/>. The wurdu ceremony is presented here: <marking-country.re.anu.edu.au/woddordda-ngarinyin-intro/>.

6   Rita Huggins and Jackie Huggins, *Auntie Rita* (Canberra: Aboriginal Studies Press, 1994). *Auntie Rita* has been published in numerous editions, with the latest published in 2023: Rita Huggins and Jackie Huggins, *Auntie Rita: The classic memoir of an Aboriginal woman's love and determination* (Sydney: Aboriginal Studies Press, 2023).

2   Good timing? Australian history's changing temporality

1   EP Thompson, *The Making of the English Working Class* (New York: Pantheon Books, 1963); Frank Bongiorno, 'Australian labour history: Contexts, trends and influences', *Labour History*, no. 100 (2011): pp. 1–18; Ann Curthoys, 'Towards a feminist labour history', *Labour History*, no. 29 (1975): pp. 88–95; Ann Curthoys, 'Historiography and women's liberation', *Arena*, no. 22 (1970): pp. 35–40.

2   Michel-Rolph Trouillot, *Silencing the Past: Power and the production of history* (Boston: Beacon Press, 1995); Gayatri Chakravorty Spivak, 'Can the subaltern speak?', in *Marxism and the Interpretation of Culture*, Cary Nelson and Lawrence Grossberg (eds) (Champaign: University of Illinois Press, 1988), pp. 271–313; Patrick Wolfe, *Traces of History: Elementary structures of race* (London: Verso, 2016); Aileen Moreton-Robinson, *The White Possessive: Property, power, and Indigenous sovereignty* (Minneapolis: University of Minnesota Press, 2015); Dipesh Chakrabarty, 'Empire, ethics, and the calling of history: Knowledge in the postcolony', in *Unsettling History: Archiving and narrating in historiography*, Sebastian Jobs and Alf Lüdtke (eds) (Frankfurt: Campus Verlag, 2010), pp. 63–88; La Garrett J King, 'What is black historical consciousness?', in *Contemplating Historical Consciousness: Notes from the field*, Anna Clark and Carla Peck (eds) (New York: Berghahn Books, 2020), pp. 163–74; Linda Tuhiwai Smith, *Decolonizing Methodologies: Research and Indigenous peoples*, 2nd ed. (London: Zed Books Ltd, 2012); Leigh Boucher, 'New cultural history and Australia's colonial past', in *Australian History Now*, Anna Clark and Paul Ashton (eds) (Sydney: NewSouth Publishing, 2013), pp. 288–304; Anna Clark, *Making Australian History* (Sydney: Penguin Random House, 2022); Patricia Grimshaw, Marilyn Lake, Ann McGrath and Marian Quartly, *Creating a Nation* (Melbourne: McPhee Gribble, 1994).

3   Peter Novick, *That Noble Dream: The 'objectivity question' and the American historical profession* (Cambridge: Cambridge University Press, 1988).

4   Ann Curthoys and John Docker, *Is History Fiction?* (Ann Arbor: University of Michigan Press, 2005); Novick, *That Noble Dream*; Tom Griffiths, *The Art of Time Travel: Historians and their craft* (Melbourne: Black Inc., 2016).

5   Wolfgang von Leyden, 'History and the concept of relative time', *History and Theory*, vol. 2, no. 3 (1963): pp. 263–85.

6   Reinhart Koselleck, *Futures Past: On the semantics of historical time* (Cambridge, Mass: MIT Press, 1985); Juhan Hellerma, 'Koselleck on modernity, historik, and layers of time', *History and Theory*, vol. 59, no. 2 (2020): pp. 188–209; David Carr, 'Place and time: On the interplay of historical points of view', *History and Theory*, vol. 40, no. 4 (2001): pp. 153–67.
7   Berber Bevernage and Chris Lorenz, 'Breaking up time – negotiating the borders between present, past and future: An introduction', in *Breaking up Time – Negotiating the borders between present, past and future*, Berber Bevernage and Chris Lorenz (eds) (Göttingen: Vandenhoeck & Ruprecht, 2013): p. 13; Chris Lorenz and Marek Tamm, 'Who knows where the time goes?', *Rethinking History*, vol. 18, no. 4 (2 October 2014): pp. 499–521.
8   Anna Clark, 'Just a matter of time: Reviewing temporality in Australian historiography', *Rethinking History*, vol. 25, no. 2 (2023): pp. 1–27.
9   Leigh Boucher, 'Victorian liberalism and the effect of sovereignty: A view from the settler periphery', *History Australia*, vol. 13, no. 1 (2016): p. 18; Leigh Boucher, 'Trans/national history and disciplinary amnesia: Historicising White Australia at two fins de siècles', in *Creating White Australia*, Jane Carey and Claire McLisky (eds) (Sydney: Sydney University Press, 2009), pp. 44–64; Bain Attwood, 'Settler histories and Indigenous pasts: Australia and New Zealand', in *The Oxford History of Historical Writing: Historical writing since 1945*, Axel Schneider and Daniel Woolf (eds), vol. 5, (Oxford: Oxford University Press, 2015): pp. 594–614; Bain Attwood, 'Denial in a settler society: The Australian case', *History Workshop Journal*, vol. 84, no. 1 (2017): pp. 24–43.
10 Warwick Anderson, '1. Decolonizing histories in theory and practice: An introduction', *History and Theory*, vol. 59, no. 3 (2020): pp. 369–75; Miranda Johnson, '7. Toward a genealogy of the researcher as subject in post/decolonial Pacific histories', *History and Theory*, vol. 59, no. 3 (2020): pp. 421–29; Deborah Bird Rose, *Reports from a Wild Country: Ethics for decolonisation* (Sydney: UNSW Press, 2004).
11 Ann McGrath and Mary Anne Jebb (eds), *Long History, Deep Time: Deepening histories of place* (Canberra: ANU Press, 2015); Ann McGrath, Laura Rademaker and Jakelin Troy (eds), *Everywhen: Australia and the language of deep history* (Sydney: UNSW Press, 2023).
12 See, for example: Alex Lichtenstein, 'Decolonizing the AHR', *American Historical Review*, vol. 123, no. 1 (2018): pp. xiv–xvii.
13 Priya Satia, *Time's Monster* (Cambridge: Harvard University Press, 2020): pp. 6–7.
14 Dipesh Chakrabarty, 'The politics and possibility of historical knowledge: Continuing the conversation', *Postcolonial Studies*, vol. 14, no. 2 (2011): p. 247.
15 Satia, *Time's Monster*: p. 70.
16 GW Rusden, *History of Australia* (London: Chapman and Hall Ltd, 1883): p. 2.
17 Author unknown, *The History of New Holland, from Its Discovery in 1616, to the Present Time* (London: John Stockdale, 1787): pp. 1–2.
18 John Dunmore Lang, *An Historical and Statistical Account of New South Wales, Both as a Penal Settlement and as a British Colony*, 2nd ed., vol. 1 (London: A.J. Valpy, 1837): p. 1.
19 David Collins, *An Account of the English Colony in New South Wales, From Its First Settlement in January 1788, to August 1801: With remarks on the dispositions, customs, manners, &c. of the native inhabitants of that country*, 2nd ed. (London: T Cadell and W Davies, 1804), p. 10.

20 George ('An Old Hand') Hamilton, *Experiences of a Colonist Forty Years Ago: A journey from Port Phillip to South Australia in 1839 and a voyage from Port Phillip to Adelaide in 1846* (Adelaide: J Williams, 1880): p. 38.
21 Author unknown, *The History of New Holland*, p. ix.
22 William Westgarth, *Australia Felix; or a historical and descriptive account of the settlement of Port Phillip, New South Wales; Including full particulars of the manners and condition of the Aboriginal natives; with observations on emigration, on the system of transportation; and on colonial policy* (Edinburgh: Oliver and Boyd, 1848): pp. 2–3.
23 F Algar, *A Handbook to New South Wales* (London: 'Australian and New Zealand Gazette' Office, 1870): p. 2.
24 Denis Byrne, 'Deep nation: Australia's acquisition of an Indigenous past', *Aboriginal History Journal*, vol. 20 (1996): p. 91.
25 Mark McKenna, 'A preference for forgetting: Some reflections on publishing: *Looking for Blackfellas' Point: An Australian history of place*', *Aboriginal History Journal*, vol. 27 (January 2011): p. 132. See also: Paul Carter, *The Road to Botany Bay: An exploration of landscape and history* (Minneapolis: University of Minnesota Press, 1987).
26 Jeanine Leane, 'Historyless people', in *Long History, Deep Time*, Jebb and McGrath (eds): p. 156; Lorenzo Veracini, 'Historylessness: Australia as a settler colonial collective', *Postcolonial Studies*, vol. 10, no. 3, (March 2015 [2007]): pp. 271–85. See also: Patrick Wolfe, *Traces of History: Elementary structures of race* (London, New York: Verso, 2016); 'Settlercolonialism and the elimination of the native', *Journal of Genocide Research*, vol. 8, no. 4 (2006): pp. 387–409.
27 EJ Hobsbawm and David J Kertzer, 'Ethnicity and nationalism in Europe today', *Anthropology Today*, vol. 8, no. 1 (1992): p. 3.
28 Grace Karskens, 'Life and death on Dyarubbin', *Griffith Review*, no. 63 (2019): p. 105.
29 Ian Tyrrell, *Historians in Public: The practice of American history, 1890–1970* (Chicago: University of Chicago Press, 2005); Stefan Berger, 'Introduction', in *Writing the Nation: A global perspective*, Stefan Berger (ed.) (Hampshire: Palgrave Macmillan, 2007): pp. 1–29; Kerwin Lee Klein, *Frontiers of Historical Imagination: Narrating the European conquest of North America, 1890–1990* (Berkeley: University of California Press, 1999); Peter Mandler, *History and National Life* (London: Profile Books, 2002).
30 'Editorial', *Sydney Morning Herald*, 21 April 1900; 'Editorial: An historical society', *Sydney Morning Herald*, 22 October 1900; KR Cramp, 'The Australian Historical Society – The story of its foundation', *Australian Historical Society: Journal and proceedings*, vol. 4, no. 1 (1917): pp. 1–14.
31 Attwood, 'Denial in a settler society', pp. 24–43.
32 Alexander Sutherland, *Victoria and Its Metropolis: Past and present*, vol. 1 (Melbourne: McCarron, Bird & Co., Publishers, 1888): p. 29.
33 GV Portus, *Australia Since 1606*, 2nd ed. (Melbourne: Oxford University Press, 1955): p. 18.
34 Russel Ward, *Man Makes History* (Sydney: Shakespeare Head Press, 1952): p. 2. See also: AL Meston, *A Junior History of Australia*, 3rd ed. (Oxford, Melbourne: Oxford University Press, 1941): pp. 115–16.
35 Peter Board, 'History and Australian history', *Australian Historical Society: Journal and proceedings*, vol. 3, no. 6 (1916): p. 291.
36 William Austin Horn, 'The scientific exploration of Central Australia', *Proceedings of the Royal Colonial Institute*, vol. 27 (1895–96): pp. 88–110; Amy Way, 'Displacing

history, shifting paradigms: Erasing Aboriginal antiquity from Australian anthropology', *History Australia*, vol. 19, no. 4 (2022): pp. 1–21; Laura Rademaker, 'A history of deep time: Indigenous knowledges and deep pasts in settler-colonial presents', *History Australia*, vol. 18, no. 4 (2021): pp. 658–75.
37   Andrew Markus, 'William Cooper and the 1937 Petition to the King', *Aboriginal History Journal*, vol. 7 (2011): pp. 46–60; John Patten and William Ferguson, *Aborigines Claim Citizen Rights! A statement of the case for the Aborigines Progressive Association* (Sydney: The Publicist, 1937); Jack Horner and Marcia Langton, 'The Day of Mourning', in *Australians 1938*, Bill Gammage and Peter Spearitt (Eds), vol. 3, *Australians: A historical library* (Sydney: Fairfax, Syme & Weldon Associates, 1987), pp. 29–36; Gavin Souter, 'Skeletons at the feast', in *Australians 1938*, Bill Gammage and Peter Spearitt, *Australians: A historical library* (Sydney: Fairfax, Syme & Weldon Associates, 1987): pp. 13–28.
38   Xavier Herbert, *Capricornia* (London: Angus & Robertson, 1938); Eleanor Dark, *The Timeless Land*, 5th ed. (London: Collins, 1946); Judith Wright, 'N___s Leap New England', *Meanjin*, vol. 4, no. 2 (1945): p. 85.
39   Ian J McNiven and Lynette Russell, *Appropriated Pasts: Indigenous peoples and the colonial culture of archaeology* (Washington: AltaMira Press, 2005): pp. 8, 52.
40   Tom Griffiths, *Hunters and Collectors: The Antiquarian imagination in Australia* (Melbourne: Cambridge University Press, 1996): p. 45.
41   Graeme Osborne and WF Mandle (eds), New History: Studying Australia Today (Sydney: George Allen & Unwin, 1982).
42   DJ Mulvaney, *The Prehistory of Australia* (Melbourne: Penguin, 1969): p. 15.
43   Billy Griffiths, *Deep Time Dreaming: Uncovering ancient Australia* (Melbourne: Black Inc., 2018): p. 2. See also: Ann McGrath, Laura Rademaker and Ben Silverstein, 'Deep history and deep listening: Indigenous knowledges and the narration of deep pasts', *Rethinking History*, 13 September 2021: pp. 1–20; Ann McGrath and Lynette Russell (eds), *The Routledge Companion to Global Indigenous History* (Milton Park: Routledge, 2022).
44   Oodgeroo Noonuccal, *The Dawn Is at Hand: Poems* (Brisbane: Jacaranda Press, 1966); Oodgeroo Noonuccal, *My People: A Kath Walker collection*, 2nd ed. (Brisbane: Jacaranda Press, 1981); Kevin Gilbert, *Because a White Man'll Never Do It* (Sydney: Angus & Robertson, 1973); Kevin Gilbert, *Living Black: Blacks talk to Kevin Gilbert* (Melbourne: Penguin, 1978); Gary Foley, 'Black Power, land rights and academic history', *Griffith Law Review*, vol. 20, no. 3 (January 2011): pp. 608–18; Marnie Kennedy, *Born a Half Caste* (Canberra: Australian Institute of Aboriginal Studies, 1985); Margaret Tucker, *If Everyone Cared* (Sydney: Ure Smith, 1977).
45   Moreton-Robinson, *The White Possessive*.
46   RHW Reece, 'The Aborigines in Australian historiography', in *Historical Disciplines and Culture in Australasia*, John A Moses (ed.) (Brisbane: University of Queensland Press, 1979): p. 274. See also: G Osborne and WF Mandle (eds), *New History: Studying Australia today* (Sydney: George Allen & Unwin, 1982).
47   Dipesh Chakrabarty, 'Empire, ethics, and the calling of history: Knowledge in the postcolony', in *Unsettling History: Archiving and narrating in historiography*, Sebastian Jobs and Alf Lüdtke (eds) (Frankfurt: Campus Verlag, 2010): pp. 63–88; 'Minority histories, subaltern pasts', *Perspectives on History*, 1 November 1997, <www.historians.org/publications-and-directories/perspectives-on-history/november-1997/minority-histories-subaltern-pasts>; Dipesh Chakrabarty, 'The time of history and the times of gods', in *The Politics of Culture in the Shadow of Capital*, Lisa Lowe and David Lloyd (eds) (Durham: Duke University Press, 1997), p. 50;

Durba Ghosh, 'Another set of imperial turns?', *American Historical Review*, vol. 117, no. 3 (2012): p. 782; Edward Said, *Culture and Imperialism* (New York: Vintage Books, 1994); Spivak, 'Can the subaltern speak?': pp. 280–81; Epeli Hau'ofa, *We Are the Ocean: Selected works* (Honolulu: University of Hawai'i Press, 2008); Tracey Banivanua Mar, *Decolonisation and the Pacific: Indigenous globalisation and the ends of empire* (Cambridge: Cambridge University Press, 2016).

48 Jeanine Leane, 'Historyless people', in *Long History, Deep Time*, Jebb and McGrath (eds): p. 151.
49 John Maynard, 'Across "Koori time" and space', in *Everywhen*, McGrath, Rademaker and Troy (eds): pp. 221–28.
50 Tony Birch, 'The trouble with history', in *Australian History Now*, Anna Clark and Paul Ashton (eds) (Sydney: NewSouth Publishing, 2013): pp. 232–50; Leane, 'Historyless people'; Alison Whittaker (ed.), *Fire Front: First Nations poetry and power today* (Brisbane: University of Queensland Press, 2020); Larissa Behrendt, *Finding Eliza: Power and colonial storytelling* (Brisbane: University of Queensland Press, 2016).
51 Miranda Johnson, 'Writing Indigenous histories now', *Australian Historical Studies*, vol. 45, no. 3 (2014): pp. 317–30.
52 Krim Benterrak, Stephen Muecke and Paddy Roe, *Reading the Country: Introduction to nomadology* (Melbourne: Re.Press, 2014): p. 144.
53 Warwick Anderson, '8. Finding decolonial metaphors in postcolonial histories', *History and Theory*, vol. 59, no. 3 (2020): p. 438. See also: Ann McGrath, 'People of the footprints: Rediscovery, Indigenous historicities and the science of deep time', *Interventions*, vol. 20, no. 2, 2021: pp. 181–207.
54 Sebouh David Aslanian, Joyce E Chaplin, Ann McGrath and Kristin Mann, 'AHR conversation how size matters: The question of scale in history', *The American Historical Review*, vol. 118, no. 5 (1 December 2013): p. 1436.
55 McGrath, Rademaker and Troy (eds), *Everywhen*.
56 Cited in: Clark, *Making Australian History*: p. 300.

3 Deep Time history goes to school: How the new Australian curriculum is learning from the past

1 CEW Bean, 'The old inhabitants', Victorian Education Department, *Victorian Readers; Eighth book* (Melbourne: Victorian Education Department, 1928): p. 6.
2 Bean, 'The old inhabitants', 1928: p. 6.
3 Ann McGrath and Mary Ann Jebb (eds), *Long History, Deep Time: Deepening histories of place* (Canberra: ANU Press, 2015).
4 Australian Curriculum and Reporting Authority (ACARA), 'Year 7 History: Deep Time History of Australia', Australian Curriculum (2022). The full course title used by ACARA is 'Deep Time History of Australia'. In this chapter, I use 'Deep Time History'.
5 Ann McGrath and Laura Rademaker, 'The languages and temporalities of "Everywhen" in Deep History', in Ann McGrath, Laura Rademaker and Jakelin Troy (eds), *Everywhen: Australia and the language of deep history* (Sydney: UNSW Press, 2023): p. 4.
6 McGrath and Rademaker, 'The languages and temporalities of "Everywhen" in Deep History', p. 8.
7 Tanya Kohvakka, 'The absent curriculum in Finnish history textbooks: The case of colonialism', *Nordisk tidsskrift for pedagogikk og krittikk*, vol. 10, no. 3 (2024): p. 47.

8   Beth Marsden, 'The compulsory system is failing: Assimilation, mobility, and Aboriginal students in Victorian state schools, 1961–1968', *History of Education Review*, vol. 47, no. 2: pp. 143–54; Matthew Keynes and Beth Marsden, 'Ontology, sovereignty, legitimacy: Two key moments when history curriculum was challenged in public discourse and the curricular effects, Australia 1950s and 2000s', *History of Education Review*, vol. 50, no. 2: pp. 130–45.
9   Clare Bradford, *Reading Race: Aboriginality in Australian children's literature* (Melbourne: Melbourne University Press, 1997): p. 64.
10 Ross L Jones, James Waghorne and Marcia Langton, *Dhoombak Goobgoowana: A history of Indigenous Australia and the University of Melbourne* (Melbourne: Melbourne University Press, 2024): p. 13.
11 Baldwin Spencer, 'The Australian Aborigines', *School Paper* (Melbourne: Victorian Education Department, 1900): p. 4.
12 Victorian Education Department, *School Paper*, Class 3 (Melbourne: Victorian Education Department, 1911): p. 36.
13 Anna Clark, 'Just a matter of time: Reviewing temporality in Australian historiography', *Rethinking History: The journal of theory and practice*, vol. 28, no. 1 (2024): p. 8; Tom Griffiths, *The Antiquarian Imagination in Australia: Hunters and collectors* (Melbourne: Cambridge University Press, 1996): p. 56.
14 Penelope Edmonds, 'The intimate, urbanising frontier: Native camps and settler colonialism's violent array of spaces around early Melbourne', *Making Settler Colonial Space: Perspectives on race, place and identity* (London: Palgrave Macmillan: 2010): pp. 129–54.
15 Victorian Education Department, *School Paper*, Grades VII and VIII, February 1920: p. 7.
16 Bean, 'The old inhabitants'.
17 Victorian Education Department, *School Paper* Grades V and VI, November 1929: p. 4.
18 Richard Broome, *Aboriginal Victorians: A history since 1800* (Sydney: Allen & Unwin, 2005): p. iii.
19 Griffiths, *The Antiquarian Imagination in Australia*: pp. 55–85; Dr Aunty Doris Paton, Beth Marsden and Jessica Horton, '"No time for a history lesson": The contest over memorials to Angus McMillan on Gunaikurnai Country', *Aboriginal History*, vol. 46 (2022): pp. 3–27.
20 Victorian Education Department, *Social Studies: Course of study* (Melbourne: Victorian Education Department, 1955): p. 12.
21 For example, in April 1968, the *School Paper* for Grades 5 & 6 included 'Why parrots cannot sing …', written by Dorothy Carnegie. It began: 'The Dream-time was the very beginning of everything so long that only the very wisest of the birds and creatures can guess, and it was then that the Great Bunyip called his tribe together …'
22 Jan Keane, *National Identity and Education in Early Twentieth Century Australia* (Bingley: Emerald Publishing Limited Studies, 2024): p. 101. Danielle Hradsky, 'Education for reconciliation? Understanding and acknowledging the history of teaching First Nations content in Victoria, Australia', *History of Education*, vol. 51, no. 1 (2022): p. 141.
23 Mati Keynes, Beth Marsden and Archie Thomas, 'Does the curriculum fail Indigenous political aspirations? Sovereignty and Australian history and social studies curriculum', *Nordic Journal of Educational History*, vol. 10, no. 2 (2023): p. 71.

24　*Koori History Syllabus*, Melbourne: Victorian Curriculum and Assessment Board, 1994.
25　Kevin Lowe, Nikki Moodie and Sara Weuffen, 'Refusing reconciliation in Indigenous curriculum', in Bill Green, Philip Roberts and Marie Brennan (eds), *Curriculum Challenges and Opportunities in a Changing World: Curriculum studies worldwide* (Cham: Palgrave McMillian, 2021): pp. 71–86; Jacinta Maxwell, Kevin Lowe and Peta Salter, 'The re-creation and resolution of the "problem" of Indigenous education in the Aboriginal and Torres Strait Islander cross-curriculum priority', *The Australian Educational Researcher*, vol. 45, no. 2 (2018): pp. 161–77.
26　Bruce Pascoe, *Dark Emu: Black seeds: Agriculture or accident?* (Broome: Magabala Books, 2014); Larissa Behrendt (dir.), *The First Inventors*, SBS, 2023.
27　First Peoples' Assembly of Victoria, *Tyerri Yoo-Rrook (seed of truth): Report to the Yoo-Rrook Justice Commission from the First People's Assembly of Victoria*, June 2021.
28　Commonwealth of Australia, *Final Report of the Referendum Council*, 30 June 2017.
29　Melitta Hogarth, 'Talkin' bout a revolution: The call for transformation and reform in Indigenous education', *The Australian Educational Researcher*, vol. 45, no. 5 (2018): pp. 663–74.
30　Melitta Hogarth, 'An analysis of education academics' attitudes and preconceptions about Indigenous Knowledge in initial teachers' education', *Journal of Indigenous Education*, vol. 51, no. 2 (2022), pp. 1–18.
31　Daniel Hurst, 'Alan Tudge says he doesn't want students to be taught "hatred" of Australia in fiery Triple J interview', *Guardian*, 8 September 2021, <www.theguardian.com/australia-news/2021/sep/08/alan-tudge-says-he-doesnt-want-students-to-be-taught-hatred-of-australia-in-fiery-triple-j-interview>.
32　Calla Wahlquist, 'Rio Tinto blasts 46,000-year-old Aboriginal site to expand iron ore mine', *Guardian*, 26 May 2020, <www.theguardian.com/australia-news/2020/may/26/rio-tinto-blasts-46000-year-old-aboriginal-site-to-expand-iron-ore-mine>; Keira Proust, 'Calls for better education after sacred Aboriginal cultural sites vandalised on NSW Central Coast', ABC News, 5 November 2023, <www.abc.net.au/news/2023-11-06/aboriginal-sacred-sites-vandalised-nsw-central-coast-education/103039536>.
33　Tasmania was the only state to implement the new Australian Curriculum in 2023.
34　The timeline for implementing this new curriculum is determined by state and territory education authorities. The Victorian Curriculum and Assessment Authority (VCAA) released their new curriculum late in June 2024, when this chapter was already complete; in October 2024 it was announced that the NSW Education Standards Authority's new syllabus (to be implemented from 2027) did not include 'deep time history of Australia' in Year 7 history.
35　Nikki Moodie, 'Decolonising race theory: Place, survivance and sovereignty' in Greg Vass, Jacinta Maxwell, Sophie Rudolph and Kalervo N Gulson (eds), *The Relationality of Race in Education Research* (Abingdon: Routledge, 2017): p. 38.
36　ACARA Teachers Guide 4, 'The Deep Time history of Australia: Preparing to teach the Version 9.0 Australian Curriculum: History Year 7', a Teacher's Guide released by ACARA in June, 2024.
37　Bryan Smith, 'The disciplined winds blow in from the West: The forgotten epistemic inheritance of historical thinking', *History Encounters: A journal of historical consciousness, historical cultures, and history education*, vol, 7, no. 3 (2020): pp. 21–32.
38　For example, June Bam, *Ausi Told Me: Why Cape herstoriographies matter* (Johannesburg: Jacana Media, 2021); Ann McGrath, Laura Rademaker and Ben Silverstein, 'Deep history and deep listening: Indigenous knowledges and the

narration of deep pasts', *Rethinking History*, vol. 25, no. 3 (2021): pp. 307–26; McGrath and Jebb, *Long History, Deep Time: Deepening histories of place*, 2015.
39 Clark, 'Just a matter of time', 2024: p. 4.
40 Lou Netana-Glover, 'Indigenous futures and deep time connections to place', in *The Routledge Handbook of Australian Indigenous Peoples and Futures*, Bronwyn Carlson et al. (eds) (London: Routledge, 2023): p. 300.
41 Joe Sambono, *First Nations Perspectives in the Classroom*, Curriculum Connect Symposium, 2022, <curriculumconnect.slq.qld.gov.au/resources/first-nations-perspectives-classroom-joe-sambono>.
42 Research Centre for Deep History, *Marking Country* website, <marking-country.re.anu.edu.au/>; Global Encounters Monash website, <globalencounters.net/>.

4 Archaeology and Aboriginal sovereignty
1   Hamish Hastie, 'State swings axe on iconic Kimberley Falls experience', *WA Today*, 15 March 2024, </www.watoday.com.au/politics/western-australia/state-swings-axe-on-iconic-kimberley-horizontal-falls-experience-20240315-p5fcsu.html>.
2   Valda Blundell, Kim Doohan, Daniel Vachon, Malcolm Allbrock, Mary Anne Jebb and Joh Bornman (eds), *Barddabardda Wodjenangorddee: We're telling all of you: The creation, history and people of Dambimangaddee Country* (Derby: Dambimangari Aboriginal Corporation, 2017); Sylvester Mangolamara, Lily Karadada, Janet Oobagooma, Donny Woolagoodja, Jack Karadada and Kim Doohan, *We are coming to see you* (Derby: Dambimangari Aboriginal Corporation/Wunambal Gaambera Aboriginal Corporation, 2019); Yornadaiyn Woolagoodja, *Yornadaiyn Woolagoodja* (Broome: Magabala Books, 2020).
3   Martin Porr, 'Art, representation, and the ontology of images: Some considerations from the *Wanjina Wunggurr* tradition, Kimberley, Northwest Australia', in *Ontologies of Rock Art: Images, relational approaches, and Indigenous knowledges*, Oscar Moro Abadía and Martin Porr (eds) (Abingdon: Routledge, 2021): pp. 192–95.
4   Billy Griffiths, *Deep Time Dreaming: Uncovering ancient Australia* (Carlton: Black Inc., 2018).
5   Benedict Anderson, *Imagined Communities: Reflections on the origin and spread of nationalism* (London: Verso, 2006).
6   'The Uluru Statement from the Heart', Australian Human Rights Commission website, <humanrights.gov.au/our-work/aboriginal-and-torres-strait-islander-social-justice/publications/uluru-statement-heart>.
7   Chris Clarkson et al., 'Human occupation of northern Australia by 65,000 years ago', *Nature*, vol. 547 (2017): p. 306.
8   See, for example, James F O'Connell et al. 'When did Homo sapiens first reach Southeast Asia and Sahul?' *Proceedings of the National Academy of Sciences*, vol. 115, no. 34 (2018): pp. 8482–90. A series of forum pieces published in 2018 provide an overview of some of the issues that are discussed in connection to the dating of Madjedbebe in the journal of *Australian Archaeology* (vol. 83, no. 3 and vol. 84, no. 4).
9   Martin Porr, 'Digging into the human past: Archaeology, time, and the object', in *Engaging with the Past and Present: The relationship between past and present across the disciplines*, Paul M Dover (ed.) (Abingdon: Routledge, 2023).
10 Billy Griffiths and Lynette Russell, 'What we were told: Responses to 65,000 years of Aboriginal history', *Aboriginal History*, vol. 42 (2018): pp. 31–54, 32.
11 Catherine J Frieman, 'Innovation, continuity, and the punctuated temporality of archaeological narratives', in *Everywhen: Australia and the language of deep history*,

Ann McGrath, Laura Rademaker and Jakelin Troy (eds), (Sydney: UNSW Press, 2023).
12　Justin Pollard, *The Story of Archaeology: An illustrated history of 50 great discoveries* (London: Quercus, 2011): p. 30.
13　Pollard, *The Story of Archaeology*: p. 32.
14　Bruce Trigger, *A History of Archaeological Thought, 2nd Edition* (Cambridge: Cambridge University Press, 2006).
15　Pratik Chakrabarti, *Inscriptions of Nature: Geology and the naturalization of antiquity* (Baltimore: John Hopkins University Press, 2020).
16　Clive Gamble, *Making Deep History: Zeal, perseverance, and the time revolution of 1859* (Oxford: Oxford University Press, 2021); Michael Taylor, *Impossible Monsters: Dinosaurs, Darwin, and the war between science and religion* (Dublin: Penguin, 2024).
17　Julian Thomas, *Archaeology and Modernity* (New York: Routledge, 2004).
18　Gamble, *Making Deep History*.
19　Simon Holdaway, 'Absolute dating', in *Archaeology in Practice: A student guide to archaeological analyses*, Jane Balme and Alistair Paterson (eds): pp. 85–117 (Chichester: Wiley Blackwell, 2014).
20　Zenobia Jacobs, 'Optically stimulated luminescence (OSL) dating', in *Encyclopedia of Geoarchaeology*, Allan S Gilbert (ed.), (Dordrecht: Springer, 2017).
21　Porr, 'Digging into the human past'.
22　Griffiths, *Deep Time Dreaming*.
23　Rachel J Crellin, *Change and Archaeology* (Abingdon: Routledge, 2020); Assaf Nativ and Gavin Lucas, 'Archaeology without antiquity', *Antiquity*, vol. 94, no. 376 (2020): pp. 852–63; Catherine J Frieman, *Archaeology as History: Telling stories from a fragmented past* (Cambridge: Cambridge University Press, 2023).
24　Harry Lourandos, *Continent of Hunter-Gatherers: New perspectives in Australian prehistory* (Cambridge: Cambridge University Press, 1997): p. 9.
25　Peter Hiscock, *Archaeology of Ancient Australia* (New York: Routledge, 2007).
26　Hiscock, *Archaeology of Ancient Australia*: p. 17.
27　Hiscock, *Archaeology of Ancient Australia*: p. 17.
28　Hiscock, *Archaeology of Ancient Australia*: p. 17.
29　Clarkson et al., 'Human occupation of northern Australia by 65,000 years ago': p. 306.
30　Jane Balme and Alistair Paterson (eds), *Archaeology in Practice: A student guide to archaeological analyses* (Malden: Wiley-Blackwell, 2013).
31　Tim Murray, *From Antiquarian to Archaeologist: The history and philosophy of archaeology* (Barnsley: Pen & Sword Books Ltd, 2014); Tim Murray (ed.), *Time and Archaeology* (London: Routledge, 2014).
32　Frieman, *Archaeology as History*.
33　Ann McGrath and Mary Anne Jebb (eds), *Long History, Deep Time: Deepening histories of place* (Canberra: ANU Press, 2015); Ann McGrath, Laura Rademaker and Jakelin Troy (eds), *Everywhen: Australia and the language of deep history* (Sydney: UNSW Press, 2023).
34　Christopher Witmore, 'Chronopolitics and archaeology', in *The Encyclopedia of Global Archaeology*, Claire Smith (ed.) (New York: Springer, 2014).
35　Maria Stavrinaki, 'All the time in the world', *Artforum*, vol. 56, no. 7 (2018): pp. 202–14; Aleida Assmann, *Is Time out of Joint? On the rise and fall of the modern time regime* (Ithaca: Cornell University Press, 2020).

36 Amy Way, 'Displacing history, shifting paradigms: Erasing Aboriginal antiquity from Australian anthropology', *History Australia*, vol. 19, no. 4 (2022): pp. 710–30.
37 Thomas, *Archaeology and Modernity*.
38 Daniel Lord Smail and Andrew Shryock, 'History and the "pre"', *American Historical Review*, vol. 118, no. 3 (2013): pp. 709–57.
39 Chakrabarti, *Inscriptions of Nature*; see also Dipesh Chakrabarty, 'The muddle of modernity', *The American Historical Review*, vol. 116, no. 3 (2011): pp. 663–75.
40 See also: Stefanos Geroulanos, *The Invention of Prehistory: Empire, violence, and our obsession with human origins* (New York: Liveright Publishing Corporation, 2024).
41 Johannes Fabian, *Time and the Other: How anthropology makes its object* (New York: Columbia University Press, 1983).
42 Tim Ingold, *The Perception of the Environment: Essays in livelihood, dwelling and skill* (London: Routledge, 2000).
43 Walter D Mignolo, *The Darker Side of Western Modernity: Global futures, decolonial options* (Durham: Duke University Press, 2011): pp. 155–56.
44 Gavin Lucas, *The Archaeology of Time* (London: Routledge, 2005): pp. 12–13.
45 Martin Porr, 'The temporality of humanity and the colonial landscape of the deep human past', in *Interrogating Human Origins: Decolonisation and the deep human past*, Martin Porr and Jacqueline Maree Matthews (eds) (London: Routledge, 2020).
46 Lucas, *The Archaeology of Time*; Gavin Lucas, *Writing the Past: Knowledge and literary production in archaeology* (New York: Routledge, 2019).
47 Christopher Witmore, 'A question of chronopolitics', in *Reclaiming Archaeology: Beyond the tropes of modernity*, Alfredo González-Ruibal (ed.), (New York: Routledge, 2013).
48 François Hartog, *Chronos: The west confronts time* (New York: Columbia University Press, 2023).
49 Tim Ingold, 'Evolution without inheritance: Steps towards an ecology of learning', *Current Anthropology*, vol. 63 (2022): pp. S32–S55.
50 Hartog, *Chronos*.
51 Laurent Olivier, 'The business of archaeology is the present', in *Reclaiming Archaeology: Beyond the tropes of modernity*, Alfredo González-Ruibal (ed.), (New York: Routledge, 2013).
52 Witmore, 'A question of chronopolitics'.
53 Margarita Diaz-Andreu, *A World History of Nineteenth-Century Archaeology: Nationalism, colonialism, and the past* (Oxford: Oxford University Press, 2008); Margarita Díaz-Andreu, 'Nationalism and archaeology', *Nations and Nationalism*, vol. 7, no. 4 (2001): pp. 429–40.
54 Dan Edelstein, Stefanos Geroulanos and Natasha Wheatley (eds), *Power and Time: Temporalities in conflict and the making of history* (Chicago: The University of Chicago Press, 2020).
55 Kathleen Davis, *Periodization and Sovereignty: How ideas of feudalism and secularization govern the politics of time* (Philadelphia: University of Pennsylvania Press, 2008); Gavin Lucas and Orri Vésteinsson, 'The future of periodization: Dissecting the legacy of culture history', *Cambridge Archaeological Journal*, vol. 34, no. 4 (2024): pp. 637–52, doi:10.1017/S0959774324000015.
56 Dipesh Chakrabarty, *Provincializing Europe: Postcolonial thought and historical difference* (Princeton: Princeton University Press, 2000); Jean M O'Brien, *Firsting and Lasting: Writing Indians out of existence in New England* (Minneapolis: University of Minnesota Press, 2010); Gustavo Verdesio, 'Indigeneity and time: Towards

a decolonization of archaeological temporal categories and tools', in *Reclaiming Archaeology: Beyond the tropes of modernity*, Alfredo González-Ruibal (ed.), (New York: Routledge 2013); Priya Satia, *Time's Monster: History, conscience and Britain's empire* (Cambridge: Harvard University Press, 2020).

57 See, for example, Ann McGrath and Mary Anne Jebb, *Long History, Deep Time*; McGrath, Rademaker and Troy, *Everywhen*.
58 Griffiths, *Deep Time Dreaming*.
59 Lynette Russell, *Savage Imaginings: Historical and contemporary constructions of Australian Aboriginalities* (Melbourne: Australian Scholarly Publishing, 2001); Ian J McNiven and Lynette Russell, *Appropriated Pasts: Indigenous peoples and the colonial culture of archaeology* (Oxford: Altamira Press, 2005).
60 Martin Porr and Henny Piezonka, 'Indigenous concerns, archaeology, and activism', *Forum Kritische Archäologie*, vol. 12 (2023): pp. 58–62.
61 Rachel Wood, '50 years of radiocarbon dating in Australian archaeology', *Australian Archaeology*, vol. 90, no. 1 (2024): pp. 136–37.
62 Andrew Shryock and Daniel Lord Smail (eds), *Deep History: The architecture of past and present* (Berkeley: University of California Press, 2011).
63 Steve Brown, 'Making Indigenous archaeology Indigenous: Will it ever happen?', *Australian Archaeology*, vol. 90, no. 1 (2024): pp. 17–19; Kellie Pollard, 'Year of the voice: Third space archaeology for decolonised interdisciplinary collaboration', *Australian Archaeology*, vol. 90, no. 1 (2024): pp. 96–98; Claire Smith, 'A transformative archaeology: Archaeology as a tool for public good', *Australian Archaeology*, vol. 90, no. 1 (2024): pp. 106–08.
64 Bruce Pascoe, *Dark Emu: Black seeds: Agriculture or accident?* (Broome: Magabala Books, 2014).
65 Alan Barnard, 'Defining hunter-gatherers: Enlightenment, romantic and evolutionary perspectives', in *The Oxford Handbook of the Archaeology and Anthropology of Hunter-Gatherers*, Vicki Cummings, Peter Jordan and Marek Zvelebil (eds) (Oxford: Oxford University Press, 2014).
66 Michel-Rolph Trouillot, *Silencing the Past: Power and the production of history* (Boston: Beacon Press, 1995).
67 The book and the supporters of its project have also been the target of horribly vicious attacks by right-wing commentators and conservative media; I will not engage with these here.
68 Peter Sutton and Keryn Walshe, *Farmers or Hunter-Gatherers? The Dark Emu debate* (Melbourne: Melbourne University Press, 2021).
69 Tom Griffiths, 'Reading Bruce Pascoe', *Inside Story*, 2019, <insidestory.org.au/reading-bruce-pascoe/>; Martin Porr and Ella Vivian-Williams, 'The tragedy of Bruce Pascoe's *Dark Emu*', *Australian Archaeology*, vol. 87, no. 3 (2021): pp. 300–04.
70 Porr and Vivian-Williams, 'The tragedy of Bruce Pascoe's *Dark Emu*'.
71 S Anna Florin and Xavier Carah, 'Moving past the "Neolithic problem": The development and interaction of subsistence systems across northern Sahul', *Quaternary International*, vol. 489 (2018): pp. 46–62; Ian Keen, 'Foragers or farmers: *Dark Emu* and the controversy over Aboriginal agriculture', *Anthropological Forum*: pp. 1–23, doi:10.1080/00664677.2020.1861538; Tim Denham and Mark Donohue, 'Putting the *Dark Emu* debate into context', *Archaeology in Oceania*, vol. 58, no. 3 (2023): pp. 275–95.
72 Black Trowel Collective et al., 'Archaeology in 2022: Counter-myths for hopeful futures', *American Anthropologist*, vol. 126 (2023): pp. 135–48.

73 Porr, 'The temporality of humanity and the colonial landscape of the deep human past'.
74 Martin Porr and Jacqueline Maree Matthews (Eds), *Interrogating Human Origins: Decolonisation and the deep human past* (London: Routledge, 2020).
75 Clive S Gamble, *Origins and Revolutions: Human identity in earliest prehistory* (Cambridge: Cambridge University Press, 2007); Clive S Gamble and Erika Gittins, 'Social archaeology and origins research: A Paleolithic perspective', in *A Companion to Social Archaeology*, Lynn Meskell and Robert W Preucel (Eds), (Malden: Blackwell, 2004).
76 Russell, *Savage Imaginings*; McNiven and Russell, *Appropriated Pasts*; Bruno David, Marcia Langton and Ian McNiven, 'Re-inventing the wheel: Indigenous peoples and the master race in Philip Ruddock's "wheel" comments', *Philosophy Activism Nature*, vol. 2 (2002): pp. 31–45.
77 Damien Finch et al., 'Ages for Australia's oldest rock paintings', *Nature Human Behaviour*, vol. 5, no. 3 (2021): pp. 310–18.
78 Sean Ulm et al., 'Early Aboriginal pottery production and offshore island occupation on Jiigurru (Lizard Island group), Great Barrier Reef, Australia', *Quaternary Science Reviews* (2024): 108624. doi:10.1016/j.quascirev.2024.108624.
79 Commonwealth of Australia, 'A way forward: Inquiry into the destruction of 46,000 year old caves at the Juukan Gorge in the Pilbara Region of Western Australia' (Canberra: Commonwealth of Australia, 2021), <https://www.aph.gov.au/Parliamentary_Business/Committees/Joint/Former_Committees/Northern_Australia_46P/CavesatJuukanGorge/Report#:~:text=About%20this%20inquiry&text=30%20September%202020%3A-,The%20destruction%20of%2046%2C000%20year%20old%20caves%20at%20the%20Juukan,report%20by%2018%20October%202021.>.
80 Porr, 'Art, representation, and the ontology of images'; Commonwealth of Australia, 'A way forward'.
81 Claire Smith et al., 'Pursuing social justice through collaborative archaeologies in Aboriginal Australia', *Archaeologies*, vol. 15, no. 3 (2019): pp. 536–69; Claire Smith et al., 'Social justice: Material culture as a driver of inequality', in *The Cambridge Handbook of Material Culture Studies*, Lu Ann De Cunzo and Catherine Dann Roeber (Eds) (Cambridge: Cambridge University Press, 2022).
82 Deborah Bird Rose, *Nourishing Terrains: Australian Aboriginal views of landscape and wilderness* (Canberra: Australian Heritage Commission, 1996); Minoru Hokari, *Gurindji Journey: A Japanese historian in the outback* (Sydney: UNSW Press, 2011); Olivia Guntarik, '"Dangerous" historiographies: Minoru Hokari's observations and lived Aboriginal practices of history', *AlterNative: An international journal of Indigenous peoples*, vol. 9, no. 1 (2013): pp. 30–44; Martin Porr, 'Country and relational ontology in the Kimberley, Northwest Australia: Implications for understanding and representing archaeological evidence', *Cambridge Archaeological Journal*, vol. 28, no. 3 (2018): pp. 395–409.
83 Mark Rifkin, *Beyond Settler Time: Temporal sovereignty and Indigenous self-determination* (Durham: Duke University Press, 2017): p. 2.
84 Nativ and Lucas, 'Archaeology without antiquity'.
85 Alfredo González-Ruibal (ed.), *Reclaiming Archaeology: Beyond the tropes of modernity* (New York: Routledge, 2013).
86 Martin Porr and Jacqueline Maree Matthews, 'Thinking through story', *Hunter Gatherer Research*, vol. 2, no. 3 (2016): pp. 249–74; Frieman, 'Innovation,

continuity, and the punctuated temporality of archaeological narratives'; Annie Ross, 'Challenging metanarratives: The past lives in the present', *Archaeology in Oceania*, vol. 55 (2020): pp. 65–71; Frieman, *Archaeology as History*. While the topic has certainly not received enough attention in Australian archaeology, I also want to note that the theme of the Australian Archaeological Association Annual Conference 2024 was *Sharing Archaeological Narratives* and this initiative will certainly enhance awareness of this important aspect of archaeological theory and practice.

5 Difficult temporalities: Indigenous and Western archaeological ways of knowing the past in Oceania

1 For a more extended discussion of these case studies, see: Chris Urwin, Lynette Russell and Robert Skelly, 'Building culturally meaningful chronologies: Negotiating Indigenous and Western temporalities in Oceania', *Archaeology in Oceania*, vol. 59, no. 3 (2025): pp. 465–78.
2 Richard Bradley, *The Past in Prehistoric Societies* (London: Routledge, 2002): p. 155; Cristián Simonetti, 'Between the vertical and the horizontal: Time and space in archaeology', *History of the Human Sciences*, vol. 26, no. 1 (2013): pp. 90–110.
3 For example, see Billy Griffiths, *Deep Time Dreaming: Uncovering ancient Australia* (Melbourne: Black Inc., 2017).
4 Chris Clarkson et al., 'Human occupation of northern Australia by 65,000 years ago', *Nature*, vol. 547 (2017): pp. 306–10.
5 John McPhee, 'Set piece on geologic time from annals of the former world', in *The Earth Around Us*, Jill S Schneiderman (ed.) (London: Routledge, 2010): p. 25.
6 The deepest soil layer containing artefacts at Madjedbebe (dating older than 65 000 years ago) was found c. 260 cm below the surface.
7 For a detailed exploration of Pacific historicities, see: Chris Ballard, 'Oceanic historicities', *The Contemporary Pacific*, vol. 26, no. 1 (2014): pp. 95–154.
8 Denis Byrne, *Surface Collection: Archaeological travels in Southeast Asia* (Lanham: Altamira Press, 2007): p. ix; Shannon Foster, 'On the shores of the Narinya: Contemporary D'harawal interactions with ancestral knowledges', in *Everywhen: Australia and the language of deep history*, Ann McGrath, Laura Rademaker and Jakelin Troy (eds) (Sydney: UNSW Press, 2023): p. 286; Diana James, 'Tjukurpa time', in *Long History, Deep Time: Deepening histories of place*, Ann McGrath and Mary Anne Jebb (eds) (Canberra: ANU Press, 2015).
9 Nganyinytja Ilyatjari quoted in James, 'Tjukurpa time': p. 33; Ian McNiven, 'Theoretical challenges of Indigenous archaeology: Setting an agenda', *American Antiquity*, vol. 81, no. 1 (2016): pp. 27–41; Deborah Bird Rose, *Country of the Heart: An Indigenous Australian homeland* (Canberra: Aboriginal Studies Press, 2002); papers in Alan Rumsey and James F Weiner (eds), *Emplaced Myth: Space, narrative, and knowledge in Aboriginal Australia and Papua New Guinea* (Honolulu: University of Hawai'i Press, 2001).
10 Ann McGrath, 'People of the footprints: Rediscovery, Indigenous historicities and the science of deep time', *Interventions*, vol. 24, no. 2 (2021): doi:10.1080/136980 1X.2021.1972822.
11 See chapters in Ann McGrath, Laura Rademaker and Jakelin Troy (eds), *Everywhen: Australia and the language of deep history* (Sydney: UNSW Press, 2023).
12 Alison Bashford, 'Deep genetics: Universal history and the species', *History and Theory*, vol. 57, no. 2 (2018): pp. 312–22; Pratik Chakrabarti, 'Is deep history white?', lecture given to the New Earth Histories Program, University of New South Wales, Sydney, July 2020.

13 Stephanie Mawson, 'The deep past of pre-colonial Australia', *The Historical Journal*, vol. 64, no. 5, (2021): p. 1478.
14 A handful of authors, such as Bruce Pascoe and Bill Gammage, have had some success narrating small parts of Indigenous Deep History for a wide readership, exploring the creative ways Aboriginal people made the continent of Australia through fire, plant management and aquaculture. Yet Gammage's characterisation of fire use and land management, and Pascoe's characterisation of Indigenous food production, as 'agriculture' have come under criticism for making generalisations that do not hold across Aboriginal Australia. See: Bill Gammage, *The Biggest Estate on Earth: How Aborigines made Australia* (Sydney: Allen & Unwin, 2011); Bruce Pascoe, *Dark Emu: Aboriginal Australia and the birth of agriculture* (Broome: Magabala Books, 2014).
15 For a more extended discussion of these ideas and examples, see Chris Urwin, Lynette Russell and Robert Skelly, 'Building culturally meaningful chronologies: Negotiating Indigenous and Western temporalities in Oceania', *Archaeology in Oceania*, vol. 59, no. 3 (2025): pp. 465–78.
16 The people of Orokolo Bay speak the Orokolo language, which belongs to the Eleman language group. The language group is often known by the ethnonym 'Elema' in anthropological and material culture literature. For further details of the culture and their ceremonies in the 1920s–1930s – some forty years after Britain and Australia colonised the Territory of Papua – see Francis Edgar Williams, *Drama of Orokolo: The social and ceremonial life of the Elema* (Oxford: Oxford University Press, 1940).
17 Chris Urwin, 'Excavating and interpreting ancestral action: Stories from the subsurface of Orokolo Bay, Papua New Guinea', *Journal of Social Archaeology*, vol. 19, no. 3 (2019): pp. 279–306; Chris Urwin, *Building and Remembering: An archaeology of place-making on Papua New Guinea's South Coast* (Honolulu: University of Hawai'i Press, 2022).
18 Williams, *Drama of Orokolo*: p. 340.
19 The ceremony was documented assiduously by the Australian anthropologist Francis Edgar Williams (1940) during many months of fieldwork in Orokolo Bay between 1923 and 1937. At that time, he was the Australian Government Anthropologist for the Territory of Papua.
20 Urwin, *Building and Remembering*: pp. 100–17.
21 Houhii Iaupa quoted in Urwin, *Building and Remembering*: p. 83.
22 For further details of the story, see Urwin, *Building and Remembering*: p. 197.
23 Nigel Oram, 'Pots for sago: The *hiri* trading network', in *The Hiri in History: Further aspects of long distance Motu trade in Central Papua*, Tom Dutton (ed.) (Canberra: Australian National University, 1982: pp. 1–34; Robert Skelly and Bruno David, *Hiri: Archaeology of long-distance maritime trade along the south coast of Papua New Guinea* (Honolulu: University of Hawai'i Press, 2017).
24 Urwin, *Building and Remembering*: pp. 195–97.
25 Chris Urwin, Quan Hua and Henry Arifeae, 'Combining oral traditions and Bayesian chronological modeling to understand village development in the Gulf of Papua (Papua New Guinea)', *Radiocarbon*, vol. 63, no. 2 (2021): pp. 647–67.
26 Urwin, *Building and Remembering*: pp. 199–200.
27 Urwin et al., 'Combining oral traditions and Bayesian chronological modeling'.
28 Clarkson et al., 'Human occupation of northern Australia by 65,000 years ago'.
29 Billy Griffiths and Lynette Russell, 'What we were told', *Aboriginal History*, vol. 42 (2018): pp. 31–54.

30 Lynette Russell, *Savage Imaginings: Historical and contemporary constructions of Australian Aboriginalities* (Melbourne, Australian Scholarly Publishing, 2001).
31 Mary Graham and Morgan Brigg, 'Indigenous international relations: Old peoples and new pragmatism', *Australian Journal of International Affairs*, vol. 77, no. 6 (2023): p. 598.
32 Eric Wilmot, 'The dragon principle', in *Who Owns the Past? Papers from the annual symposium of the Australian Academy of the Humanities*, Isabel McBryde (Ed.) (Oxford: Oxford University Press, 1985): p. 45.
33 Sonya Atalay, 'Multivocality and Indigenous archaeologies', in *Evaluating Multiple Narratives: Beyond nationalist, colonialist, imperialist archaeologies*, Junko Habu, Clare Fawcett and John M Matsunaga (eds) (New York: Springer, 2008): pp. 29–44.
34 Atalay, 'Multivocality and Indigenous archaeologies'.
35 For example, see: Atalay, 'Multivocality and Indigenous archaeologies'; Chip Colwell-Chanthaphonh and TJ Ferguson, 'Memory pieces and footprints: Multivocality and the meanings of ancient times and ancestral places among the Zuni and Hopi', *American Anthropologist*, vol. 108, no. 1 (2006): pp. 148–62; James L Flexner, 'Archaeology and Kastom: Island historicities and transforming religious traditions in southern Vanuatu', *Journal of Archaeological Method and Theory*, vol. 29 (2022): pp. 1367–86; McNiven, 'Theoretical challenges of Indigenous archaeology'.

6 Songs, stories, and Deep Histories from Mutthi Mutthi, Ngiyampaa, Barkindji and Tati Tati Water Country

1 'Margooya Lagoon cultural flows management plan Tati Tati Kaiejin', Tati Tati Keiajin website, <www.kaiejin.org.au/pdf/Margooya%20Lagoon%20Cultural%20 Flows%20Management%20Plan>.
2 Barry Hart, Neil Byron, Carmel Pollino and Michael Stewardson (eds), 'Murray-Darling Basin: Its Future Management' (United States: Elsevier, 2020): p. xxii.
3 'Margooya Lagoon Cultural Flows management plan', Tati Tati Keiajin.
4 'Willandra Lakes Region', NSW Department of Environment and Heritage website, <www.environment.nsw.gov.au/topics/parks-reserves-and-protected-areas/types-of-protected-areas/world-heritage-listed-areas/willandra-lakes-region>.
5 'Willandra Lakes Region', NSW Department of Environment and Heritage.
6 'Share Mungo Culture: The Three Tribal Groups', Mungo National Park website, <visitmungo.com.au/share-culture.html#:~:text=Visitors%20to%20Mungo%20 National%20Park,for%20their%20Country%20at%20Mungo.>.
7 'Share Mungo Culture: The tribal groups', Mungo National Park.
8 A series of extensive trackways or footprints mark a lakebed that existed in the last ice age. The footprints have been radio-carbon dated to be at least 20 000 years old. These footprints are recognised to have been made by the Ancestors of the traditional tribal groups of the Willandra Lakes Region.
9 Michael Bird et al., 'Australia's epic story: A tale of amazing people, amazing creatures and rising seas', *Conversation*, 18 April 2019, <theconversation.com/australias-epic-story-a-tale-of-amazing-people-amazing-creatures-and-rising-seas-115701>.
10 In the face of a changing climate and threatened ecosystems, it is crucial to understand First Nations' ecological and historical Knowledges as equal to Western knowledges, and essential to addressing the climate crisis and polluted waterways. To read more on 'historicities' see: Laura Rademaker and Ben Silverstein, 'Deep historicities', *Interventions*, vol. 24, no. 2 (2022): pp. 137–60.

11 If interested in the work of Deep Historians, the reader may be interested in seeking out the work of Ann McGrath, Lynette Russell, Billy Griffiths, Ben Silverstein and Laura Rademaker, to name a few. See various references cited throughout this book, and chapters in this book.
12 *Terra nullius* is a legal fiction meaning, 'land over which no sovereignty has previously been exercised,' used to justify the British settlement of Aboriginal and Torres Strait Islander lands. It was overturned with the *Native Title Act 1993* (Cth).
13 William Adams and Martin Mulligan, 'Introduction', in *Decolonizing Nature: Strategies for conservation in a post-colonial era*, William Adams and Martin Mulligan (eds) (London: Routledge, 2003): p. 3.
14 Sebouh David Aslanian, Joyce E Chaplin, Ann McGrath and Kristin Mann, 'How size matters: The question of scale in history', *The American Historical Review*, vol. 118, no. 5 (2013): p. 1436.
15 Rademaker and Silverstein, 'Deep historicities': p. 137.
16 Brendan Kennedy (Tati Tati Traditional Owner), in discussion with the author, April 2024.
17 Emily O'Gorman, *Wetlands in a Dry Land: More-than-human histories of Australia's Murray-Darling Basin* (Seattle: University of Washington Press, 2021): p. 7.
18 Sarah Laborde and Sue Jackson, 'Living waters or resource? Ontological differences and the governance of waters and rivers', *Local Environment*, vol. 27, no. 3 (2022): p. 6.
19 Lana D Hartwig, Sue Jackson and Natalie Osborne, 'Trends in Aboriginal water ownership in New South Wales, Australia: The continuities between colonial and neoliberal forms of dispossession', *Land Use Policy*, vol. 99 (2020): pp. 1–13.
20 Damien Short, 'The social construction of Indigenous "Native Title" land rights in Australia', *Current Sociology*, vol. 55, no. 6 (2007): pp. 857–76.
21 Virginia Marshall, *Overturning Aqua Nullius: Securing Aboriginal water rights* (Canberra: Aboriginal Studies Press, 2017).
22 *Aqua nullius* is the unjustified and erroneous assumption that water belonged to no-one when the British invaded Australia.
23 Hartwig, Jackson and Osborne, 'Trends in Aboriginal water ownership in New South Wales': p. 14.
24 The Willandra Lakes were an expansive system of thirteen different lakes in the height of the last ice age, covering an area of 2400 square kilometres. Billy Griffiths, *Deep Time Dreaming: Uncovering ancient Australia* (Melbourne: Black Inc., 2018): p. 84.
25 Malcolm Allbrook and Ann McGrath, 'Collaborative histories of the Willandra Lakes: Deepening histories and the deep past', in *Long History, Deep Time: Deepening histories of Place*, Ann McGrath and Mary Anne Jebb (eds) (Canberra: ANU Press, 2015): p. 243.
26 A lunette is a bow-shaped sand dune. Within the Willandra Lakes some are 33-kilometre-long dunes where erosion has exposed the internal strata and opened a window on the past.
27 Jim Bowler, Rhys Jones, Harry Allen and AG Thorne, 'Pleistocene human remains from Australia: A living site and human cremation from Lake Mungo, Western New South Wales', *World Archaeology*, vol. 2, no. 1 (1970): p. 56.
28 Bowler, Jones, Allen and Thorne, 'Pleistocene human remains from Australia': p. 60.
29 Griffiths, *Deep Time Dreaming*: p. 25.
30 Malcolm Allbrook, 'Mungo Lady', *Australian Dictionary of Biography*, <adb.anu.edu.au/biography/mungo-lady-27703>.

31 Mary Pappin, 'Working together', in Helen Lawrence (ed.), *Mungo over millennia* (Sorell: Maygog Publishing, 2006): pp. 50–51.
32 Lynette Russell and Chris Urwin provide further discussion on 'beginnings' in this volume.
33 Ann McGrath, 'People of the footprints', *Interventions*, vol. 24, no. 2 (2022): p. 186.
34 'Share Mungo Culture: Mungo Lady and Mungo Man', Mungo National Park.
35 Jim Bowler et al., 'New ages for human occupation and climatic change at Lake Mungo, Australia', *Nature*, vol. 421, no. 6925 (2003): p. 837.
36 'Share Mungo Culture: Mungo Lady and Mungo Man', Mungo National Park.
37 Ann McGrath, 'Deep Histories in time, or crossing the great divide?', p. 2.
38 Ann McGrath and Andrew Pike, *Message from Mungo*, Ronin Films, Mitchell, 2014, DVD.
39 Alice Kelly, 'Letter as quoted in Isabel McBryde to John Mulvaney [1973]', Mulvaney Papers 70, quoted in: Griffiths, *Deep Time Dreaming*: p. 92.
40 Adams and Mulligan, 'Introduction': p. 3.
41 For readers who wish to hear the views of Aunty Mary Pappin Senior and others as directly expressed, *Message from Mungo*, a documentary film made in close collaborations with Community members, may be useful. See: Ann McGrath and Andrew Pike, *Message from Mungo*.
42 Mary Pappin Junior (Mutthi Mutthi Traditional Owner), in discussion with the author, April 2024.
43 Steve Webb (Professor of Australian Studies, Bond University), in discussion with the author, April 2024, 'Willandra Lakes Region Trackways', e-mail to author, 29 November 2022.
44 'Share Mungo culture: Ancient footprints', Mungo National Park website.
45 McGrath, 'People of the Footprints': p. 201.
46 Deborah Smith, 'Revealed: The runners of 20,000 BC', *Sydney Morning Herald*, 22 December 2005, <www.smh.com.au/national/revealed-the-runners-of-20-000bc-20051222-gdmo6y.html>.
47 Dr Steve Webb (Professor of Australian Studies, Bond University), in discussion with the author, April 2024.
48 'No distance between us', National Museum of Australia website, <australian.museum/about/organisation/media-centre/no-distance-between-us/>.
49 'Mungo footprint mould', National Museum of Australia website, <australian.museum/learn/first-nations/unsettled/unsettled-introduction/mungo-footprint-mould/>.
50 Christian Little et al., paper, (Proceedings of the 3rd International Conference on Best Practices in World Heritage: Integral Actions, Menorca, 2–5 May 2018).
51 Janet C Pritchard and John Kalish, 'Linking fish growth and climate across modern space and through evolutionary time: Otolith chronologies of the Australian freshwater fish, Golden Perch' (PhD Thesis, Australian National University, 2004): p. 45.
52 Colin Macgregor, 'Preserving the ancient human trackways site in the Willandra Lakes World Heritage Area', *Studies in Conservation*, vol. 67, no. S1 (2022): p. 151.
53 Steve Webb, 'An echo from a footprint: A step too far', in *Reading Prehistoric Human Tracks*, Andreas Pastoors and Tilman Lenssen-Erz (eds) (Cham: Springer International Publishing, 2021): p. 405.
54 Tjukurrpa refers to origins and powers embodied in Country. It is a way of seeing and understanding the world and connects people to Country and to each other

through shared social and knowledge networks. Tjukurrpa is often associated with the Dreaming.
55 'Artists: Mitjili Napanangka Gibson', Gallery Gondwana website, <www.gallerygondwana.com.au/category/Mitjili-Napanangka-Gibson>.
56 'Mitjli Napanangka Gibson masterpiece New York bound', Japingka Aboriginal Art website, <japingkaaboriginalart.com/articles/mijili-napanangka-gibson-masterpiece-new-york-bound/>.
57 Webb, 'An echo from a footprint': p. 407.
58 Webb, 'An echo from a footprint': p. 405.
59 Webb, 'An echo from a footprint': p. 407.
60 Aunty Bernadette Pappin (Mutthi Mutthi Traditional Owner), in discussion with the author, April 2024.
61 'Cultural flow: Indigenous connections and rights to water – a Mutthi Mutthi film', YouTube video, 9:24, posted by 'Anti-Nuclear Archives', January 2023, <www.youtube.com/watch?app=desktop&v=90WptDjh11U>.
62 'Cultural flow: Indigenous connections and rights to water – a Mutthi Mutthi film'.
63 Miki Perkins, 'Reversing "aqua nullius": Traditional owners seek cultural water rights', *Sydney Morning Herald*, 21 August 2021, <www.smh.com.au/environment/sustainability/reversing-aqua-nullius-traditional-owners-seek-cultural-water-rights-20210827-p58mgn.html>.
64 Brendan Kennedy (Tati Tati Traditional Owner), in discussion with the author, April 2024.
65 'Government needs to deliver on cultural flows', Environmental Justice Australia website, <envirojustice.org.au/press-release/government-needs-to-deliver-on-cultural-flows/>.
66 Yoorrook Justice Commission, 'Transcript of day 10 – Public hearing (Lagoon session)', 24 April 2024, <yoorrookjusticecommission.org.au/wp-content/uploads/2024/05/WUR.HB06.0010.0077.pdf>.
67 Yoorrook Justice Commission, 'Transcript of day 10'.
68 Margo Neale and Lynne Kelly, *Songlines: The power and promise* (Melbourne: Thames & Hudson Australia Pty Ltd, 2020): p. 26.
69 'The Statement', Uluru Statement from the Heart website, <ulurustatement.org/the-statement/view-the-statement/>.
70 O'Gorman, *Wetlands in a Dry Land*: p. 15.
71 Yoorrook Justice Commission, 'Transcript of day 10'.
72 The Murray Lower Darling Rivers Indigenous Nations, 'Echuca Declaration', 2010, <culturalflows.com.au/~culturalflowscom/images/documents/Echuca_declaration.pdf>.

7 Kai Māori spaces and temporalities in Tāmaki Makaurau
1 Russell Stone, *From Tāmaki-Makau-Rau to Auckland* (Auckland: Auckland University Press, 2001): pp. 243–44.
2 Te Aka Māori Dictionary, 'Tino Rangatiratanga', Te Aka Māori Dictionary, <maoridictionary.co.nz/search?&keywords=rangatira#:~:text=rangatira%20in%20rank.-,rangatiratanga,birth%2C%20attributes%20of%20a%20chief>.
3 Ian Hugh Kawharu, *Waitangi: Māori and Pākehā perspectives of the Treaty of Waitangi* (Auckland: Oxford University Press, 1989): p. 314.
4 Nin Tomas, 'Maori concepts and practices of rangatiratanga: "Sovereignty"?', in *Sovereignty: Frontiers of possibility*, Julie Evans, Ann Genovese, Alexander Reilly and Patrick Wolfe (eds) (Honolulu: University of Hawai'i Press, 2013): p. 222.

5   La Via Campesina, 'La Via Campesina political declaration: 30 years of collective struggle, hope and solidarity', La Via Campesina website, 2022, <https://viacampesina.org/en/2022/04/la-via-campesina-political-declaration-30-years-of-collective-struggle-hope-and-solidarity/>.
6   Hannah Wittman, Nettie Wiebe and Annette Aurélie Desmarais, *Food Sovereignty: Reconnecting food, nature & community* (Halifax: Fernwood, 2010): pp. 2–4.
7   Herbert W Williams, *A Dictionary of the Māori Language* (Wellington: Government Printer, 1957): pp. 85–86; Te Aka Māori Dictionary, 'kai'.
8   According to Reverend Māori Marsden, Te Ao Mārama is the world of being, earth sphere or sphere of day. See: Māori Marsden and Te Ahukaramū Charles Royal, *The Woven Universe: Selected writings of Rev. Māori Marsden* (Otaki: Estate of Rev. Māori Marsden, 2003): pp. 19–20.
9   Marsden and Royal, *The Woven Universe*: pp. 44–46.
10 Jessica Hutchings, *Te Mahi Māra Hua Parakore: A Māori food sovereignty handbook* (Otaki, Te Tākupu, Te Wānanga o Raukwa, 2015): p. 38.
11 Graeme Murdoch, 'Maungawhau e Tū Tonu Mai Ana', in Helen Laurenson (ed.), *The History of Mount Eden: The district and its people* (Auckland: Epsom & Eden District Historical Society Inc, 2019): p. 12.
12 Taimoana Turoa and Te Ahukaramū Charles Royal, *Te Takoto o Te Whenua o Hauraki: Hauraki landmarks* (Auckland: Reed, 2000): p. 215.
13 In one account the isthmus formed between the familial conflicts between Mataaho and Mahuika. See: Agnes Sullivan, *Māori Gardening in Tāmaki before 1840* (Auckland: Unpublished Manuscript, undated): pp. 39–40.
14 Murdoch, 'Maungawhau e Tū Tonu Mai Ana': p. 12.
15 Auckland Council, 'Te Tū whakahira me ngā kōrero tuku iho mō ngā Tūpuna Maunga: Tūpuna Maunga significance and history', Auckland Council website, <www.aucklandcouncil.govt.nz/about-auckland-council/how-auckland-council-works/kaupapa-maori/comanagement-authorities-boards/tupuna-maunga-tamaki-makaurau-authority/Pages/tupuna-maunga-significance-history.aspx>.
16 Janet Davidson, 'Auckland', in Kevin L Jones (ed.), *The Penguin Field Guide to New Zealand Archaeology* (Auckland: Penguin Books, 2007): p. 36.
17 Atholl Anderson, 'A fragile plenty: Pre-European Māori and the New Zealand environment', in *Environmental Histories of New Zealand*, Eric Pawson and Tom Brooking (eds) (Melbourne: Oxford University Press, 2002): pp. 41–49; Davidson, 'Auckland': p. 30; Agnes Sullivan, 'Intensification in volcanic zone gardening in Northern New Zealand', in *Prehistoric Intensive Agriculture in the Tropics*, IS Farrington (ed.) (Oxford: British Archaeological Reports, 1985): p. 480.
18 Stone, *From Tāmaki-Makau-Rau to Auckland*: p. 4.
19 Davidson, 'Auckland', p. 36; Sullivan, 'Intensification in volcanic zone gardening in northern New Zealand': p. 480; Ian Smith, *Estimating the Magnitude of Pre-European Māori Marine Harvest in Two New Zealand Study Areas* (Wellington: Ministry of Fisheries, 2011): p. 53.
20 Bruce Hayward, 'Prehistoric pa sites of metropolitan Auckland', *Tane*, vol. 29, no. 2 (1983): pp. 3–14; Sullivan, 'Intensification in volcanic zone gardening in northern New Zealand': p. 481.
21 This sequence comes from archaeological evidence of Maungarei (Mt Wellington), and it can be broadly assumed to be the same. See: Jones, *The Penguin Field Guide to New Zealand Archaeology*: p. 92.
22 Sullivan, 'Intensification in volcanic zone gardening in northern New Zealand': p. 480.

23 This analysis was arrived at by combining the proposed sequences from Janet Davidson and Agnes Sullivan. See: Sullivan, 'Intensification in volcanic zone gardening in northern New Zealand': p. 481; Davidson, 'Archaeological investigations at Maungarei: A large Māori settlement on a volcanic cone in Auckland, New Zealand', *Tuhinga*, vol. 22 (2011): p. 84.
24 Jones, *The Penguin Field Guide to New Zealand Archaeology*: p. 92.
25 Susan Bulmer, 'Settlement patterns in Tāmaki-Makau-Rau revisited', in *Oceanic Culture History: Essays in honour of Roger Green*, Roger Green and Janet Davidson (eds) (Dunedin North: New Zealand Journal of Archaeology, 1996): p. 645.
26 Agnes Sullivan, 'Stone-walled complexes of Central Auckland', *New Zealand Archaeological Association Newsletter*, vol. 15 (1972): p. 7.
27 Bulmer, 'Settlement patterns in Tāmaki-Makau-Rau revisited': pp. 642–45; Susan Bulmer, 'City without a state? Urbanisation in pre-European Taamaki-Makau-Rau (Auckland, New Zealand)', in *The Development of Urbanism from a Global Perspective*, Paul Sinclair (ed.) (Uppsala: Uppsala University, 1993): pp. 9–10.
28 Bulmer, 'City without a state?': p. 7.
29 Davidson, 'Auckland': p. 37.
30 Estimated from Auckland Council, 'Māori identity and wellbeing – Tangata Whenua', Auckland Council website, <www.aucklandcouncil.govt.nz/plans-projects-policies-reports-bylaws/our-plans-strategies/auckland-plan/maori-identity-wellbeing/Pages/default.aspx>.
31 Angela Ballara, 'Settlement patterns in the early European Māori phase of Māori society', *The Journal of the Polynesian Society*, vol. 88, no. 2 (1979): p. 201.
32 Stone, *From Tāmaki-Makau-Rau to Auckland*: p. 2.
33 Williams, *A Dictionary of the Maori Language*: p. 180; Te Aka, 'Māori Dictionary'.
34 Sullivan, 'Stone-walled complexes of Central Auckland': p. 152.
35 Agnes Sullivan, 'Scoria mounds at Wiri', *New Zealand Archaeological Association Newsletter*, vol. 17, no. 3 (1974): p. 129; Louise Furey, *Māori Gardening: An archaeological perspective* (Wellington: Department of Conservation, 2006): p. 33.
36 Sullivan recorded 10 000 scoria mounds in the Matukutūruru (Wiri) field alone; it's then probable to estimate that over 100 000 scoria modifications were made across the entirety of the isthmus. See: Sullivan, 'Scoria mounds at Wiri': p. 128.
37 Sullivan, 'Scoria mounds at Wiri': p. 135.
38 Lucy Mackintosh, 'Shifting grounds: History, memory and materiality in Auckland landscapes c.1350–2018' (PhD Thesis, University of Auckland, 2019): p. 38.
39 Elsdon Best, *Māori Agriculture* (Wellington: Whitcombe and Tombs, 1925); William Phillipps, *Māori Houses and Food Stores* (Wellington: Government Printer, 1952).
40 Sullivan, *Māori Gardening in Tamaki before 1840*: p. 83.
41 Furey, *Māori Gardening*: p. 18; Best, *Māori Agriculture*: p. 142.
42 Furey, *Māori Gardening*: pp. 17–18.
43 Best, *Māori Agriculture*: p. 215.
44 David Veart, 'Stone structures and landuse at three South Auckland volcanic sites' (MA Thesis, University of Auckland, 1986): p. 102.
45 Nick Roskruge, *Rauwaru, the Proverbial Garden: Ngā-Weri, Māori root vegetables, their history and tips on their use* (Palmerston North: Institute of Agriculture and Environment, 2014): p. 110.
46 Sullivan, *Māori Gardening in Tāmaki before 1840*: p. 79.
47 Paul Moon, *A Tohunga's Natural World: Plants, gardening and food* (Auckland: David Ling Publishing, 2005): pp. 67–68.

48 Roskruge, *Rauwaru, the Proverbial Garden*: p. 111.
49 Best, *Maori Agriculture*: p. 145.
50 Graeme Murdoch, 'Part One: The land', in *Waitakere Ranges: Ranges of inspiration: Nature, history, culture*, Bruce Harvey and Trixie Harvey (eds) (Waitakere City: Waitakere Ranges Protection Society, 2006): p. 20.
51 Graeme Murdoch, *Whatipu: Our history* (Auckland: Auckland Regional Council, 2007): p. 4.
52 Murdoch, 'Part One: The land': pp. 30–33.
53 Murdoch, *Whatipu*: p. 4.
54 Sally McAra, 'Māori fishing nets in the Canterbury Museum', *Records of the Canterbury Museum*, vol. 15 (2001): p. 88.
55 Auckland Council, 'Māori identity and wellbeing – Tangata Whenua'.
56 The full list from a Waitangi Tribunal describes Māori catching: flounder, mullet, pioke shark, skate, trevally, snapper, kahawai, kingfish, parore, tarakihi, moki, herring, stringray, lemonfish, hapuku, limpet, crayfish, toheroa, pipi, scallops, mussels, paua, kina, pupu, oysters, toitoi, karengo, sea fungus, eels, koura, trout, whitebait and watercress: Waitangi Tribunal, *Report of the Waitangi Tribunal on the Manukau Claim* (Wai 8), Waitangi Tribunal, 1989: pp. 39–41.
57 For example, fish, lobsters, mussels, pipi, pupu and oyster beds could be gathered from Puketutu Island, Pukaki Creek and the Waiuku channel, all the way along the eastern coast of Awhitu Peninsula to the south head of the Manukau Harbour and from the Wairopa channel to the Mangere inlet. Sharks, stingray scallops, and other fish could be gathered from the Papakura Channel, Pahurehre Inlet, Oruarangi Creek and Karore banks, Waitangi Tribunal 1989: p. 39.
58 Stone, *From Tāmaki-Makau-Rau to Auckland*: p. 4.
59 Specific species featured in this area is pipi, haku, eels, pātiki (flounder), kanae (mullet), kahawai, haku (yellowtail kingfish), tītiko (sea snail) and tio (oyster). See: John La Roche and Sue La Roche, *The Pourewa Valley Story* (Auckland: Self published, 2022): p. 9, <www.pourewa.nz/wp-content/uploads/2022/10/Ch-1-The-Pourewa-Valley-Story.pdf>.
60 For example, shark fishing appears to be associated with Kauri Point, Waikokota (Freemans Bay), the upper Waitemata Harbour and Puponga Point. See: Stone, *From Tāmaki-Makau-Rau to Auckland*, p. 4; Chris Paulin, 'Perspectives of Māori fishing history and techniques: Ngā Āhua Me Ngā Pūrākau Me Ngā Hangarau Ika O Te Māori', *Tuhinga*, vol. 18 (2007): p. 17; Sullivan, *Māori Gardening in Tamaki Before 1840*: pp. 59, 96.
61 Another name for Puketutu is Motu-o-Hiaroa, the island of Hiaroa, named after a Tainui Ancestor; Paul Goldsmith and Michael Bassett, *Puketutu and Its People* (Auckland: David Ling Publishing, 2008): p. 12.
62 Rosalie Stanley, *Puketutu Island: A brief history* (Auckland: University of Auckland, 1991), p. 2; TW Taua, 'Te Kaweau a Maki', in *West: The history of Waitakere*, Finlay Macdonald and Ruth Kerr (eds) (Auckland: Random House, 2009): p. 29.
63 FG Fairfield, 'PUKETUTU PA On Weekes' Island, Manukau Harbour', *Journal of the Polynesian Society*, vol. 47, no. 3 (1938): p. 120.
64 Fairfield, 'PUKETUTU PA On Weekes' Island, Manukau Harbour': pp. 120–23.
65 Paul Monin, *Waiheke Island: A history* (Palmerston North: Dunmore Press, 1992): p. 18; Vivien Rickard, *Archaeological sites of Waiheke Island* (Auckland: New Zealand Historic Places Trust, 1984): p. 9.
66 Rickard, *Archaeological Sites of Waiheke Island*: p. 9. Many examples of taro and karaka plantations can be found in surveys such as: E Gael Atwell, *Site Recording in*

the *Eastern Half of Waiheke Island* (Auckland: New Zealand Historic Places Trust, 1975): pp. 21–46.
67   Monin, *Waiheke Island*: pp. 28–29.
68   New Zealand Government, *Ngāti Paoa and the Trustees of the Ngāti Paoa Iwi Trust and Crown: Deed of Settlement of Historical Claims*, 2021: p. 4.
69   New Zealand Government, *Ngāti Paoa and the Trustees of the Ngāti Paoa Iwi Trust and Crown*: p. 5.
70   Sullivan, *Māori Gardening in Tāmaki before 1840*: p. 86.
71   Sullivan, *Māori Gardening in Tāmaki before 1840*: p. 86.
72   Sullivan, *Māori Gardening in Tāmaki before 1840*: p. 89.
73   Sullivan, *Māori Gardening in Tāmaki before 1840*: pp. 89–90.
74   Sullivan, *Māori Gardening in Tāmaki before 1840*: p. 87.
75   Sullivan, *Māori Gardening in Tāmaki before 1840*: p. 93.
76   Bulmer, 'City without a state?': pp. 24–25.

8   For the common good: Local sovereignty and ra'ui in the Cook Islands
1   We note that this population figure does not include the large diaspora of Mangaians on Rarotonga, and in other nations such as Aotearoa and Australia.
2   In the sense that Edward Said described in *Orientalism: Western conceptions of the Orient* (New York: Vintage Books, 1979).
3   Jared Diamond, *Collapse: How societies choose to fail or succeed* (London: Viking, 2005); see also Jared Diamond, 'Easter's end', *Discover*, vol. 9 (1995): 62–69.
4   See the essays on the practice of ra'ui across the islands of Polynesia in Tamatoa Bambridge (ed.), *The Rahui: Legal pluralism in Polynesian traditional management of resources and territories* (Canberra: ANU Press, 2016).
5   Rod Dixon, 'I uta i tai – a preliminary account of *ra'ui* on Mangaia, Cook Islands', in *The Rahui: Legal pluralism in Polynesian traditional management of resources and territories*, Tamatoa Bambridge (ed.) (Canberra: ANU Press, 2016): pp. 79–104.
6   Only one of the authors, marine biologist Antony Vavia, pictured in photo on page 148, has Cook Islander heritage (from Mitiaro Island). The other two authors, Bronwen Neil and Tom Murray, write with an appreciation of their Australian convict-settler-colonial upbringing. White settlers are called *pākehā* in Māori and *papa'ā* in Cook Islands Māori: Jasper Buse and Raututi Taringa, *Cook Islands Māori dictionary with English finderlist* (Canberra: ANU Press, 1996): p. 314. The two languages are closely related but not identical.
7   Linda Tuhiwai Smith, *Decolonizing Methodologies: Research and Indigenous peoples*, 3rd ed. (Bloomsbury: London, 2021): p. 3.
8   Diamond, *Collapse*: pp. 100–10, 287.
9   Diamond, *Collapse*: p. 118; also Diamond, 'Easter's end': p. 68.
10   See: Terry Hunt, 'Rethinking Easter Island's ecological catastrophe', *Journal of Archaeological Science*, vol. 34 (2007): pp. 485–502; Valentí Rull, 'Natural and anthropogenic drivers of cultural change on Easter Island: Review and new insights', *Quaternary Science Reviews*, vol. 150, no. 15 (2016): pp. 31–41; Mauricio Lima et al., 'Ecology of the collapse of Rapa Nui society', *Proceedings of the Royal Society B, Biological Science*, vol. 287 (2020): 20200662. A decolonising lens on the socio-ecological challenges facing Polynesian populations would also highlight the role of epidemic diseases introduced by Europeans in the 19th century.
11   Lidia Guzy, 'Indigenous Shamanic worldviews as dialogical eco-cosmology', *Lagoonscapes: The Venice journal of environmental humanities*, vol. 1, no. 2 (2021): pp. 281–94, 282.

12　Kristina Tiedje and Lucas Johnston, 'Ecocosmologies and "western" epistemologies: Contestation, conflict, and collaboration', *Special Issue of the Journal for the Study of Religion, Nature & Culture*, vol. 11, no. 2 (2017): pp. 153–56.
13　Jo Anne Rey, 'Indigenous identity as country: The "ing" within connecting, caring, and belonging', *Genealogy*, vol. 5, no. 2 (2021). Rey's work has focussed on the unceded lands of the Dharug people in western Sydney, including the country where Macquarie University's Wallumattagal Campus now stands.
14　A framework described by Ani James, Jean Mitaera and Apii Rongo-Raea, *Turanga Māori: A Cook Islands conceptual framework transforming family violence – restoring wellbeing* (Wellington: Ministry of Social Development, 2012), <https://pasefikaproud.co.nz/assets/Resources-for-download/PasefikaProudResource-Nga-Vaka-o-Kaiga-Tapu-Pacific-Framework-Cook-Islands.pdf>.
15　John Maynard quoted in: Ann McGrath, Laura Rademaker and Jakelin Troy (eds), *Everywhen: Australia and the language of deep history* (Sydney: UNSW Press, 2023): p. 23.
16　Christina A Newport, 'Vaka moana as policy space: Navigating the Cook Islands case of climate change mobility' (PhD Thesis, University of Auckland, 2019).
17　Figure 12, in Dixon, '*I uta i tai* – a preliminary account of *ra'ui* on Mangaia, Cook Islands': p. 86, also shows the six punas and the *marae* located around the swamps in each district.
18　Arno Pascht, 'Land rights in Rarotonga (Cook Island): Traditions and transformations', *Pacific Studies*, vol. 34, no. 2 (2011): pp. 195–222.
19　Despite earlier European attempts to portray the majority of the population as open to land reform, resistance to the Land Courts and other reforms remained particularly strong in Mangaia. See: Michael Reilly, *Ancestral Voices from Mangaia: A history of the ancient gods and chiefs*, Memoirs of the Polynesian Society, vol. 54, Polynesian Society, Auckland (2009): p. 157. The situation is different on Rarotonga, as described by Ronald Gordon Crocombe, *Land Tenure in the Cook Islands* (New York: Oxford University Press, 1964): pp. 190–210.
20　Michael Reilly, 'Reading into the past: A historiography of Mangaia in the Cook Islands' (PhD Thesis, Australian National University, 1991): p. ix.
21　Resident Commissioner to the Cook Islands, Walter Edward Gudgeon, cited cultural conservatism and marked dislike of Europeans as the reasons for such strong resistance amongst Mangaians. Walter Edward Gudgeon, *Appendices to the Journals of the House of Representatives* (Wellington: New Zealand Ministry for Heritage and Culture, 1903), A3, No. 56, p. 23 & A.3, No. 1: p. 3.
22　Adam Johann von Krusenstern, *Atlas de l'Océan Pacifique* (St Petersburg 1824–1835).
23　*The Cook Islands and Other Islands Government Act, 1901.*
24　Food and food distribution in general have long played a central role in power politics in Mangaia: Michael Reilly, *Ancestral Voices from Mangaia: A history of the ancient gods and chiefs*, Memoirs of the Polynesian Society, vol. 54, Polynesian Society, Auckland (2009): pp. 153–56.
25　Buse and Taringa, *Cook Islands Māori dictionary with English finderlist*, p. 75, s.v. 'ariki, 1'. See: Dixo, '*I uta i tai* – a preliminary account of *ra'ui* on Mangaia, Cook Islands': p. 99, on the 'Ruler of food' in the Ngariki period of Mangaian history.
26　William Wyatt Gill, *Myths and Songs from the South Pacific* (London: 1876): pp. 634–36.
27　See: Charlotte Chambers, 'European contact and systems of governance on

Tongareva', in *The Rahui: Legal pluralism in Polynesian traditional management of resources and territories*, Tamatoa Bambridge (ed.) (Canberra: ANU Press, 2016): pp. 165–76.
28 Tegan Churcher Hoffmann, 'The reimplementation of the Ra'ui: Coral reef management in Rarotonga, Cook Islands', *Coastal Management*, vol. 30, no. 4 (2002): pp. 401–18.
29 Anna Tiraa, 'Ra'ui in the Cook Islands: Today's context in Rarotonga', *Traditional Marine Resource Management and Knowledge Information Bulletin*, vol. 19 (2006): pp. 11–15.
30 Hoffmann shows that ra'ui on Rarotonga is an effective conservation management tool and is improving coral reef health, with the ra'ui site showing significantly higher species diversity. See: Hoffmann, 'The reimplementation of the Ra'ui: Coral reef management in Rarotonga, Cook Islands': pp. 401–18.
31 The concept of tapu (English for 'taboo', 'sacred') and its relation to mana are explained by Manuka Henare, 'Tapu, mana, mauri, hau, wairua: A Māori philosophy of vitalism and cosmos', in *Indigenous Traditions and Ecology: The interbeing of cosmology and community*, John A Grim (ed.) (Cambridge: Harvard University Press, 2001): pp. 197–221.
32 See also: Patrick Nunn, William Aalbersberg, Shalini Lata and Marian Gwilliam, 'Beyond the core: Community governance for climate-change adaptation in peripheral parts of Pacific Island countries', *Regional Environmental Change*, vol. 14 (2013): pp. 221–35.
33 Tiraa, 'Ra'ui in the Cook Islands'.
34 Sonja Lee Miller, *'A quantitative assessment of ra'ui (a traditional approach to marine protected areas) on the fishes and invertebrates of Rarotonga, Cook Islands'* (PhD Thesis, Victoria University, 2008).
35 Philippa J Cohen and Timothy J Alexander, 'Catch rates, composition and fish size from reefs managed with periodically-harvested closures', *PLoS One*, vol. 8, no. 9 (2013): e73383; Kevin Leleu et al., 'Fishers' perceptions as indicators of the performance of marine protected areas (MPAs)', *Marine Policy*, vol. 36, no. 2 (2012): pp. 414–22.
36 Paul Bahn and John Flenley, *Easter Island, Earth Island* (New York: Thames and Hudson, 1992): p. 214.

9 History on the rocks

1 Gabriel Maralngurra, in conversation, 10 August 2022.
2 Gabriel Maralngurra, in conversation, 10 August 2022.
3 This argument and the ideas in this chapter are expanded upon in our recent book *Aboriginal Rock Art and the Telling of History* (Cambridge: Cambridge University Press, 2024). See also, for example, Erich Kolig, 'Social causality, human agency and mythology: Some thoughts on history-consciousness and mythical sense among Australian Aborigines', *Anthropological Forum*, vol. 10, no. 1 (2000): pp. 9–30; Tony Swain, *A Place for Strangers: Towards a history of Australian Aboriginal being* (Melbourne: Cambridge University Press, 1993); Peter Sutton, 'Myth as history, history as myth', in *Being Black: Aboriginal Cultures in 'settled' Australia*, Ian Keen (ed.) (Canberra: Aboriginal Studies Press, 1988): p. 251.
4 Penelope J Corfield, 'Primevalism: Saluting a renamed prehistory', in *Time and History in Prehistory*, Stella Souvatzi, Adnan Baysal and Emma L Baysal (eds) (Abingdon: Routledge, 2018): p. 265.

5   Bruce G Trigger, 'Alternative archaeologies: Nationalist, colonialist, imperialist', vol. 19, no. 3 (1984): pp. 355–70; Bruce G Trigger, *A History of Archaeological Thought* (Cambridge: Cambridge University Press: 2007).
6   See Evert Baudou, *Den nordiska arkeologin – historia och tolkningar* (Stockholm: Almqvist & Wiksell International, 2004): pp. 91–111; Joakim Goldhahn, 'To let mute stones speak – On the becoming of archaeology', in *Giving the Past a Future: Essays in archaeology and rock art studies in honour of Dr. Fil. H.C. Gerhard Milstreu*, Ellen Meijer and James Dodd (eds) (Oxford: Archaeopress, 2018): pp. 37–57.
7   Joakim Goldhahn, 'Bredarör on Kivik: A monumental cairn and the history of its interpretation', *Antiquity*, vol. 83, no. 320 (2009): pp. 359–71.
8   Nils Wessman, 'Berättelse om sin Resa genom Blekinge och Skåne till undersökande af desse provincers Antiquiteter och historia', *Den Swenska Mercurius*, vol. 3, no. 3 (1758): pp. 1310–17.
9   Goldhahn, 'To let mute stones speak'.
10 See: Schnapp, *The Discovery of the Past*. For the folklore of rock engravings in northern Europe. See: Joakim Goldhahn, 'On the archaeology of elves', in *Cognitive Archaeology: Mind, ethnography, and the past in South Africa and beyond*, David S Whitley, Johannes Loubster and Gavin Whitelaw (eds) (New York: Routledge, 2019), pp. 270–310.
11 Souvatzi, Baysal and Baysal, *Time and History in Prehistory*: p. 4; Bo Gräslund, *The Birth of Prehistoric Chronology: Dating methods and dating systems in nineteenth-century Scandinavian archaeology* (Cambridge: Cambridge University Press, 1987); Peter Rowley-Conwy, *From Genesis to Prehistory: The archaeological three age system and its contested reception in Denmark, Britain, and Ireland* (Oxford: Oxford University Press, 2007).
12 For example, Alain Schnapp, *The Discovery of the Past: The origins of archaeology* (London: British Museum Press, 1996).
13 Severin Fowles and Lindsay M Montgomery, 'Rock art counter-archives of the American West', *Murals of the Americas* (2019): p. 101.
14 Claire Smith and Gary Jackson, 'Decolonizing Indigenous archaeology: Developments from down under', *American Indian Quarterly*, vol. 30, no. 3 (2006): p. 316.
15 Ann McGrath and Lynette Russell (eds), 'History's outsiders? Global Indigenous histories', in *The Routledge Companion to Global Indigenous History*, (London: Routledge, 2022), pp. 11–16.
16 Adele Perry, 'The colonial archive on trial', in *Archive Stories: Facts, fictions, and the writing of history*, Antoinette Burton (ed.) (Durham: Duke University Press, 2006), p. 333; Souvatzi, Baysal and Baysal, *Time and History in Prehistory*: p. 13; Ian J McNiven and Lynette Russell, *Appropriated Pasts: Indigenous peoples and the colonial culture of archaeology* (Lanham: Rowman Altamira, 2005): pp. 11–49.
17 Eric R Wolf, *Europe and the People without History* (Berkeley: University of California Press, 1982).
18 Sue McKemmish, Shannon Faulkhead and Lynette Russell, 'Distrust in the archive: Reconciling records', *Archival Science*, vol. 11, no. 3/4 (2011): p. 225.
19 Stephen A Mrozowski and Peter R Schmidt (eds), *The Death of Prehistory* (Oxford: Oxford University Press, 2013): p. 3.
20 Adele Perry, 'The colonial archive on trial', in *Archive Stories: Facts, fictions, and the writing of history*, Antoinette Burton (ed.) (Durham: Duke University Press, 2006): p. 236.

21 RG Craven, 'The pre – (whose?) – history debate: Where are our Manning Clarks of archaeology and anthropology?', *Australian Archaeology*, vol. 49 (1999): p. 64; Smith and Jackson, 'Decolonizing Indigenous archaeology': p. 316.
22 McNiven and Russell, *Appropriated Pasts*: p. 5; Maxine Oland, Siobhan M Hart and Liam Frink (eds), *Decolonizing Indigenous Histories: Exploring prehistoric/colonial transitions in archaeology* (Tuscon: University of Arizona Press, 2012): p. 1; Corfield, 'Primevalism': p. 265; Kent G Lightfoot, 'Culture contact studies: Redefining the relationship between prehistoric and historical archaeology', *American Antiquity* (1995): pp. 199–217; Daniel Lord Smail and Andrew Shryock, 'History and the "pre"', *American Historical Review*, vol. 118, no. 3, (2013): pp. 709–37.
23 Craven, 'The pre – (whose?) – history debate': p. 65. See also the debate in *Australian Archaeology* in 2000.
24 Joe Watkins, 'Through wary eyes: Indigenous perspectives on archaeology', *Annual Review of Anthropology*, vol. 34 (2005): pp. 429–49; Sonya Atalay, 'Indigenous archaeology as decolonizing practice', *American Indian Quarterly*, vol. 30, no. 3/4 (2006): pp. 280–310; Smith and Jackson, 'Decolonizing Indigenous archaeology', p. 312; McNiven and Russell, *Appropriated Pasts*.
25 Joe Watkins, *Indigenous Archaeology: American Indian values and scientific practice* (New York: Rowman & Littlefield, 2000): p. 6.
26 Mrozowski and Schmidt, *The Death of Prehistory*: p. 10.
27 Alistair Paterson, 'Rock art as historical sources in colonial contexts', in Oland, Hart and Frink (eds), *Decolonizing Indigenous Histories*: p. 67.
28 Lindsay M Montgomery and Severin Fowles, 'An Indigenous archive: Documenting Comanche history through rock art', *The American Indian Quarterly*, vol. 44, no. 2 (2020): p. 197.
29 McKemmish, Faulkhead and Russell, 'Distrust in the archive': p. 218.
30 Ann McGrath and Mary Anne Jebb (eds), *Long History, Deep Time: Deepening histories of place* (Canberra: ANU Press, 2015); Andrew Shryock and Daniel Lord Smail, *Deep History: The architecture of past and present* (Oakland: University of California Press, 2011). See also project websites such as <re.anu.edu.au/> and <marking-country.re.anu.edu.au/>.
31 Shryock and Smail, *Deep History*.
32 McKemmish, Faulkhead and Russell, 'Distrust in the archive': pp. 212, 220; Terry Cook, 'What is past is prologue: A history of archival ideas since 1898, and the future paradigm shift', *Archivaria* (1997): p. 18.
33 Eric Ketelaar, 'The archive as a time machine', in *European Archives News, Proceedings of the DLM-Forum* (2002): p. 577.
34 Ketelaar, 'The archive as a time machine': p. 579.
35 Souvatzi, Baysal and Baysal, *Time and History in Prehistory*: p. 1.
36 Darren Jorgensen and Ian McLean, *Indigenous Archives: The making and unmaking of Aboriginal art* (Crawley: UWA Publishing, 2017).
37 Gabriel Maralngurra, in conversation, 12 August 2022.
38 Wakaman Elder Carol Chong, cited in Paul SC Taçon and Liam M Brady, 'The place of rock art in the contemporary world', in *Relating to Rock Art in the Contemporary World: Navigating symbolism, meaning, and significance*, Liam M Brady and Paul SC Taçon (eds) (Boulder: University Press of Colorado, 2016): p. 12.
39 Quoted in Paul SC Taçon, 'Connecting to the Ancestors: Why rock art is important for Indigenous Australians and their well-being', *Rock Art Research*, vol. 36, no. 1 (2019): pp. 6–7.

40 Taçon, 'Connecting to the Ancestors': p. 7.
41 Taçon, 'Connecting to the Ancestors': p. 10.
42 Taçon, 'Connecting to the Ancestors': p. 8.
43 See also Ian McLean, *Rattling Spears: A history of Indigenous Australian Art* (London: Reaktion Books, 2016): p. 26.
44 Taçon and Brady, 'The place of rock art in the contemporary world': p. 4.
45 Robert Layton, *Australian Rock Art: A new synthesis* (Cambridge: Cambridge University Press, 1992): p. 75.
46 Howard Morphy, 'Recursive and iterative processes in Australian rock art: An anthropological perspective', in *A Companion to Rock Art*, Jo McDonald and Peter Veth (eds) (New York: John Wiley & Sons, 2012): pp. 296–97.
47 Morphy, 'Recursive and iterative processes in Australian rock art', p. 297.
48 Paul SC Taçon and Christopher Chippindale, 'An archaeology of rock-art through informed methods', in *The Archaeology of Rock-Art*, Christopher Chippindale and Paul SC Taçon (ed.) (Cambridge: Cambridge University Press, 1998): p. 1.
49 Suzanne Briet, *What Is Documentation? English translation of the classic French Text, translated and edited by Ronald E Dayet* (Lanham: Scarecrow Press, 2006); Geir Grenersen, Kjell Kemi and Steinar Nilsen, 'Landscapes as documents: The relationship between traditional Sámi terminology and the concepts of document and documentation', *Journal of Documentation*, vol. 72, no. 6 (2016): p. 1186.
50 Geoffrey Yeo, 'Concepts of record (2): Prototypes and boundary objects', *American Archivist*, vol. 71, no. 1 (2008): p. 140; Joan M Schwartz and Terry Cook, 'Archives, records, and power: The making of modern memory', *Archival Science*, vol. 2, no. 1/2 (2002).
51 Montgomery and Fowles, 'An Indigenous archive': p. 198.
52 Montgomery and Fowles, 'An Indigenous archive': pp. 198–202; Francesca Merlan, 'The interpretive framework of Wardaman rock art: A preliminary report', *Australian Aboriginal Studies*, vol. 2 (1989): p. 19.
53 For a discussion of historians' reverence for archives and the limits of this sacralising view, see: Mike Jones, 'The temple of history: Historians and the sacralisation of archival work', *History Australia*, vol. 18, no. 4 (2021): pp. 676–93.
54 McKemmish, Chandler and Faulkhead, 'Imagine': p. 284; McLean, *Rattling Spears*: p. 17.
55 Gay'wu Group of Women, *Songspirals: Sharing women's wisdom of Country through Songlines* (Sydney: Allen & Unwin, 2019); Margo Neale, *Songlines: Tracking the Seven Sisters* (Canberra: National Museum of Australia, 2017).
56 Faulkhead, 'Connecting through records': p. 84.
57 Lynette Russell, 'Indigenous records and archives: Mutual obligations and building trust', *Archives and Manuscripts*, vol. 34, no. 1 (2006): pp. 32–43.
58 Sue McKemmish et al., 'Decolonizing recordkeeping and archival praxis in childhood out-of-home care and Indigenous Archival Collections', *Archival Science*, vol. 20, no. 1 (2020): p. 21; Shannon Faulkhead et al., 'Australian Indigenous knowledge and the archives: Embracing multiple ways of knowing and keeping', *Archives and Manuscripts*, vol. 38, no. 1 (2010): p. 34.
59 Sue McKemmish, Tom Chandler and Shannon Faulkhead, 'Imagine: A living archive of people and Place "somewhere beyond custody"', *Archival Science*, vol. 19, no. 3 (2019): p. 286.
60 Terri Janke and Livia Iacovino, 'Keeping cultures alive: Archives and Indigenous cultural and intellectual property rights', *Archival Science*, vol. 12, no. 2 (2012): p. 156; Livia Iacovino, 'Rethinking archival, ethical and legal frameworks for records

of Indigenous Australian communities: A participant relationship model of rights and responsibilities', *Archival Science*, vol. 10, no. 4 (2010): p. 360.
61   Janke and Iacovino, 'Keeping cultures alive': p. 160.
62   Lynette Russell, 'Indigenous knowledge and archives: Accessing hidden history and understandings', *Australian Academic & Research Libraries*, vol. 36, no. 2 (January 2005): p. 162.
63   Terri Janke, *True Tracks: Respecting Indigenous knowledge and culture* (Sydney: UNSW Press, 2021): p. 254.
64   Faulkhead et al., 'Australian Indigenous knowledge': p. 34; Natalie Harkin, 'The poetics of (re) mapping archives: Memory in the blood', *Journal of the Association for the Study of Australian Literature*, vol. 14, no. 3 (2014).
65   Margo Neale and Lynne Kelly, *Songlines: The power and promise* (Thames & Hudson, 2020), p. 50; Petra Lundy, '"Giving life to the truth": Indigenous art as a pathway to archival decolonization' (MA Thesis, University of Manitoba, 2018).
66   Fowles and Montgomery, 'Rock art counter-archives of the American west': p. 105.
67   Liz Conor and Jane Lydon, 'Double take: Reappraising the colonial archive', *Journal of Australian Studies*, vol. 35, no. 2 (2011): p. 137; Paul S Taçon and Sally K May, 'Rock art evidence for Macassan-Aboriginal contact in Northwestern Arnhem Land', in *Macassan History and Heritage: Journeys, encounters and influences*, Marshall Clark and Sally K May (eds) (Canberra: ANU Press, 2013): pp. 127–39.
68   Paterson, 'Rock art as historical sources': p. 70, see also Sally K May et al., 'The missing Macassans: Indigenous sovereignty, rock art and the archaeology of absence', *Australian Archaeology*, vol. 87, no. 2 (2021): pp. 127–43.
69   Morphy, 'Recursive and iterative processes': p. 296; Taçon, 'Connecting to the Ancestors': p. 7.
70   Jeff Doring, *Gwion Gwion: Secret and sacred pathways of the Ngarinyin, Aboriginal people of Australia* (Cologne: Koneman, 2000): p. 20.
71   Liam M Brady and John J Bradley, '"That painting now is telling us something": Negotiating and Apprehending contemporary meaning in Yanyuwa Rock Art, Northern Australia', in *Relating to Rock Art in the Contemporary World: Navigating symbolism, meaning, and significance*, Liam M. Brady and Paul SC Taçon (eds) (Boulder: University Press of Colorado, 2016): p. 86.
72   Brady and Bradley, '"That painting now is telling us something"': p. 102.
73   John A Walsh, '"Images of God and friends of God": The Holy Icon as document', *Journal of the American Society for Information Science and Technology*, vol. 63, no. 1 (2012): p. 188.
74   Perry, 'The colonial archive on trial': p. 335.
75   Laura Rademaker and Ben Silverstein, 'Deep historicities', *Interventions*, vol. 24, no. 2 (2022): pp. 137–60; Ann McGrath, Laura Rademaker and Ben Silverstein, 'Deep history and deep listening: Indigenous knowledges and the narration of deep pasts', *Rethinking History*, vol. 25, no. 3 (2021): pp. 307–26.
76   Jane Lydon, '"Behold the tears": Photography as colonial witness', *History of Photography*, vol. 34, no. 3 (2010): pp. 234–50; Jane Lydon, 'Return: The photographic archive and technologies of Indigenous memory', *Photographies*, vol. 3, no. 2 (2010): pp. 173–87.
77   Michelle Caswell, '"The archive" is not an archives: On acknowledging the intellectual contributions of archival studies', *Reconstruction*, vol. 16, no. 1 (2016).
78   Joakim Goldhahn et al., '"Our dad's painting is hiding, in secret place": Reverberations of a rock painting episode in Kakadu National Park, Australia', *Rock Art Research*, vol. 38, no. 1 (2021): pp. 59–69.

79 Terri Janke, *True Tracks: Respecting Indigenous knowledge and culture* (Sydney: UNSW Press, 2021).
80 McNiven and Russell, *Appropriated Pasts*: p. 234.
81 Gabriel Maralngurra, in conversation, 10 August 2022.

10   Language has Country: Memory, transmission and sovereignty in Tara June Winch's *The Yield*

1 Aileen Moreton-Robinson, 'Introduction' in *Sovereign Subjects: Indigenous sovereignty matters*, Aileen Moreton-Robinson (Ed.) (Sydney: Allen & Unwin, 2007): p. 2.
2 Rosanne Kennedy and Ben Silverstein, 'Beyond presentism: Memory studies, deep history and the challenges of transmission', *Memory Studies*, vol. 16, no. 6 (2023): pp. 1609–27. We borrow this term from Linda Barwick, who argues that, in the creative period referred to in Warlpiri as jukurrpa and often translated as the Dreaming in English, 'totemic ancestors ... performed actions in a "time out of time" that created and structured today's experiential world – including the landscape, all beings that live in it, and the laws and codes (languages, ceremonies, kinship systems) that enable them to interact and be fecund. This creative period can be thought of as belonging to a deep present rather than a deep past, in that ancestral power continues to reside in and activate the experiential world': Linda Barwick, 'Songs and the deep present', in *Everywhen: Australia and the language of deep history*, Ann McGrath, Laura Rademaker and Jakelin Troy (eds) (Sydney: UNSW Press, 2023): pp. 92–93.
3 Tara June Winch, *The Yield* (London: Hamish Hamilton, 2019).
4 The Uluru Statement represents an outcome of a years-long process of discussion regarding future reform to the Australian Constitution to recognise Indigenous peoples in that document. It was supported by a majority of Indigenous delegates to the 2017 National Constitutional Convention held at Uluru. It begins by recognising Aboriginal and Torres Strait Islander sovereignties, and calls for the 'establishment of a First Nations Voice enshrined in the Constitution', and a Makarrata Commission that would supervise a process of 'agreement making between governments and First Nations and truth-telling about our history': <ulurustatement.org/the-statement/view-the-statement/>.
5 The exhibition, curated by Brenda Croft, was on show at the National Gallery of Australia from 13 October 2007 – 10 February 2008, <nga.gov.au/exhibitions/national-indigenous-art-triennial-culture-warriors/>. It closed three days before Kevin Rudd's national Apology to Indigenous Peoples, issued on 13 February 2008. Archie Moore's *kith and kin* won the coveted Golden Lion, awarded to the best national pavilion at the Venice Biennale 2024, the first time an Australian artist has won: <www.theguardian.com/artanddesign/video/2024/apr/21/kamilaroi-bigambul-artist-archie-moore-wins-gold-lion-award-at-venice-biennale>.
6 On storying as a way of making meaning that both moves towards decolonisation and evokes a resonance with Country, see: Jason de Santolo, 'Indigenous storywork in Australia', in *Decolonizing Research: Indigenous storywork as methodology*, Jo-Ann Archibald et al. (eds) (London: Zed Books, 2019): p. 171.
7 See, for example, Tonya Stebbins, Vicki Louise Couzens, Christina Eira, and Victorian Aboriginal Corporation for Languages, Language revival factsheets, Melbourne, Victoria, 2015, <www.vaclang.org.au/images/projects/meeting%20point%20fact%20sheets/Language%20Revival%20Factsheets%20Set.pdf>.
8 Winch, *The Yield*: pp. 313–38.
9 Winch, *The Yield*: p. 1.

10 In contrast to historiography and law, the novel is a relatively unregulated form for transmitting images of the past, and as such, can accommodate a range of sources and voices. See Ann Rigney, 'Portable monuments: Literature, cultural memory and the case of Jeanie Deans', *Poetics Today*, vol. 25, no. 2 (2004): p. 375.
11 Winch, *The Yield*: p. 2.
12 This 'Plea' is archived in the National Library of Australia and the Warangesda Aboriginal Mission has been listed on the NSW heritage register since 2010. See JB Gribble, *A Plea for the Aborigines of New South Wales* (Jerilderie, 1879), available from <nla.gov.au/nla.obj-52756199>. Other parts of Greenleaf's letters take inspiration from JB Gribble, 'The Warangesda Mission: In the newly formed diocese of Riverina, New South Wales', in *Mission Life* (London: Wells Gardner, Darton & Co, 1884): pp. 368–78, available from <nla.gov.au/nla.obj-52785264>.
13 Winch, *The Yield*: p. 257.
14 Winch, *The Yield*: p. 2.
15 Jedda references the Aboriginal heroine of the 1950s classic, *Jedda*, in which a black baby is taken from her Community after her mother dies in childbirth, to be raised in white culture. See *Jedda*, Charles Chauvel (dir.) (Chauvel Film Enterprises Pty Ltd, 1955).
16 Winch, *The Yield*: pp. 6–8.
17 Winch, *The Yield*: p. 1.
18 Bawaka Country et al., 'Co-becoming Bawaka: Towards a relational understanding of place/space', *Progress in Human Geography*, vol. 40, no. 4 (2016): p. 456.
19 Ann McGrath and Laura Rademaker, 'The languages and temporalities of "everywhen" in deep history', in *Everywhen: Australia and the language of deep history*, Ann McGrath, Laura Rademaker and Jakelin Troy (eds) (Sydney: UNSW Press, 2023): p. 2.
20 McGrath and Rademaker, 'The languages and temporalities of "everywhen" in deep history': p. 2.
21 Brenda Croft, 'Still in my mind: Gurindji location, experience and visuality: Teachers' notes' (Artback NT, n.d.) <artbacknt.com.au/wp-content/uploads/sites/31/SIMM-EDUCATION-RESOURCE-TEACHERS-NOTES-1.pdf>: p. 9.
22 McGrath and Rademaker, 'The languages and temporalities of "everywhen" in deep history': p. 2. See also Nick Enfield and Jakelin Troy, 'Jaky Troy on the Sydney Language', audio recording, *Sydney Centre for Language Research*, 12 August 2020, <soundcloud.com/sydneylanguageresearch/jaky-troy-on-the-sydney-language>.
23 Anne Brewster and Kim Scott, '"Can you anchor a shimmering nation state via regional Indigenous roots?" Kim Scott talks to Anne Brewster about *That Deadman Dance*', in *History, Power, Text: Cultural studies and Indigenous studies*, Timothy Neale, Crystal McKinnon and Eve Vincent (eds) (Sydney: CSR Books, 2014): p. 505; Rosanne Kennedy, 'Orbits, mobilities, scales: Kim Scott's *That Deadman Dance* as transcultural remembrance', *Australian Humanities Review*, vol. 59 (2016): pp. 114–35.
24 Jan Assmann, 'Collective memory and cultural identity', *New German Critique*, vol. 65 (1995): pp. 125–33.
25 Aleida Assmann, 'Canon and archive', in *Cultural Memory Studies: An international and interdisciplinary handbook*, Astrid Erll, Ansgar Nünning, and Sara B Young (eds) (Berlin: Walter de Gruyter, 2008): pp. 97–107.
26 Winch, *The Yield*: p. 1.
27 Winch, *The Yield*: pp. 3, 6.

28 Rigney, 'Portable monuments': p. 381.
29 Winch, *The Yield*: pp. 11–12, 23, 312.
30 Jane Simpson, 'Making dictionaries', in *Language and Culture in Aboriginal Australia*, Michael Walsh and Colin Yallop (eds) (Canberra: Aboriginal Studies Press, 1993): p. 132. See also Laura Rademaker, *Found in Translation: Many meanings on a North Australian Mission* (Honolulu: University of Hawai'i Press, 2018): p. 9.
31 Sophia Compton, 'Reading sovereignty in the fiction of Tara June Winch' (MA Thesis, UNSW, 2022): p. 53.
32 Winch, *The Yield*: pp. 126, 160, 204.
33 Winch, *The Yield*: p. 160.
34 Winch, *The Yield*: pp. 33, 175, 203, 256.
35 Winch, *The Yield*: pp. 205–06.
36 Winch, *The Yield*: p. 26.
37 Rademaker, *Found in Translation*: p. 118; Rachel Gilmour, *Grammars of Colonialism: Representing languages in colonial South Africa* (Basingstoke: Palgrave Macmillan, 2006): p. 111.
38 Winch, *The Yield*: p. 25.
39 Stephen Muecke, *No road (bitumen all the way)* (Fremantle: Fremantle Arts Centre Press, 1997): p. 70; Morgan Brigg and Mary Graham, 'The relevance of Aboriginal political concepts (6): Relationalism, not sovereignty', *ABC Religion & Ethics*, 5 December 2020, <www.abc.net.au/religion/aboriginal-political-philosophy-relationalism/12954274>.
40 Winch, *The Yield*: p. 36.
41 Technologies of memory – sometimes referred to as 'mnemotechnologies' – are those technologies and techniques – photography, commemorative ritual, body art, literature and many other cultural forms – through which 'shared images of the past are actively produced and circulated': Rigney, 'Portable monuments': pp. 366, 369.
42 The history and meaning of native title in Australia has been contentious but has been a part of settler state law since a native title claim, lodged by Eddie Mabo and other Meriam plaintiffs from the Eastern Torres Strait in 1982, was upheld by the High Court in 1992. Native title is now one way that Australian common law recognises, in certain limited circumstances, 'the rights and interests of Aboriginal and Torres Strait Islander people in land and waters according to their traditional laws and customs'. See <nativetitle.org.au/learn/native-title-and-pbcs/native-title-rights-and-interests>.
43 Winch, *The Yield*: p. 6.
44 Winch, *The Yield*: p. 1.
45 Winch, *The Yield*: p. 312.
46 Ellen van Neerven, '*The Yield* by Tara June Winch', *Australian Book Review*, no. 413 (August 2019), <www.australianbookreview.com.au/abr-online/archive/2019/371-august-2019-no-413/5676-ellen-van-neerven-reviews-the-yield-by-tara-june-winch>.
47 'A note on this narration from Tara June Winch' in Tara June Winch, *The Yield*, audiobook, narrated by Tony Briggs (Penguin Random House Australia, 2019).
48 Assmann, 'Canon and archive': p. 98.
49 Assmann, 'Canon and archive': pp. 100–02, 104.
50 Shaunnagh Dorsett and Shaun McVeigh, *Jurisdiction* (Oxford: Routledge, 2012): pp. 5, 6, 32.
51 JL Austin, *How to Do Things with Words* (Oxford: Clarendon Press, 1962).
52 Winch, *The Yield*: p. 34.

53 Martuwarra RiverOfLife et al, 'Recognizing the Martuwarra's first law right to life as a living ancestral being', *Transnational Environmental Law*, vol. 9, no. 3 (2020): p. 544.
54 Shaun McVeigh and Sundhya Pahuja, 'Thinking with jurisdiction', *Zeitschrift für ausländisches öffentliches Recht und Völkerrecht / Heidelberg Journal of International Law*, vol. 82, no. 2 (2022): p. 301.
55 Shiri Pasternak, *Grounded Authority: The Algonquins of Barriere Lake against the state* (Minneapolis: University of Minnesota Press, 2017).
56 Taiaiake Alfred, 'Sovereignty', in *A Companion to American Indian History*, Phil Deloria and Neal Salisbury (eds) (New York: Blackwell, 2002): pp. 460, 464.
57 Brigg and Graham, 'The relevance of Aboriginal political concepts (6): Relationalism, not sovereignty'.
58 Crystal McKinnon, 'Expressing Indigenous sovereignty: The production of embodied texts in social protest and the arts' (PhD Thesis, La Trobe University, 2018): p. 9.
59 Joanne Barker, 'For whom sovereignty matters', in *Sovereignty Matters: Locations of contestation and possibility in Indigenous struggles for self-determination*, Joanne Barker (ed.) (Lincoln: University of Nebraska Press, 2005): p. 21. See also Patricia A Monture, 'Women's words: Power, identity, and Indigenous sovereignty', *Canadian Woman Studies/Les Cahiers de la Femme*, vol. 26, no. 3/4 (2008): p. 158; Leanne Betasamosake Simpson, 'The place where we all live and work together: A gendered analysis of "sovereignty"' in *Native Studies Keywords*, Stephanie Nohelani Teves et al. (eds) (Tucson: University of Arizona Press, 2015): p. 19.
60 Jean Dennison, 'Entangled sovereignties: The Osage Nation's interconnections with governmental and corporate authorities', *American Ethnologist*, vol. 44, no. 4 (2017): p. 685. See also: Ben Silverstein, 'Reading sovereignties in the shadow of settler colonialism: Chinese employment of Aboriginal labour in the Northern Territory of Australia', *Postcolonial Studies*, vol. 23, no. 1 (2020): pp. 43–57.
61 Aileen Moreton-Robinson, 'Introduction' in *Sovereign Subjects: Indigenous sovereignty matters*, Aileen Moreton-Robinson (ed.) (Sydney: Allen & Unwin, 2007): p. 2.
62 Aileen Moreton-Robinson, 'Incommensurable sovereignties: Indigenous ontology matters', in *Routledge Handbook of Critical Indigenous Studies*, Brendan Hokowhitu et al. (eds) (London: Routledge, 2021): p. 259.
63 Aileen Moreton-Robinson, 'Incommensurable sovereignties': p. 263.
64 Aileen Moreton-Robinson, 'Incommensurable sovereignties': p. 263.
65 Christine F Black, *The Land Is the Source of Law: A dialogic encounter with Indigenous jurisprudence* (Oxford: Routledge–Cavendish, 2011): p. 167 (emphasis in original). See also Mary Graham, 'Some thoughts about the philosophical underpinnings of Aboriginal worldviews', *Worldviews: Environment, culture, religion*, vol. 3, no. 2 (1999): pp. 105–06.
66 Kevin Gilbert, *Because a White Man'll Never Do It* (Sydney: HarperCollins, 1994): p. 3.
67 Stan Grant Sr and John Rudder, *A New Wiradjuri Dictionary* (Canberra: Restoration House, 2010): pp. 7, 20.
68 *The Yield* 'does not purport purism, but embraces modernity, collage and collaboration if it serves the regeneration, continuation and flourishing of life', Bartha-Mitchell writes. At the same time, the particularity of language is 'invaluable' as it grounds knowledge in place. Kathrin Bartha-Mitchell, *Cosmological Readings of Contemporary Australian Literature: Unsettling the Anthropocene* (London: Routledge, 2023): pp. 95–96.

69 Winch, *The Yield*: p. 127.
70 Wendy Brady, 'That sovereign being: History matters', in *Sovereign Subjects: Indigenous sovereignty matters*, Aileen Moreton-Robinson (ed.) (Sydney: Allen & Unwin, 2007): p. 142.
71 Winch, *The Yield*: p. 283.
72 Winch, *The Yield*: pp. 16, 270.
73 Winch, *The Yield*: p. 162.
74 Winch, *The Yield*: p. 253.
75 Winch, *The Yield*: p. 278.
76 Hayden White, *The Content of the Form: Narrative discourse and historical representation* (Baltimore: Johns Hopkins University Press, 1987).
77 Winch, *The Yield*: p. 253.
78 Winch, *The Yield*: p. 289.
79 Winch, *The Yield*: p. 3.
80 Winch, *The Yield*: p. 84.
81 Winch, *The Yield*: p. 251.
82 Winch, *The Yield*: p. 253.
83 Winch, *The Yield*: p. 88.
84 Kennedy, 'Orbits, mobilities, scales': p. 127.
85 Winch, *The Yield*: p. 294.
86 See also Barwick, 'Songs and the deep present': p. 94.

11 A place for a stranger: The Wardandi history of Thomas Timothée Vasse

1 The Baudin expedition, conceived during the French revolution and then approved by Napoleon, was the first to produce a complete map of Australia, as a rival English expedition led by Matthew Flinders was delayed when the Governor of Mauritius detained him there for seven years.
2 François Péron et al., *Voyage de Découvertes aux Terres Australes. Volume I. [Historique]: Exécuté par ordre de Sa Majesté l'empereur et roi, sur les corvettes le Géographe, le Naturaliste, et la goélette le Casuarina, pendant les années 1800, 1801, 1802,1803 et 1804* (De l'Imprimerie Impériale, 1807): p. 68. Geographe Bay is spelled as 'Geographe' these days, although it was named after Baudin's vessel the *Géographe*.
3 Alain Sérieyx and Neville Weston, *Wonnerup: The sacred dune* (Perth: Abrolhos Publishing, 2001): p. 157.
4 Sérieyx and Weston, *Wonnerup*: p. 157.
5 William Webb, 'Interview with Bill Webb August 2021 SLWA OH4759', State Library of Western Australia (ed.) (2021), <encore.slwa.wa.gov.au/iii/encore/record/C__Rb7359986>. See also: Mary Blight, 'The story of Vasse and the Wardandi Noongar: A new perspective' (Honours Thesis, University of Western Australia, 2021). I am grateful to Bill Webb for sharing this oral history and to my supervisors, Dr Paul Gibbard and Dr Len Collard.
6 Blight, 'The Story of Vasse and the Wardandi Noongar'.
7 Tony Birch, '"The invisible fire": Indigenous sovereignty, history and responsibility', in *Sovereign Subjects: Indigenous Sovereignty Matters*, Aileen Moreton-Robinson (ed.) (Taylor and Francis: 2008): p. 108. For a discussion on Indigenous sovereignty and oral history tradition see: Jennifer Nez Denetdale, 'The value of oral history on the path to Dine/Navajo sovereignty', in *Dine Perspectives: Revitalizing and reclaiming Navajo thought*, Lloyd Lee (ed.) (Tucson: University of Arizona Press, 2014).

8   Blight, 'The story of Vasse and the Wardandi Noongar': p. 59.
9   Blight, 'The story of Vasse and the Wardandi Noongar': p. 60.
10 Len Collard, *A Nyungar Interpretation of Ellensbrook and Wonnerup Homesteads* (Perth: Heritage Council of Western Australia, 1994): p. 53.
11 Neville Green, *Broken Spears: Aborigines and Europeans in the Southwest of Australia* (Perth: Focus Education Services, 1984): p. 5.
12 Len Collard and Dave Palmer, 'Noongar and non-Aboriginal people going along together (Ngulla wangkiny, ni, katitjin Noongar nyidyung koorliny, kura, yeye, boorda)', in *New Perspectives on Exploration Archives*, Shino Konishi, Maria Nugent, and Tiffany Shellam (eds) (Canberra: ANU Press, 2015): p. 192.
13 Clint Bracknell, 'Old dogs and ice ages in Noongar country', in *Everywhen: Australia and the language of deep history*, Ann McGrath, Laura Rademaker and Jakelin Troy (eds) (Sydney: UNSW Press, 2023): p. 79.
14 Mary Durack, *To Be Heirs Forever* (London: Corgi Books, 1979): p. 51.
15 Bracknell, 'Old dogs and ice ages in Noongar country': p. 85.
16 Blight, 'The story of Vasse and the Wardandi Noongar': p. 51.
17 Eliza Dawson married a convict called Joseph Hill and they had ten children. Joseph Hill worked in the timber industry, and also was employed carting stone for the construction of the Leeuwin lighthouse in 1895 or 1896. See: Gail Cresswell, *The Light of Leeuwin: The Augusta-Margaret River Shire history* (Margaret River: The Augusta-Margaret River Shire History Group, 1989): p. 27.
18 List of Noongar Apical Ancestors – Attachment A1 of the Application, 2003, National Native Title Tribunal, <www.nntt.gov.au/searchRegApps/NativeTitleClaims/Pages/details.aspx?NTDA_Fileno=WC2003/007>.
19 Collard and Palmer, 'Noongar and non-Aboriginal people going along together': p. 194.
20 *The Deadwater Chant* by Margot Edwards with Wardandi elder Vilma Webb, produced by Arts Margaret River, co-directed by Phil Thomson, Kelton Pell and Margot Edwards; musical director Guirec Martin; production/design by Alan Surgener, <spongedoll.com/2020/11/03/deadwater-chant/>. This project was supported by the Australia Council for the Arts, Regional Arts Fund WA and Arts Margaret River.
21 Linda Barwick, 'Songs and the deep present', in *Everywhen*, McGrath, Rademaker, and Troy (eds) (Sydney: UNSW Press, 2023): p. 93.
22 Bracknell, 'Old dogs and ice ages in Noongar country': pp. 81–82.
23 George Fletcher Moore, 'Correspondence', *The Perth Gazette and Western Australian Journal*, Volume 6, Saturday 5 May 1838, <trove.nla.gov.au/newspaper/article/639547>.
24 Jean Fornasiero, Peter Monteath and John West-Sooby, *Encountering Terra Australis: The Australian Voyages of Nicolas Baudin and Matthew Flinders* (Adelaide: Wakefield Press, 2004): p. 144. Paul Gibbard, *The French Collector: Journal and Letters of Theodore Leschenault, Botanist of the Baudin Expedition* (Perth: UWA Publishing, 2023): p. 71.
25 Fornasiero, Monteath and West-Sooby, *Encountering Terra Australis*: p. 144; Leslie Ronald Marchant, *France Australe: A study of French explorations and attempts to found a penal colony and strategic base in South Western Australia, 1503–1826* (Perth: Artlook Books, 1982): p. 144; Graham Seal, *The Savage Shore: Extraordinary stories of survival and tragedy from the early voyages of discovery* (Sydney: Allen & Unwin, 2015): pp. 198–99.

26 Collard, *A Nyungar Interpretation of Ellensbrook and Wonnerup Homesteads*: p. 49.
27 Len Collard and Dave Palmer, 'Looking for the residents of Terra Australis: The importance of Nyungar in early European coastal exploration', in *Strangers on the Shore: Early coastal contacts in Australia*, Margo Neale, Peter Veth and Peter Sutton (eds) (Canberra: National Museum of Australia Press, 2008): p. 165; Thomas Brendan Cullity, *Vasse: An account of the disappearance of Thomas Timothée Vasse* (Perth: T.B. Cullity, 1992): p. 3.
28 See: Frank Horner, *The French Reconnaissance: Baudin in Australia 1801–1803* (Melbourne: Melbourne University Press, 1987), p. 150; Henry William Bunbury, *Lieutenant Bunbury's Australian Sojourn: The letters and journals of Lt. H.W. Bunbury, 21st Royal North Fusiliers, 1834–1837*, JMR Cameron and Phyllis Barnes (eds) (Perth: Hesperian Press, 2014): p. 175. John Dunmore, *French Explorers in the Pacific II* (Oxford: Clarendon Press, 1965): p. 17.
29 Lester-Irabinna Rigney, 'Internationalization of an Indigenous anticolonial cultural critique of research methodologies: A guide to Indigenist research methodology and its principles', *Wicazo Sa Review*, vol. 14, no. 2 (1999): pp. 109–21.
30 In Noongar culture, there are six seasons in the south-west of Western Australia: Birak from December to January, Bunuru from February to March, Djeran from April to May, Makuru from June to July, Djilba from August to September and Kambarang from October to November. See 'Noongar Six Seasons', *Kurongkurl Katitjin Cultural Leadership*, <www.ecu.edu.au/centres/kurongkurl-katitjin/cultural-leadership/nyoongar-six-seasons>.
31 Len Collard, Clint Bracknell and David Palmer, 'Nyungar of Southwestern Australia and Flinders: A dialogue on using Nyungar intelligence to better understand coastal exploration', *ab-Original: Journal of Indigenous Studies and First Nations and First Peoples' Cultures*, vol. 1, no. 1 (2017): p. 7.
32 Edward Duyker, 'Timothée Vasse: A biographical note', *The French Australian Review* (2016), <www.isfar.org.au/wp-content/uploads/2016/10/51_EDWARD-DUYKER-Timoth%C3%A9e-Vasse-A-Biographical-Note.pdf>.
33 Horner, *The French Reconnaissance*: p. 150.
34 Shino Konishi, 'Early encounters in Aboriginal place: The role of emotions in French readings of Indigenous sites', *Australian Aboriginal Studies*, no. 2 (2015): p. 12.
35 Konishi, 'Early encounters in Aboriginal place': p. 15.
36 Bill Gammage, *The Biggest Estate on Earth: How Aborigines made Australia* (Sydney: Allen & Unwin, 2011): p. 18.
37 Nicolas Baudin, Christine Cornell and Jean-Paul Faivre, *The Journal of Post Captain Nicolas Baudin, Commander-in-Chief of the Corvettes Geographe and Naturaliste, Assigned by Order of the Government to a Voyage of Discovery* (Adelaide: Libraries Board of South Australia, 1974): p. 106.
38 Pierre Bernard Milius et al., *Pierre Bernard Milius: Le dernier commandant de l'expédition Baudin: Le journal 1800–1804* (Perth: Australian Capital Equity Pty Limited conjointement avec la National Library of Australia, 2013): p. 62.
39 Péron et al, *Voyage de découvertes aux Terres Australe*: p. 97.
40 François Michel Ronsard, 'Journal nautique de François Michel Ronsard (tome 1)' (1801): p. 23, <baudin.sydney.edu.au/wp-content/uploads/2019/07/ronsardjournalnautiquevol15jj29.pdf>.
41 Baudin, Cornell and Faivre, *The Journal of Post Captain Nicolas Baudin*: p. 183.
42 Milius et al., *Pierre Bernard Milius*: pp. 63–64.
43 Léon Brèvedent, 'Journal nautique historique de Léon Brèvedent (cahier 1)',

(1801): p. 8, <baudin.sydney.edu.au/wp-content/uploads/2019/07/brevedentjournalnautiquehistoriquecahier1.pdf>.
44 Milius et al., *Pierre Bernard Milius*: p. 64.
45 Milius et al., *Pierre Bernard Milius*: pp. 63–64.
46 Baudin, Cornell and Faivre, *The Journal of Post Captain Nicolas Baudin*: p. 183.
47 Milius et al., *Pierre Bernard Milius*: p. 64.
48 Brèvedent, 'Journal nautique historique de Léon Brèvedent (cahier 1)': p. 8.
49 Milius et al, *Pierre Bernard Milius*: p. 64. The dog's name was Kismy and it belonged to Brèvedent, who had been persuaded to lend it to Milius.
50 François-Désiré Breton, 'Journal de François-Désiré Breton' (1801): p. 68, <baudin.sydney.edu.au/wp-content/uploads/2019/07/breton.pdf>.
51 Milius et al., *Pierre Bernard Milius*: pp. 64–65.
52 Milius et al., *Pierre Bernard Milius*: pp. 64–65.
53 Baudin, Cornell and Faivre, *The Journal of Post Captain Nicolas Baudin*: p. 183.
54 Fornasiero, Monteath and West-Sooby, *Encountering Terra Australis*: p. 300.
55 Ann McGrath, Laura Rademaker and Ben Silverstein, 'Deep History and deep listening: Indigenous knowledges and the narration of deep pasts', *Rethinking History*, vol. 25, no. 3 (2021): p. 308.
56 Patrick D Nunn and Nicholas J Reid, 'Aboriginal memories of inundation of the Australian coast dating from more than 7000 years ago', *Australian Geographer*, vol. 27, no. 1 (2016): p. 39.
57 Bracknell, 'Old dogs and ice ages in Noongar country': p. 77.
58 George Edward Webb, 'Interview with George Webb – transcript – interviewed by Ramona Johnson SLWA Call Number OH2522/13', State Library of Western Australia (ed.) (1989): p. 20.
59 Nunn and Reid: p. 42.
60 David Rose, 'Phylogenesis of the Dreamtime', *Linguistics and the Human Sciences*, vol. 8, no. 3 (2013): p. 356.
61 Nunn and Reid, 'Aboriginal memories of inundation of the Australian coast dating from more than 7000 years ago': p. 40.
62 Martha Rose Beard, 'Re-thinking oral history – a study of narrative performance', *Rethinking History*, vol. 21, no. 4 (2017): p. 529, <www.tandfonline.com/doi/full/10.1080/13642529.2017.1333285>. Beard says that this performance of oral history offers insights into the subjective experiences and feelings of those recounting it, giving a greater understanding of the significance of the story as it is told.
63 Blight, 'The story of Vasse and the Wardandi Noongar': p. 52.
64 Blight, 'The story of Vasse and the Wardandi Noongar': p. 52.
65 Blight, 'The story of Vasse and the Wardandi Noongar': p. 52.
66 Blight, 'The story of Vasse and the Wardandi Noongar': p. 52.
67 Blight, 'The story of Vasse and the Wardandi Noongar': p. 52.
68 Blight, 'The story of Vasse and the Wardandi Noongar': p. 52.
69 A video of these locations can be viewed here: <www.youtube.com/watch?v=NcUXIQxinNQ>. Illustration and video are courtesy of Sam Blight.
70 Barwick, 'Songs and the deep present': p. 94.
71 The *Naturaliste*, under the command of Hamelin, had returned to France from Sydney, carrying the many specimens and animals that the Baudin expedition had already collected; it also carried crew members whom Baudin judged unable to continue the expedition. The second boat for the expedition, the *Casuarina*, was purchased in Sydney and Louis De Freycinet was appointed captain: Dunmore, *French Explorers in the Pacific II*: p. 29.

72 Edward Duyker, *François Péron: An impetuous life: Naturalist and voyager* (Melbourne: Miegunyah Press, 2006): p. 182. Quoting François Péron, *Voyage of Discovery to the Southern Lands by François Péron: Translated from the French by Christine Cornell* (Adelaide: Friends of the State Library of South Australia, 2006): p. 130.
73 Péron et al., *Voyage de découvertes aux Terres Australe*: p. 197.
74 Konishi, 'Early encounters in Aboriginal place': p. 13.
75 François Michel Ronsard, 'Journal nautique de François Michel Ronsard (tome 2)', (1803): pp. 38–39, <baudin.sydney.edu.au/wp-content/uploads/2019/07/ronsardjournalnautiquevol25jj30.pdf>. The expedition then went up to Shark Bay and on to Île de France, where Baudin died of tuberculosis; then back to France under the command of Milius.
76 Péron et al., *Voyage de découvertes aux Terres Australe*.
77 Péron et al., *Voyage de découvertes aux Terres Australe*: p. 99.
78 Péron et al., *Voyage de découvertes aux Terres Australe*: p. 99.
79 Sérieyx and Weston, *Wonnerup*: p. 150.
80 Hannah McGlade, 'The McGlade case: A Noongar history of land, social justice and activism', *The Australian Feminist Law Journal*, vol. 43, no. 2 (2017): pp. 186–87, doi:10.1080/13200968.2017.1400371.
81 EOG Shann, *Cattle Chosen: The story of the first group settlement in Western Australia, 1829 to 1841*, Facsimile ed., Historical reprint series (Perth: University of Western Australia Press, 1978 reprint of 1926 edition): p. 100.
82 John Bussell was away in England at the time looking for a bride. He had left in December 1826 and returned to Western Australia in May 1839: *Rodger Jennings, Busselton: '…outstation on the Vasse', 1830–1850* (Busselton: Shire of Busselton, 1983): pp. 98, 150.
83 Shann, *Cattle Chosen*: pp. 104–08. See also the Massacre Map produced by the University of Newcastle <c21ch.newcastle.edu.au/colonialmassacres/detail.php?r=1035> for the entry concerning this massacre.
84 James Cameron, *The Millendon Memoirs: George Fletcher Moore's Western Australian diaries and letters, 1830–1841* (Perth: Hesperian Press, 2006): p. 436. Moore accompanied Governor Stirling and a party of others selected to deal with a serious disagreement between the Government Resident and the chief magistrate at Albany. See: Pamela Statham-Drew, *James Stirling: Admiral and founding governor of Western Australia* (Perth: University of Western Australia Press, 2003): p. 349.
85 See Rupert Gerritsen, *Early Records of the Wardandi Language* (Canberra: I P Publications, 2011): p. 1. Also James Cameron, 'George Fletcher Moore (Paper in: *The Irish in Western Australia*. Edited by Bob Reece)', *Studies in Western Australian History*, no. 20 (2000): p. 28.
86 Cameron, *The Millendon Memoirs*: p. 439.
87 George Fletcher Moore, *Diary of Ten Years Eventful Life of an Early Settler in Western Australia, and also A Descriptive Vocabulary of the Language of the Aborigines*, Facsimile ed., Historical reprint series (Perth: University of Western Australia Press, 1978): p. 341. The location of Vasse's bones was actually nearer to Quindalup, south of Wonnerup, as told by Bill Webb.
88 Moore, *Diary of Ten Years Eventful Life of an Early Settler in Western Australia*.
89 Cameron, 'George Fletcher Moore': p. 23. This expedition showed him this was not the case, although he and explorer George Grey continued to speculate about this possibility.

90   Cameron, *The Millendon Memoirs*: p. 432.
91   See William J Lines, *An All Consuming Passion: Origins, Modernity, and the Australian Life of Georgiana Molloy* (Sydney: Allen & Unwin, 1994): p. 301. When Georgiana Molloy moved to the Vasse in 1839, she had a guide called Calgood, whom she continued to employ even during the violence at the Vasse in February 1841; this violence was a punitive action led by her husband, Captain John Molloy.
92   Lines, *An All Consuming Passion*: pp. 149–50.
93   Alexandra Hasluck has stated that this was Dr Carpenter, medical officer for the Australind settlement of 1840, whereas Brendan Cullity says that it was a Dr Carr, who was succeeded by Dr Carpenter at Australind. See: Alexandra Hasluck, *Portrait with Background: A life of Georgiana Molloy* (Melbourne: Oxford University Press, 1955): p. 226. Also Cullity, *Vasse*: p. 18.
94   Hasluck, *Portrait with Background*: p. 226.
95   Hasluck, *Portrait with Background*: p. 226.
96   Cullity, *Vasse*: p. 19.
97   Bill Webb also holds Wardandi oral history on this massacre, which will be explored in further research.
98   Warren Bert Kimberly, *History of West Australia: A narrative of her past together with biographies of her leading men* (Melbourne: F.W. Niven and Co., 1897): p. 116; James Sykes Battye, *Western Australia: A history from its discovery to the inauguration of the Commonwealth* (Perth: Reprint of 1924 edition, University of Western Australia Press, 1978): p. 161.
99   Hasluck, *Portrait with Background*: p. 226.
100 Augustus Oldfield, 'On the Aborigines of Australia', *Transactions of the Ethnological Society of London*, no. 3 (1865): pp. 218–19.
101 Webb, 'Interview with Bill Webb August 2021'.
102 Jackie Huggins, 'Experience and identity: Jackie Huggins and writing history', *Limina: A journal of historical and cultural studies*, no. 2 (1996): p. 2.

12 Walking as a practice of sovereignty

1   The term was suggested as the title for the project by Paul Girrawah House, as a means of encapsulating its cultural concept and context. House is a senior Ngambri–Ngunawal custodian of the Canberra region with Wiradyuri, Walgalu and Ngunawal ancestry; and Senior Community Engagement Officer, First Nations Portfolio and Bandalang Fellow at the Australian National University, Ngambri/Kamberri/Canberra. For further reading, see the Wiradyuri Condobolin Language Program website, <https://wcclp.com.au/>. Additionally, I honour the deep Wiradyuri Knowledges ontology of Dr Stan Grant AM, with the Wiradyuri Community-guided research support of Dr John Rudder and Marion Wighton-Packham. Additionally, the Dhurga/Thurga term 'Muruda' means footprint, indicating an etymological affiliation between the two language groups – Dhurga/Thurgha Language from the Yuin/Yuwinj People from Nowra to Narooma on the New South Wales South Coast, inland to Araluen and Braidwood, while Wiradyuri Country encompasses three rivers – the Wambool (Macquarie), the Kalare (Lachlan) and the Murrumbidgee/Murrumbidjeri; the southern border being from the Milawa Bila (Murray River) at Albury, upstream to Tumbarumba, north along the edges of the mountains, past Tumut/Dumut, Gundagai to Lithgow, then up to Dubbo, west across the plains to Willandra Creek near Mossgiel, central western New South Wales.

2   'National Heritage Places – Wave Hill Walk-Off Route', Australian Government, Department of Climate Change, Energy, The Environment and Water (DECCEEW) website, <www.dcceew.gov.au/parks-heritage/heritage/organisations/australian-heritage-council/national-heritage-assessments/wave-hill>.
3   This Indigenous Health and Wellbeing project is funded by an initiative of the Australian National University known as the Grand Challenge program, which aims to combine multi-disciplinary expertise for projects of national significance.
4   Some Indigenous scholars consider the ongoing colonial project in their respective homelands to be continuing unsettlement and displacement, challenging the concept of 'settler/settled/settlement'.
5   'Australia's National Heritage List', Australian Government, DECCEEW website, <www.dcceew.gov.au/parks-heritage/heritage/places/national-heritage-list>.
6   GP Whitley, 'John Lhotsky (1795–1866)', *Australian Dictionary of Biography* vol. 2 (1967; online 2006), <adb.anu.edu.au/biography/lhotsky-john-2357>.
7   Gather, 'Great Dividing Range: A song of the women of the Menero tribe near the Australian Alps, 1834', State Library of New South Wales website, <gather.sl.nsw.gov.au/digital-heritage/great-dividing-range-song-women-menero-tribe-near-australian-alps-1834>.
8   John Lhotsky, 'A song of the women of the Menero [ie, Monaro] tribe near the Australian Alps [music], arranged with the assistance of several musical gentlemen for the voice and pianoforte; [collected] by J. Lhotsky', National Library of Australia website, Bib ID 2881730, <catalogue.nla.gov.au/catalog/2881730>. The song published by Lhotsky is now recognised as the second published Australian song including First Nations Language, the first being 'A song of the natives of New South Wales' (1793). See: Keith Smith, '1793: A song of the natives of New South Wales', *Electronic British Library Journal*, vol. 2 (2011): pp. 1–7.
9   Lhotsky, 'A song of the women of the Menero [ie, Monaro] tribe near the Australian Alps'.
10 John Lhotsky, 'Some remarks on a short vocabulary of the natives of Van Diemen Land; And also of the Menero Downs in Australia', *The Journal of the Royal Geographical Society of London*, vol. 9 (1839): pp. 157–62.
11 John Lhotsky, *A Journey from Sydney to the Australian Alps, undertaken in the months of January, February, and March, 1834* (Sydney: By Commission at R. Ackerman's Repository of Arts, 1835).
12 Lhotsky, *A Journey from Sydney*: p. 19.
13 John Gale, *Canberra: History of and legends relating to the federal capital territory of the Commonwealth of Australia* (Canberra: A.M. Fallick & Sons, 1927): p. 123.
14 Samuel Shumack, *An Autobiography or, Tales and Legends of Canberra Pioneers* (Canberra: ANU Press, 1967): p. 150.
15 'Nellie "Queen Nellie" Hamilton', Find a Grave website, <www.findagrave.com/memorial/159923567/nellie-hamilton#source>.
16 'New South Wales', *Argus*, 16 April 1862: p. 6.
17 Laurie Bamblett, 'Nangar (c. 1848–1927), *Australian Dictionary of Biography*, <adb.anu.edu.au/biography/nangar-33736>.
18 Laurie Bamblett and Wendy Bunn, 'Ooloogan (c. 1840–1928)', *Australian Dictionary of Biography*, <adb.anu.edu.au/biography/ooloogan-33760>.
19 'Aborigine defends his rights', *Argus*, 10 May 1927: p. 19.
20 'Gaanha-bula (Mount Canobolas) Aboriginal Dreaming Story as told by Uncle Neil Ingram Senior, Wiradjuri Elder', Orange City Council website, <www.orange.nsw.gov.au/wp-content/uploads/2022/01/CP_LakeCanobolas_Mural_stories_01.

pdf>. Additional reading on Wiradyuri Community determination to reclaim the traditional names of these significant sites: Mollie Gorman, 'Wiradjuri elder Neil Ingram seeks official return of traditional name for Mount Canobolas, near Orange', ABC News website, 19 December 2022, <www.abc.net.au/news/2022-12-19/wiradjuri-npws-geographical-names-board-canobolas-gaanha-bula/101782698>; Dan Butler, 'Traditional Wiradjuri name approved for Macquarie River', NITV News website, 9 November 2021, <www.sbs.com.au/nitv/article/traditional-wiradjuri-name-approved-for-macquarie-river/kkgtljh4z>. Guhanal wanyi has also been stated as the traditional name for Mount Macquarie, see: 'Cultural heritage', Canobolas Conservation Alliance (CCA) – Save Mt Canobolas website, <savemtcanobolassca.com/the-sca/heritage/cultural-heritage/>.

21   Sincere thanks to First Nations historian and senior lecturer Dr Laurie Bamblett (Wiradyuri People) for permission to include his comprehensive research on Nangar, and jointly with Wendy Bunn (Walbunja/Djirringanj/Yuin Peoples), a descendant of Ooloogong, on the latter. See also: Mark McKenna and Peter Read, 'The quest for Indigenous recognition: 1927 – Jimmy Clements, John Noble, and the Opening of Parliament House', *Australian Dictionary of Biography*, <adb.anu.edu.au/the-quest-for-indigenous-recognition/jimmy-clements>.

22   'From little things, big things grow' by songwriters Kevin Daniel Carmody and Paul Maurice Kelly, Copyright held by WB Music Corp., Sony/Atv Music Publishing (Australia) Pty Ltd Paul Kelly Music, Song Cycles Pty Ltd, 1991.

23   'National Heritage Places – Wave Hill Walk-Off Route', Australian Government, DECCEEW.

24   Dr Aunty Matilda House, Ngambri Elder, speaking in initial video pitch to the ANU Indigenous Health and Wellbeing Collaborative Scheme Grand Challenge, 2019.

25   'From little things, big things grow' lyrics © Carmody and Kelly, 1991.

26   Brungle Aboriginal Station was established by the New South Wales Aborigines Protection Board and closed in 1950.

27   The Aborigines Protection Board, which came under the Department of Police, was established in the 1880s to manage reserves and the 'welfare' of an estimated 9000 Australian First Nations Peoples living in New South Wales. 'Aborigines Protection Board, State Government of New South Wales', Find and Connect, Australian Government website, <www.findandconnect.gov.au/entity/aborigines-protection-board/>.

28   Aunty Bronwyn Penrith, in conversation with Brenda L Croft, ANU School of Art and Design Photography studios, June 2019.

29   Aunty Bronwyn Penrith, in conversation with Brenda L Croft, June 2019.

30   See: Nicholas Biddle and Hannah Swee, 'The relationship between wellbeing and Indigenous Land, Language and Culture in Australia', *Australian Geographer*, vol. 43, no. 3 (2012): pp. 215–32; Leanne Betasamosake Simpson, 'Land as pedagogy: Nishnaabeg intelligence and rebellious transformation', *Decolonization: Indigeneity, education & society*, vol. 3, no. 3 (2014): pp. 1–25; Leanne Betasamosake Simpson, 'New nature – Opening keynote', Goethe-Institut Montreal, 17 July 2020, video via YouTube, <www.youtube.com/watch?v=rGFxqR2BLI4>; Nancy Van Styvendale, JD McDougall, Robert Henry and Robert Alexander Innes (eds), *The Arts of Indigenous Health and Well-Being* (Manitoba: University of Manitoba Press, 2021).

31   'Black Space Manifesto', Canada College website, <canadacollege.edu/eapc/docs/blackspace-manifesto.pdf>.

32 'Naabámi (thou shall/will see): Barangaroo (army of me)', Australian Embassy and Consulates website, <usa.embassy.gov.au/naabami>.
33 Professor Jamie Pittock, Professor, Fenner School of Environment, Australian National University. Co-team leader on *Murrudha: Sovereign Walks*, ANU Indigenous Health and Wellbeing Collaborative Scheme Grand Challenge, project video pitch, early 2019.
34 The team included Professor Brenda L Croft, Aidan Hartshorn, ANU Murrudha Research Assistant/SOMAD On Country Studio Workshop Tutor/Brungle Community member; Emily Fishpool, ANU First Nations student; Dave Johnson, ANU First Nations graduate, archaeologist and cultural consultant; Professor Ray Lovett, Mayi Kuwayu Study Director, National Centre for Epidemiology and Population Health, ANU; Maeve Powell ANU First Nations PhD Candidate, Research Associate, Resources, Environment and Development; Sam Provost, ANU First Nations PhD Candidate, Associate Lecturer, Fenner School of Environment and Society; and Ngunawal/Wiradyuri Community member Billy Tompkins.
35 Panel participants included: Professor Brenda L Croft, Dr Aunty Matilda House-Williams, Aidan Hartshorn, Shane Herrington, Rohit Rao, Murrudha R/A ANU graduate student (Panel one); Dr Jilda Andrews, Will Kepa, Cheryl and Michelle Davison (Djinama Yilaga leader and member), Dr Lisa Slater, Associate Dean (Equity, Diversity and Inclusion), School of Humanities and Social Inquiry; Associate Professor, School of Humanities and Social Inquiry, University of Wollongong; Aunty Sue Bulger, Chairperson Brungle Tumut Local Aboriginal Land Council, Brungle Community member.
36 Dr Jilda Andrews, Research Fellow, Australian National University. Yuwaalaraay cultural practitioner and museum ethnographer based in Canberra, Australia, chairing *Murrudha: Sovereign Walks* (panel #2), AIATSIS National Indigenous Research Conference, 'Navigating the spaces in between: Indigenous ways of knowing, seeing, and being', 31 May 2022.
37 Shane Herrington, Wolgalu, Aboriginal Discovery Ranger, National Parks Association, NSW, *Murrudha: Sovereign Walks* (panel #2), AIATSIS National Indigenous Research Conference, 31 May 2022.
38 Rohit Rao is an ANU Graduate student with GIS mapping skills who has been working as part of the Murrudha team, *Murrudha: Sovereign Walks* (panel #2), AIATSIS National Indigenous Research Conference, 31 May 2022.
39 Sue Bulger, Walgalu/Wiradyuri, then-Chairperson, Brungle Tumut Local Aboriginal Land Council, *Murrudha: Sovereign Walks* (panel #2), AIATSIS National Indigenous Research Conference, 31 May 2022.
40 Dr Lisa Slater, Associate Professor, School of Humanities and Social Enquiry, University of Wollongong. Critical Indigenous Studies and Cultural Studies scholar who has been working closely with Brungle Community members on environmental research projects, *Murrudha: Sovereign Walks*, panel #2, AIATSIS National Indigenous Research Conference, 31 May 2022.
41 Will Kepa, PhD candidate, ANU School of Music; Manager, Yil Lull Studio, *Murrudaha: Sovereign Walks*, panel #1, AIATSIS National Indigenous Research Conference, 30 May 2022.
42 Cheryl Davison, Ngarigo/Walbunja Peoples, founder of Djinama Yilaga, creative and cultural practitioner, *Murrudha: Sovereign Walks*, panel #1, AIATSIS National Indigenous Research Conference, 30 May 2022.

43 Community participants included Dr Aunty Matilda House-Williams, Aunty Bronwyn Penrith, Aunty Lois Peeler AM, Professor Julie Andrews, Aunty Sue Bulger, Aunty Coral Bulger, Aunty Soni Piper, Wendy Bunn, Cheryl Spencer, Will Kepa, Cheryl Davison, Iris Walker-White, Maria Walker, James Ingram, Aidan Hartshorn, Monika Duggan and non-Indigenous participants Dr Lisa Slater, Dr Harold Koch, Rohit Rao and Prue Hazelgrove.
44 Dr Lois Peeler AM (Victorian Senior Australian of the Year 2017, NAIDOC 2022 Female Elder of the Year) Elder-in-Residence, Worawa Aboriginal College Ltd., Healesville, Victoria, personal communications, 25 November 2023.
45 Coral Bulger, CEO, Brungle Tumut Local Aboriginal Land Council, Tumut, NSW, personal communications, 30 November 23.
46 Wendy Bunn, personal communications, 30 November 2023.
47 Iris Walker-White, Djinama Yilaga co-leader, eldest sister of Cheryl Davison, Michelle Davison, cousin to Maria Walker, personal communications, 15 July 2024.
48 Michelle Davison, Djinama Yilaga member, younger sister to Iris Walker-White, personal communications, 15 July 2024.
49 Brenda Gifford, award-winning composer and performer, member of Ngarra Burria: First Peoples Composers, School of Music, ANU, personal communications, 15 July 2024.
50 Maria Walker, Djinama Yilaga member, cousin/sister to Cheryl and Michelle Davison, and Iris Walker-White, personal communications, 15 July 2024.
51 Leah House, grand-daughter of Dr Aunty Matilda House-Williams, personal communications, 15 July 2024.
52 Prue Hazelgrove, artist/photographer, assisted the multidisciplinary author, Brenda L Croft, on the photoshoots for Naabámi from its inception in 2019, and assisted with the exhibition installation at the Embassy of Australia, Washington DC, USA.
53 Kobi Davison, the youngest member of Djinama Yilaga, nephew of Cheryl and Michelle Davison, and Iris Walker-White, aged 11 years, personal communications, 21 July 2024.

Index

*Numbers in italics denote illustrations and photos.

Aboriginal people
  Aboriginal and Torres Strait Islander Voice to parliament 9–10, 21–22, 54–55, 69
  age determination of presence on Australian continent 69–71
  ancestral remains and footprints of 108–11, 111–15, 116
  ancestral values 3
  and assimilationism 23, 50, 226
  continuous culture of 69–70, 86–88, 98–101, 103–18, 168
  Creation stories 116
  destruction of heritage of 11, 55, 81, 86
  dispossession of as inevitable 35
  as 'dying race' 47, 48–49, 212
  homogenising narratives about 51
  knowledge and history of 68, 87–88, 98–101
  land rights 38, 60–61, 93, 117–18, 207–208; see also Native Title
  material culture of 61
  missions 226
  'mythologies' 51
  politicisation of 50, 213
  in pre-contact era as agriculturalists 82–84
  in pre-contact era as hunter-gatherers 49, 82–83
  in pre-contact era as 'primitive' 46–47, 50, 82–83
  reciprocal relationships and 13, 164, 194
  Stolen Generations 19, 21–25, 167–68, 170, 176, 228, 234
  water rights 107, 116, 117–18
  see also language, Indigenous; sovereignty; Uluru Statement from the Heart
Aboriginal Tent Embassy 8
Aboriginals Protection Act 1897 19
Aborigines Act 1957 50
ACARA see Australian Curriculum and Reporting Authority
Acknowledgment of Country 8–9, 20
Akutagawa, Malia 3
Algar, Frederic 31
American Indigenous people 157, 161, 234, 239
Anderson, Warwick 40
Andrews, Jilda 223–24, *223*, *229*
Aotearoa (New Zealand) 1, 2, 4, 8–9, 12–13, 64, 121–35, 138
  and Cook Islands 141–47
  see also Māori people
archaeology
  and Aboriginal social justice 88–89
  and Aboriginal sovereignty 81–88, 88–89
  archaeological temporality 78, 86–87, 93
  Australian 81–88
  and chronopolitics 69, 70–71, 77–81, 81–88
  and collaborations with Indigenous people 90–101
  and colonialism 79, 85, 89
  and dating 76, 84; see also radiometric dating; time/temporality
  definitions 80, 87
  and excavation 37–38, 72, 76–77, 93–98, *97*, 110
  future of 88–89
  history of 69, 78, 153–55
  importance in negotiations surrounding heritage 68–69
  interpretation of evidence 78
  multidisciplinary strengths of 67, 89
  prehistory 33–36, 75, 108, 110, 153, 154–55, 156
  role in nation-building 80–81, 88–89
  and sensationalism 84
  stratigraphic analysis 72–73, 77, 88, 90, 96, 108
  and time 12, 67, 68–69, 71, 71–77, 78–80, 81–88, 89, 90–91
  see also Deep History; deep time; history
archives 15, 157
  colonial 157, 160–61
  Country as 160–62

First Nations 157, 158–64
  language as 169–78
  rock art as 158–64
  written 6, 91, 173, 190
Arnhem Land 7, 70, 158, 161, 162, 164
  West Arnhem landscape *165*
  West Arnhem rock art *152*
Assmann, Aleida 179
Atalay, Sonya 100
Attwood, Bain 34
Auckland *see* Tāmaki Makaurau
Austin, JL 179
Australia *94*
  Australia Day 8, 36
  Federation 33–34
  National Heritage List 208, 209, 217, 218, 225
Australian Archaeological Association 81–82
Australian Curriculum and Reporting Authority 11–12, 43, 56–58, 59–64
  curriculum development 58
  Deep Time History curriculum 43–45, 51–64
  and First Nations educators 54–55
  politicisation of history curriculum 55
  Teacher's Guide for Deep Time History 56, 58–60, 62
Australian National University (ANU)
  excavations at Lake Mungo 108
  Murrudha: Sovereign Walks project 208, 209, 221, 222, *229*, 230, 233

Bahn, Paul 146
Barangaroo 234, 236
Barker, Joanne 180–81
Barkindji people 12, 104–105, 107–108, 114
Barwick, Linda 190, 196
Bashford, Alison 91
Bates, Daisy 194
Baudin, Nicolas 191–94, 198
Baudin expedition to Geographe Bay, WA 14, 187–203
Bean, CEW 42–43, 46, 48
Beard, Martha Rose 194
Behrendt, Larissa 39
Bentarrak, Krim 40
Bevernage, Berber 27
Bibbulmun people 188, 195

Bidjara
  Country 20–25
  language 24–25
  people 3, 11, 16, 20
Bininj people 158, 161
Birch, Tony 39, 188
Black, Christine 182
Blak Sovereign Movement 10
Blight, Mary 14, 187–203, 242
Board, Peter 36
Bonner, Neville 100
Bowler, Jim 38, 104, 108–109
Bracknell, Clint 189–90, 194
Brady, Liam M 159
Brady, Wendy 183
Brèvedent, Léon 192–93
Brigg, Morgan 176, 180
Brungle Aboriginal Community walk to Canberra 1927 207–16, *210*; *see also Murrudha: Sovereign Walks*
Brungle Aboriginal Station 219–21, 225, 226
Bulger, Coral *231*, 232
Bulger, Sue *223*, 226
Bunda, Tracey 55
Bunn, Wendy *231*, 232
Bussell family 199–201
Byrne, Denis 32, 91

Carmody, Kev 230
Carnarvon Gorge 3, 11, 19–23
ceramics, ancient Aboriginal 85
Chakrabarti, Pratik 78, 91
Chakrabarty, Dipesh 28–29
Charles, Tanya 115
Chong, Carol 158
chronopolitics 69, 70–71, 77–88
Chronos 80
Clark, Anna 11, 26–41, 43, 48, 242
Clarkson, Chris 70, 76
Clements, Jimmy *see* Nangar, Jimmy
clever men (walamira) 14, 209, 214, *215*, *216*
climate change 12, 136, 138, 140, 146–47
Coghlan, Timothy 34
Collard, Len 188–90
Collins, David 29–30
colonialism
  colonial histories 1–2, 6–7, 28–34, 39, 42–43, 46–47, 49, 54

colonial law 6–7, 107, 213
coloniser sovereignty 6, 185
resistance to 141–43
Combes, Edward 34
Conway, Fred 11, 16, 20, 22, 25, 241
Cook, Captain James 39, 55, 142
Cook Islands 12–13, 136–48
  map *137*
  ocean-going canoes 140–41, *147*, *148*
Cooper, William 36
Country 2
  Acknowledgment of 8–9, 20
  Ancestors and 99, 101, 104–105, 109, 110, 112–14, 116, 117, 153, 170, 175, 178, 181
  as archive 160–62
  caring for 105, 112, 140, 162, 175
  connection to 22–25, 111–18, 177
  definitions 172
  and Indigenous history and sovereignty 2, 116–18, 172
  language and connection to 168–69, 172–74, 178–79
  Marking Country website 22, 24, 63
  obligations to 187–203
  Welcome to 8–9, 218
Croft, Brenda 14–15, 172, 207–40, 242
Cronin, Kathryn 23
curriculums *see* Australian Curriculum and Reporting Authority

Dark, Eleanor 36
Dark Emu 54, 82–84
dating *see* radiometric dating
Davison, Cheryl 227–28, 234, *236*
Davison, Kobi 234, *235*, *236*, 240
Davison, Michelle 234, *235*, *236*, 237
Day of Mourning 36
Deep History 4–8
  Aboriginal 98–101, 116–18, 151–65, 167, 194
  Australian 37–41, 81–88, 109, 116–18
  collaborative 101
  and deep sovereignty 1–3, 5, 28, 91, 117, 167
  definitions 5, 44, 91, 157
  Finnish 44–45
  and Indigenous voices 91
  of Oceania 92–93
  teaching of 42–64

in the Victorian school curriculum 42–43, 45–52
  see also Australian Curriculum and Reporting Authority, Deep Time History curriculum; deep time; history
deep time
  Aboriginal articulations of 167
  and deep present 167–69, 182, 184
  definitions 28, 53, 90–91
  and historical time 37, 43
  as outside of empirical history 35–36
  scientific orientation of 90–91
Dennison, Jean 181
Dharawal/Dhurga/Djirringanj/Walbunja/Yuin peoples 208
Dhurga language 223, 227, 234
Diamond, Jared 137, 138, 146
dictionaries 174, 176
  missionary 174, 175–76
  Noongar 199
  Wiradjuri 14, 168–69, 171, 173–79, 182, 185–86
Djinama Yilaga choir 223, 227, 230, 233, 234, *235*
Dorsett, Shaunnagh 179
Dreaming 51, 182, 189; *see also* Everywhen

ecocosmologies 139–41, 146
education *see* Australian Curriculum and Reporting Authority
environmental mismanagement 137–39
ethnography 140, 180
  collaborative autoethnography 217, 221
  ethnographers 140, 194, 202
  ethnographic analogy 75–76, 78
  ethnographical texts 122, 128
European imperialism, and history *see* history/histories
Evans, Raymond 23
Everywhen 15, 116–18, 189, 209; *see also* Dreaming
Everywhen: Australia and the language of deep history 2, 40, 172
evolution, racist understandings of 46–47, 75, 84–85, 99
Ewing, Thomas 34

Faulkhead, Shannon 160
Ferguson, Bill 36
fiction 13, 166–86

296

First Fleet 29–31, 34, 39, 43, 44
First Inventors, The 54
Flenley, John 146
Fletcher, Grace 12, 103–18, 243
Foley, Gary 38
food
    Cook Islands food practices 136–47
    foodscapes 12–13, 121–35, 136–48
    Māori food practices 13, 16, 121–35
Fowles, Severin 161
Freeman, Dean 222, 225, *229*, *231*
Frere, John 71

Gamble, Clive 85
Geographe Bay, WA 187–203
    Baudin/French expedition to 187–203
    map *197*
geology 36, 48, 72, 75, 90, 106
Gibbs, Pearl 36
Gifford, Brenda *236*, 237, 239
Gilbert, Kevin 38, 182
Gill, William Wyatt 143
Gilmour, Rachel 176
Gittins, Erica 85
Goenpul people 181
Goldhahn, Joakim 13, 151–65, 243
Gondiwindi, Albert (fictional character) 167–68, 169–70, 174–79, 182–85
Gondiwindi, August (fictional character) 169–71, 176–77, 183–86
Graham, Mary 100, 176, 180–81
Grant, Stan Sr 169, 182
Greenleaf, Reverend (fictional character) 169–71, 176, 178
Gribble, Reverend John B 170
Griffiths, Billy 38, 70, 98
Gurindji/Malngin/Bilinara peoples 207–208, 217, 218, 229–30
    Gurindji Walk-Off 1966 207–208, 216–19, *217*, 229
Guzy, Lidia 139

Hamelin, Jacques Félix Emmanuel 191–92
Hamilton, George 30
Hamilton, (Queen) Nellie 213, 214–15, 220
Hartog, François 80
Hawai'i 3–4, 8–10, 13, 142
Hazelgrove, Prue *236*, 238
Herbert, Xavier 36

Herrington, Shane *223*, 224–25, 226, *229*
Hervey Islands 142; *see also* Cook Islands
Hill, Elizabeth 189, 194
Hiscock, Peter 75–76
historians 11
    Indigenous 38–41
    as 'time police' 11, 41
historiography
    ancient texts 154
    Australian 33–36, 37–41, 108, 116–18
    colonial 27, 33–34
    critiques 27, 36, 37–41, 92, 153
    definition 27
    post–Second World War 37–41
history/histories
    academic 22, 33–34, 153, 155, 158, 163
    Australian 27, 33–36, 37–41, 42–64
    colonial narratives 1–2, 6–7, 28–34, 39, 42–43, 46–47, 49, 54
    curricula 34, 43–45, 51–52, 52–64; *see also* Australian Curriculum and Reporting Authority
    decolonisation of 2, 27–28, 37–41, 156–57
    definitions 5, 39, 153, 157
    exclusion of First Nations people from 6–7, 23, 28–36, 38–39, 42–44, 49, 153–57
    First Nations 6, 7–8, 22–23, 40, 196, 232
    'history wars' 52
    'hyphenated' 39–40
    and imperialism 27–33, 80–81, 85–86, 156–57
    inclusive narratives 9, 15, 44, 54
    Indigenous-led 15–16, 28, 36, 156–57, 232
    'Koori history' 51–52
    Māori history 64
    multitemporal 1, 5, 74–75
    multivocal 93, 100–101
    and 'myth' 153–55, 156
    and narratives of 'progress' 28–36, 37, 43, 46–47, 75, 79–80, 81, 85
    and nation-making 33–36
    'New History' 37–41, 157
    non-written recording of 155–57
    objectivity and 26–27
    oral 12, 14, 95, 100, 156–57, 169, 194–99

precolonial 28–36, 37, 42–43, 46–48, 75, 155–57
prehistory 33–36, 75, 108, 110, 153, 154–55, 156
professionalisation of 27, 33–34
'scientific' 47, 48–49, 100
and sovereignty 6–7, 15
starting dates for 154–55
subjectivity of 6–7, 26–27, 83
and time 26–27, 32
and truth-telling 26, 39, 54
Western-style 7–8, 15, 29, 32, 80, 83, 91, 100, 153–55, 155–57
and writing 154–55
see also archaeology; Deep History
History of New Holland, The 29, 30–31
Hobsbawm, Eric 33
Hogarth, Melitta 55, 56
House, Leah 229, 234, *236*, 238
House-Williams, Matilda 218, *233*, 234, *236*, 237
Howitt, Mary EB 46–47
Huggins, Jack 19
Huggins, Jackie 1, 3, 4, 10–11, 19–25, 202, 243
Huggins, Rita 11, 19, 21, 24

Indigenous peoples
  acknowledgment of history and sovereignty of 1, 55, 156
  archives 157, 158–64
  land rights 156
  see also Aboriginal people; American Indigenous people; Māori people
Indigenous sustainability knowledge systems *see* ecocosmologies
Injalak Hill, Arnhem Land, NT 151, *152*, 153, 164

Janke, Terri 161, 163
Japanangka, Paddy 114
Johnson, Dave 222
Johnson, Miranda 39
Johnston, Lucas 140
Jupurulla, Johnny 114
Juukan Gorge 55, 86

Kairos 80
Kaivakovu, PNG 2, 93, 95–96, *97*; *see also* Orokolo Bay, PNG

Kammingurt 189, 194
Karingbal people 20
Kelly, Alice 110, 115
Kennedy, Brendan 12, 103, 105, 111, 115–16, 117
Kennedy, Marnie 38
Kennedy, Rosanne 13, 166–86, 244
Kepa, Will 222–23, 227
Kertzer, David 33
Ketelaar, Eric 157
Kimberley
  people 24, 68
  rock art 68, 85, 162
King Billy *see* Nangar, Jimmy
knowledge systems
  embodied and relational 163–64
  hierarchy of 156, 160–61
  Indigenous 26, 43–44, 56–58, 61–63, 77, 81, 88, 139–40, 153–57, 161, 162–64
  scientific 32, 88, 163–64
Kohvakka, Tanja 44–45
Konishi, Shino 191, 198
Koori history 51–52

Lake Mungo, NSW 7, 38, 104–105, 108–11, 111–15; *see also* Mungo National Park, NSW; Willandra Lakes, NSW
Lamilami, Leonard 158
Lamilami, Patrick 158–59
Lamilami, Ronald 158
land rights 38, 60–61, 93, 117–18, 207–208
  water rights 107, 116, 117–18
  see also Native Title
Lang, John Dunmore 29
language, Indigenous
  archiving 169–78
  colonial efforts to extinguish 173, 184, 226
  and connection to Country 168–69, 172–74, 178–79
  revival/reclamation 14, 166–86, 208, 221, 223
  and sovereignty 169, 172–73, 176, 178, 183
  and ways of thinking 182–83
  see also dictionaries
languages, specific
  Bidjara l 24–25

Dhurga 223, 227, 234
Māori 8
Tati Tati 106
Wiradjuri/Wiradyuri 167–69, 171–74, 177–79, 182–83, 186, 207, 226
Larihairu, PNG 2, 93, 96; *see also* Orokolo Bay, PNG
law 179–80
  colonial 6–7, 107, 213
  Indigenous 14, 164, 169, 179–80, 181–82, 183, 187–88, 195
  international, and sovereignty 5–6
Layton, Robert 159
Le Bas de Sainte Croix, Alexandre 192–93
Leane, Jeanine 33, 39
Lhotsky, Johann 211–13
Lhotsky trek from Canberra to Ngarigo/Meneroo High Country 1834 209, 211–13, 220
Lingiari, Vincent 216
Lorenz, Chris 27
lou haera 7, 95
Lourandos, Harry 74–75
Lydon, Jane 162–63

Mabo judgment 9, 20; *see also* Native Title
Madagammana, Bhaveeka 13, 121–35, 244
Madjedbebe rock shelter, Arnhem Land, NT 70, 76, 98
Mangaia, Cook Islands 2, 16, 136–48
  ecocosmologies 139–41
  ra'ui and seafood conservation 143–47
  sovereignty on 141–43
  see also Cook Islands
Māori people
  ancestors 124–26, 131, 138
  culture 8
  dispossession 122–23, 128
  fishing 129–31, 133–34
  food 13, 16, 121–35
  food cultivation 126–35
  food sovereignty 122, 123–24, 126, 130–32
  history 64
  language 8
  lunar calendar 128–29, 133
  provisioning of colonial settlers 121, 132
  seasonal movements 132–35
  sovereignty 122, 123–24, 126, 130–32, 135

spiritual and place-specific knowledge 124–26
Treaty of Waitangi 9, 122
Maralngurra, Gabriel 13, 16, 151–65, 245
Margooya Lagoon 103, 107
Marking Country website 22, 24, 63
Marks, Ron 159
Marsden, Beth 11, 42–64, 245
Marvellous *see* Ooloogan
Mawson, Stephanie 92
May, Sally Kate 13, 151–65, 245
Maynard, John 39, 140
McGrath, Ann 1–16, 22, 40, 44, 106, 109, 155, 172–73, 244
McKenna, Mark 32
McNiven, Ian 36,
McPhee, John 91
McVeigh, Shaun 179
Meneroo/Monaro/Ngarigo/Ngarigu
  Country 209, 211, 220
  peoples 208, 212
Meston, AL 35
Meyer, Manulani Aluli 3
Milius, Pierre Bernard 192–93, 196
Molloy, Georgiana 201
Molloy, Captain John 201
Montgomery, Lindsay 161
Moodie, Nikki
Moore, Archie 168, 176
Moore, George Fletcher 190–91, 199–202
Moreton-Robinson, Aileen 166–67, 181
Morphy, Howard 159–60, 162
Muecke, Stephen 40, 176
Mulvaney, John 37–38
Mungo Lady 104, 108–11
Mungo Man 104, 108–11
Mungo National Park, NSW 104, 105, 111
  ancestral trackways 105, 111–15
  see also Lake Mungo, NSW; Willandra Lakes, NSW
Murray, Tom 13, 136–48, 245
Murray River 3, 37, 48, 103, 115, 117
Murray-Darling Basin 103–18
Murrudha 14–15, 207–40
Murrudha: Sovereign Walks 207–40
  historical framework 209–19
  Lhotsky trek from Canberra to Ngarigo/Meneroo High Country 1834 209, 211–13, 220

Nangar/Ooloogan walk 1927 209, *210*, 214–16
Queanbeyan to Cooma walk 1873 209, 213–14, 220
timeline 221–40
Wave Hill Walk-Off Route 1966 207–208, 216–19, *217*, 229
Murrumbidgee River 115, 225–26
Mutthi Mutthi people 12, 103–105, 106–107, 109–12, 114–16

Naabámi (thou shall/will see): Barangaroo (army of me) research project and exhibition 230, 233, 234, *235*, *236*, 237, 238
NAIDOC Week
   celebrations in Washington DC 2024 221, 233, *235*, *236*, 239
   Elder of the Year 2023 *233*
Nangar, Jimmy Wiradyuri walamira (Jimmy Clements) 14–15, 209–11, 214, *215*, 218–20, 225, 230, *231*, 232
Nangar/Ooloogan walk 1927 209, *210*, 214–16, 232
Napanangka, Mitjili 113–14
nationalism, Australian 34
Native Title 20–21, 68, 177, 185
   Native Title Act 1993 20
   see also land rights
Neil, Bronwen 13, 136–48, 246
New Zealand *see* Aotearoa
Newport, Christina 140
Ngambri/Ngunawal/Walgalu
   Country 214, 219
   peoples 208, 218
Ngarigo
   people 208, 209, 211–14, 218, 219
   song 211–12
Ngiyampaa people 104–105, 107, 114
Noble, George John *see* Ooloogan
Noongar
   Country 3, 187
   dictionary 199
   history 194–97, 199–203
   people 14, 188–91; *see also* Wardandi/Wardanji Noongar people
   prophesy and Thomas Timothée Vasse 187–90
Noonuccal, Oodgeroo 38
Novick, Peter 26
Nunn, Patrick 194

Oceania 1, 2, 90–102
Olivier, Laurent 80
Ooloogan (George John Noble) 14–15, 209–11, 214, *216*, 218–20, 225, 230, *231*, 232
Osage people 181
Orokolo Bay, PNG 2, 7, 12, 92, 93–98, 101

Pahuja, Sundhya 180
palaeontology 36, 72, 90
Palmer, Dave 189–90
Pappin, Bernadette 105, 111, 114
Pappin, Mary Junior 105, 111–12, 114–15
Pappin, Mary Senior 109, 112
Papua New Guinea 1, 4, 70, 90, 92–93, *94*, 105
   earliest human presence in 70
   excavations on south coast of 93–98
   see also Larihairu, PNG; Orokolo Bay, PNG
Pascoe, Bruce 54, 82–84
Patai, Peia 140–41, 146
Patten, Jack 36
Peeler, Lois *231*, 232
Penrith, Bronwyn 219–20, *231*, *236*, 237, 239
periodisation 6
Péron, François 191, 198
Pintubi trackers 113–14
Pittock, James 208, 221, *229*
Polynesians 2, 122, 125–27, 131, 136–39, 141; *see also* Māori people
Porr, Martin 7, 12, 67–89, 246
Portus, GV 35
postcolonial studies 26, 37, 39

Queanbeyan to Cooma walk 1873 209, 213–14, 220

Rademaker, Laura 2, 13, 44, 151–65, 172–73, 175–76, 246
radiometric dating 67, 69–71, 73, 86, 88
   calibration 73–74
   error ranges 101
   importance 84, 86
   optically stimulated luminescence (OSL) 70, 73
   radiocarbon dating 37, 82, 101
Rao, Rohit *223*, 225
Rapa Nui (Easter Island) 138–39, 146

Rarotonga, Cook Islands 136, *137*, 140–41, 144; *see also* Cook Islands
ra'ui 13, 136–48
   and seafood conservation 143–47
   Te Mana Ra'ui Act 143–44
recognition of Indigenous peoples 8–10, 37–38, 54, 85, 86, 105–106, 107, 117, 209
Reece, Bob 39
referendums
   of 1967 (Aboriginals) 109
   of 2023 (Voice) 9–10, 21–22, 54–55, 69
Reid, Nicholas 194
Rey, Jo 140
rock art
   as archive 158–64
   Carnarvon Gorge 22
   as complement to written sources 154
   as cultural identity and law 164
   destruction of 11, 55, 86
   as history 13, 151–54
   importance of in Indigenous culture 151, 158–62
   Indigenous American 161
   Injalak Hill, Arnhem Land, NT 151, *152*, 153, 164
   Kimberley 68, 85, 162
   photographs *152*
   'readers' 162–64
   Swedish 154
   Western scholarship on 153–55
Roe, Paddy 40, 116
Ronsard, François-Michel 198
Rose, David 194
Rudd, Kevin 218, *233*, 234, *236*
   Apology to Stolen Generations 234
Rudder, John 169, 182
Rusden, GW 35–36
Russell, Lynette 12, 36, 70, 90–102, 155, 161, 247

sacred sites *see* Country; rock art
Sambono, Joe 55, 56
Satia, Priya 28–29
Saunders, Kay 23
scar trees 103
Scott, Kim 173
Sea, Sky, and Land conference 2023 3
Serieyx, Alain 187

settler colonial violence 7, 47, 174, 176, 201
Silverstein, Ben 13, 166–86, 247
Simpson, Jane 174
Slater, Lisa *223*, 226–27
Society for the Study of Social Sciences (4S) 3, 8
songlines 62, 160
sovereignty
   archaeology and Aboriginal sovereignty 81–89
   coloniser 6, 185
   deep, and Deep History 1–3, 5, 28, 91, 117, 167
   definitions 5, 180–81
   everyday 8–10
   food 123
   historical practices and 1–2, 5
   imperial 6–7
   Indigenous 8, 28, 81–88, 141–43, 166–86, 214
   Indigenous language and 169, 172–73, 176, 178, 183
   international law and 5–6
   Māori food 122, 123–24, 126, 130–32
   memory and 178–86
   non-Indigenous recognition of Indigenous sovereignty 8–10, 28
   performative/embodied Indigenous sovereignty *see Murrudha: Sovereign Walks*
   relationality and 181, 184
   resistance to acknowledging Indigenous sovereignty 55, 166
   sovereign walks *see Murrudha: Sovereign Walks*
   spiritual notion of 70
   temporal 2, 86–87
   Western legal concept 180
   see also Country; language, Indigenous
Spencer, Baldwin 46–47, 63
Stanner, WEH 38
Steadman, Brad 11, 40–41
Stolen Generations 19, 21–25, 167–68, 170, 176, 228, 234
stone tools 46, 71
storytelling/storywork 2, 37, 169, 174, 176, 194, 208, 220–21, 226–27; *see also* history, oral
Sutherland, Alexander 35

Taçon, Paul SC 159–60
Tāmaki Makaurau (Auckland), NZ 12–13, 121–35; *see also* Māori people
Tasmania 4, 105, 142
Tasmanian Aboriginal people 212
Tati Tati
  language 106
  people 12, 103, 107–108, 115–16, 117–18
terra nullius 9, 20, 30, 106; *see also* land rights; Native Title
Thorne, Alan 108–109
Tiedje, Kristina 140
time/temporality 87, 163
  archaeological notions of 12, 67, 68–69, 71, 71–77, 78–80, 81–88, 89, 90–91
  as colonising 28–33
  decolonisation of 2, 27
  difficult temporalities 90–102
  fictional 170–71
  historical relativity of 27
  Indigenous conceptualisations of 2, 7, 27–28, 71, 74–75, 77, 90–91, 93–101, 186, 202
  as linear 71
  multiple temporalities 167, 170–71
  non-linear 2, 71, 116–18
  and power 86
  temporal scales 74–75, 77
  temporal sovereignty 2, 86–87
  Western conceptualisations of 93, 99
  see also deep time
Tol Tol *see* Margooya Lagoon
trackways, ancestral 105, 111–15
Treaty 10, 20, 21–22; *see also* Native Title
Treaty of Waitangi 9, 122
Troy, Jakelin 2
Truth-Telling 2, 9, 21, 54, 168; *see also* Uluru Statement from the Heart
  Truth Telling Commission, Qld 10, 21–22
  Truth-Telling Commission, Vic 22
Tucker, Margaret 38
Tudge, Alan 55
Tyrrell, Ian 33

Uluru Statement from the Heart 9, 54, 69–70, 117, 168
Urwin, Chris 12, 90–102, 247
Urwin, Jess 165, 241

Vasse, Thomas Timothée 14, 187–203
  colonial settlers find out about Vasse's survival 199–203
  death of 195–96, 200, 201, 202
  and Noongar prophesy 187–90, 202
  how Vasse was left behind 191–94
  Wardandi oral history about 189–90, 194–99, 200, 202
Vaughan, Mehana Blaich 3
Vavia, Antony 13, 136–48, *148*, 248
Veracini, Lorenzo 33
Victorian Education Department 42, 45–52, 59
Victorian Readers 42, 45, 59, 63
Voice Referendum 2023 9–10, 21–22, 54–55, 69

Walgalu/Wiradyuri
  Country 14, 214, 219
  language 226
  peoples 208, 218
  stories 227
Walker, Maria *235*, *236*, 237–38
Walker-White, Iris 234, *235*, *236*
walking on Country 14–16, 207–40
Wanjina Wunggurr Traditional Owners 68
Ward, Russel 35
Wardandi/Wardanji Noongar people 14, 187–203
  massacre of at Wonnerup 199, 201
Watkins, Joe 156
Wave Hill Walk-Off 1966 207–208, 216–19, *217*, 229; *see also* Gurindji/Malngin/Bilinara peoples
Way, Amy 22
Webb, Bill 187, 189–90, 194–97, 199, 201–202
Webb, George 194
Webb, Steve 110, 111–14
Welcome to Country 8–9, 218
Western Australia 187–203
Westgarth, William 31
Whittaker, Alison 39
Willandra Lakes, NSW 3, 7, 12, 104, 108–15; *see also* Lake Mungo, NSW; Mungo National Park, NSW
Williams, Shayne 159
Wilmot, Eric 100
Winch, Tara June 13, 166–86
Wiradjuri/Wiradyuri

Country 170, 183
dictionary 14, 168–69, 171, 173–79, 182, 185–86
language 167–69, 171–74, 177–79, 182–83, 186, 207, 226
people 3, 186
see also Walgalu/Wiradyuri; Winch, Tara June
Witmore, Christopher 78
Wolfe, Patrick 33
Wonnerup Inlet, WA 194, 196, *197*, 200
Wonnerup massacre of Wardandi people 199, 201
Wright, Judith 36
Yangar *see* Nangar, Jimmy

Yield, The 13, 166–86
Yorta Yorta people 208
Yuin people 208, 219, 223, 227
Yulidjirri, Thompson 151, 153

www.ingramcontent.com/pod-product-compliance
Lightning Source LLC
Chambersburg PA
CBHW021936290426
44108CB00012B/857